T0375324

China's Path to Innovation

Over the past three decades, China has experienced rapid economic growth and a fascinating transformation of its industry. However, much of this success is the result of industrial imitation and China's continuing success now relies heavily on its ability to strengthen its indigenous innovation capability. In this book, Xiaolan Fu investigates how China can develop a strategy of compressed development to emerge as a leading innovative nation. The book draws on quantitative and qualitative research that includes cross-country, cross-province and cross-firm analysis. Large multi-level panel datasets, unique survey databases, and in-depth industry case studies are explored. Different theoretical approaches are also used to examine the motivations, obstacles and consequences of China's innovation with a wider discussion around what other countries can learn from China's experience. This book will appeal to scholars and policy-makers working in fields such as innovation policy, technology management, development and international economics and China studies.

XIAOLAN FU is Professor of Technology and International Development and Founding Director of the Technology and Management Centre for Development at the University of Oxford. Her research interests include innovation, technology and industrialisation; trade, foreign direct investment and economic development; emerging Asian economies; and innovation and productivity in the UK and US. She also has first-hand experience working in the business and academic sectors in China before coming to the UK.

'Professor Fu has integrated a variety of scholarly articles from the firm level to the industry level to the national policy level, to produce the first comprehensive treatment of Chinese innovation activities from an open innovation perspective. Her masterful book points the way towards 'open innovation with Chinese characteristics'.'

Henry Chesbrough, Professor at UC Berkeley's Haas School of Business and author of *Open Innovation*

'That China is the workshop of the world is now a 'given'. Professor Fu has invested years in the search for clues to how the goods in the China workshop have moved from being 'assembled in China' through 'invented in China' to 'invented and commercialised in a complex open engagement with the world's capital and skilled labour'. This book is the authoritative result and is essential reading.'

Barbara Harriss-White, Emeritus Professor of Development Studies, Oxford University and co-editor of *China-India: Pathways of Economic and Social Development*

'This fascinating book by a leading Chinese scholar is hugely informative of the challenges China faces in its quest to become a major global innovative economy. It populates a knowledge gap, challenges our conventional wisdom and provides important insights for corporate and government policy makers alike.'

Raphael Kaplinsky, Professor of International Development, The Open University

'China achieved an average annual growth rate of 9.8% for 35 years, made possible only by continuous technological innovations, after the transition from a planning economy to a market economy in 1979. Such a long period of extra-ordinary growth was unprecedented in human history. This book carefully studies China's open national innovation system at national, regional and firm levels. It deciphers how China was able to achieve such a remarkable success in the past, examines how China may sustain dynamic growth in the future and suggests what other countries can learn from China's success. The book is a must-read for anyone who wants to understand Chinese economic development.'

Justin Yifu Lin, Professor, Peking University and Former Chief Economist, The World Bank

'Finally, we have an analytical volume that combines economic theory, interna-tional experience, and China's socio-economic conditions to formulate a most credible strategy to greatly strengthen China's capacity to innovate. Xiaolan Fu's 'Open National Innovation System' approach deserves careful study by other developing countries because it is also applicable to them.'

Wing Woo, Professor, University of California at Davis and President, Jeffrey Cheah Institute on Southeast Asia, Malaysia

China's Path
to Innovation

XIAOLAN FU
University of Oxford

CAMBRIDGE
UNIVERSITY PRESS

University Printing House, Cambridge CB2 8BS, United Kingdom

Cambridge University Press is part of the University of Cambridge.

It furthers the University's mission by disseminating knowledge in the pursuit of education, learning and research at the highest international levels of excellence.

www.cambridge.org
Information on this title: www.cambridge.org/9781107046993

First published 2015

A catalogue record for this publication is available from the British Library.

Library of Congress Cataloguing in Publication data
Fu, Xiaolan, 1967–
China's path to innovation / Xiaolan Fu.
  pages   cm
ISBN 978-1-107-04699-3 (hardback)
1. Economic development – China.   2. Industrial policy – China.
3. Information technology – Management – China.   I. Title.
HC427.95.F798   2015
338′.0640951–dc23

2014048687

ISBN 978-1-107-04699-3 Hardback

Contents

Figures

Tables

Preface

This book is an outcome of my research on innovations in China over the past 10 years. I started my research on innovation as a project team member of a Cambridge-MIT joint project on 'International Innovation Benchmarking', which compared innovation activities in Europe, the UK in particular, and the United States. Innovations were a key area of concern for policy makers and business managers, as well as the academic scholars. Although China's economic reforms started in 1978, up to the early 2000s the Chinese economy had been driven by system reforms, investment, exports and foreign direct investment (FDI) at different periods. Innovation was still a concept that had never really come to the centre of China's development strategy, nor had it arrived at the debate on the drivers of its long-term economic growth. Having witnessed the competition among industrialised countries for leadership in innovation and the priority that has clearly been given to skills and innovation in policy making in these countries, I started my pursuit to understand how to build innovation capabilities in a developing country such as China. I strongly believe that this will be a crucial area for China, not only for academic research but also for policy making and business management in the real-world context. In fact, without much waiting, the Chinese government began to change its development strategy in 2006. It placed development of indigenous innovation as the top priority in its official national development plan.

As a researcher who has a strong interest in China's industrial competitiveness and its external trade and investment, I have worked extensively in these areas; hence, I started my research quest from my understanding of the sources of innovative knowledge and technology in China and the processes of innovation diffusion. I gradually moved on to researching the conditions and processes of innovation creation in developing countries. I also examined the relationship between different paths at different stages of development of a country, their advantages and disadvantages and the conditions for effectiveness of each path. My past work experiences and interest in studying innovations in the developed and other developing countries allowed me to examine China's path from an international comparative perspective. This has formed the basic structure and approach of research that I present in this book.

China's Path to Innovation is a combination of a selected number of my published journal papers and several new studies on some of the most recent topics regarding China's ongoing transformation from imitation to innovation. It is a serious academic book based on 10 years of research and reflection. All published and unpublished new papers are selected and organised to provide a systematic, comprehensive and coherent study of China's path to innovation, although each chapter is fairly self-contained. Journal publication offers a great advantage that one's research comes under close scrutiny through the peer review process and can benefit greatly from it. My aim is to publish the more original parts of the book in this way with updated data and information. The hope is that the whole will add up to more than the sum of its parts and that we can identify and develop a general model of the technology development strategy of the developing countries based on a series of peer-reviewed, in-depth studies of individual factors, mechanisms and cases.

Many acknowledgements and thanks are due. Since 2005, my research on innovation and on China has been supported by substantial grants from the Economic and Social Sciences Research Council (ESRC), the Engineering and Physics Sciences Research Council (EPSRC), the British Academy, the Cairncross Foundation and the State Administration of Foreign Experts Affairs (SAFEA) of China. I thank these bodies for their financial support and for the confidence that they have shown in my research.

I am grateful to the copyright holders of the following journals for permitting me, with acknowledgement, to present full or part of the papers that have appeared in their journals in suitably revised form: Xiaolan Fu, Carlo Pietrobelli and Luc Soete, 'The role of foreign technology and indigenous innovation in emerging economies: technological change and catch-up', *World Development*, 39 (2011) (part of the Introduction); Xiaolan Fu, 'Foreign direct investment, absorptive capacity and regional innovation capabilities in China', *Oxford Development Studies*, 36 (2008) (Chapter 3); Xiaolan Fu, 'Processing-trade, FDI and exports of indigenous firms: firm-level evidence from high-technology industries in China', *Oxford Bulletin of Economics and Statistics*, 73 (2011) (Chapter 4); Xiaolan Fu and Yundan Gong,

'Indigenous and foreign innovation efforts and drivers of technological upgrading', *World Development*, 39 (2011) (Chapter 5); Xiaolan Fu and Hongru Xiong, 'Open innovation in China: policies and practices', *Journal of Science & Technology Policy in China*, 2 (2011) (Chapter 6); Xiaolan Fu, Hongru Xiong and Jizhen Li, 'Open innovation as a response to constraints and risks and the moderating role of governance', *Asian Economic Papers*, 13 (2014) (Chapter 7); Xiaolan Fu, Jizhen Li and Martin Johnson, 'Internal and external sources of tacit knowledge: evidence from the optical fibre and cable industry in China', *Journal of Chinese Economic and Business Studies*, 9 (2011) (Chapter 9); Xiaolan Fu and Jing Zhang, 'Technology transfer, indigenous innovation and leapfrogging in green technology: solar-PV panel industries in China and India', *Journal of Chinese Economic and Business Studies*, 9 (2011) (Chapter 10); Xiaolan Fu and Qing Gong Yang, 'Exploring the cross-country gap in patenting: a stochastic frontier approach', *Research Policy*, 38 (2009) (part of Chapter 13); Xiaolan Fu and Rongping Mu, 'Enhancing China's innovation performance: the policy choice', *China & World Economy*, 22 (2014) (part of Chapter 14).

Chapter 8 is based on a paper written jointly with Jizhen Li published by the Oxford University Technology and Management Centre for Development Working Paper series. Chapter 11 is based on a new unpublished paper written jointly with Zhongjuan Sun. I would like to thank my co-authors for allowing results of our joint research to be included in this volume. Prototypes of various chapters have been presented, in the past years, at seminars at many universities and various conferences, which cannot be acknowledged here in detail. I am grateful to the organisers and participants for providing me with these opportunities to obtain helpful feedback on the research from experts.

Among the numerous colleagues and friends whom I wish to thank for helpful and constructive comments and discussions are Luc Soete, Henry Chesbrough, Alan Hughes, Adrian Wood, Jinglian Wu, Justin Yifu Lin, Barbara Harriss-White, Edmund Valpy FitzGerald, Wing Thye Woo, Anne Miroux, Carlo Pietrobelli, Angang Hu, Rongping Mu, Erniu Xuan, Rajneesh Narula, Pierre Mohnen, Raphie Kaplinsky, Mammo Muchie, Xin Fang, Wei Lv, Jiangang Victor Zhang, Mingjie Ma, Jian Gao, Poh Kam Wong, Jin Chen, Guisheng Wu, Jizhen Li, V. N. Balasubramanyam, Cyril Lin, John Knight, Andy Cosh, Michael Kitson, Carl Dahlman, David Kaplan, Jose Katz, Frances Stewart, Steve Rayner, Christine Greenhalgh, Yongding Yu, Linda Yueh, Yang Yao,

Jing Zhang, Yundan Gong, Hongru Xiong, Qing Gong Yang, Marc
Ventresca, Diego Sanchez-Ancocher, Eric Thun, Bin Hao, Chunyan
Zhang and Xiaming Liu.

I am grateful to Jun Hou, Martin Johnson, Peter Luke and Zifu Wang
for excellent research assistance. The support of Paula Parish and Claire
Wood of Cambridge University Press was essential for the publication
of the book.

I thank the Department of International Development of Oxford
University for hosting the research and providing financial support
and the Centre for Business Research of Cambridge University for
support during the early stage of my research on innovation and
China. I also thank colleagues and students of the Technology and
Management Centre for Development, Oxford University, for stimulat-
ing discussions and help. The collegiality of the Fellowship of Green
Templeton College, Oxford, has also been an inspirational support.

Finally, I can hardly express the debt of gratitude I owe to my family,
especially my husband, Shaohui, and my son, Yujie, for their great love
and support. Without their support, the book would not have come to
fruition.

Xiaolan Fu

Abbreviations

ABC	Absorptive capacity
CDB	China Development Bank
CDMA	Code division multiple access
CILG	Central innovation leading group
CIS	Community Innovation Survey
COEs	Collective-owned enterprises
CPO	Chinese State Intellectual Property Office
DEA	Data envelopment analysis
EIS	European Innovation Scoreboard
EP	Export processing
EPZs	Export processing zones
EU	European Union
FDI	Foreign direct investment
FIEs	Foreign invested enterprises
GDP	Gross domestic products
GLLAMMs	Generalized linear latent and mixed models
GMM	Generalised method of moments
GVC	Global value chains
HKTM firms	Hong Kong, Taiwan and Macao firms
HMT	Hong Kong, Macau and Taiwan
ICT	Information and communication technology
IMD	Institute for Management Development
IPR	Intellectual property rights
ITU	International Telecommunication Union
JV	Joint venture
MLEs	Medium- and large-sized enterprises
MNEs	Multinational enterprises
MOST	Ministry of Science and Technology of China
MSTI	Main science and technology indicators
NIEs	Newly industrialised economics

NIP	National innovation performance
NIS	National innovation system
OBM	Original brand manufacturers
ODM	Original design manufacturers
OECD	Organisation for Economic Co-operation and Development
OEM	Original equipment manufacturers
OFDI	Outward foreign direct investment
OI	Open innovation
OLS	Ordinary least squares
ONIS	Open national innovation system
OT	Ordinary trade
POEs	Privately owned enterprises
PRIs	Public research institutions
PT-FDI	Processing trade–FDI
R&D	Research and development
REF	Research excellence framework
S&T	Science and technology
SEZs	Special economic zones
SFA	Stochastic frontier analysis
SHCs	Shareholding companies
SMEs	Small and medium enterprises
SOEs	State-owned enterprises
SSB	State Statistical Bureau
STP	Strategic technology partnering
TFP	Total factor productivity
UNCTAD	United Nations Conference on Trade and Development
USPTO	United States Patent and Trademark Office
WBDI	World Bank development indicators
WCY	World Competitiveness Yearbook
WFO	Wholly foreign owned
WTO	World Trade Organization
ZTE	Zhongxing Telecommunications Equipment Corporation

Introduction

1 | *Introduction*

The past three decades have witnessed rapid economic growth and a fascinating transformation of China's economy and industry, from an economy dominated by agriculture to one that is referred to as a 'world manufacturing plant', from a small exporter of resource- and unskilled-labour–intensive products to a major producer of manufactured exports. The total industrial output of China increased from US$91 million in 1980 to US$3,728 million in 2013, and the share of industrial products in total exports has increased from 50 per cent in 1980 to more than 95 per cent in 2012 (NBS, 2013).

Increasing industrial competitiveness as revealed through surging exports and upgraded export composition has also astonished the rest of world. China's total exports and imports increased from US$38 billion in 1980 to US$4,265 billion in 2012. China's share in the world markets for exports of goods rose from 0.9 per cent in 1980 to 11 per cent in 2012. More significant is the export of manufactured products from China, which increased from US$9 billion in 1980 to US$1,948 billion in 2012, 38 per cent of which constituted high-technology products, accounting for 16.5 per cent of the world's total high-technology exports (UNCTAD, 2014). China is now the world's largest economy in terms of trade. The country has also maintained a fast growth rate despite the recent global economic crisis that severely affected the industrialised economies.

However, the country also faces significant criticisms of its growth model because of its heavy dependency on foreign technology transfer and imitation and its lack of creativity and indigenous capabilities in core technology. Moreover, with the amount of surplus unskilled labour in China falling, and the resource and environmental constraints for sustainable growth becoming increasingly significant, China is being forced towards a more skill-intensive and technology-intensive growth path as its own Lewis Turning Point approaches, that is, when the surplus labour in the subsistence sector is fully absorbed into the modern sector. China now faces significant challenges in moving from imitation to innovation. The success of this transformation will be of crucial importance for China to avoid the middle-income trap and sustain its long-term economic growth (Wu, 2013).

Therefore, given China's remarkable achievement in industrialisation and modernisation in the past three decades as well as the challenges of sustainable development and structural change ahead, it is pertinent to ask the following questions: What was China's path to innovation in the past, and whither the future? How has China managed to develop and upgrade its technological capabilities at such a remarkable speed? In the twenty-first century, how can China significantly enhance its indigenous innovation capability and accomplish the transition from imitation to innovation, thereby becoming an innovative nation? As one of the major economies in the world, how can China develop a path of compressed development and leapfrog the conventional latecomer path of imitative industrialisation, progressing up the value chain, taking a lead in the low-carbon industrial revolution and reemerge as the world's leading innovation power as documented for an earlier era in Joseph Needham's (1954) seminal work? Is there a China model of innovation? What are the lessons that other countries can learn from China's experience? These are all important questions of great interest not only to academic researchers but also to policy makers and practitioners.

As the world's second largest economy and one that is still firmly on a path of stable and promising economic growth, any fundamental changes in China will have significant impact on global business and global economies. Moreover, China has increasingly been seen as an exemplary model for other emerging economies. Its successes and challenges will thus be closely watched by policy makers in both developed and emerging economies. Therefore, findings from this book will have significant policy and practical implications for both developed and other developing countries.

Innovation and its sources

Innovation is a process of creative destruction, taking place as a 'process of industrial mutation that incessantly revolutionises the economic structure from within, incessantly destroying the old one, incessantly creating a new one" (Schumpeter, 1942: 83). It is widely recognised as a major driver of long-term growth and a key element of industrialisation and catch-up in developing countries (Romer, 1990). In the present context, innovation concerns not only novel innovations but also innovation via diffusion of existing ideas and techniques. It includes not only technological innovations but also non-technological innovations, such as new management practices and new institutional structures. In other words, innovation refers to the introduction or adoption of new products, new production processes, new ways of organisation and management, new methods of marketing and new business models. A complete innovation chain includes both the creation and commercialisation of new knowledge.

Innovation can occur as a result of a concerted focus by a range of different agents, by chance or as a result of changes in industry structure, in market structure; in local and global demographics; in human perception, mood and meaning; in the amount of already available scientific knowledge, and so on (Drucker, 1985). At the micro level, the sources of innovation may come from internal focus efforts, for example, R&D activities or other organised innovation efforts, or externally from the acquisition of useful technology or knowledge created by other organisations or by users of the technology, that is, the so-called end-user innovation identified by von Hippel (1988). Currently, with the innovation paradigm shifting from closed to open, firms may also open up their innovation process and create new products and processes by tapping into external resources and collaborating with other partners (Chesbrough, 2003). At the macro level, innovations may be created by focused efforts or by chance from a range of different agents in the country, such as firms, universities and research institutions. They may also emerge as a result of acquisition of innovations created in foreign countries through several channels.

Innovation can be diffused between firms and across regions and countries through various transmission mechanisms. These include (1) licensing; (2) movement of goods through international trade, especially imports; (3) movement of capital through inward and outward foreign direct investment (FDI and OFDI); (4) movement of people through migration, travel, and foreign education of students and workers; (5) international research collaboration; (6) diffusion through media and the Internet of disembodied knowledge; and (7) integration into global value chains to benefit from the foreign technology transferred within the supply chain. Some knowledge is transferred intentionally from the knowledge owner to the recipient – and this may spur a learning process – but a large proportion of knowledge spillovers take place as unintended knowledge leakage. In recent years, the mode of innovation is becoming more and more open and good use is made of external resources. International knowledge diffusion can therefore benefit firms' innovation at every stage of the innovation process. The growing technological diversification of companies makes successful integration of new external knowledge into the innovation process increasingly important. Such successful integration further fosters innovation performance. The factors that explain the accelerating trend of utilising external sources of knowledge include, among others, technological convergence, declining transaction costs of acquiring external R&D inputs and shortening product cycle times (Narula, 2003).

The development strategies for industrialisation and catch-up in latecomer developing countries, the relative role of international technology transfer and indigenous innovation and the role of industry policy in the process have been the most important but also controversial issues in development studies and science and technology studies. One of the controversies is whether the sources of technological change are indigenous or rather based on foreign innovation efforts or a combination of the two, and which combination of different foreign sources of innovation with different degrees of emphasis. On the one hand, innovation is costly, risky and path dependent. Hence, it is more efficient for developing countries simply to acquire foreign technology created in developed countries. In principle, if innovations are easy to diffuse and adopt, a technologically backwards country can catch up rapidly, even leapfrog through the acquisition and more rapid deployment of the most advanced technologies (Soete, 1985; Grossman and Helpman, 1991, 1994; Romer, 1994; Eaton and Kortum, 1995).

On the other hand, there is the view that technology diffusion and adoption are neither costless nor unconditional. They rely on substantial and well-directed technological efforts (Lall, 2001) and on absorptive capacity (Cohen and Levinthal, 1989). An additional related difficulty in the debate on indigenous versus foreign technology upgrading is that technical change is often biased in a particular direction so that foreign technologies developed in industrialised countries may not be appropriate to the economic and social conditions of developing countries (Atkinson and Stiglitz, 1969; Basu and Weil, 1998; Acemoglu, 2002; Fu and Gong, 2010). In addition, we cannot simplistically assume that the private interests of multinationals coincide with the social interests of the host countries (Lall and Urata, 2003). The available empirical evidence on the effects of the sources of indigenous or foreign innovation is mixed. Studies largely fail to provide convincing evidence indicating significant positive technological transfer and spillover effects of FDI on local firms (Gorg and Strobl, 2001).

Accompanying this ongoing and inclusive debate on the role of technology transfer and indigenous innovation, the role of state and industry policy in the process of industrialisation and economic development is also subject to a wide, ongoing debate. While some argue that industry policy is crucial for the success of the newly industrialised economics (NIEs) such as Japan, South Korea and Signapore (Amsden, 2001; Chang, 2003; Pack and Saggi, 2006), there are also strong arguments for the role of the market and free competition in allocating resources efficiency and enhancing the productive efficiency of the enterprises in an economy based on the recent success of the East Asian Tigers such as Malaysia, Thailand and the Philippines (Kruger, 1974; Bhagwati, 1982; World Bank, 1996, 2005).

Some argue for a third way for structural change to occur, suggesting that sustained economic development is driven by changes in factor endowments and continuous technological innovation; therefore, industry policy should encourage the development of sectors that comply with a country's comparative advantage while the private sector and the market should be the major players in the process (Lin, 2011). Market forces and private entrepreneurship would be in the driving seat of this agenda, but governments would also perform a strategic and coordinating role in the productive sphere beyond simply ensuring property rights, contract enforcement, and macroeconomic stability (Rodrik, 2004). This debate on the role of the state and policy is relevant for our analysis of national innovation capabilities and performance because of the nature of innovation as a public product, the significant positive externalities that knowledge and ideas may generate and the presence of market failures resulting from the great uncertainty related to the innovation process.

The literature

China's experience with innovation and technological upgrading is also the subject of wide-ranging interests amongst a variety of stakeholders in economics and politics. The literature in this area can be broadly classified into several categories. The first category relates to studies of the impact of China's rising innovation and technological capabilities on the rest of the world, for example, MacDonald et al. (2008), Barlow (2013) and Someren and Someren-Wang (2013). These studies argue that the United States, the EU and China have reached a crossroads, and whether China will be a threat or an opportunity depends on the main players in government and public and private organisations rethinking their innovation policies and business development paths (Someren and Someren-Wang, 2013). They also contend that the 'rules for survival' in R&D and education are changing in favour of China, in terms of basic R&D parameters such as research expenditure, scientists trained, papers published and patents awarded (MacDonald et al., 2008).

The second category in the literature on China's innovation capabilities concerns one or several individual factors in the national innovation system or one type of innovation in China, for example, university-industry linkages, state-firm coordination, high-end talents, disruptive innovation in China and cost innovations (e.g., Zeng and Williamson, 2007; Feng, 2009; Simon and Cao, 2009; Tan, 2011). The third stream of literature relates to industry case studies, most of which focus on the high-technology industries, the information and communication technology (ICT) sector and green technologies (e.g., Lu, 2000; Jakobson, 2007; Wang, 2012; and Liu et al., 2012).

All these studies have provided useful insights about the development of innovation and technological capabilities in China. However, they are based on studies of a particular industry, a particular type of innovation, or one specific driver of innovation. What is China's national strategy and path to innovation? Comprehensive and systematic analysis of China's overall innovation strategy, driver and outcome is rare with very few exceptions (e.g., Varum et al., 2007; OECD, 2008). Varum et al. (2007) present a comprehensive description of the transformation of innovation policies and the reform of science and technology systems in China from 1978 to 2004. OECD (2008) provides a comprehensive and systematic review of China's national innovation system. Features and performances of each of the major players, that is, government, industry and universities, and the role of policy and governance are examined. Both of these studies set up their analysis under the national innovation system framework. They provide a valuable description of the relevant policies and the status and performance of the important agencies in China's national innovation system. However, *how* China achieved its current success and how china can achieve its new objective to transform itself into an innovation-driven economy is still underresearched. Our understanding is limited with regard to the evolution of China's path to innovation, in particular the evolution of strategies, processes and drivers of innovation at different stages of development and their impact on China's innovation capabilities and technological upgrading.

The objective and structure of the book

The objective of this book is to provide a systematic, comprehensive and rigorous study of China's drive towards innovation in the past and for the future. It draws on my research of more than a decade to understand, analyse and evaluate this process. The research employs the rigorous analysis and empirical methodology of modern economics as well as in-depth case studies of representative industries and leading Chinese companies. Much of the evidence is based on either survey data or longitudinal data at firm-, industry-, regional- or country-level. But a systematic approach is adopted: economic and management theory, development and evolutionary theory, institutional analysis and political economy are used to explain the motivation, sources, obstacles, policy measures, firm responses and consequences of China's drive towards being an innovative nation, and the roles played by the state, the market, the private sector and the non-market, non-state institutions such as universities and public research institutions.

In addition to the analysis of China's experience in the past three decades, the book also investigates some of China's most recent efforts in innovation, for example, internationalisation of Chinese MNEs and outward direct investment for technology acquisition and upgrading, international innovation collaboration, reforms of incentive structure at multiple levels, and the development of green technologies. Moreover, the research places China in a global context, and an international comparative perspective is taken comparing China with other emerging economies such as India and more advanced countries such as the UK. The book also critically reviews China's experience, provides an in-depth discussion of the likely way forward, and what other countries can learn from China's experience.

In light of the economic and management theories on the sources of innovation, taking on board the innovation systems framework and the capabilities approach, the book is organised into three parts focusing on the drivers of innovation at different stages of development, in addition to the Introduction and Conclusions chapters. Part I examines the role of international knowledge transfer and technological takeoff in China at the early stage of the reforms. Part II analyses the development of indigenous innovation capability in the catch-up stage of industrial development in China. Part III focuses on China's current efforts to leapfrog the country into the role of global innovation leader and assesses the role of incentive structure, institutional arrangement and unconventional knowledge sourcing and co-creation measures in the process. Before embarking on these analyses, an overview of China's innovation efforts and performance in the past three decades since the reforms is presented in Chapter 2.

Part I on the role of international knowledge transfer and technological takeoff in China includes four chapters. Chapter 3 investigates the impact of foreign direct investment on the development of regional innovation capabilities using a panel data set of Chinese regions. It finds that FDI has a significant positive impact on the overall regional innovation capacity. FDI intensity is also positively associated with innovation efficiency in the host region. The strength of this positive effect depends, however, on the availability of the absorptive capacity and the presence of innovation-complementary assets in the host region. This increased regional innovation and technological capability has contributed further to regional economic growth in China's coastal regions but not in the inland regions. It concludes that the type and quality of FDI inflows and the strength of local absorptive capacity and complementary assets in the host regions are crucial for FDI to serve as a driver of knowledge-based development. Policy implications are discussed.

Chapter 4 examines the impact of processing trade-oriented FDI on the export competitiveness of indigenous firms using disaggregated firm-level production data and product-level trade data from China covering 2000 to 2007. The estimation results show that processing trade-FDI has generated significant positive information spillover effects on the export performance of indigenous firms. However, the effect of technology spillovers on the development of international competitiveness in indigenous firms is limited and in fact exerts a significant depressive effect on the propensity to export in these firms. Indigenous innovation, economies of scale and productivity are found to be the main drivers of export performance in indigenous firms in the high-technology industries.

Chapter 5 explores the role of indigenous and foreign innovation efforts in technological upgrading in developing countries, taking into account sectoral specificities in technical change. Using a Chinese firm-level panel data set covering 2001 to 2005, the chapter decomposes productivity growth into technical change and efficiency improvement and examines the impact of indigenous and foreign innovation efforts on these changes. Indigenous firms are found to be the leading force on the technological frontier in the low- and medium-technology industries, whereas foreign-invested firms enjoy a clear lead in the high-technology sector. Collective indigenous R&D activities at the industry level are found to be the major driver of technology upgrading of indigenous firms that pushes out the technology frontier. While foreign investment appears to contribute to static industry capabilities, R&D activities of foreign-invested firms have exerted a significant negative effect on the technical change of local firms over the sample period.

Part II on the development of indigenous innovation capability in the catch-up stage includes five chapters. Chapter 6 attempts to review the evolution of policies and practices of open innovation in China using historical archives and case study approaches, covering policies and practices at both the macro and micro levels. It finds that Chinese firms have in practice employed a variety of open innovation models since the reforms of science and technology systems in the mid-1980s. Policies introduced by the Chinese government with respect to inbound and outbound open innovation as well as policies encouraging open innovation networks have encouraged Chinese firms to adopt various open innovation modes and practices. With the increasing internationalisation of R&D and globalisation of production, open innovation is diffusing rapidly in China. Challenges to adoption of open innovation for latecomer firms and the implications for latecomer firms in building indigenous innovation capability are also discussed.

Chapter 7 examines how Chinese firms use open innovation as a response to the constraints and risks of innovation that they face. A national firm-level survey of 1,400 firms in the manufacturing sector is used as the basis of the analysis. It found that institutional-, financial- and knowledge/skills-related risks and constraints are all significantly associated with firms' depth and breadth of openness in innovation. The responses, however, vary across firms of different ownership types. Foreign invested firms appear to be most responsive and take action to widen and deepen their openness in innovation. Privately owned firms have made significant responses to market/institution-related and finance/risk-related impediments but not to knowledge/skills-related ones. State-owned firms appear to be least responsive in the use of open innovation. Firm size and industry-specific effects also appear to have significant moderating effects on firms' responses to the various constraints. These findings are supported by an in-depth study of the Chinese semiconductor industry.

Chapter 8 attempts to investigate the role of universities in industrial innovation in emerging economies using a firm-level survey database from China. It also benchmarks the Chinese pattern against that of the UK. It finds that domestic universities have played a significant role in the promotion of the diffusion of frontier technology and the creation of new country- or firm-level innovation outcomes in China. In contrast to the traditional view that collaboration with universities will lead to greater novel innovation (an outcome that is supported by evidence from the UK), the contribution of domestic universities to the creation of groundbreaking innovations is limited in China. International innovation collaboration with foreign universities, especially those in the NIEs and the emerging South, appears to be fruitful in enhancing the creation of groundbreaking innovations in Chinese firms.

Chapter 9 provides an analysis of the relative significance of various methods of acquiring tacit knowledge within the Chinese optical fibre and cable industry. The chapter contributes to the definition, understanding and investigation of tacit knowledge using firm-level data in a developing country context, helping complete a gap in the existing broader literature on technological learning. The research suggests that in industries where tacit knowledge is a more important component of technological learning than codified knowledge, internal R&D activities and domestic peers are important knowledge sources. Additionally, universities are shown to be an important asset in creating learning organisations, and they provide effective knowledge sources of both tacit and codified knowledge. However, imports of equipment and licensing are a less effective learning channel in the acquisition of tacit foreign technology.

In recent years, China and India have achieved tremendous technological progress and development in the solar photovoltaic (PV) industry. Using case studies, Chapter 10 analyses and compares the technology progress processes in the solar PV industry in China and India, and it discusses the role national innovation systems played in sustaining technology acquisition, adaptation and development. It illustrates that both countries adopted a strategy of mixing and sequencing different technology transfer and indigenous innovation mechanisms. The experiences of both countries also suggest that a functional national environmental innovation system is important in sustaining and advancing technology acquisition, adaptation and development. This chapter provides an alternative pathway for developing countries to follow in catching up with developed countries in the emergent green industries and leapfrogging towards an internationally competitive green economy.

Part III on China's current efforts to leapfrog the country into a global innovation leader includes four chapters. Chapter 11 analyses the patterns of reverse learning and sequential capabilities development in Huawei and ZTE, China's two successful ICT multinational enterprises. The chapter analyses the internationalisation process of Huawei and ZTE, their learning activities in the host countries, channels for reverse knowledge transfer from one subsidiary located in developed countries to headquarters and other subsidiaries worldwide. Findings from this chapter reveal three processes of reverse learning and capabilities upgrading: learning from customers, collaborators and other subsidiaries of the company group. Findings from this case study have valuable implications for organisational learning in MNEs from developing countries.

Chapter 12 examines the role of international innovation collaboration in the process of radical innovation in China. Radical innovations represent major departures from existing practices and involve the disruptive creation of new insights. Accordingly, the launch of radical innovation requires an extension of both the depth and breadth of knowledge. This chapter investigates the patterns of international and domestic innovation collaboration in 819 Chinese firms from 2006 to 2008. It finds that collaborations with foreign partners have made a significant positive impact of the creation of novel innovation in Chinese firms. The type of foreign partners that Chinese firms may benefit by collaborating with covers a wide range, including foreign customers, suppliers, universities, private research institutions and firms in the same industry. Collaboration with foreign customers generates the largest benefits in the creation of novel innovation. Collaboration with foreign universities also proved to be fruitful for the generation of novel innovations that are new to the world, which is consistent with the findings of Chapter 8.

Chapter 13 benchmarks the patent activities of countries against the world frontier and explores the sources of the cross-country differences in innovation (proxied by patenting). A patent production frontier is first estimated for a panel of 21 OECD countries from the 1990 to 2002 period using stochastic frontier analysis. Patenting performance for each country is decomposed into basic patenting capacity and patenting efficiency. The gap between Europe and the world leaders in terms of basic patenting capacity remains substantial with little sign of convergence over the sample period. In terms of patenting efficiency, Japan, Germany and Italy have improved their relative positions in recent years. Institutional factors are found to be significantly associated with the patenting efficiency of an economy. Then, China and other emerging economies are brought into this benchmarking exercise using cross-country panel data covering 2005 to 2011. The gap in patenting performance between China and the world frontier results from China's relative underperformance mainly in the efficiency of innovation production.

Chapter 14 examines the policy choices for China's drive to transforming the country into an innovation-driven economy. Innovation capabilities, incentives and institutional frameworks are examined. The chapter argues that China should continue to increase its investment in R&D and in education, and that there should also be an attempt to strengthen the incentive system at the macro, meso and micro levels. This strengthening may include the following reforms: release the power of competition and guide resources towards innovative sectors; adopt appropriate human resource management policies, such as appraisal and remuneration systems; create effective policies for research funding management; and evaluate the efficiency of research to encourage the creativity of researchers, managers and employees. The chapter also discusses the space for industrial policy in the twenty-first century.

Chapter 15 summarises the main findings of the book, discusses the implications for other countries and identifies issues for further research. Based on the comprehensive analysis of China's path to innovation that is presented in the book, a model of an open national innovation system (ONIS) is developed and the stage-specific mixing and sequencing characteristics of the model and implications for other developing countries are discussed. Instead of being the often presented 'state-led model of innovation' in China or a pure market-driven model of innovation, the ONIS model in China is a multi-driver model led by the state, the private sector and the MNEs, with each of them playing a leading role in different segments of the economy and the innovation system.

2 | Innovation in China since the reforms: An overview

2.1 Introduction

The intensive investment and rapid development in science and technology (S&T) in China has attracted growing attention. The unprecedented increase in expenditure on R&D activities and human capital for innovation together with industrial structure upgrading and knowledge-intensive trade are strengthening China's transformation from a labour-intensive economic growth model into a knowledge-based one.

As outlined in China's 12th Five-Year Plan, innovation is a key element to promote a more balanced pattern of development. The 15-year science and technology development blueprint 'National Innovation Strategy' launched in 2006 calls for R&D spending to rise from 1.2 per cent of GDP to more than 2.5 per cent, which is slightly above the average for OECD nations, by 2020. Demonstrating its commitment to boosting investment in science and technology to build a high-performing innovation-oriented economy, the government allocated more than US$ 77.82 billion to invest in science and technology in 2011 with nearly a 20 per cent annual growth rate since 2005. As a result, China has moved faster than most of its peers in the developing world in establishing the foundations of a world-class innovation system.

This chapter provides a detailed description of the state of China's innovation and the rapid ongoing transformation of the country into an innovation-driven economy. It first presents an overall assessment of China's progress in building innovation capabilities, based on aggregate national statistics on innovation inputs and outputs. It then gives a concise picture of the innovation behaviours across industries, ownership structures, and geographic regions.

2.2 Innovation inputs: R&D and research personnel

Starting in the 1980s, China began to reform its science and technology system through a series of policies such as Key Technologies R&D in 1982, High-Technology Research and Development in 1986 and the Torch Plan in 1988. After 1990, the focus shifted to innovation. In early 2006, China convened a National Science & Technology Summit that issued the outline of the National Medium- and Long-Term Science and Technology Development Plan 2006–2020. A distinct feature of the plan is the adoption of innovation as a new national strategy and goal to propel China into the ranks of innovation-oriented countries by 2020. Since then, innovation has been recognised as the engine to shift China's long-standing export-led, low-cost manufacturing growth model to a knowledge-based sustainable growth model. The traditional focus on development relying on exports and heavy fixed-asset investment must give way to more knowledge-intensive, higher-quality growth driven by innovation.

Financial and human resource inputs, in particular into R&D, directly contribute to the development of science and technology. We start with illustrating financial inputs and the stock of research human capital, followed by indicators of measuring innovation performance.

R&D investment and composition of R&D

As a key indicator of its innovative efforts, R&D[1] expenditure in China has steadily increased at an exceptional rate from RMB 34.9 billion in 1995 to RMB 10,298 billion in 2012 – a growth factor of almost 30. With close to 20 per cent annual real growth in R&D spending, China has become the third largest global investor in R&D, just behind the United States and Japan but ahead of individual economies of the EU.[2] Figure 2.1 shows the huge increase in investment in R&D and R&D spending as a percentage of GDP from 1995 to 2012. The R&D intensity of China's economy, measured as R&D expenditure as a

---

[1] Research and development involves the creative work undertaken on a systematic basis to increase the stock of knowledge (including knowledge of humanity, culture and society) and the use of this knowledge to devise new applications.

[2] This is the authors' calculation based on data collected from the OECD Structural Analysis (STAN) database published by the OECD and the World Development Indicators published by the World Bank.

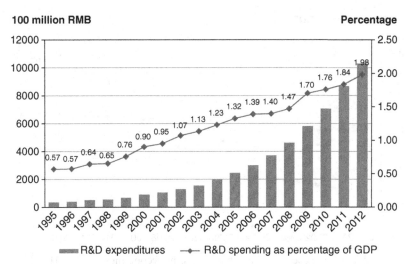

Figure 2.1 China's R&D expenditure, 1995–2012
Source: China Statistical Yearbook (1996–2013).

percentage of GDP, has also greatly increased since 1995. As a proportion of GDP, R&D was at a low of 0.57 per cent of GDP in 1995, rising to 1.32 per cent in 2005 and 1.98 per cent in 2012.

Among OECD countries, the United States, Japan and Germany are the main performers. Their ratios of R&D spending to GDP maintain stable levels between 2.5 and 3.5 per cent, while the ratio has been growing the fastest in South Korea, with average annual growth rates around 10 per cent as depicted in Figure 2.2. Although it has experienced a remarkable increase, the R&D intensity in China is still low in comparison with OECD countries. The highest ratio of R&D to GDP in China was 1.98 per cent in 2012, which is still far behind the OECD average at 2.39 per cent. The National Guidelines for S&T Development outlines an ambitious target for R&D investment: it should reach 2 per cent of GDP by 2010 and 2.5 per cent or more by 2020. As the goal of reaching 2 per cent by 2010 was not met (1.75 per cent in 2010 as shown in Figure 2.1), increasing the R&D intensity to 2.5 per cent by 2020 is a serious challenge taking into account the fast growth rate of GDP. This indicates that R&D expenditure needs to increase at least 25 per cent annually starting from 2012.

According to the classification given by the OECD, R&D covers three activities: basic research, applied research and experimental

R&D spending in GDP

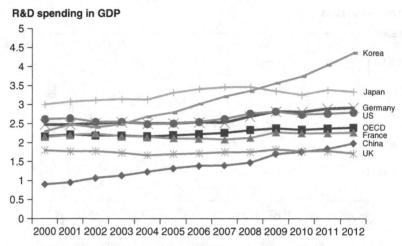

Figure 2.2 R&D expenditure in China and other economies, 1995–2012
Source: China Statistical Yearbook (1996–2013).

development.[3] The breakdown of R&D expenditure by type of activity reveals important structural features of the innovation system in China. A notable feature of China's R&D is that the share of basic research is considerably lower, whereas spending on experimental development accounts for relatively higher share, as shown in Figure 2.3. Expenditure on experimental development has grown the fastest, accounting for 84 per cent of total R&D in 2006 (72 per cent in 1998). In contrast to experimental development, the expenditure on applied research has declined from 5.3 per cent in 1998 to 4.8 per cent in 2012. Spending on basic research has remained at a stable level of around 5 per cent. The composition of R&D activities implies that a

---

[3] Basic research is experimental or theoretical work undertaken primarily to acquire new knowledge of the underlying foundation of phenomena and observable facts, without any particular application or use in view. Applied research is also original investigation undertaken to acquire new knowledge. It is, however, directed primarily towards a specific practical aim or objective; experimental development is systematic work, drawing on existing knowledge gained from research and/or practical experience, which is directed to producing new materials, products or devices; to installing new processes, systems and services; or to improving substantially those already produced or installed. More information can be found at www.oecd-ilibrary.org/sites/factbook-2013-en/08/01/01/index.html?itemId=/content/chapter/factbook-2013-60-en.

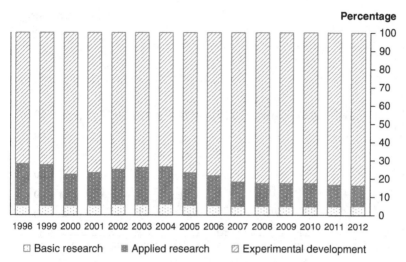

Figure 2.3 Composition of R&D by types of activities: basic research, applied research and experimental development
Source: China Statistical Yearbook (1999–2013).

big proportion of the increase in R&D expenditure in the past decades can be attributed to the investment in experimental development.

To sustain the rapid growth of R&D expenditure, strong financial supports from various channels are essential driving forces. R&D expenditure can be classified according to the funding origins: government funding, enterprise funding, foreign funding and other funding.[4] In the comparison between 2003 and 2011, Figure 2.4 shows that the growth of R&D expenditure is mainly supported by enterprises. It reflects, to some extent, that enterprises in the business sector have become an important player in the level of innovative sophistication and the structural change of the innovation system in China. Enterprises and government funding (noted as 'public institutions' in the figure) are the two largest financial resources; together they have accounted for up to 90 per cent of R&D spending in China since 2004, in particular enterprises stood at about 74 per cent of total R&D funding in 2011. In contrast, foreign-funded R&D in China has been very limited.

---

[4] Other funding may include self-raised funding, in particular for independent research institutions and the higher education sector, and leftover government money from previous years/grants.

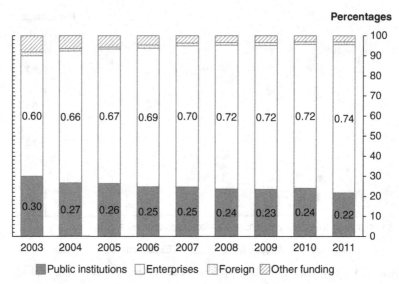

Figure 2.4 R&D composition by funding sources, 2003–2011
Source: China Statistical Yearbook (2004–2012).

R&D personnel

Human resources are equally important as R&D inputs and are a
crucial building block in forming an innovation pool. R&D personnel
include all persons employed directly on research and development
activities, as well as those providing direct services such as R&D managers, administrators and clerical staffs (OECD, 2002). The success of
transforming to a knowledge-based economy requires a large number
of R&D personnel to carry out the corresponding large-scale increase in
R&D activities. Since 2006, China has had the second highest number
of researchers in the world, just behind the United States. As shown
in Figure 2.5a, the number of R&D personnel in China, calculated in
full-time equivalents (FTE), has increased steadily since 1995. Breaking
down R&D personnel by type of activity shows that the notable
increase in the number of researchers is a response to the tremendous
growth of experimental development activities. There is also a moderate
rise in the number of researchers for basic research and applied research
during the period shown.

The number of R&D personnel is further broken down by R&D
executive entities. Enterprises have the largest share of R&D personnel,

Researchers per 10,000 people

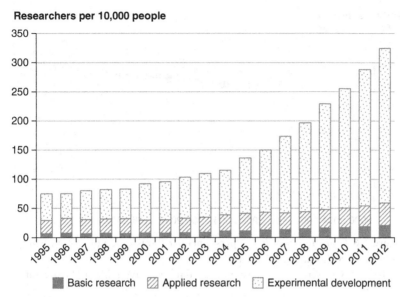

Figure 2.5a Total number of R&D personnel
Source: China Statistical Yearbook (1996–2013).

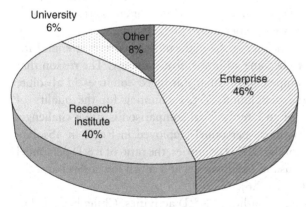

Figure 2.5b R&D personnel by executive entity, 2009
Source: China Statistical Yearbook (2010).

while research institutes take almost an equally important share, 46 per cent and 40 per cent respectively in 2009 (Figure 2.5b). The distribution of R&D personnel across different performing entities is in line with the type of R&D activities carried out in China. For

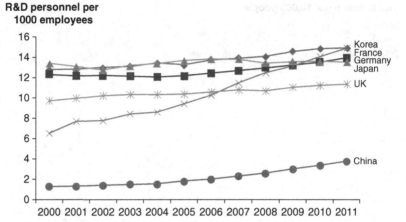

Figure 2.6 Comparison of R&D personnel per thousand employees in China and OECD economies, 2000–2011
Source: OECD science and technology database available at http://stats.oecd.org.

example, universities absorb only 6 per cent of R&D researchers, similar to the amount of money spent in basic research activities, and the majority of R&D personnel are working for enterprises in which the main R&D activity is experimental development.

The large R&D workforce is one of the most important strengths for China on its path to become an innovative economy. The reason that China is able to compete with other advanced countries in absolute numbers is its large population. Yet, accounting for the quality of innovation by way of an international comparison is still a challenge. Although China has more personnel employed in R&D in absolute numbers than most of the OECD countries, the ratio of R&D personnel weighted by per thousand employees is at a much lower level and the growth is modest (Figure 2.6).

Apart from relying on in-house R&D activities, China has tried to acquire advanced technologies via various sources. Importing technologies from foreign countries, complementing indigenous efforts, has been commonly acknowledged as a substantial driver to technological upgrading in China. One of the most straightforward ways to obtain foreign technology is through global market transaction such as purchasing licenses, patents and copyrights. Figure 2.7a exhibits

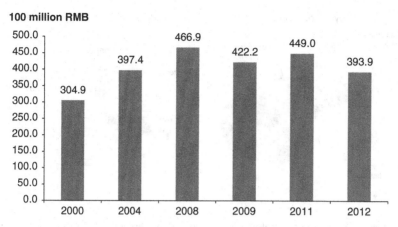

100 million RMB

Figure 2.7a Expenditure for acquisition of foreign technology in China, 2000–2012
Source: China Statistical Yearbook (2001–2013). The 2013 Statistical Yearbook does not cover the expenditure for acquisition of technology import in 2002, 2003, 2005, 2006, 2007 or 2010.

the trend of expenditure for purchasing foreign technology in China from 2000 to 2012. Since joining the World Trade Organisation (WTO) in 2001, the scale of foreign technology acquisition in China had a 30 per cent annual increase and reached a peak in 2008 with RMB 46.69 billion. After the financial crisis in 2008, the annual expenditure for foreign technology import has gone through some fluctuations but the volume has always been above 39.39 billion RMB.

Among different types of foreign technology imports in 2012, the majority of spending was for technology licensing (37 per cent) and foreign technology consultation (32 per cent) as the left pie graph in Figure 2.7b shows. In 2012, China spent about 15 per cent of its budget for technology import for patent technology licensing and transfer, while the remaining 16 per cent went for importing computer software (6 per cent), trade mark license (1 per cent) and other technology imports (9 per cent). Noticeably, a regional disparity has also been shown for the technology imports. The right pie graph in Figure 2.7b shows the total expenditure for technology import across different regions of China. The eastern region as the most economically developed area absorbed nearly 68 per cent of imported

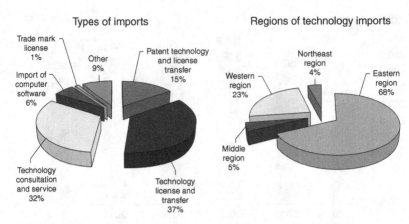

Figure 2.7b Foreign technology imports in China, percentages, 2012
Source: China Statistical Yearbook on Science and Technology (2013).

technologies. The western region accounted for 23 per cent, while the middle and northeast region in total received 9 per cent of the imported technology in 2012.

2.3 Innovation outputs: patents and published journal articles

Patents

Beyond the increasing tendency for the use of innovation inputs, equal attention is being paid to the performance of innovation, which is of interest in assessing the quality of the innovation. One of the commonly used indicators at the aggregated level to measure innovation is the total number of patent applications. Domestic patent applications to the Chinese State Intellectual Property Office (SIPO) increased nearly sixfold between 1995 and 2005, while the number of granted patents increased slightly less, about fivefold during the same period of time as illustrated in Figure 2.8. Foreign applications, though fewer in absolute numbers, rose at an even higher rate by more than sixfold and tenfold for applications and patents granted, respectively. Such a surge in patent applications can be explained by the persistent efforts devoted to R&D, as well as the increasing awareness of the value of IPR protection. The growth of patent applications increased even more after the launch of National Innovation Strategy in 2006.

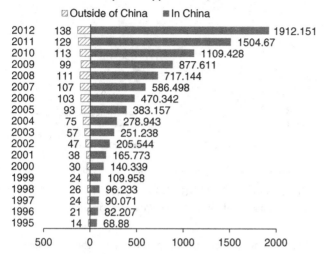

Number of patent applications, 1000 units

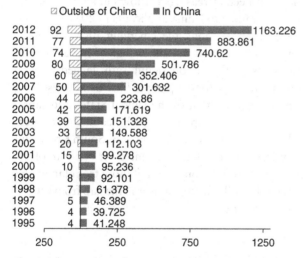

Number of granted patents, 1000 units

Figure 2.8 Number of patent applications vs number of granted patents, 1995–2012
Source: China Statistical Yearbook (1996–2013).

Patent applications to the SIPO reached 1.912 million during all of 2012, whereas the number of granted patents reached 1,163,000, nearly five and seven times, respectively, higher compared to the levels in 2005.

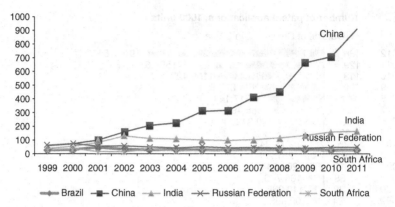

Figure 2.9 Triadic patent families across BRICS, 1999–2011
Source: OECD patent database available at http://stats.oecd.org.

As in the United States, the European Union and Japan, the number of Chinese triadic patents,[5] which are acknowledged as a better measure of the value of innovation, has been increasing, as shown in Figure 2.9. The number of triadic patents granted to China applicants in 2011 was 909, which was the highest number among the emerging BRIC countries (Brazil, Russia, India and China) and five times that of India.[6] Brazil, South Africa and the Russian Federation significantly lagged behind. Nevertheless, the total number of triadic patents filed by Chinese residents is still less than one-tenth of that of the United States and Japan (Figure 2.10). The United States and Japan are still the leading performers in triadic patent families, followed by Germany, France, South Korea and the UK. Application numbers from China accounted for one-fifth of the number from Germany, and less than one-tenth of those from Japan and the United States. This level is still low for China and the gap from OECD countries remains extremely large.

Journal articles

The higher education sector not only contributes to innovation development through its direct participation in various innovation activities but

---

[5] Triadic patents are a series of corresponding patents filed at the European Patent Office, the United States Patent and Trademark Office and the Japan Patent Office, for the same invention, by the same applicant or inventor.
[6] The data come from www.wipo.int/ipstats/en/statistics/patents.

**Number of triadic
patent families**

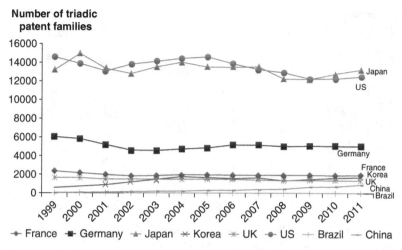

Figure 2.10 Number of triadic patent families in China and other OECD economies, 1999–2011
Source: OECD science and technology database available at http://stats.oecd.org

also through its education mission, which ensures a future supply of human resources for innovation. One of the indicators to measure innovation performance in the higher education sector is the volume of articles published worldwide. Beyond the substantial increase of domestic publications, the articles published in international peer-reviewed journals by Chinese authors or Chinese co-authors collaborating with foreign researchers have also experienced a noticeable increase. As shown in Figure 2.11, the number of articles from Chinese universities published in international journals has been increasing gradually since 2005. In 2010, the number reached 320,345, double the number in 2005.

Yet bare numbers of publications can hardly indicate the quality by themselves, and there is continuous debate about the productivity of Chinese innovation personnel. The number of citations assesses the productivity and influence of scientific literature and also serves as a measurement of the visibility of scientific research. The study conducted by Hu (2011) shows that Chinana citation ranking shifted from 19th place to 10th during the 1992–2008 period. The 12th Five-year Science and Technology Development Plan launched in 2011 aimed to further raise China's citation ranking from 8th in 2010 to 5th by the end of 2015 (World Bank, 2013). Figure 2.12 calculates the number of accumulated publications and frequency of citations between 2000

1000 articles

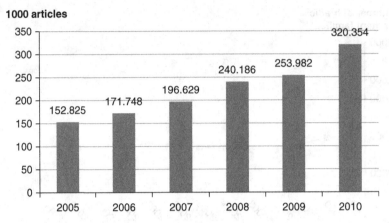

Figure 2.11 Output of R&D: index articles published in international journals
Source: China Statistical Yearbook (2006–2011).

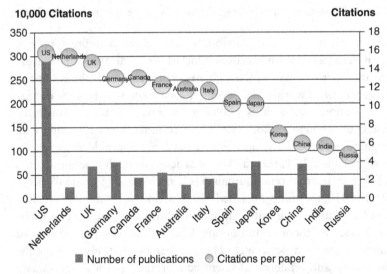

Figure 2.12 Citations of scientific papers published, 2000–2010
Source: China Statistical Yearbook (2011).

and 2010. China ranks fourth in the output of publications during the period under review, after the United States, Japan and Germany. Not surprisingly, and consistent with the findings from other studies (Simon and Cao 2009; Royal Society 2011), the citation frequency ranking of

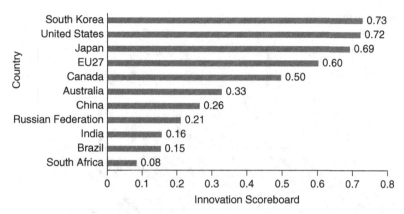

Figure 2.13 Innovation performance: international comparison, 2012
Source: EC Innovation Scoreboard (2013).

publications from China is in general lower compared to OECD economies. Given the immense investment of R&D and the large number of
R&D personnel, the lower level of productive research clearly shows
that the quality of innovation in China is severely limited. Further
efforts should be exerted to improve quality rather than quantity.

2.4 Overall innovation performance: an international comparison

Consistent findings are obtained when evaluating China's national innovation capabilities using another comprehensive index, the Innovation
Scoreboard created by the European Commission.[7] China's score is only
one-third that of the United States, South Korea and Japan, although it
the best performer among BRIC countries (Figure 2.13). Despite these
remarkable achievements, China faces significant challenges in enhancing
its innovation capability.

2.5 Industry distribution

The extent to which enterprises generate and exploit knowledge
varies across industries. To gauge the nature and underlying role of

---

[7] This index is based on 25 indicators covering a wide range of innovation enablers,
firm activities and outputs.

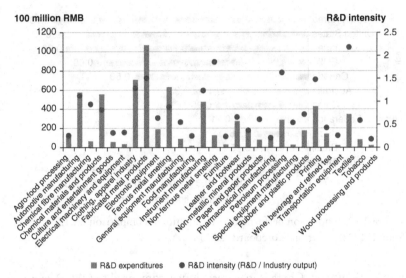

Figure 2.14 R&D expenditures and intensity of enterprises in the above-scale manufacturing industries, 2012
Source: China Statistical Yearbook (2013).

technology in economic growth, it is essential to assess the innovation activities and performance on the basis of industrial specificities. R&D expenditure by industry provides valuable information on the technological strengths of industries. In particular, the association of R&D with industries permits the link between technology and different dimensions of industries' economic performance. Figure 2.14 shows that the technology-intensive industries such as electronic equipment and electrical machinery attract the most R&D investment, while, among low-tech industries, the level of R&D spending remains substantially low.[8] The decomposition of the Chinese R&D portfolio by industry shows the emergence of Chinese high-tech sectors, which reported a higher share of technological efforts.

[8] On the basis of industry classification by technology intensity introduced by the OECD, manufacturing industries are classified in four exclusive categories: high technology, medium-high technology, medium-low technology and low technology. The classification is based on indicators such as R&D expenditures divided by value added and R&D expenditures divided by production, reflecting to different degrees 'technology producer' and 'technology adopter' aspects.

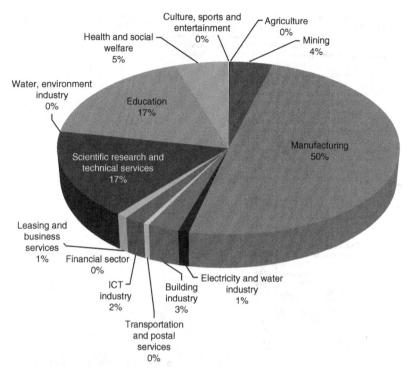

Figure 2.15 Number of R&D personnel across sectors, 2009
Source: China Statistical Yearbook (2010).

Figure 2.15 breaks down the total number of the R&D workforce across sectors. The pie graph highlights the dominance of the manufacturing sector and how it absorbs most of the R&D personnel. In 2009, the education and technical service sectors shared an equal amount of R&D personnel in China (17 per cent), followed by health and social welfare (5 per cent) and the mining sector (4 per cent).

Turning to the innovation output across industries, a significant part of patent applications is attributed to high-tech industries. Calculated at the aggregate level, the patent application share of high-tech industries accounted for 75 per cent, whereas that of low-tech industries equalled 25 per cent in 2010.[9] The sum of the electronic equipment and

---

[9] The Technology Intensity Definition is in accordance with OECD classification. For more details, please see www.oecd.org/sti/ind/48350231.pdf

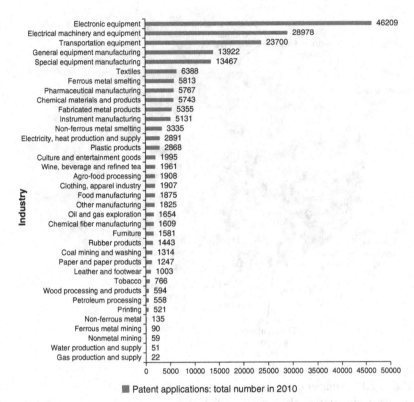

Figure 2.16 Innovation output across industries: number of patent applications, 2010
Source: China Statistical Yearbook (2011).

electrical machinery industries was responsible for 38.9 per cent of total patent applications to China's State Intellectual Property Office (Figure 2.16), followed by medium-high-technology industries such as transportation equipment and equipment manufacturing. Medium-low and low-tech industries share only fractions in the total number of patent applications in China.

A similar pattern was observed for new product sales and new product exports across industries, as shown in Figure 2.17. In response to the large R&D expenditures in high-tech industries, both sales and exports due to new products are remarkably higher in 2012 because of new products, notably for industries such as electronic equipment, electrical machinery and chemical material. Medium-low

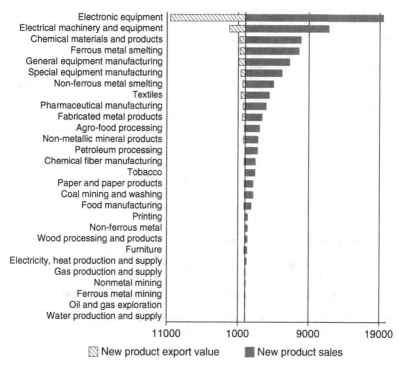

Figure 2.17 Innovation outputs across industries: new product sales and new product export values, 2012
Source: China Statistical Yearbook (2013).

and low-tech industries are in general less productive in sales and exports from new products.

The high-tech product export and import volumes are presented in Figure 2.18. From 1995 to 2012, exports of high-technology products from China increased from RMB 101 billion to RMB 6,012 billion. This rapid increase in high-tech product trade reflects the increasing importance of this trade for the Chinese economy. China has gradually become a major exporter of high-technology final products in the world. Interestingly, between 1995 and 2012, imports and exports of high-tech goods have increased almost at the same pace. With reference to the volumes, the exports of products from high-tech industries were not substantially higher than those of imports before 2005. The gap between exports and imports in high-tech industries gradually widened after 2005. The highest surplus in high-technology product

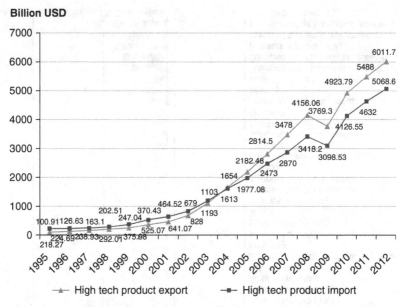

Billion USD

Figure 2.18 Export and import volume of high-tech products, 1995–2012
Source: China Statistical Yearbook (1996–2013).

trade occurred in 2012. The total of exports is US$943 billion (18.6 per cent) higher than total imports in the high-technology sector. This, to a certain extent, reflects that China's export-oriented manufacturing industry is still engaged in processing and assembly operations. Export competitiveness is predominantly based on low factor costs (Fu, 2003).

The extent of innovation outputs in China that accrues to foreign invested firms should not be neglected. As shown in Figure 2.19, foreign-owned firms produce almost a quarter of new product sales (24 per cent), and they had the highest share of new product exports in 2012, accounting for 44 per cent of total new product exports value. Domestic firms occupy the leading role in new product sales and account for nearly 66 per cent of total sales due to new products in 2012. The new-product exports from domestic Chinese firms take up to 41 per cent, which is slightly less than for foreign owned firms. Hong Kong, Macau and Taiwan invested firms account for one-tenth of total new product sales, and their share of total new-product export value is about 15 per cent.

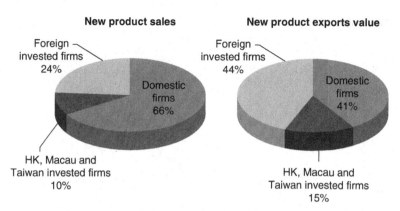

Figure 2.19 Innovation outputs by ownership of firms: new product sales and new product export values, 2012
Source: China Statistical Yearbook (2013).

2.6 Innovativeness across ownership structures

The paradigm of the National Innovation System suggests that heterogeneous national innovation output may be explained by institutional divergences (Lundvall, 1992; Freeman, 1995). Chinese firms have distinctive characteristics of corporate governance, including concentrated ownership structures: state ownership (SOEs), other domestic ownership and the emergence of foreign investors. Differences in ownership structures explain R&D activity and innovation performance across countries (Hoskisson et al., 2002). As shown in Figure 2.20, although the total amount of R&D investment increased significantly over the 2006 to 2012 period, the ownership composition of R&D investment has remained relative stable. Figure 2.21 compares the ownership structures of R&D spending in 2006 and 2012. Domestic firms (excluding SOEs) hold the dominant role, while the share in the total R&D expenditure by SOEs and foreign owned enterprises declined 2 per cent and 3 per cent, respectively. The proportions shared by Hong Kong, Macau and Taiwan (HMT) owned enterprises did not differ from 2006 to 2012.

A similar pattern is displayed when we look at the ownership structure of R&D personnel in China (Figure 2.22). Domestic enterprises absorbed the majority of the R&D workforce, 66 per cent, for both 2006 and 2012. There has been a slight increase in R&D personnel

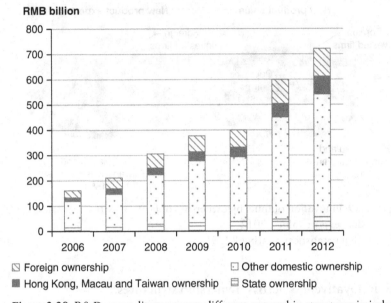

□ Foreign ownership   □ Other domestic ownership
■ Hong Kong, Macau and Taiwan ownership   ▤ State ownership

Figure 2.20 R&D expenditures across different ownership structures in industrial enterprises above designated size, 2006–2012
Source: China Statistical Yearbook on Science and Technology (2007–2013).

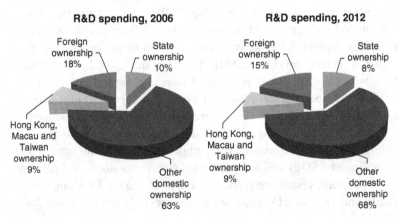

Figure 2.21 R&D expenditures across different ownership structures in industrial enterprises above designated size, 2006 and 2012
Source: China Statistical Yearbook (2007 and 2013).

1000 people, per year

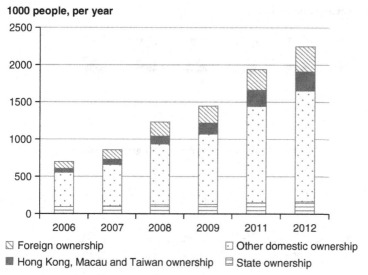

Foreign ownership / Other domestic ownership / Hong Kong, Macau and Taiwan ownership / State ownership

Figure 2.22 R&D personnel across different ownership structures in industrial enterprises above designated size, 2006–2012
Source: China Statistical Yearbook on Science and Technology (2007–2013). Data for 2010 were not published in the Yearbook.

shares for both foreign owned (from 7 per cent to 12 per cent) and HMT owned enterprises (from 13 per cent to 15 per cent), whereas the share for SOEs has dropped to half, from 14 per cent in 2006 to only 7 per cent in 2012, although the number of R&D personnel in absolute terms in this sector increased.

With respect to innovation outputs, ownership composition of patent applications is well matched with the corresponding structures of R&D expenditure and R&D personnel. With relatively higher scales of input of R&D and human capital, domestic firms take up the greatest part of patent applications in China, followed by enterprises with foreign and HMT ownership (Figure 2.23). In terms of the absolute number, patent applications filed by domestic firms in 2012 reached 348,421, nearly seven times higher compared to 2006. In parallel with the small shares in R&D and human capital investment, SOEs take the lowest proportion with respect to the number of patent applications in China.

Interesting findings are uncovered if innovation output is measured by the sales and exports due to new products. Accompanied by the

38   *Introduction*

Pieces of patent in percentages

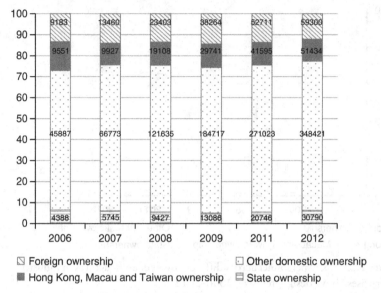

Foreign ownership Other domestic ownership
Hong Kong, Macau and Taiwan ownership State ownership

Figure 2.23 Patent applications across different ownership structures in industrial enterprises above designated size, 2009–2012
Source: China Statistical Yearbook on Science and Technology (2007–2013). Data for 2010 were not published in the Yearbook.

intensive investment in innovation inputs, the value of new product sales generated by domestic firms has experienced remarkable growth and surged to RMB 6,532 billion in 2012 as shown in Figure 2.24. Although the absolute value of new product sales generated by SOEs increased, the corresponding share has declined gradually from 10 per cent in 2009 to 7 per cent in 2012. The only observed increasing trend in the share of new product sales during the period under review is for domestic enterprises, from 54 per cent to 59 per cent. Such moderate change may be considered evidence of improvement in innovation efficiency among domestic enterprises in China. Having reached RMB 957 billion in 2012, foreign owned enterprises account for 44 per cent of total new product exports. Corresponding values reported for domestic enterprise is RMB 869 billion, nearly double the value in 2009. SOEs have had a less important performance in exporting innovative products with a share of 2 per cent in 2012.

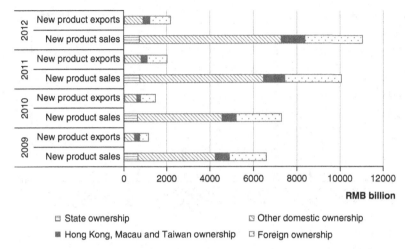

Figure 2.24 New product sales and new product exports across different ownership structures in industrial enterprises above designated size, 2009–2012
Source: China Statistical Yearbook on Science and Technology (2010–2013)

2.7 Regional disparity

Given China's vast size and diversity, its municipalities and provinces have distinct characteristics and substantial populations. Statistics of national averages under these circumstances can be particularly misleading. One of the notable features of the Chinese innovation system is the large regional disparity of R&D, as illustrated by Figure 2.25. The investment of R&D concentrated in several provinces and cities, such as Jiangsu, Beijing, Guangdong and Shandong, amounted to 45 per cent of total R&D expenditure in 2012.

In 2000, the highest R&D expenditures were found in Beijing, followed by Gansu, Shanghai and Jiangxi as shown in Figure 2.26. Southern and western China were evidently less innovative and R&D expenditures were scarce. Benefiting from the reform and opening policy and export-oriented industrialisation, the East and coastal regions were catching up at a remarkable pace, especially in Guangdong and Zhejiang provinces. With R&D expenditure below RMB 80 thousand in 2000, Guangdong has successfully become one of the most active provinces in R&D investment, which reached more than RMB 123

40 *Introduction*

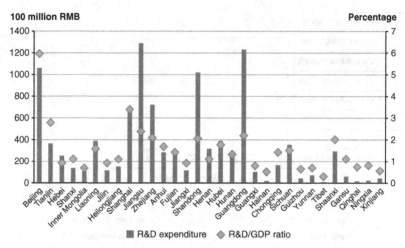

Figure 2.25 R&D expenditures and R&D/GDP ratios across China, 2012
Source: China Statistical Yearbook (2013).

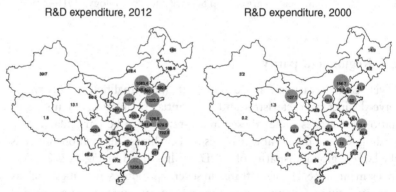

Figure 2.26 R&D expenditures across China, 2000 and 2012
Source: China Statistical Yearbook (2000 and 2013).

million in 2012. Similar exceptional increases have also been observed for Zhejiang, Jiangsu and Shandong provinces, while inland China was also catching up but at a moderate speed. It is clearly shown by Figure 2.26 that profound disparities of R&D investments are still prevalent across China, where coastal areas absorbed a large proportion of R&D spending and inland China, especially the western part, remains less innovative.

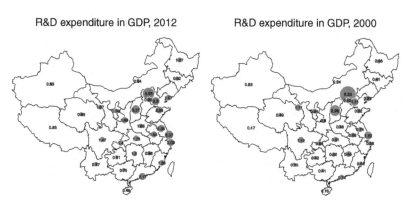

Figure 2.27 Ratio of R&D expenditures in GDP across China, 2000 and 2012
Source: China Statistical Yearbook (2000 and 2013).

Figure 2.27 presents the ratios of R&D spending in regional GDP across provinces in China. Except for Beijing and Gansu, innovation intensities rose from 2000 to 2012 across China. The highest R&D intensity was found in Beijing, at 6.28 per cent of GDP in 2000 and 5.95 per cent in 2012. The ratio for Beijing in 2012 was nearly three times that of the national average and the lowest for that year was in Tibet, at only 0.25 per cent of GDP, or just above one-eighth of the national average.

Being aware of the divergence among regions and the risk that the gap will further enlarge, the central government launched the 'Go West' strategy in 2000 to accelerate convergence. R&D expenditure and intensity in the middle and the western regions have been increasing, but the levels of knowledge stocks still remain at a lower level. It is worth noting that the large R&D spending and R&D intensity in the Gansu, Shaaxi and Shaanxi regions may be explained by the inherited R&D facilities, including military research bases, government research institutions and universities, which were located there for strategic reason during the cold war.

In addition to R&D expenditure, the large regional disparities are also observed in relation to innovation output. Figure 2.28 displays the mean value of patent applications across China in 2000 and 2012. The mean value of patent application, indicated by the horizontal bar, has risen significantly from 2,757 pieces in 2000 to 60,824 pieces in 2012. The statistics on the map clearly show that the pattern of disparity is similar to the innovation input indicators: the municipalities and

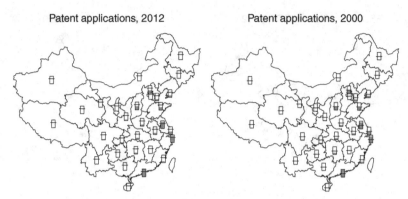

Figure 2.28 Mean patent application numbers across China, 2000 and 2012
Note: Grey area indicates the ratio of patent applications weighted by local population (10,000 people) in each regions; the bar denotes the mean of patent application numbers at the national level.
Source: China Statistical Yearbook (2000 and 2013).

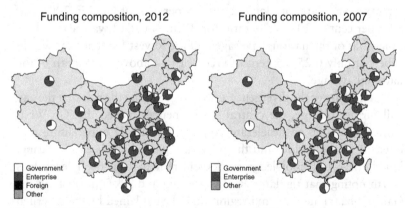

Figure 2.29 R&D funding sources across China, 2009
Source: China Statistical Yearbook (2008 and 2013).

provinces with the highest R&D intensity are in the lead, with other parts of the country following at a staggered pace.

Accordingly, adopting effective innovation policies as a tool together with other government incentives to narrow the existing gap is imperative. The breaking down of R&D funding source across regions is shown in Figure 2.29. Whereas enterprises funding plays a dominant role in sustaining R&D activities in the East and coastal regions, including Beijing, Shanghai, Guangdong, Jiangsu and Zhejiang, the government funds are mainly assimilated by the central and west provinces. Comparing the composition from 2012 to that of 2000 shows a tendency of increasing funding from enterprises, whereas the government funding becomes less prevalent. With respect to the foreign funding for innovation, only limited proportions have emerged among the giant cities such as Beijing and Shanghai.

PART I

International knowledge transfer and technological takeoff

3 | Foreign direct investment, absorptive capacity and regional innovative capabilities: Evidence from China

3.1 Introduction

Technological capabilities are a key component of competitiveness at national, regional and firm levels. The development of regional innovation capabilities has been of crucial importance for competitiveness building in both developed and developing countries. The past decade has seen increasing research on the regional innovation system. It is argued that there is something distinctive and systemic about innovation as a localised phenomenon that cannot be predicted by the more familiar national innovation systems frameworks (Metcalfe, 1997; Braczyk, Cooke and Heidenreich, 1998). Although knowledge is a non-rival public production asset, which can generate positive externalities or spillovers to others (Nelson, 1959; Arrow, 1962; Griliches, 1979), knowledge spillovers are geographically localised (Jaffe, Trajtenberg and Henderson, 1993; Audretsch and Feldman, 1996; Almeida and Kogut, 1997, Anselin, Varga and Acs, 1997). Knowledge and information may flow more easily among agents located within the same area because of social bonds that foster reciprocal trust and frequent face-to-face contacts (Breschi and Lissoni, 2001). Therefore, there may be geographic boundaries to information flows or knowledge spillovers among the firms in an industry (Krugman, 1991). These spatially bounded knowledge spillovers allow companies operating nearby important knowledge sources to introduce innovations at a faster rate than rival firms located elsewhere. This is particularly the case for 'tacit' knowledge, that is, highly contextual and difficult to codify information, which is therefore more easily transmitted through face-to-face contacts and personal relationships. Therefore, regional systems can much better capture the local nature of innovation than other wider eco-geographical systems.

Among the important players in the regional innovation system are the multinational enterprises (MNEs) and their affiliates. MNEs are a major force conducting cutting-edge research and innovation. Multinational companies are often regarded as possessing certain advantages that enable them to succeed in the global market. Their advantages, their firm-specific assets, are often of a technological nature. From 1970 to 1985, more than 80 per cent of royalty payments for international technology transfers were made by affiliates to their parent companies (UNCTAD, 2005a). Therefore, openness of the local economy to multinational enterprises located in the region may have a significant impact on regional innovation performance. The strength of the effect of FDI on regional innovation capacity may, however, depend on the absorptive capacity of the host regions. Innovation is an evolutionary and accumulative process. Only with the necessary capability to identify, assimilate and develop useful external knowledge can the host regions effectively benefit from the advanced technology embedded in FDI. Although there has been some research on the role of absorptive capacity at the firm level, empirical studies of the role of absorptive capacity in the evolving regional innovation system in the developing countries have been rare.

In this chapter, I investigate the impact of FDI on regional innovation capabilities in China with special emphasis on the role of absorptive capacity and complementary assets in determining the strength of the assimilation and modification. This chapter is organised as follows: Section 3.2 presents the theoretical framework for understanding relations between FDI, absorptive capacity and regional innovation performance. Section 3.3 provides an overview of FDI and innovation in China. Section 3.4 discusses the impact of FDI on regional innovation capacity. Section 3.5 analyses FDI and regional innovation efficiency. Section 3.6 examines the linkage between FDI, innovation, and regional economic growth in China. Section 3.7 concludes with some policy implications.

3.2 Foreign direct investment, absorptive capacity and regional innovation capabilities in developing countries: a theoretical framework

The development of technological capabilities is the outcome of a complex interaction of incentive structure with human resources, technology efforts and institutional factors. The incentive structure includes macroeconomic incentives – incentives from competition and factor markets, and the institutions include market and non-market institutions such as the legal framework, industrial institutions and training and technology institutions. It is the interplay of all these factors in particular country settings that determines at the regional level how well the regions employ the resources and develop their technological capabilities (Lall, 1992). In other words, it is the efforts of the agents in a region (i.e., business, government and the universities) and the strength of the linkages between these agents that determine the performance of a regional innovation system (Braczyk, Cooke and Heidenreich, 1998; Fu et al., 2006a).

Foreign direct investment contributes to regional innovation in four ways. First, R&D and other forms of innovation generated by foreign firms and R&D labs of MNEs increase the innovation outputs in the region directly. Increasing FDI contributes to the emergence of newer economies with more sophisticated technology generation (Athreye and Cantwell, 2007). Globalisation of R&D activities by MNEs has been a major shift in international business in recent decades. MNEs have three types of global R&D programmes: support laboratories, locally integrated laboratories and internationally interdependent laboratories (Pearce, 1999). When the operations of MNEs in host countries move from being cost based towards the supply of higher-value parts, their R&D activities may eventually accede to locally integrated laboratory status. Increases in the international spread of subsidiary research efforts in MNEs have tended on average to reinforce the position of established centres of higher-grade technological activity (Athreye and Cantwell, 2007). Depending on the availability of low-cost but high-end skilled human capital, MNEs may even establish international interdependent laboratories that are oriented to basic research in one or more scientific disciplines. These independent laboratories have the potential to reinforce a country's developing strength in basic research that may provide technological inputs to radical innovation (Pearce, 2005).

Second, spillovers emanating from foreign innovation activities may affect the innovation performance in the region in which they are located. Several channels exist for knowledge to spill over from foreign to local firms. These include knowledge transfers through the supply chain, skilled labour turnovers and demonstration effects. Knowledge transfer via supply chain requires effective quality linkages between foreign firms and local suppliers and customers. When cross-regional labour mobility is low, any benefits from MNEs are likely to mainly go to local firms (Greenaway, Upward and Wright, 2002). Demonstration effects may also be local if firms only closely observe and imitate those in the same region (Blomstrom and Kokko, 1998). Convincing evidence suggests a productivity advantage of MNEs over domestic firms in developing countries and some industrialised countries (e.g., Girma, Greenaway and Wakelin, 2001). Empirical evidence on the actual extent of spillovers from MNEs to domestic firms is, however, mixed (Blomstrom and Kokko, 1998; Görg and Greenaway, 2004).

Third, FDI may affect regional innovation capacity through competition effects. Market competition may also be a two-edged sword in terms of its effect on innovation. Geroski (1990) argues that lack of competition in a market will give rise to inefficiency and result in sluggish innovative activity. On the other hand, the traditional Schumpeterians claim that monopoly power makes it easier for firms to appropriate the returns from innovation and thereby provides the incentive to invest in innovation (Cohen and Levin, 1989; Symeonidis, 2001). Foreign R&D activities may also crowd out domestic innovation activities as they attract the most talented researchers and compete in the markets of innovation products that threaten local firms, SMEs in particular (Fu, 2004a, 2007; Aghion et al., 2005; UNCTAD, 2005b). In the Chinese electronics industry, Hu and Jefferson (2002) find significant productivity depression rather than positive spillover effects of FDI on domestic firms.

Finally, in addition to greater R&D investments by MNEs and their affiliates, FDI may contribute to regional innovation capabilities by advanced practices and experiences in innovation management and thereby greater efficiency in innovation. Innovation is not a simple linear transformation with basic science and other inputs at one end of a chain and commercialisation at the other (Hughes, 2003). Successful innovation requires more than brilliant scientists. It involves everyone from top management to employees in its R&D, finance, production and marketing divisions. It requires high-quality decision-making; long-range planning; motivation and management techniques; coordination; and efficient R&D, production and marketing. Therefore, the innovation performance of a firm is determined not only by 'hard' factors such as R&D personnel and R&D investment but also by certain 'soft' factors such as management practices and governance structures (Aghion and Tirole, 1994; Bessant, Caffyn and Gilbert, 1996; Cosh, Fu and Hughes, 2004). MNEs are major participants in innovation and are more experienced in innovation management. They may contribute to the local innovation system by transferring managerial know-how to local firms through spillover effects.

However, two main conditions are needed for significant spillovers from FDI: one is the absorptive capacity of the local firms and organisations (Cohen and Levinthal, 1989; Girma, 2005), and the second is sufficient effective linkages generated between the foreign and domestic economic activities (Balasubramanayam, Salisu and Sapsford, 1996; Fu, 2004b). Absorptive capacity refers to the ability of an organisation or region to identify, assimilate and exploit knowledge from the environment (Cohen and Levinthal, 1989). Absorptive capacity is usually proxied by the technology gap between the foreign and the domestic firms, R&D intensities of the local firms or human capital embodied in local firms. Studies using the first approach find that spillovers are present when the technology gaps are moderate (Kokko, Tansini and Zejan, 1996); smaller plants or plants with a low share of skilled workers in the workforce lack the necessary absorptive capacity to benefit from FDI. R&D activities of organisations have two faces (Aghion and Howitt, 1992, 1998; Griffith, Redding and Van Reenen, 2003). One is the widely acknowledged knowledge creation function; the other is their role in learning and promoting 'absorptive capacity', given the fact that innovation is cumulative and path dependent. It is argued that a certain level of R&D intensity is needed before firms benefit from FDI-generated externalities. The absorptive capacities of the local firms and organisations in turn determine the overall absorptive capacities of the host region, as they are the basic elements in a regional innovation system.

In addition to absorptive capacity, complementary assets (ingredients) may play an important role in forming the overall dynamic capabilities required to convert technological opportunities into innovative sales and competitive market advantage (Teece, 1986; Teece, Pisano and Shuen, 1997; Hughes and Scott Morton, 2006; Cosh, Fu and Hughes, 2012; Fu, 2012). The introduction of substantially new or improved products requires parallel shifts in the strategy of organisations, the structure of organisations and practices in management. MNEs are also more likely to locate in regions with sound scientific and educational infrastructure, the potential for intra- and interindustry spillovers or locally embedded specialisation because they are seeking complementary assets to most effectively transfer and commercialise their technological advantage (Cantwell and Santangelo, 1999; Cantwell and Piscitello, 2002). Therefore, a region's receptiveness to new ideas, the strength of its entrepreneurship, information and communication infrastructure as well as the presence of clusters of high-technology industries may all enhance its capability in the assimilation of new ideas and technology generated internally or transferred from external sources.

In summary, FDI impacts on regional innovation capabilities in several ways. First, FDI may contribute to the overall regional innovation performance directly as a result of the greater innovation intensity in MNEs. Second, FDI may contribute to regional innovation performance through greater innovation efficiency in MNEs. Third, FDI may affect innovation capability of local indigenous firms through technological and managerial knowledge spillovers. The strength of the FDI effect on regional innovation capabilities depends on the absorptive capacity of and the complementary assets in the domestic sector, the linkages between the foreign and the domestic sectors and the technology content of the FDI.

3.3 FDI and innovation in China

FDI in China

Since it launched economic reforms and called for foreign capital participation in its economy in 1979, China has received a large part of international direct investment flows. China has become the second largest FDI recipient in the world, after the United States, and the largest host country among developing countries. The fastest growth of FDI inflows into China started in the spring of 1992 after Deng Xiaoping circuited China's southern coastal areas and Special Economic Zones (SEZs). Since then, China has adopted a new approach, which turned away from special favourable regimes to FDI in the SEZs and selected coastal regions towards more nationwide implementation of open policies for FDI. Inflows of FDI into China reached a peak level of US$45.463 million in 1998. After a drop in 1999, mainly because of the impact of the Asian financial crisis and the rise of acquisition transactions in both OECD and non-OECD countries, FDI inflows into China resumed their fast-growing trend and reached a historical peak of US$60.63 billion in 2004 (Figure 3.1).

Figure 3.1 Trade and FDI in China, 1985–2004
Source: China Statistical Yearbook (1986–2005).

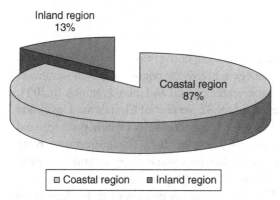

Figure 3.2 Regional distribution of FDI stock in China, 2005
Source: www.fdi.gov.cn/.

This huge inflow of FDI is, however, highly concentrated geographically in the coastal region. By 2005, total FDI stock in the coastal provinces accounted for 87 per cent of total FDI stock in China (Figure 3.2). This uneven distribution of FDI in China has economic, policy and geographic attributes and generates an uneven impact on regional competitive performance in China. As a result, the average FDI intensity measured by foreign assets in total industrial assets was 28 per cent in the coastal region, which was three times higher than that in the inland region at only 7 per cent. In Guangdong, Fujian and Shanghai, nearly half of the net fixed industrial assets are foreign invested (Table 3.1).

The sources and entry modes of inward FDI in China have also evolved over time. While investment from overseas Chinese in Hong Kong, Macao and Taiwan was the major source of inward FDI in the 1980s, the 1990s has seen increasing inward FDI from the major industrialised countries and other OECD countries. The entry modes of foreign firms have also evolved from joint ventures in the 1980s to wholly foreign-owned enterprises in the 1990s, which accounted for more than 70 per cent of all FDI projects in the late 1990s. Some large MNEs have started to set up their global R&D centres in China, mostly in its large coastal cities such as Beijing and Shanghai. With the launch of the Western Region Development Strategy by the Chinese government, the relocation of some foreign-invested enterprises into the inland regions has been increasing. They are, however, mostly in labour- or land-intensive industries.

Innovation

As one of the important drivers of competitiveness, innovation effort and performance in China are not even across the regions. Again, a significant gap in innovation exists between the coastal and inland regions. In 2004, the coastal provinces accounted for 82 per cent of China's total invention patent applications, 79 per cent of the total sales of new products and 73 per cent of total industrial R&D expenditure. The innovation activity in the coastal provinces is further concentrated in several provinces including Guangdong, Shanghai, Jiangsu, Shangdong and Zhejiang (Figures 3.3, 3.4, 3.5). Expenditure on acquisition of technology from abroad by the coastal region accounted for 67 per cent of China's total expenditure on foreign technology acquisition in 2004 and was about twice that of the inland region (Table 3.2). Jiangsu, Shanghai, Beijing and Guangdong are the top four regions that spend most on foreign technology acquisition. While Shanghai and Beijing acquire mainly foreign technology, Jiangsu and Guangdong rely on both foreign and domestic technology. The inland regions, with the exception of Chongqin, spend much less than most of the coastal regions, with one-third relying more on foreign technology and two-thirds acquiring more domestic technology.

Table 3.1 *FDI intensity: share of foreign assets in total industrial assets*

	1999	2004	1999–2004 average
Guangdong	50%	51%	51%
Fujian	48%	50%	50%
Shanghai	40%	49%	44%
Jiangsu	28%	37%	32%
Tianjin	28%	28%	27%
Beijing	19%	22%	20%
Zhejiang	19%	22%	19%
Liaoning	16%	16%	15%
Hainan	19%	14%	15%
Shandong	13%	16%	14%
Guangxi	9%	14%	13%
Hebei	12%	12%	12%
Coastal average	**25%**	**28%**	**26%**
Chongqing	13%	16%	16%
Anhui	9%	12%	12%
Jilin	11%	12%	11%
Hubei	11%	9%	10%
Jiangxi	6%	9%	7%
Henan	8%	7%	7%
Hunan	4%	8%	6%
Shaanxi	6%	4%	6%
Yunnan	6%	5%	6%
Sichuan	4%	6%	5%
Shanxi	2%	7%	5%
Ningxia	4%	8%	5%
Heilongjiang	6%	5%	5%
Inner Mongolia	3%	4%	4%
Gansu	3%	2%	2%
Guizhou	2%	3%	2%
Xinjiang	2%	1%	1%
Qinghai	1%	1%	1%
Tibet	1%	NA	1%
Inland average	**5%**	**7%**	**6%**

Source: Statistical Yearbook of China.

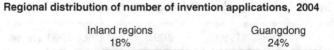

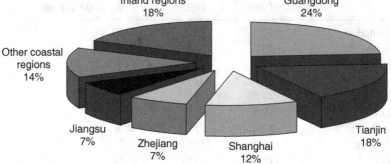

Figure 3.3 Regional distribution of number of invention applications, 2004
Source: First Economic Census of China (2004).

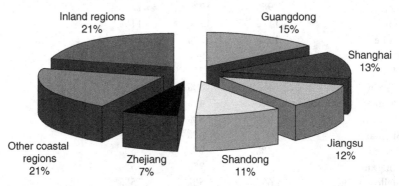

Figure 3.4 Regional distribution of sales of new products, 2004
Source: First Economic Census of China (2004).

Innovation by foreign firms

Since the late 1990s, with the increasing globalisation in innovation, the R&D activities of foreign firms in China have been increasing at a faster pace than those of the domestic firms. The average annual growth of R&D expenditure from 1998 to 2004 was 38 and 33 per cent in foreign invested enterprises and ethnic Chinese invested firms, respectively.[1]

---

[1] Ethnic Chinese invested firms refer to foreign firms that have owners from Hong Kong, Macao and Taiwan.

Table 3.2 *Expenditure on technology acquisition, 2004 (¥10th)*

Provinces	Expenditure on acquisition of technology from abroad	Expenditure on acquisition of technology from domestic sources	Expenditure on acquisition of technology from abroad Percentage	Expenditure on acquisition of technology from domestic sources Percentage
Whole	3679496	699192	100.0%	100.0%
Jiangsu	549744	90289	14.9%	12.9%
Shanghai	540190	33743	14.7%	4.8%
Beijing	314287	2865	8.5%	0.4%
Guangdong	258259	61465	7.0%	8.8%
Liaoning	210968	14075	5.7%	2.0%
Tianjin	163259	6578	4.4%	0.9%
Zhejiang	151700	40682	4.1%	5.8%
Shandong	138257	80177	3.8%	11.5%
Fujian	64123	25842	1.7%	3.7%
Guangxi	33388	11368	0.9%	1.6%
Hainan	486	1108	0.0%	0.2%
Coastal region total			65.9%	52.7%
Chongqin	253162	36568	6.9%	5.2%
Hubei	154054	38464	4.2%	5.5%
Hebei	137388	29658	3.7%	4.2%
Henan	127227	27226	3.5%	3.9%
Anhui	85003	10095	2.3%	1.4%
Jilin	84493	2695	2.3%	0.4%
Heilongjian	74177	29977	2.0%	4.3%
Hunan	66696	7769	1.8%	1.1%
Shaanxi	60553	27010	1.6%	3.9%
Shanxi	54788	18144	1.5%	2.6%
Jiangxi	48822	24384	1.3%	3.5%
Sichuan	47248	41492	1.3%	5.9%
Inner Mongolia	20988	6157	0.6%	0.9%
Gansu	16013	5579	0.4%	0.8%
Yunnan	9627	15479	0.3%	2.2%
Ningxia	9012	1850	0.2%	0.3%
Guizhou	3966	4525	0.1%	0.6%
Xinjiang	1529	3925	0.0%	0.6%

Table 3.2 (*cont.*)

Provinces	Expenditure on acquisition of technology from abroad	Expenditure on acquisition of technology from domestic sources	Expenditure on acquisition of technology from abroad Percentage	Expenditure on acquisition of technology from domestic sources Percentage
Qinghai	90	4	0.0%	0.0%
Tibet	na	na		
Inland region total			34.1%	47.3%

Source: First Economic Census of China, 2004.
Note: Expenditure on technology acquisition refers to expenditure on purchasing technology, including for product design, process design, blueprints, prescription, patents and relevant key equipment, instruments and samples from foreign or domestic sources.

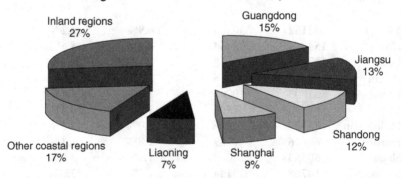

Regional distribution of industrial R&D, 2004

Inland regions 27%
Guangdong 15%
Jiangsu 13%
Shandong 12%
Shanghai 9%
Liaoning 7%
Other coastal regions 17%

Figure 3.5 Regional distribution of industrial R&D, 2004
Source: First Economic Census of China (2004).

This is much higher than that in indigenous firms at 25 per cent over the same time period (Table 3.3).

In 2004, the number of foreign firms was about one-third of China's total number of enterprises. Although the R&D expenditure and R&D staff of the foreign firms accounted for only 27 per cent and 18 per cent

Table 3.3 *Growth rate of R&D expenditure*

	1998	1999	2000	2001	2002	2003	Average annual change (1998–2003)
Indigenous enterprises	18%	44%	19%	18%	22%	32%	25%
FIEs by HKTM	50%	23%	12%	25%	27%	59%	33%
FIEs	7%	73%	19%	25%	53%	49%	38%

Source: First Economic Census of China, 2004.

of China's total industrial R&D expenditure and R&D staff, innovation outputs by foreign firms in terms of percentage of total sales of new products and the percentage of invention patent applications by foreign firms were both more than 40 per cent. This suggests higher productivity in innovation and better innovation management in foreign firms than in indigenous firms. The expenditure on acquisition of foreign technology by foreign firms accounted for nearly half of China's total expenditure on foreign technology acquisition, suggesting greater effort by foreign firms in acquiring advanced technology (Figure 3.6).[2]

3.4 FDI and innovation capacity: empirical evidence

The econometric analysis of the impact of FDI on regional innovation capacity starts from a basic region's innovation production function as follows:

$$Y_{i,t} = \alpha + \beta RDS_{i,t-1} + \lambda RDP_{i,t-1} + \gamma HC_{i,t-1} + \delta FDI_{i,t-1} + \varepsilon \quad (3.1)$$

where Y is innovation output, RDS is R&D expenditure, RDP is the number of people involved in research and development activity, HC is human capital, FDI is FDI intensity measured by the ratio of net fixed assets of FIEs to total industrial net fixed assets in the region and ε is the error term that has the normal property. All the variables are in

---

[2] Expenditure on absorption of foreign technology refers to expenditure on assimilation of foreign technology; this includes expenses for training, assimilation, imitation, and development of foreign technology and relevant staff costs and equipment costs.

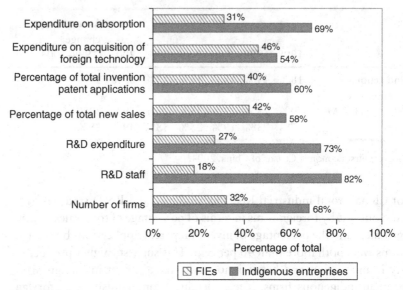

Figure 3.6 Innovation activities: foreign and indigenous enterprises in China, 2004
Source: First Economic Census of China (2004).

logarithm. We use one-year lagged values for all the explanatory variables. In other words, we assume that innovation production in a given year is reflected in the patents that are granted one year in the future. Another advantage in using one-year lag for the independent variables is that it removes the possible endogeneity between FDI and the dependent variable, number of patents, as FDI may choose to locate in regions that have high innovation capacity.

Here, following Jaffe (1989) and Acs, Luc and Varga (2002), we measure innovation output by number of patents granted to domestic applicants per 10,000 population. Although patent number has its advantages, it also suffers from the low face validity problem that patents do not fully reflect the commercial success and the value of new and renewed products (Acs and Audretsch, 1990; Kleinknecht, 1996). Investment in research and development is often found to be a significant determinant of innovation performance. Regions that invest more in R&D are more likely to innovate because R&D directly creates new products and processes. Labour force skills and the availability of qualified scientists and engineers, particularly the qualified research staff directly involved in R&D activities, are other widely recognised critical factors that contribute to firm innovation performance (Hoffman et al., 1998; Porter and Stern, 1999).

To capture the effects of absorptive capacity and complementary assets, we expend the model by including the interaction terms of FDI and absorptive capacity (ABC) and FDI and complementary assets (CA) alternatively. According to the literature discussed earlier, absorptive capacity is measured in two ways: regional R&D intensity (RDS) measured by the R&D spending to GDP ratio and labour force quality (HC) measured by the percentage of the population with 15 years of schooling. Absorptive capacities serve to enhance a region's capacity to recognise and absorb relevant external resources for innovation (Cohen and Levinthal, 1990). Complementary assets (CA) are also measured in three ways: (1) number of computers per thousand households (COMP), which may capture many innovative characteristics of a region, for example, information infrastructure and receptiveness to new ideas; (2) the share of value added from high-technology industry in regional total value added (HITECS), which indicates the industry and technology structure in a region and the industry infrastructure to assimilate and develop the R&D externalities from FDI; and (3) transaction value in technological markets (TECHMKT), which measures the extensiveness and depth of technology linkages, flows and transactions in the regions and reflects the development level and activeness of the institutions that facilitate the transfer of technology within a region.[3] Equation (3.1) is thus extended to the following:

$$Y_{i,t} = \alpha + \beta RDS_{i,t-1} + \lambda RDP_{i,t-1} + \gamma HC_{i,t-1} + \delta FDI_{i,t-1} \\ + \theta ABC_{i,t-1} * FDI_{i,t-1} + CA_{i,t-1} * FDI_{i,t-1} + \varepsilon_{i,t} \quad (3.2)$$

All the variables are in logarithm.

The three types of patents are invention, utility model and external design. Invention is a new technical solution related to a product, process or improvement thereof. Utility model refers to practical and new technological proposals on the shape and structure of a product or the combination of shape and structure. External design involves a new

---

[3] Technological transactions include technology transfer, technology consultation, technical service, technical training, technology-equity share exchange, technology intermediation and various research-production co-operations.

design of shape, pattern or combination of colour or aesthetic properties. Invention patents are regarded as major innovations. To obtain a patent for invention, an application must meet the requirements of novelty, inventiveness and practical applicability according to patent law. It usually takes about one to one and a half years to process an invention patent application in China, but six months or even less for utility model and design patents (Cheung and Lin, 2004). Given the different novelty and importance of the three types of patents, we run regression against Equation (3.2) using these three types of patent as the dependent variable alternatively to examine the impact of FDI on innovations of different degrees of novelty.

The data used relate to a provincial-level panel data set for the 31 provinces and municipality cities in China from 1998 to 2004. The data are collected from the China Statistical Yearbook and the Ministry of Science and Technology of China (MOST) online database. This study differs from some existing studies in that it uses the data from MOST for R&D expenditure and R&D staff rather than using the data of 'investment in innovation' published in the China Statistical Yearbook. The MOST data are more precise on R&D expenditure because 'investment in innovation' includes, in addition to spending on research and development, expenditure on renewal of fixed assets, capital construction, new site construction and expenditure on corresponding supplementary projects for production or welfare facilities and related activities.[4] The MOST measurement of R&D is also better than using expenditure and staff on science and technology because, according to the definition

---

[4] It includes (1) projects listed in the innovation plan of the current year of the central government and the local governments at various levels as well as projects that, although not listed in the innovation plan of the current year, are to continue being constructed in this year, using the investment listed in the plan of innovation of previous years and carried forward to this year; (2) projects of technological innovation or renewal of the original facilities, arranged both in the plan of innovation and in the plan of capital construction; extension projects (main workshops or a branch of the factory) with newly increased production capacity (or project efficiency) not up to the standard of a large and medium-sized project; and projects moving the whole factory to a new site so as to meet the requirements of urban environmental protection or safe production; (3) projects of reconstruction or technological innovation with a total investment of 500,000 RMB yuan and more by state-owned units, though listed neither in the plan of capital construction nor in the plan of innovation; the projects in the state-owned units of moving the whole factory to a new site so as to meet the requirements of urban environmental protection or safe production.

given by MOST and the State Statistical Bureau (SSB), science and technology include the broad social science disciplines in addition to the natural science and engineering disciplines.

Table 3.4 reports the estimation results of Equation (3.2) on the impact of FDI on regional innovation capacity. The estimated coefficient of the FDI variable is positive and statistically significant at the 99 per cent significance level. This fact suggests a significant contribution of FDI to regional innovation capacity. The magnitude of the estimated FDI coefficient in the base equation is 0.356, suggesting a 1 per cent increase in FDI intensity increases regional patent output by 0.35 per cent. These magnitudes are of a similar level to the R&D expenditure variable and sometimes even higher than that of the human capital variable.

The estimated coefficients of the two proxies of absorptive capacity – RD intensity and labour force skills – bear the expected positive sign and are statistically significant at the 99 per cent significance level. The estimated coefficients of the interaction terms between the absorptive variables and the FDI variable are positive and statistically significant as well. This evidence provides strong support to the proposition of the important role of absorptive capacity in assimilation of the knowledge spillovers from FDI.

We have three proxies to capture the complementary assets for innovation in the regions: number of computers per thousand households, the share of the high-technology sector in regional total value added and the transaction value in the technological market. The interaction terms between FDI and the first two complementary assets variables are positive and statistically significant.[5] This evidence suggests that better information and communication infrastructure, greater receptiveness to new ideas and a better developed cluster of high-technology sectors in the local economy will complement the advanced technology embodied in FDI, facilitate the innovation process and therefore lead to greater innovation capacity of the region. The

---

[5] The correlation coefficients between FDI intensity on one hand and computer usage, share of high-technology industry and technological market transaction values are as high as 0.57, 0.54 and 0.40, respectively, and statistically significant at the 1 per cent significance level. Inclusion of FDI and these complementary assets variables in the regression simultaneously raises significant multicolinearity problems. We, therefore, include FDI and the interaction terms only in the regression in addition to other variables of interest.

Table 3.4 Impact of FDI on regional innovation capacity

	Dependent variable: log (patents per thousand population)											
	Coef	p-value	Coef	p-value	Coef	p-value	Coef	p-value	Coef	p-value	Coef	p-value
C	1.309***	0.000	1.506***	0.000	2.591***	0.000	1.383***	0.000	1.265***	0.000	1.321***	0.000
LOG(RDGDP?(−1))	0.354***	0.002	0.690***	0.000	0.243**	0.043	0.392***	0.001	0.403***	0.001	0.411***	0.000
LOG(RDSTAF?(−1))	0.149*	0.058	0.147**	0.041	0.173**	0.025	0.157**	0.047	0.148*	0.061	0.118	0.132
LOG(HC?(−1))	0.316***	0.000	0.304***	0.001	0.724***	0.000	0.337***	0.000	0.287***	0.001	0.334***	0.000
LOG(FDIS?(−1))	0.357***	0.000	0.474***	0.000	0.816***	0.000	0.310***	0.000	0.299***	0.000	0.302***	0.000
LOG(FDIS?(−1))* LOG(RDGDP?(−1))	0.138***	0.008										
LOG(FDIS?(−1))* LOG(HC?(−1))					0.134**	0.018						
LOG(FDIS?(−1))* LOG(COMP?(−1))							0.020*	0.086				
LOG(FDIS?(−1))* LOG(HITECS?(−1))									0.041***	0.007		
LOG(FDIS?(−1))* LOG(TECHMKT?(−1))											0.010	0.291
LM	258.21***		175.27***		247.74***		212.76**		250.77**		268.82	
Hausman	0.07		2.18		7.74		6.53		7.85		32.18***	
Model	RE		RE		RE		RE		RE		FE	

Note: ***Significance at 99 per cent level; **significance at 95 per cent level; *significance at 90 per cent level.

estimated coefficient of the interaction variable between FDI and the technological market transaction value bears the expected positive sign but is not statistically significant. This may be explained by the lack of foreign participation in the technological market as evidenced in the survey that we discussed in an earlier section (Zhou, 2006).

3.5 FDI and regional innovation efficiency

Statistical analysis to investigate the impact of FDI on regional innovation efficiency involves two steps. We first evaluate the innovation efficiency using data envelopment analysis (DEA), which allows for multi-output and multi-input in the model. Second, we explore the role of FDI in the determination of regional innovation efficiency.

The three main approaches to the measurement of efficiency are ratio analysis, such as labour productivity and capital productivity; the normal econometric approach, such as the Solow-type total factor productivity (TFP) index; and the frontier approach, such as data envelopment analysis. TFP provides a more comprehensive guide to efficiency than does partial productivity. It takes into account the contribution of factors other than raw labour and capital, such as managerial skills and technical know-how. The conventional Solow-type total factor productivity defines TFP growth as the residual of output growth after the contribution of labour and capital inputs has been subtracted from total output growth. This method, however, attributes all the deviations from the expected output to TFP, without taking into account measurement error. It is subject to several well-known assumptions: (1) the form of production function is known, (2) there are constant returns to scale, (3) firms exhibit optimising behaviour, and (4) technical change is neutral. If these assumptions do not hold, TFP measurements will be biased (Coelli et al., 1998; Arcelus and Arocena, 2000).

The frontier approach evaluates a firm's efficiency against a measure of best practice. Two main methods are used for the estimation. One is a non-parametric programming approach, data envelopment analysis; another is a parametric production function approach, stochastic frontier analysis (SFA). In the DEA approach, a best-practice function is built empirically from observed inputs and outputs. The efficiency measure of a firm's innovation activity is defined by its position relative to the frontier of best performance established mathematically by the ratio of the weighted sum of outputs to the weighted sum of inputs (Charnes, Cooper and Rhodes, 1978). The strength of the programming approach lies not only in its lack of parameterisation but also in that no assumptions are made about the form of the production function. In addition, the programming approach allows us to estimate efficiency with multi-output and multi-input. This technique has a major shortcoming in that it has no provision for statistical noise, or measurement error, in the model (Norman and Stoker, 1991; Greene, 1997).

Given the advantages and disadvantages of the different efficiency estimation approaches, we use the DEA approach in the estimation of innovative efficiency because this method allows us to evaluate a firm's efficiency in innovation against best practice, and it allows us to estimate efficiency with multi-output and multi-input.

In the DEA approach, for a sample of n firms, if X and Y are the observations on innovation inputs and outputs, assuming variable returns to scale, the firm's innovative efficiency score, θ, is the solution to the linear program problem,

$$Max_{\theta,\lambda}\ \theta$$

$$\text{st.} -\theta y_i + Y\lambda \geq 0$$

$$x_i - X\lambda \geq 0$$

$$\lambda_i \geq 0$$

$$\Sigma\lambda_i = 1 \qquad i = 1,...,n. \tag{3.3}$$

where θ is a scalar and λ is an nx1 vector of constants. The efficiency score ranges from 0 to 1. If $\theta_k = 1$ and all slacks are zero, the kth firm is deemed to be technically efficient (Cooper, Seiford and Tone, 2000).

In the analysis, as our major objective is to maximise innovation output, we concentrate on output-oriented efficiency, which reflects a firm's efficiency in producing maximum innovation output with given inputs, under constant returns to scale. Innovation output is measured by the number of patents granted to each region. Given the differences in degrees of novelty across the three types of patents – invention, utility model and design – we include these three measures of innovation as outputs in our multi-output DEA model. Inputs in our models include the R&D expenditure to GDP ratio and the total number of R&D staff as a share of the total population. As invention patents are of higher degrees of novelty, we assume their importance is twice that of the utility models and design. Therefore, the weights restriction we use in the three-output DEA model is as follows:

$$Q_{\text{invention}} = 2\, q_{\text{utilitymodel}} = 2\, q_{\text{design}} \qquad (3.4)$$

The estimated regional innovation efficiency is then regressed on FDI intensity in each region. In the estimation of firm innovative efficiency, the efficiency scores have an upper bound of 1.0 and a lower bound of 0.0; the ordinary least squares estimates would be inconsistent. Therefore, the regression model for technical efficiency is specified in the form of the Tobit model as follows (Tobin, 1958; Fu and Balasubramanyam, 2003):

$$IE = \begin{cases} \alpha + \beta X_i + \mu & \text{if } \alpha + \beta X_i + \mu < 1 \\ 1 & \text{otherwise} \end{cases} \qquad (3.5)$$

where *IE* = innovative efficiency, and X_i is a vector of explanatory and control variables including FDI intensity, labour force skills and industry structure in the region.

Figure 3.7 shows the distribution of the estimated regional innovation efficiency. Patterns revealed from this figure suggest that the innovation efficiency of Chinese regions has been increasing over time from

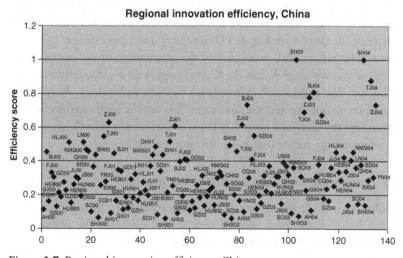

Figure 3.7 Regional innovation efficiency, China
Source: Author's estimation.

Table 3.5 *Impact of FDI on regional innovation efficiency*

	Dependent variable: *LOG(IE)*			
Variable	Coefficient	Prob.	Coefficient	Prob.
C	–0.963***	0.000	1.481***	0.001
LOG(FDIS?(–1))	0.157**	0.044	0.192**	0.021
LOG(HC?(–1))			0.596***	0.000
LOG(HITECS?(–1))			–0.263**	0.012
Random Effects				
Hausman statistics	0.16		0.05	
Adjusted R-squared	0.14		0.50	

Note: ***Significance at 99 per cent level; **significance at 95 per cent level; *significance at 90 per cent level.

2000 to 2005. Two observations form the regional innovation frontier: Shanghai in 2003 and 2004. Other regions close to the frontier are the several coastal provinces and municipalities including Tianjin, Beijing, Zhejiang and Guangdong.

Table 3.5 reports the estimated results on the impact of FDI on regional innovation efficiency. The estimated coefficients of the FDI variable are positive and statistically significant at the 5 per cent significance level. The results are robust across different specifications, suggesting a significant positive impact of FDI on regional innovation efficiency. Regions with higher FDI intensity are more efficient in innovation. Human capital, measured by the percentage of the population with a university degree, has the largest impact on regional innovation efficiency. The estimated coefficient of the high-technology share variable bears an unexpected negative sign. This may be explained by heavy investment in R&D and large R&D personnel numbers in the domestic high-technology sector that have not been used efficiently.

3.6 Innovation and regional economic growth

Finally, we include the innovation output variable in a growth function in the light of the new growth theory and estimate the impact of innovation on regional economic growth:

$$y_{it} = \alpha + \phi t_{it} + \beta l_{it} + \gamma k_{it} + \lambda x_{it} + v_{it} \qquad (3.6)$$

where i and t denote regions and time, respectively. The disturbance term, v_{it}, varies across regions and time and has the usual properties. The dependent variable, y_{it}, is the real growth rate of GDP; the explanatory variables are the number of patents granted, t_{it}; the growth rate of labour, l_{it}; the growth rate of the capital stock, k_{it}; and real growth rate of exports, x_{it}, and y_{it-1}, which is the one-year lag of y_{it}. Lowercase denotes logarithm. We introduce exports into the production function explicitly for three reasons. First, the incentives associated with export orientation are likely to lead to higher total factor productivity because of economies of scale and competition effects. Second, exports are likely to alleviate serious foreign exchange constraints and thereby enable the country to import more advanced machinery and materials. Third, exports are likely to result in a higher rate of technological innovation and dynamic learning from abroad, although the direction of causality is debatable (Balasubramanyam, Salisu and Sapsford, 1996).

We estimate Equation (3.6) for all the regions in the country and for the coastal and inland region subgroups separately. To examine the FDI-innovation-growth link in the two regional groups, we also estimate Equation (3.2) for the coastal and inland region subsample separately. The estimated results are reported in Table 3.6. In the coastal region, FDI has been a significant contributor to regional innovation performance, and innovation again contributes significantly to output growth. The story in the inland region is, however, not the same. In the inland region, the estimated coefficient of the FDI variable, though bearing the expected positive sign in the innovation function, is not statistically significant. Again, the estimated coefficient of the innovation variable is not statistically significant although the sign is positive as expected. These facts suggest that FDI is not a significant driver of innovation capability in the inland region, nor does innovation lead to regional economic growth. The estimated coefficients of the exports and innovation variables show the expected positive sign and are statistically significant when they enter the regressions alternatively. However, the estimated coefficient of innovation marginally loses its significance when it enters the regression together with exports. This is likely due to the fact that the two variables are correlated because greater innovation enhances competitiveness and hence more exports, and greater openness by exporting may contribute to more innovation.

Table 3.6 The FDI-innovation-growth linkage in the coastal and inland regions

Coastal — Log(rgdp)

Coastal	Coef	p-value	Coef	p-value	Coef	p-value
LGL	−0.085	0.481	−0.075	0.537	−0.087	0.467
LKY	0.072***	0.004	0.095***	0.000	0.077***	0.002
LGREX	0.097***	0.003			0.072**	0.045
LPATENT			0.010***	0.008	0.006	0.119
Constant	0.166***	0.000	0.128***	0.002	0.125***	0.002
LM	0.02		0.48		0	
Hausman	5.9		1.49		5.01	
	C		C		C	

Coastal — Log(patent)

	Coef	p-value
FDIS	2.834**	0.018
RDGDP	0.513**	0.023
HC	6.176**	0.010
Constant	6.648***	0.000
LM	85.93	
Hausman	6.54	
	C	

Inland — Log(rgdp)

Inland	Coef	p-value	Coef	p-value	Coef	p-value
LGL	−0.465*	0.050	−0.468**	0.036	−0.469**	0.037
LKY	0.055***	0.001	0.077***	0.000	0.078***	0.000
LGREX	0.006	0.714			−0.001	0.949
LPATENT			0.006	0.154	0.006	0.155
Constant	0.138***	0.000	0.116***	0.000	0.116***	0.000
LM	4.55		5.71**		5.71**	
Hausman	1.86		3.08		3.08	
	C		RE		RE	

Inland — Log(patent)

	Coef	p-value
FDIS	2.694	0.143
RDGDP	0.199	0.129
HC	4.231*	0.069
Constant	6.268***	0.000
LM	133.36	
Hausman	6.3	
	C	

Note: ***Significance at 99 per cent level; **significance at 95 per cent level; *significance at 90 per cent level.

3.7 Conclusions

This chapter has investigated the impact of FDI on regional innovation capabilities and efficiency in a fast-growing developing country that has received phenomenal amounts of foreign direct investment. We find that FDI can contribute significantly to overall regional innovation capacity. The strength of this positive effect depends, however, on the availability of the absorptive capacity and the presence of innovation-complementary assets in the host region. In the coastal region of China, which possesses a pool of intelligent educated R&D staff and skilled labour and hosts most of China's R&D activities and top universities and research institutes and where inward FDI has evolved from labour-intensive processing activities to more strategic asset-seeking types of FDI by major MNEs, FDI has played a significant role in promoting regional innovation capacity as well as regional innovation efficiency from 2000 to 2004. This increased regional innovation and technological capability contribute further to the fast regional economic growth in this region. However, the inland provinces have not experienced a similar innovation-growth-promotion effect of FDI. The type and quality of FDI they have attracted and the lack of absorptive capacity and complementary assets may all be blamed for this failure in the inland region. FDI into the inland regions of China is mainly in labour-, land- or resource-intensive production activities. The newly increased relocated FDI may also be motivated by tax holidays provided by local government and low labour and land costs in the inland region. The technology content of this FDI is low and spillovers are limited. The lack of absorptive capacity and complementary assets may become another bottleneck that hinders the upgrading of the local economy towards the higher end of the value chain and the transition of the local economy to a knowledge-based economy.

Our attention to innovation has long been mistakenly placed on R&D expenditure. R&D spending is, however, only one of the important inputs of innovation. In many cases, huge R&D spending on innovation activities has not generated sufficient innovation output, as we had expected. The productivity of innovation and the management of innovation are of crucial importance, especially for developing countries whose resources for innovation are limited. This research indicates that FDI contributes not only to the outputs of the regional innovation system but also to the productivity of innovation in developing countries.

The sample period under study is anchored in an era with increasing globalisation of R&D activities. Findings from this study have important policy implications. First, globalisation of R&D may provide an opportunity for developing countries to catch up on the technology frontier. MNEs' can become an embedded driver of knowledge-based development. However, the quality and type of FDI are important for a significant innovation promotion effect of FDI. Technology-intensive, R&D-related FDI may play an important role in this process. FDI into the coastal regions of China in the twenty-first century with greater participation of global leading MNEs has been much different from the labour-intensity, export-oriented FDI in the early stage. Second, enhancement of local absorptive capacity has been crucial to the effective assimilation of the knowledge and technology spillovers from FDI. Finally, the development of complementary assets in the local innovation system has also been crucial for greater success in assimilation and development of external knowledge. Therefore, a role remains for government policies in promoting these necessary conditions for a successful FDI-assisted technological advancement.

Evidence from the current study, however, provides little information on whether FDI has promoted the indigenous innovation capability of the developing countries. According to a report by Zhou (2006), most of the foreign R&D labs in China are independent and wholly foreign owned for better protection of intellectual property rights. More than 90 per cent of these MNEs' labs do not apply for patents to avoid disclosure of technology know-how. About 80 per cent of the foreign firms do not have any plan to collaborate with indigenous labs or firms or universities. Moreover, these foreign-owned R&D labs are again unevenly distributed geographically, with Beijing, Shanghai and Shenzhen accounting for nearly 84 per cent of total foreign R&D labs in China. A study by Fu et al. (2006b) based on 12 British enterprises operating in East Asia reveals that firms intend to use technology that is superior to that at the local level rather than world-class technology in their subsidiary or joint ventures in China. One of the main reasons is their concern about the poor intellectual property rights protection in China. All this raised concerns that these active foreign R&D firms may remain as isolated innovation poles in the developing economy. Though they have increased the overall innovation inputs and outputs in the

developing economy, their benefits to the technological capability building of the indigenous sector remain to be seen. This may also give rise to
another form of brain drain, in which intelligent research staff members
have been lost from the domestic sector to the foreign sector, although
they stay physically in the country. Evidence from this study also
suggests that the lack of effective protection of intellectual property
rights has been a significant barrier preventing MNEs from introducing
more advanced technology into China and investing more in innovation. Another important step for the governments of developing countries is to strengthen the protection of intellectual property rights to
attract more technology-intensive FDI and to encourage innovation.

4 | *Processing trade, FDI and international competitiveness of the Chinese high-technology industries*

4.1 Introduction

The fragmentation and segmentation of production at the global level has been one of the major trends driven by multinational enterprises (MNEs). Encouragement of the processing trade, especially foreign direct investment (FDI) in export-oriented processing activities in export processing zones (EPZs), has become a policy tool widely utilised by developing countries to enter the global production network and build up international competitiveness. The number of EPZs increased from 79 in 1975 to more than 3,500 in 2006 (ILO, 2003).

The literature on the impact of FDI on local firms has concerned itself mainly with ordinary FDI, which engages with substantial production activities using materials from domestic or international markets. The evidence is mixed, in general. Some find positive export spillovers from FDI; some find no or negative impact (e.g., Aitken, Hanson and Harrison, 1997; Kokko, Transini and Zejan, 2001; Greenaway, Upward and Wright, 2004; Buck et al., 2007; Kneller and Pisu, 2007). In reality, different factors are at work and the relative magnitudes of these channels depend on host country conditions and the type of FDI inflows (Javorcik, 2008). So far, little is known about the effects of processing trade–FDI (PT-FDI), a type of FDI engaged in export-oriented processing trade activities aiming to take advantage of the low-cost unskilled or semi-skilled labour in developing countries and the preferential policies provided in the EPZs. This type of FDI involves mainly importing duty-free materials and spare parts, assembling or processing them into final products and exporting them to the international markets. The literature on EPZs has mostly focused on employment gains. The study of the impact of EPZs on the development of international competitiveness of local firms is limited, with the exception of a few case studies. An in-depth understanding and a rigorous evaluation of the impact of the PT-FDI on local firms are crucial for policy making. Is PT-FDI an effective channel for the development of the global competitiveness of indigenous firms? Has such FDI helped indigenous firms gain international competitiveness in technology-intensive industries in developing countries? What can the indigenous firms learn from PT-FDI? In industries where the processing trade is pervasive, what is the impact of PT-FDI on local firms' export market participation? Research on these questions is limited.

Using firm-level panel data from China, this chapter examines these research questions in China's high-technology industries. The technology-intensive industries in China have significant involvement with PT-FDI. Exports resulting from the processing trade accounted for about 85 to 90 per cent of China's total exports of high-technology products (Ma and Assche, 2010).[1] This chapter contributes to the literature in several ways. First, it seeks to fill the gap in the literature on the impact of processing trade–FDI on the international competitiveness of local firms through a systematic theoretical and empirical analysis. Second, it is one of the first major empirical examinations to have a special focus on processing trade. Recent research by Yu (2010) examined the effect of engagement with the processing trade on productivity growth in a sample of 31,000 foreign invested and local firms in China in all manufacturing industries and found that firms (both foreign and local) engaged in the processing trade experienced higher productivity growth. By contrast, this research focuses on the spillover effects of PT-FDI on the export performance of local firms in high-technology industries. Third, unlike most of the existing literature, this chapter constructs the FDI knowledge pools at a more disaggregated level, in order to distinguish the different channels at work. It also takes into account the time lag that is needed for knowledge spillover to take effect.

The chapter is organised as follows: Section 4.2 reviews the literature and presents a theoretical framework for the research. Section 4.3 briefly reviews the background of the processing trade and exports of high-technology products in China. Sections 4.4 and 4.5 discuss the methodology and data. Sections 4.6 and 4.7 present the results of the estimations together with robustness checks. Finally, Section 4.8 presents conclusions.

---

[1] Defined as products in industries with a high ratio of R&D expenditure to sales.

4.2 The theory and literature

Knowledge spillovers from FDI occur when multinationals find it difficult to protect the leakage of firm-specific assets, such as superior production technology, management practices or marketing information to local firms (Caves, 1996). As a result, FDI may affect the export competitiveness of domestic firms in two ways. One of the channels is technology spillovers, which could strengthen the core competitiveness of the local firms through demonstration effects and labour movement. Spillovers of advanced technology may contribute to the international competitiveness of local firms that have strong absorptive capacity. Of course, an important precondition for effective spillovers is that the production activities in the FIEs should be technology or skill intensive (Sjoholm, 1999). There may also be vertical spillovers within the supply chain when MNEs provide better intermediate materials for their producer customers or when they transfer knowledge to their suppliers for better quality final products. Moreover, FDI is expected to help a host country to create assets (comparative advantage) in certain areas and facilitate the transition of indigenous firms from FDI recipient to exporters (Dunning et al., 2001).

The other channel is export-related information spillovers. This refers to the leakage or spillover of information relating to export market intelligence, international marketing know-how and export operations from foreign to domestic firms. Such information spillovers may also take place through demonstration effects and labour movement (Aitken et al. 1997). Exporting involves sunk costs (Melitz, 2003; Bernard and Jensen, 2004). This includes the establishment of distribution and logistics channels, product compliance with regulations, market research to acquire information about consumer preferences and market structure in foreign countries. Moreover, because of information asymmetries, the costs of export market entry are perceived by some domestic firms to be too high. This would discourage export market participation (Greenaway and Kneller, 2004). Such fixed costs associated with the entry into export markets are significant for firms in differentiated product industries (Roberts and Tybout, 1997). Export-related information spillovers can effectively lower the sunk costs associated with export market entry (Aitken et al., 1997) so that the *marginal* firm finds it profitable to start exporting. It may also allow existing exporters to have a better understanding of their existing export market as well as potential new markets. Therefore, the possible spillovers of technological knowledge and export-related information may enhance export competitiveness and export market participation of local firms.

Moreover, FDI may also generate a competition effect on the exports of local firms. Such competition effects can serve as a double-edged sword. On the one hand, strong foreign competition may compel local firms to strengthen and improve their competitiveness for survival (e.g., Liu, 2010). On the other hand, there may be a significant depressive effect on the productivity of local firms when foreign invested firms crowd domestic firms from the product market and compete with them in the labour and resources markets (Aitken and Harrison, 1999; Hu and Jefferson, 2002; Hu, Jefferson and Qian 2005; Fu and Gong, 2011).

The empirical literature on export spillovers from foreign firms is relatively smaller. Using firm-level data from Mexico, Aitken et al. (1997) find the probability of exporting by domestic firms increases with the concentration of exports of foreign firms operating in the same industry and region. Kokko et al. (2001) also find that foreign firms positively affect the probability of domestic firms' exporting using firm-level data from Uruguay. However, Barrrios, Görg and Strobl (2003) find no evidence of an effect from MNEs on the export share in Spain. Similarly, Ruane and Sutherland (2005) find negative export spillover effects in Ireland probably because of the use of Ireland as an export platform to the rest of the EU. They argue that export spillovers are unlikely in this case because competition with domestic firms in local product markets is limited. In the case of China, Buckley et al. (2002) suggest that FDI from Hong Kong, Macao and Taiwan is more likely to transfer marketing skills to the local firms based on evidence from industry-level data. Buck et al. (2007) test the mechanisms underpinning the Trade Development Path hypothesis using firm-level panel data of Chinese firms in nine Standard Industrial Classification (SIC) two-digit industries for the period 1998–2001. They use the share of foreign workers in total employment, output, exports and R&D investment as the measure of FDI spillovers and find evidence in support of such spillovers. These studies provide useful insights, but none of them explores whether there is any difference between ordinary FDI and processing trade-FDI. The industry and regional pool of FDI presence is normally constructed at aggregate SIC two-digit and province levels. The selection bias arising from firms' export decisions has not been appropriately corrected either.

Spillovers from processing trade-FDI and export performance of domestic firms

Processing export activities include processing or assembly with imported materials and processing or assembly with supplied materials. The processing firms process duty-free materials and components supplied by foreign firms and export finished products. They are paid a fee for the assembly or processing activity. The foreign firms control both the supply of the materials as well as the entire international marketing of the processed or assembled products. In the case of processing or assembly with imported materials, the processing firms import, free of customs duty, parts and components that are used to produce finished goods and export them to international markets. The production activity related to processing trade is often semi-skilled– or unskilled-labour intensive with low value added. This is true even in technology-intensive industries such as electronics. For example, most of the latest iPhones sold globally are assembled in China. The materials and components are produced in South Korea, the United States, Germany, Italy, France, Japan and other countries. For each iPhone that is sold at the retail price of $600, the assembly fee earned by the China-based processing MNE is only US$6.54 per iPhone.[2]

As discussed earlier, knowledge spillovers from FDI may take place through different channels. The strength of the spillovers is determined by the type of FDI inflows as well as host country conditions (Javorcik, 2008). As for PT-FDI, although some of the transmission channels through which spillovers take effect remain available, the strength of the spillovers is likely to be low because of several serious constraints. First, there is little scope for technology transfer because the activity that is undertaken in processing trade in most developing countries is in fact low-skilled labour intensive. The core technologies are controlled by the MNEs and are often embedded in the imported components or the imported production lines. This constraint will be more significant when technology becomes more precise and when core technologies are increasingly embedded in imported components. As a result, although the demonstration effect and personnel movement mechanisms are still available, little advanced technology is available to be

---

[2] Source: 'Supply chain for iPhone highlights costs in China', *New York Times*, 5 July 2010. Available at www.nytimes.com/2010/07/06/technology/06iphone.html.

transferred via demonstration. The level of technical skills of assembly-line workers is low and provides limited scope of technology spillover through labour movement.

Second, technology spillovers taking place in the supply chain via backward linkages are found to be the strongest channel (Javorcik, 2004). However, given the 'two-end outside' nature of processing trade production activity, that is, both materials and markets of the products are outside the country, the linkages between PT-FDI and domestic firms are low in general. A range of 3 per cent to 9 per cent of inputs purchased domestically is often observed in developing countries (Milberg, 2007). Koopman et al. (2008) find that processing exports from China contain only 18 per cent Chinese content, whereas those for ordinary trade were as high as 89 per cent. Moreover, products under processing trade cannot be sold to other domestic firms. Therefore, vertical technology spillovers from PT-FDI will be limited too.

In respect to export information spillovers, FDI may generate positive export-related information spillovers to domestic firms through demonstration effects, movement of labour from foreign to local firms and other social learning channels. Domestic firms will thus obtain information about international demand, foreign regulations of their products and sophisticated export operations and logistics. Such export-related information spillovers may help domestic firms reduce sunk costs and become capable of entering export markets. In the case of PT-FDI, these transmission mechanisms are still at work. Moreover, in industries where processing trade is prevailing, sunk costs for export market entry are low for domestic firms, as foreign customers will provide materials, components and product design and take care of marketing and sales. As a result, the export-related information spillovers will remain to have a significant effect on export participation of domestic firms, especially in industries where processing trade prevails.

Finally, like ordinary FDI, PT-FDI will also generate a competition effect on domestic firms. However, in contrast to domestic firms in developing countries, PT-FDI has an advantage created through integration of advanced technology, low-cost labour and established international marketing channels. MNEs also have access to higher-quality components, materials and other intermediate inputs than the domestic firms do. Therefore, MNEs engaged in processing-trade activities will enjoy a clear competitive advantage over the indigenous firms in international markets. As a result, PT-FDI is likely to exert a strong negative competition effect on indigenous firms and crowd them out of the export market.

It should be noted that firms engaging in processing trade are different from original equipment manufacturers (OEMs). An OEM's products are marketed under the purchasing company's brand name. Normally, an OEM has strong technological and production capacities, although it lacks compatible capabilities in design, marketing and branding. Some OEMs have successfully upgraded to original design manufacturers (ODMs) and eventually to original brand manufacturers (OBMs). However, OEM in high-technology industries such as consumer electronics is confined to a few new industrialised economies (NIEs) with strong local capabilities, mainly in Korea and Taiwan (Hobday, 1995; Lall, 2001). In contrast, the development of the electronics industries in the 'Little Asian Tigers' such as Indonesia, Malaysia, the Philippines and Thailand was mainly driven by PT-FDI following the relocation of the labour-intensive assembly activities from the old NIEs. The upgrading of technological capabilities in indigenous firms in these Little Tigers was far less successful than that in Korea and Taiwan (Lall, 1996).

In sum, the knowledge that spills over from PT-MNEs to indigenous firms is mainly in the form of marketing intelligence and management techniques. Although there will be some spillovers of basic technology through demonstration or the movement of assembly-line workers or technicians, the scope of technology spillover in the processing activity is limited within the development of export competitiveness in the indigenous sector. In contrast, the crowding-out effect of MNEs on the domestic firms in the export market is strong. Therefore, we have the following hypotheses:

Hypothesis 4–1: Processing trade–FDI is likely to have a positive export information spillover effect on the export performance of indigenous firms.

Hypothesis 4–2: Processing trade–FDI is likely to have an insignificant or even negative technology spillover effect on the export performance of indigenous firms.

4.3 FDI and exports in technology-intensive industries in China

Since China embarked on economic reforms in 1978, its economy has been gradually opened up to foreign trade and investment. As part of its

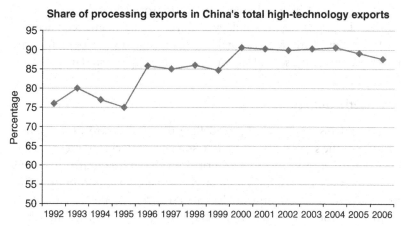

Figure 4.1 Share of processing exports in China's total high-technology exports
Source: Data from 2000 to 2006 based on author's own estimation; data from 1992 to 1999 are reproduced from Ma and Van Assche (2010) and Koopman, et al. (2008).

policy to promote integration into the global production network, the government encouraged export-oriented FDI, which mainly engaged in processing and assembling spare parts and components for the export markets. Export-oriented FDI was encouraged by fiscal and financial incentives, for example, tax holidays and tax rebates for exports. As a result, exports under the export-processing (EP) regime grew much faster than that under the ordinary-trade (OT) regime as a result of the involvement of FDI, the preferential government policy and the lower transaction costs of the EP regime. The average annual growth rate of processing exports was as high as 18 per cent in the 1990s, while that for ordinary exports was only 10 per cent (Fu, 2004). Since 1996, exports resulting from the processing trade have accounted for more than 50 per cent of China's total exports (MOFTEC, 2000).

This figure is much higher in the high-technology sector. Since 1996, the share of high-technology exports accounted for by processing trade reached 85 per cent. In 2004, the share increased to as high as 90 per cent and shows little evidence of decline over time (Figure 4.1). In the entire computer and other computer periphery equipment industries, the shares of processing exports have been as high as 99 per cent over the 2000 to 2006 period. Most foreign-invested enterprises (FIEs) in the high-technology industries in China have engaged in processing trade. As a result, exports of high-technology products from China have increased rapidly. In 2008, high-technology exports from China accounted for 13.1 per cent of the world's total exports of high-technology products, ranking China as the second largest high-technology exporter in the world.

4.4 Methodology

Two problems arise with the modelling of export performance. First, because of the sunk costs of exports, some firms decide not to enter the export market. So a number of firms have no export sales. There is, therefore, a selection effect based on the decision to export or not. This problem involves estimating a Heckman selection model for panel data controlling for sample selection bias (Hsiao, 2003; Kneller and Pisu, 2007). Second, the value of the dependent variable is censored at zero. Normal ordinary least squares estimator may produce biased estimates because the dependent variable is not normally distributed, hence imposing inappropriate restrictions on the residuals. Instead, a Tobit model should be employed for the estimation.

Therefore, the Type II Tobit model (selection in censored data) is used. It is a two-stage model incorporating two equations. The first equation of the model explains the propensity to export. Those firms that reported having positive export sales are defined as exporters. The second equation explains the export sales of a firm (if it exports). The empirical model is as follows:

(1) Decision equation (Probit model)

$$z_{it}^* = w_{it}\gamma + v_{it} \tag{4.1}$$

and
$$z_{it} = 1 \quad \text{if } z_{it}^* > 0,$$

$$z_{it} = 0 \text{ if } z_{it}^* \leq 0.$$

(2) Export performance equation (Tobit model)

$$e_{it}^* = \beta x_{it} + \sigma \lambda_i + \mu_{it} \tag{4.2}$$

and
$$e_{it} = e_{it}^* \quad \text{if } z_{it} = 1$$

$$e_{it} = 0 \text{ if } z_{it} = 0$$

$$\mu_{it} = \alpha_i + \varepsilon_{it}$$

$$v_{it} = \alpha_i' + \varepsilon_{it}'$$

$$t = 1, \dots, t \text{ and } i = 1, \dots, N, \text{ and}$$

$$\varepsilon_{it} = \rho_1 \varepsilon_{it-1} + \tau_{it}$$

$$\varepsilon'_{it} = \rho_2 \varepsilon'_{it-1} + \tau'_{it}$$

$$\tau_{it} \sim N(0, \sigma_\tau^2), \ \tau'_{it} \sim N(0, \sigma \tau'^2)$$

where e is the logarithm of total exports,[3] z is a dummy variable for exporting or not, w and x are vectors of explanatory variables for export decision and export performance equations, σ is the standard deviation and λ is the inverse Mills ratio. The components α_i and α_i' are unobserved individual specific random disturbances which are constant over time, and ε_{it} are idiosyncratic errors that vary across time and individuals. Hence, the model allows unobserved heterogeneity, first order state dependence and serial correlation in the error components. Admittedly, this approach has a drawback in terms of the difficulty of establishing a distribution of individual specific effects. When a firm decides not to export ($z = 0$), the observed exports value e is zero. The significance of the presence of the selection effects is indicated by the Rho statistics, which reflects the correlation between the error terms of the two equations (μ and υ). If there are significant selection effects, the Heckman selection model is preferred. Otherwise, we utilise the standard Tobit model.

Following the literature (e.g., Aitken et al., 1997; Buck et al., 2007; Kneller and Pisu, 2007), the explanatory variables in w and x include a vector of FDI spillovers variables and a vector of control variables. The FDI spillover variables consist of technology spillovers (fdi^{tech}) and export information spillovers (fdi^{inf}). In contrast to the existing literature, we use lagged values of the FDI spillover variables in the model to capture the fact that it takes time for knowledge and information spillovers to take effect on receiving firms' export performance. In line with the literature, the control variables consist of firm size (fs), capital intensity measured by the capital-labour ratio (kl), labour productivity (yl), innovation measured by percentage of sales on account of new products (rd) and the wage rate ($wage$) that reflects labour skills on one

---

[3] Firms whose exports values are zero are given a zero value after taking logarithms. This does not affect the data distribution because the minimum positive value of exports is greater than 1.

hand and labour costs on the other. Moreover, we also control for some industry-level characteristics that may influence a firm's export market entry. These include competition (*comp*) in the industry, innovation intensity in the industry (rd^i) and the export orientation of the industry (*exp^i*). Including these variables in the model also allows us to control for the possibility that foreign firms choose to locate in more technologically advanced or export-intensive industries.

As the vectors of covariates of x_i and w_i may be the same, a possible problem of identification exists if this is the case. Following Kneller and Pisu (2007), I include a lagged export variable in both export equations. This is theoretically consistent with the models of exports that suggest export performance is path dependent (Bernard et al., 2003; Melitz, 2003) and helps reduce the identification problem. Finally, to control for the possible unobserved spatial covariance, a vector of regional dummy variables (*reg*) is included in the model representing firms located in the Yangtze River Delta, the Pearl River Delta, Beijing and Tianjin municipalities, other coastal regions, Chongqing municipality and the remainder of the inland regions. Therefore, w and x for the export decision and export performance equations are as follows:

$$w_{it} = \left\{ fdi_{it-1}^{tech}, fdi_{it-1}^{inf}, z_{it-1}, fs_{it}, kl_{it}, yl_{it}, rd_{it}, wage_{it}, comp_{jt}, exp_{jt}, rd_{jt}, reg_i \right\}$$

(4.3)

$$x_{it} = \left\{ fdi_{it-1}^{tech}, fdi_{it-1}^{inf}, e_{it-1}, fs_{it}, kl_{it}, yl_{it}, rd_{it}, wage_{it}, comp_{jt}, exp_{jt}, rd_{jt}, reg_i \right\}$$

(4.4)

$$i \in j$$

where j is the industry that firm i belongs to. Details of the definition of the variables are described in Table 4.1. The estimation of the export performance equation involves an estimation of a Heckman sample selection model with panel data. The generalised linear latent and mixed models (GLLAMMs) developed by Skrondal and Rabe-Hesketh (2004), which enable the correction of selection bias in panel data, are employed for the estimation.

Moreover, there is possible endogeneity between exports and productivity. Whereas more efficient firms choose to enter the export market, exports may also lead to higher productivity through 'learning by exporting' (Bernard and Jensen, 2004). Therefore, an instrumental

Table 4.1 *Summary statistics of the variables*

Variable	Definition	Obs	Mean	Std.	Min	Max
z	Export dummy, equals 1 for exporters	108805	0.388	0.487	0.000	1.000
e	Ln (export value)	108805	-2.027	4.865	-5.869	12.295
pt-foex	Export-related information spillovers of PT-FDI	108805	2.076	4.542	-5.869	13.057
pt-foei	Technology spillovers of PT-FDI	108805	-0.725	4.051	-5.869	10.563
npt-foex	Export-related information spillovers of non-PT-FDI	108805	-0.313	3.008	-5.769	8.922
npt-foei	Technology spillovers of non-PT-FDI	108805	-1.246	2.706	-5.769	8.041
yl	Labour productivity	108805	4.975	1.087	0.000	11.183
size	Ln (no of employees)	108215	83.31	157.60	0.000	4981.60
kl	Capital to labour ratio	108805	287.26	295.01	15.57	1806.86
rd	Innovation measured by per cent of sales of new products in total sales	91965	0.090	0.257	0.000	23.347
wage	Ln (wage rate)	108606	2.598	0.687	-5.030	10.177
comp	Hirschman concentration index for the industry	108805	0.501	0.294	0.000	1.000
ind_exp	Export-sales ratio of the industry	108805	0.319	0.252	0.000	0.990
ind_rd	Percentage of new sales of the industry	108805	7.454	9.321	0.000	41.636
pts	Share of processing exports in total exports of the industry	108807	0.597	0.333	0.002	1.000

variables approach should be used for the estimation. Productivity of firms is hence instrumented using a vector of instrumental variables. The instruments used include (1) the lagged dependent (export) and endogenous variables (productivity); (2) variables indicating the ownership structure of the firms, in particular the share of state and private ownership in a firm; and (3) all the remaining exogenous variables in the model. Given the drawbacks in governance of state ownership in the Chinese firms, it can reasonably be argued that a firm will be less productive if it has a higher proportion of assets owned by the state. The appropriateness of the instrumental variable candidates is also carefully tested using the Sargan test for over-identifying restrictions. Reassuringly, it was found that the instruments are valid and appropriate. We formally test whether the assumption of endogeneity is borne out by the data at hand. If the regressors are not endogenous after all, the standard Tobit model would be the most efficient estimation method to use. The Davidson-Mackinnon test of exogeneity suggests that the endogeneity problem is not statistically significant at the 1 per cent level (p-value = 0.035). Therefore, the standard Tobit model estimates are preferred. Nevertheless, we report both the standard Tobit and the IV estimates as a robustness check.

4.5 Data and measurement

This chapter uses a highly disaggregated large panel data set compiled by linking a large firm-level production and export data set with data derived from a large product-level trade data set.

Firm-level production and export data

The firm-level panel data set of Chinese technology-intensive industries from 2000 to2007 was drawn from the *Annual Report of Industrial Enterprise Statistics* compiled by the National Bureau of Statistics of China, covering all state-owned firms and other types of firms with annual turnover of more than RMB 5 million (US\$0.7 million) in the technology-intensive industries. The data include firms of both domestic and foreign ownership. Foreign firms are defined as those with 25 per cent or more foreign equity investment according to the Joint Venture Law of the People's Republic of China. Following Eurostat's definition of high-technology industries (Eurostat, 2004), firms in industries involved in the manufacture of medical and pharmaceutical products (SIC 27), electronic products and communication equipment (SIC 40) and instrument, stationery and office equipment (SIC 41) are included in the sample. These include 52 industries at the SIC four-digit level.[4]

An unbalanced panel is used to allow for firm entry and exit to capture the industrial dynamics over the sample period. Data cleaning has been carried out to exclude the outliers and unreasonable data entries. The final data set consists of 108,930 observations from 53,981 firms, including 70,587 observations of domestic firms and 38,343 observations of foreign firms. Overall, 63 per cent of the firms are domestic, 21 per cent are wholly foreign owned (WFO) subsidiaries and 15 per cent are joint ventures (JVs). In the electronics industry, foreign firms accounted for almost 50 per cent of the total number of firms, and most of them (32 per cent) are WFO subsidiaries. The share of foreign firms is the lowest in the pharmaceutical industry. Only 18 per cent of the firms are foreign owned, and most of them (13 per cent) are joint ventures. In the instruments industries, the proportion of foreign invested firms is 32 per cent.

Product-level trade data

The product-level trade data were drawn from the shipment records compiled by the General Administration of Customs of China. The data records detailed trading information at Harmonised System (HS) eight-digit level for each shipment for the years 2000, 2002, 2004 and 2006. In total, 68.52 million shipments were made in the sample period. We first aggregate the export value by trade mode for each product in each year and then estimate the proportion of processing exports in total exports in each product sector in each year. The share of processing exports in the years 2001, 2003 and 2005 is estimated by interpolation, and that for 2007 is calculated using extrapolation. The HS eight-digit product-level trade data are then converted into SIC four-digit industry-level export data. Finally, these industry-level processing trade data are linked to the firm-level data according to each firm's SIC four-digit industry classification.

---

[4] The industry classification changed from GB1994 to GB2002 in 2003. So for years before 2003, all the SIC codes are recoded (00, 01, 02) at the SIC four-digit level.

Measurement

Export performance of the firms can be measured by the value of exports or the export-sales ratio. There are some differences between the two measurements. The total value of exports reflects a firm's strength of export competitiveness; export to sales ratio reflects the export market orientation of a firm. As the main concern of this chapter is the international competitiveness of domestic firms, the value of exports is used to measure the export competitiveness of firms.

Spillovers from PT-FDI are proxied using two variables that represent FDI spillovers in two different forms, that is, spillovers of technology and spillovers of export information. We first construct the overall FDI knowledge or information pool following the normal practice and then estimate the PT-FDI spillovers variable by adjusting the overall FDI spillovers variable with the processing-trade intensity in each industry for each year. We also estimate the non-processing, ordinary FDI spillovers variable and include this in the regression model to control for possible spillovers from other FDI sources.

Spillover effects from FDI are examined empirically by testing whether the performance of domestic firms changes as a result of the greater foreign presence in the same industry or region. Foreign presence is often measured in terms of the output, employment and assets of foreign firms in an industry or region. Given the fact that foreign firms may have different strengths, some literature goes further to distinguish FDI spillovers in specific areas such as technology or export information. The recent literature on foreign knowledge spillovers constructs the foreign knowledge pool using the total R&D investment or total number of patents of foreign firms (Kneller and Stevens, 2006; Singh, 2007). Given the focus on technological knowledge and export-related information spillovers from FDI in this chapter, the latter approach is more appropriate for the measurement of the FDI knowledge and information pool.

Technology spillovers from FDI are often measured by the total value of R&D capital in FIEs or the share of FIE R&D investment in total R&D investment in the same industry or region (e.g., Buck et al., 2007; Fu and Gong, 2011). Admittedly, R&D investment is only one of the major inputs in innovation and knowledge creation. Moreover, MNEs in developing countries, especially those engaged in processing trade, often carry out R&D at their headquarters and invest little in R&D in their affiliates that specialise in assembly. Therefore, sales from new products offer a better measure of the overall technology advancement in the MNEs. The total value of sales from new products by FIEs in the same industry and the same region is used to proxy the technological knowledge pool provided by FDI.

Similarly, in the estimation of *export-related information spillovers*, the pool of export information in FIEs is proxied by the total value of FIE exports in the same industry or region (e.g., Aitken et al., 1997; Kneller and Pisu, 2007; Iwasaki et al., 2010). It is expected that the larger the export-related information pool, the greater the corresponding information spillovers from foreign to domestic firms. Admittedly, export volumes are not only a result of marketing information but also reflect the technological advancement of a firm. The correlation coefficient of the technology and the export-related information spillovers variables is 0.416, indicating a certain level of overlap. By controlling for the possible technology spillovers effect in the regression, the estimated coefficient of the export information spillover variable should, to a considerable extent, reflect the net export information spillovers effect from FDI. Nevertheless, we should bear in mind the limitations in making precise measurement of spillovers and observe caution when drawing conclusions.

Based on these estimates of the export information pool and technological knowledge pool, PT-FDI spillover variables are estimated by adjusting these knowledge pool estimates with the FIE processing exports intensity in each SIC four-digit industry. Spillovers of non-processing FDI are estimated by adjusting the FDI knowledge pool with non-processing trade share in the same industry. Most of the existing literature constructs FDI knowledge pool at SIC two- or three-digit level for industry classification and provincial level for geographic division. Unlike these methods, in this chapter the FDI knowledge pool is constructed at a more disaggregated level: the SIC four-digit level for industry classification and broad-city level, which includes a city and its surrounding rural area, for regional classification.[5] The advantage of such disaggregation is, first, that technologies, especially in the technology-intensive industries, are specialised and industry specific. Second, knowledge spillovers are geographically localised (Jaffe, Trajtenberg and Henderson, 1993; Austreche and Feldman, 1996).

---

[5] A city and its surrounding area are identified using telephone area codes.

Knowledge and information may flow more easily among agents located within the same area because of social bonds that foster reciprocal trust and frequent face-to-face contacts (Breschi and Lissoni, 2001). Evidence for the United States (Acs, Luc and Varga, 2002) and Europe (Funk and Niebuhr, 2000) finds a significant decline in spillovers beyond a range of 50–75 miles and 120 kilometres, respectively. Many provinces in China are larger than most of the countries in Europe. Aggregation at the provincial level is hence too wide for effective knowledge spillovers in the standard sense. Of course, the construction of knowledge and the information pool at this disaggregated level may, on the other hand, restrict the scope of spillovers when firms observe new product ideas in markets that are not their local markets. We therefore estimate the models using alternative spillovers measurements at provincial level as a robustness check. Table 4.1 reports the summary statistics of the variables used in the test.

4.6 Results

Table 4.2 reports the main export and innovation performance indicators of domestic and foreign firms in technology-intensive industries over the sample period. In all industries, the proportion of firms participating in exporting is higher amongst foreign than domestic firms. Foreign firms also have higher export-to-sales ratios as well as higher value of exports per firm. On average, the electronics industry has the highest share of exporters among the foreign firms. About 75 per cent of the foreign firms in this industry engaged in export activity, which is three times as high as that in the indigenous firms. The average export-sales ratio in this industry is 54 per cent, which is about five times as high as that in the indigenous firms. Looking at changes over time, the propensity of export participation of foreign and indigenous firms did not change much from 2000 to 2007. Not surprisingly, the difference between foreign and indigenous firms is much smaller in respect to technology and innovation measured by the percentage of sales of new products. In the electronics and instruments industries, this ratio is even higher in indigenous firms. Most of these high-technology exports result from processing trade. The share of processing exports in total exports ranged between 85 to 90 per cent from 2000 to 2006. In the electronics and communications equipment sector, this proportion had consistently been around 89 per cent except in the communication

Table 4.2 *Exports and innovation indicators of domestic and foreign firms, 2007*

		Domestic					Foreign		
Industry SIC	Percentage of total exports	Export-sales ratio	Ln(exports)	Percentage of exporters	Percentage of new sales	Export-sales ratio	Ln(exports)	Percentage of exporters	Percentage of new sales
27	4	5.41	1.47	0.17	0.08	16.41	3.30	0.36	0.09
40	87	11.62	2.46	0.27	0.12	53.53	7.73	0.75	0.07
41	9	12.74	2.26	0.26	0.12	48.61	6.70	0.69	0.06
Total	100	9.42	2.03	0.23	0.10	47.21	6.91	0.68	0.07

Percentage of processing exports in total exports, electronics industry of China, 2006

Figure 4.2 Percentage of processing exports in total exports, electronic industry of China, 2006

Note: The sectors are placed according to the volume of exports, from largest on the top to smallest at the bottom.

Source: Author's estimation according to customs data.

transmitting equipment industry. In sectors such as computer, computer peripheral equipment, computer network and printed circuit board industries, the share of processing exports in total exports was still as high as 99 per cent in 2006 (Figure 4.2). On average, the electronics industry accounted for 87 per cent of China's total high-technology exports from 2000 to 2007.

On average, foreign invested firms produce 89 per cent of China's total exports of high-technology products. This indigenous foreign division has been relatively stable over the sample period. Disaggregating the industries at the four-digit level, Table 4.3 shows that the manufacture of electronic components and their assembly (SIC 4061) has the largest export value, followed by computer peripheral equipment manufacturing (SIC 4043). In SIC 4061, around 80 per cent of the WFO firms engaged in exporting. Foreign firms contributed to 88 per cent of China's total exports in this industry, and 84 per cent of these exports are processing exports. In the computer industry (SIC 4041, SIC 4042 and SIC 4043), almost all of these exports (99 per cent) were on account of processing trade in 2006. Moreover, again almost all of these exports were produced in FIEs. The share of FIEs' exports in total exports was as high as 97 per cent, 98 per cent and 94 per cent in these computer industries (SIC 4041,

Table 4.3 *Export performance of top 10 exporting high-technology industries: SIC four-digit level, 2007*

SIC	Industry	Percent-age of processing trade 2006	Percentage of total exports			Export-sales ratio (percentage)			Percentage of exporters		
			WFO	JV	Local	WFO	JV	Local	WFO	JV	Local
4061	Electronic components and their assembly	84	63	25	12	58	42	13	78	73	32
4043	Computer peripheral equip.	99	80	14	6	66	39	12	79	66	27
4071	Household video equip.	98	41	42	17	70	47	23	85	71	38
4053	Integrated circuit devices	85	69	26	5	65	48	8	82	74	23
4062	Printed circuit board	93	78	18	4	64	41	7	81	73	22
4059	Optical devices and other electronic devices	82	68	22	10	62	35	12	82	68	31
4014	Mobile communication and terminal equip.	84	71	23	6	46	30	8	72	56	22
4041	Entire computer	99	90	7	3	59	19	3	72	43	13
4072	Household audio equip.	99	61	28	11	81	67	27	90	84	40
4052	Semiconductor discrete devices	87	73	19	8	67	37	10	87	73	33
Total	All high-technology industries	88	63	23	14	59	31	9	77	57	22

4042 and 4043), respectively. All these provide stylised examples of PT-FDI and suggest that most of the high-technology exports from China are in fact exports of PT-cum-MNEs. High-technology exports from indigenous Chinese firms are very limited.

On the other hand, there are substantial variations in the speed of catch-up across industries. Indigenous firms in a few sectors have shown rapid export growth, including manufacturers of integrated circuit devices, vacuum electronic devices, industrial automatic control system, optical devices and mobile communication and terminal equipment. In these sectors, the indigenous firms have shown a faster export growth than FIEs and a catch-up trajectory. However, despite the high growth rate in the indigenous firms, partly because of a low starting level and strong government-funded R&D programs, strong foreign dominance in the exports of these industries is clear.

Table 4.4 reports the Probit model estimates of the spillover effects of PT-FDI on the propensity to export in the indigenous firms. Both the lagged and contemporaneous effects of PT-FDI are reported for comparison. Both the standard Probit and IV estimates are reported as a robustness check. As columns (1) to (4) show, the estimated coefficient of the lagged information spillover variable of PT-FDI is positive and significant at the 1 per cent level, suggesting positive export-related information externalities emanating from PT-FDI to the indigenous firms. The estimated results are consistent in both the baseline model and the full model when non-processing trade or ordinary FDI is controlled for. The results are also consistent in the standard Probit and the IV model indicating the robustness of the results. However, the estimated coefficients of technology spillovers of PT-FDI are negative and statistically significant at the 5 per cent level.

In other words, while the limited innovation activities in the foreign affiliates in China offer limited knowledge spillovers, the overall technological and innovation capabilities of the MNEs have posed a barrier to the indigenous firms in their export propensity. The results are also robust across different model specifications and different estimation methods. All this evidence supports hypotheses 4–1 and 4–2 suggesting that, on the one hand, PT-FDI has offered positive marketing and export-related information spillovers to local firms; on the other hand, its overall advantage in technology, mostly embodied in imported components and materials and coupled with low labour costs gained through processing trade, has formed a

Table 4.4 *Probit model estimates of export decisions in the high-technology industry*

Variables	Lagged effect				Contemporaneous effect			
	Normal (1)	IV (2)	Normal (3)	IV (4)	Normal (5)	IV (6)	Normal (7)	IV (8)
pt_forx	0.009***	0.009**	0.008**	0.008**	0.0151***	0.0145***	0.0106***	0.0100***
	(0.003)	(0.003)	(0.003)	(0.003)	(0.003)	(0.003)	(0.003)	(0.004)
pt_fori	-0.008**	-0.008**	-0.008**	-0.007**	-0.010***	-0.010***	-0.007**	-0.007**
	(0.004)	(0.004)	(0.004)	(0.004)	(0.003)	(0.003)	(0.003)	(0.003)
npt_forx			0.013***	0.013***			0.021***	0.021***
			(0.005)	(0.005)			(0.004)	(0.004)
npt_fori			-0.005	-0.006			-0.003	-0.004
			(0.005)	(0.005)			(0.004)	(0.004)
z_lag	2.474***	2.472***	2.471***	2.468***	2.437***	2.436***	2.433***	2.433***
	(0.023)	(0.023)	(0.023)	(0.023)	(0.0)20	(0.020)	(0.020)	(0.020)
yl	0.0002***	0.0001	0.0002***	0.0001	0.0001***	0.0001	0.0001***	0.0001
	(4.3E-05)	(0.0002)	(4.3E-05)	(0.0002)	(3.7E)-05	(0.0001)	(3.7E-05)	(0.0001)
size	0.230***	0.241***	0.229***	0.241***	0.234***	0.242***	0.235***	0.241***
	(0.012)	(0.020)	(0.012)	(0.020)	(0.01)0	(0.018)	(0.010)	(0.018)
kl	0.0001	0.0001	0.0001	0.0001	0.0001	0.0001	0.0001	0.0001
	(0.0001)	(0.0001)	(0.0001)	(0.0001)	(0.000)1	(0.0001)	(0.0001)	(0.0001)
rd	0.229***	0.228***	0.230***	0.229***	0.259***	0.259***	0.260***	0.260***
	(0.031)	(0.031)	(0.031)	(0.031)	(0.029)	(0.029)	(0.029)	(0.029)
wage	0.020	0.012	0.012	0.008	0.024	0.018	0.013	0.009
	(0.020)	(0.028)	(0.020)	(0.028)	(0.017)	(0.024)	(0.017)	(0.024)

Table 4.4 (*cont.*)

Variables	Lagged effect				Contemporaneous effect			
	Normal (1)	IV (2)	Normal (3)	IV (4)	Normal (5)	IV (6)	Normal (7)	IV (8)
comp	-0.019	-0.018	-0.018	-0.018	-0.003	-0.003	-0.004	-0.004
	(0.037)	(0.037)	(0.037)	(0.037)	(0.032)	(0.032)	(0.032)	(0.032)
Ind_exp	0.578***	0.564***	0.551***	0.543***	0.563***	0.551***	0.527***	0.515***
	(0.054)	(0.054)	(0.056)	(0.056)	(0.0470)	(0.047)	(0.048)	(0.048)
Ind_rd	0.002	0.002*	0.002	0.002*	0.003***	0.004***	0.004***	0.004***
	(0.001)	(0.001)	(0.001)	(0.001)	(0.001)	(0.001)	(0.001)	(0.001)
Constant	-3.143***	-3.187***	-3.090***	-3.153***	-3.184***	-3.206***	-3.110***	-3.127***
	(0.082)	(0.111)	(0.085)	(0.114)	(0.071)	(0.097)	(0.073)	(0.099)
Region dummies	Y	Y	Y	Y	Y	Y	Y	Y
Year dummies	Y	Y	Y	Y	Y	Y	Y	Y
N	32,115	31,948	31,948	31,948	42,449	42,017	42,449	42,017
Log-likelihood	-7977	-7946	-7936	-7942	-10632	-10554	-10617	-10540
Chi-squared	14162	14132	14112	14126	18264	18156	18237	18130

Note: Standard errors in parentheses; *** p<0.01, ** p<0.05, * p<0.1.

strong competitive barrier that prevents the local firms from participating in international markets.

As expected, the export-related information spillovers of non-PT-FDI have shown a positive and significant effect on the export participation of indigenous firms. The magnitude of the estimated coefficient is double the size of that of PT-FDI. This is consistent with our proposition that non-PT-FDI has more linkages and interactions with the domestic economy. As regards the technology spillovers effect, non-PT-FDI does not appear to exert significant technology spillovers effects on the export market participation of indigenous firms, which is different from the estimated effects of PT-FDI. In other words, for non-PT-FDI, its possible positive technological spillovers facilitated via linkages with domestic firms in the domestic market and the competition pressure in the international market offset each other; hence, its net effect on local firms becomes insignificant on average. Again, the estimated results are robust for both the standard Probit and IV estimation methods.

The estimated coefficient of the past export status variable is positive and statistically significant at the 1 per cent level in all specifications, suggesting the importance of past export experience in firms' current export decisions. The estimated coefficient of the labour productivity variable bears a positive sign, but it is insignificant in the IV estimation model, although it is statistically significant in the standard Probit regression. As regards the remaining control variables, larger firms appear to be more likely to enter the export market; firms with greater innovations are more likely to export; and the wage rate does appear to have a significant effect on firms' export propensity, which can be explained by the fact that it reflects labour skills on the one hand and production costs on the other. The estimated coefficient of the capital-labour ratio is not statistically significant either, probably because of the labour-intensive nature of processing trade. Looking at the three industry-level variables, firms in industries with greater export orientation are more likely to export. Firms in industries with more innovation are also more likely to export. In other words, there are significant intra-industry spillovers of indigenous innovative technology within the sectoral innovation system. Finally, domestic market competition does not appear to have significant impact on indigenous firms' export market participation in these industries, likely because the quality standard in the domestic market is substantially different from that in the export market, and for most firms, the export market is not an easy alternative in the face of fierce domestic competition.

The contemporaneous effect of PT-FDI on the propensity to export in indigenous firms reported in columns 4 to 8 presents a similar picture. The signs of the estimated coefficients are the same as those of the lagged effects, whereas there are some slight differences in the magnitude of the estimated coefficients and the level of statistical significance. In general, the size and significance of the contemporaneous information spillovers effect are greater than those of the lagged effect, whereas those of the technological spillovers remain similar with lagged effects, likely because of the difference in the speed of diffusion between export information and technological knowledge. The estimated coefficients of the control variables remain broadly consistent with the lagged effects estimates.

Turning to the estimates of export performance measured by the value of exports, Table 4.5 reports the Heckman selection estimates obtained using GLLAMM that have corrected the selection bias. The

Table 4.5 *Spillovers from PT-FDI and export value of domestic firms*

Variables	GLLAMM (selection in Tobit model)		OLS[a] (random effects)	
	Normal (1)	IV (2)	Normal (3)	IV (4)
pt_forx_lag	0.0227**	0.020**	0.012**	0.011**
	(0.010)	(0.010)	(0.005)	(0.005)
pt_fori_lag	−0.011	−0.009	−0.006	−0.005
	(0.010)	(0.010)	(0.005)	(0.005)
npt_forx_lag	0.028**	0.027**	0.010*	0.009
	(0.013)	(0.013)	(0.006)	(0.006)
npt_fori_lag	−0.025*	−0.026*	−0.008	−0.009
	(0.015)	(0.015)	(0.007)	(0.007)
e_lag	0.637***	0.638***	0.809***	0.810***
	(0.011)	(0.011)	(0.007)	(0.007)
size	0.487***	0.617***	0.278***	0.299***
	(0.035)	(0.060)	(0.028)	(0.028)
kl	0.0001	0.0001	0.0001	0.0001
	(0.0001)	(0.0001)	(0.0001)	(0.0001)

Table 4.5 *(cont.)*

Variables	GLLAMM (selection in Tobit model)		OLS[a] (random effects)	
	Normal (1)	IV (2)	Normal (3)	IV (4)
yl	0.001***	0.002***	0.004***	0.004**
	(0.001)	(0.001)	(0.001)	(0.001)
rd	0.374***	0.369***	0.351***	0.356***
	(0.097)	(0.098)	(0.106)	(0.110)
wage	−0.003	−0.088	0.036	0.032
	(0.062)	(0.083)	(0.028)	(0.036)
comp	0.001	0.006	0.000	0.001
	(0.104)	(0.105)	(0.041)	(0.040)
Ind_exp	1.415***	1.336***	0.818***	0.795***
	(0.193)	(0.194)	(0.144)	(0.145)
Ind_rd	0.009*	0.011**	0.005**	0.006**
	(0.005)	(0.005)	(0.002)	(0.002)
Constant	−3.140***	−3.430***	−2.416***	−2.528***
	(0.288)	(0.351)	(0.137)	(0.132)
Region dummies	Y	Y	Y	Y
Year dummies	Y	Y	Y	Y
N	31,948	31,948	31,948	31,948
Log-likelihood	−7809	−7831		
Chi-squared	5740	5648	88313	93688
R^2_between			0.962	0.963
R^2_overall			0.712	0.712

Note: Standard errors in parentheses. ***$p<0.01$, **$p<0.05$, *$p<0.1$.
[a] Cluster-robust standard errors are reported for OLS estimates.

Rho-statistics indicate significant selection effects in the full sample; therefore, the GMMALL estimates are preferred. Consistent with our expectations, evidence from this table shows that export-related information spillovers from FDI have a positive impact on the export performance of the local firms. A 1 per cent increase in the FIE processing exports increases the exports of domestic firms in the same industry by 0.02 per cent. The estimated coefficients are statistically significant at the 5 per cent level. On the other hand, the export performance effect of technological spillovers from PT-FDI bears a negative sign but is statistically insignificant. Comparing this result with the significant negative effect of technology spillovers of PT-FDI on domestic firms' propensity to export, the difference between the two proves a qualitative difference between the indigenous exporters and non-exporters. Firms that have made the breakthrough and entered the export market normally have already reached the threshold level of competitiveness. They possess greater capabilities than non-exporters to compete with FIEs and to learn from FIEs through reverse engineering. However, it is difficult for those firms that have not reached the export productivity threshold level to imitate the technological advancement embedded in the imported components and materials used in the FIEs.

Non-PT-FDI shows a similar significant positive information spillover effect on the export performance of indigenous firms, similar to that of PT-FDI. The technology spillover effect of non-PT-FDI on indigenous firms is negative and marginally significant at the 10 per cent level in the Tobit model. In other words, exports from non-processing foreign firms that utilise locally produced material and components impose stronger competitive pressure on the exports of indigenous exporters partly because they have similar strength and hence compete in narrow segments of the market. However, the statistical significance of the estimated coefficients is not robust. Whereas the Tobit estimates produce some significant coefficients at the 5 and 10 per cent levels, the coefficients estimated by standard panel model are not statistically significant.

Factors that significantly affect how much a domestic firm exports are in general similar to those in the export decision regression with one notable difference. A firm's past performance in exporting still plays an important role in shaping its current export performance. Larger firms export more; more innovative firms export more. Again, in industries with higher export-sales ratios and greater innovation, the export volume of individual firms is greater. The capital-labour ratio and wage rate do not appear to have a significant effect on the export performance of domestic firms, probably because of similar reasons to those discussed earlier. Unlike with the results of the export decision regression, labour productivity appears to have a significant and positive effect on export performance. The estimated coefficient is positive and significant in both the selection bias–corrected standard Tobit and

IV-instrumented Tobit estimates, suggesting a role for productivity in the determination of export performance in firms that have already entered the export markets.

Columns (3) and (4) of Table 4.5 report the ordinary least squares (OLS) estimates as a robustness check, although the selection bias has not been corrected and the left-end censored distribution of the dependent variable has not been taken into account. As the estimation is performed at the firm level but includes industry-level variables, the standard errors are biased downwards. Following Moulton (1990), standard errors are clustered at the industry level to make correct inferences. The estimated results are broadly consistent with those of the selection bias–corrected Tobit model estimates. The information spillover effect remains positive and significant for the PT-FDI. This effect of non-PT-FDI is also positive but is only marginally significant. The estimated coefficient of the technology spillovers variable remains negative but is not statistically significant. The effects of past export performance, firm size, labour productivity, in-house R&D and industry-level export orientation and innovativeness all remain consistent with the earlier estimates.

4.7 Robustness check

Table 4.6 reports the results of the robustness check using the high indigenous export industries subsample to determine whether PT-FDI

Table 4.6 *Determinants of export performance in industries with fast indigenous export growth: IV estimates*

Variables	Export decision	Export value
	Probit (1)	GLLAMM (selection in Tobit) (2)
pt_forx_lag	0.001 (0.012)	0.012 (0.034)
pt_fori_lag	0.0001 (0.010)	0.009 (0.030)
npt_forx_lag	0.0577* (0.032)	0.104 (0.101)

Table 4.6 (*cont.*)

Variables	Export decision	Export value
	Probit (1)	GLLAMM (selection in Tobit) (2)
npt_fori_lag	−0.006	−0.066
	(0.032)	(0.100)
z_lag	2.413***	
	(0.077)	
e_lag		0.613***
		(0.038)
yl	0.0001	0.002
	(0.0001)	(0.001)
size	0.346***	0.890***
	(0.060)	(0.188)
kl	0.0001	0.0001
	(0.0001)	(0.0001)
rd	0.547***	0.809**
	(0.1107	(0.366)
wage	−0.143	−0.275
	(0.090)	(0.277)
comp	0.025	0.143
	(0.119)	(0.357)
Ind_exp	0.298	1.524***
	(0.189)	(0.584)
Ind_rd	−0.003	−0.005
	(0.005)	(0.013)
Constant	−3.354***	−4.970***
	(0.357)	(1.197)
Region dummies	Y	Y
N	3,244	3,244
Log(likelihood	−742.6	−696.5
Chi-squared	1266	506.4

Note: Standard errors in parentheses. ***$p<0.01$, **$p<0.05$, *$p<0.1$. IV method is used to control for the endogeneity between labour productivity and export performance. Fast export-growth industries are those top 20 export sectors in which the difference in export growth from 2000 to 2007 between the domestic and foreign firms is greater than 10. These include SIC 4053, 4059, 4014, 4051, 4111 and 4119.

has greater and positive influence in these industries. The subsample includes industries that have achieved fast export growth in the domestic sector. Industries whose indigenous export growth rate over the 2000–2006 period is 10 times that of the FIEs are included in this subsample. It includes more than 1,000 firms with 3,244 observations in the integrated circuit devices, optical devices and other electronic devices, mobile communication and terminal equipment, vacuum electronic devices, the industrial automatic control system and auxiliary instrument and other general instrument industries. The estimated results suggest that indigenous innovation, export information spillovers and economies of scale are the important factors that contributed to the growth of exports in the indigenous firms. Only export information spillovers from non-PT-FDI appear to contribute significantly to the fast export growth in these sectors. All the remaining FDI spillover variables show no significant impact on the export performance of indigenous firms. In contrast, indigenous innovation through in-house R&D shows a positive and significant effect on both export decision and performance. The size of the estimated coefficients is much larger than those for the full sample. Moreover, larger firms appear to be more likely to export and export more.

Table 4.7 reports the robustness check results using alternative measurement of FDI spillovers. FDI information and the knowledge pool are

Table 4.7 *Spillovers from PT-FDI and export performance of indigenous firms: IV estimates of alternative spillover measurements*

Variables	Export decision Probit (1)	Export value GLLAMM (selection in Tobit) (2)
pt_forx_lag	0.010** (0.005)	0.022 (0.015)
pt_fori_lag	−0.002 (0.003)	0.005 (0.010)
npt_forx_lag	0.019*** (0.005)	0.040** (0.016)
npt_fori_lag	−0.006 (0.004)	−0.019 (0.014)

Table 4.7 (*cont.*)

Variables	Export decision Probit (1)	Export value GLLAMM (selection in Tobit) (2)
z_lag	2.428*** (0.025)	
e_lag		0.617*** (0.012)
yl	0.0003* (0.0002)	0.0018*** (0.001)
size	0.269*** (0.022)	0.668*** (0.069)
kl	0.0001 (0.0001)	0.0001 (0.0001)
rd	0.428*** (0.045)	0.515*** (0.139)
wage	0.052* (0.029)	−0.038 (0.094)
Constant	−2.656*** (0.823)	−4.281*** (1.427)
Industry dummies	Y	Y
Region dummies	Y	Y
Year dummies	Y	Y
N	31868	24757
Log-likelihood	−7753	−6085
Chi-squared	10587	4784

Note: Standard errors in parentheses. ***$p<0.01$, **$p<0.05$, *$p<0.1$.

FDI knowledge and information pool variables are constructed at the provincial level.

IV method is used to control for the endogeneity between labour productivity and export performance.

constructed at the provincial level to allow for wider export information and technological knowledge spillovers. The general picture is broadly consistent with the estimated results using FDI spillover variables constructed at a more disaggregated broad-city level. Consistent with earlier results, FDI has generated significant export information spill-overs on the propensity of export market participation in indigenous firms, and the strength of that effect of non-PT-FDI is stronger than that of PT-FDI. However, unlike the estimates of city-level spillover varia-bles, the information spillover effect of PT-FDI is insignificant at the provincial level, confirming the argument that knowledge spillovers are a localised phenomenon, and firms in the same cluster benefit the most from knowledge spillovers between firms. As regards the technology spillovers from FDI, although the estimated coefficients also bear a negative sign, which is consistent with the earlier results, they are not statistically significant in either model. There are two possible explan-ations for this change. First, technology spillovers may be transmitted to other cities through people's movement. Second, competition may be stronger between firms in the same cluster because they are more likely to compete in the same or similar segment product and factor markets. In-house R&D, firm size and labour productivity remain the significant determinants of export performance of indigenous firms.

4.8 Conclusions

This chapter examines how and to what extent processing trade-FDI influences the international competitiveness of indigenous firms using linked and highly disaggregated firm-level and product-level data sets relating to production, trade mode and exports from China. Findings show that although there had been some fast export growth in a few of the high-technology industries, by 2007 about 90 per cent of the technology-intensive exports from China were still the processing exports of MNEs. Most of the indigenous firms have not built up their international competitiveness and rely on the domestic market.

The estimated results suggest that FDI engaged in processing trade activities offers significant positive information spillovers to local firms with regards to their export activities. Such spillovers have provided domestic firms not only with foreign market intelligence but also export and marketing techniques. However, although there will still be some technology spillovers through demonstration and the movement of workers, the scope for technology spillovers in such low-skilled labour-intensive assembly activities is limited. Benefits from PT-FDI–facilitated technology spillovers are too small to build up export competitiveness in the international markets, where firms have to compete with MNEs that actively engage in R&D and innovation. Moreover, the competitive advantage enjoyed by the MNEs through the combination of technological, financial and marketing capital with low-cost labour leads to competition with indigenous firms and crowds them out of export markets. Such negative technology spillover effects pose a significant barrier for non-exporters regarding export market participation. As a result, the effect of technology spillovers of PT-FDI on the propensity of export market entry in indigenous firms is in fact negative and significant. However, exporters who already possess international competitiveness are able to compete and to learn from foreign competition. The net effect of such spillovers therefore becomes insignificant.

Non-PT-FDI, on the one hand, provides slightly stronger positive information spillovers on domestic firms; on the other hand, it still shows a negative technology spillover effect on the export value of indigenous exporters, although this is only marginally significant at the 10 per cent significance level. The estimated results suggest that indigenous innovation, economies of scale and export information spillovers from non-PT-FDI are the main drivers of export performance in the indigenous firms. Labour productivity does not appear to have a significant role in firms' export decisions, suggesting that the productivity threshold level for exporting is low in industries where processing trade is prevalent. Labour productivity serves as a significant factor determining the scale of a firm's exports. FDI spillover variables constructed at a more disaggregated broad-city level appear to better reflect the stronger information/knowledge spillovers that take place between firms in the same cluster and the stronger competition effect that occurs between firms in the same cluster compared to those taking place between firms in different cities.

Evidence from this research has important policy implications. The establishment of export processing zones and the encouragement of process-trade–cum–FDI have been used by many developing countries as a major policy tool to facilitate technological learning and upgrading in indigenous firms as well as to promote job creation. Evidence from this research suggests that although there are significant export information spillovers, the direct technological learning effect is limited and the benefits are not provided quickly. The technology advantage of the MNEs even poses a significant barrier deterring the export market participation of the indigenous firms. In the case of the technology-intensive industries in China, although some catch-up is taking place in a few industries, the overall FDI spillover effects are not strong enough to increase the international competitiveness of the indigenous firms. In the high-technology industries, where technology becomes increasingly sophisticated and precise, the opportunities for learning and catch-up through labour-intensive processing-trade–based production activities have become smaller than those experienced by Japanese and Korean firms in the 1960s and 1970s. Complementary policy tools are needed to provide real commitments to technology transfer and opportunities for indigenous technological learning and local capabilities building.

Admittedly, processing-trade FDI will contribute to employment and income growth in the host country. Income from processing trades may be reinvested in education, which eventually will raise the skills level of the next generation in the host country. In the long run, the host country may gradually move up the technology ladder with improved labour skills. Even such an indirect slow upgrading process will not come about automatically without redistribution of the income into education and indigenous innovation. Therefore, effective government policies and a favourable national culture to ensure that the income from processing trade is reinvested in skills building and indigenous innovation are crucial in the development of technological capabilities and the international competitiveness of indigenous firms.

5 | Indigenous and foreign innovation efforts and technological upgrading in China

5.1 Introduction

Technology upgrading is a key element of industrialisation in developing countries. International technology transfer through foreign direct investment (FDI) has long been regarded as a major engine of technology upgrading in developing countries. Many developing countries combined competition for FDI with the expectation that advanced technological knowledge embedded in FDI can drive technological upgrading in their countries. On the other hand, in recent years more and more developing countries have started to question the effectiveness of such a FDI-led technology upgrading strategy and have called for greater emphasis on indigenous innovation as a driver of the development of indigenous technological capabilities. It is therefore timely to assess the following two questions: (1) what are the major drivers of technological upgrading in developing countries, and (2) can developing countries rely on foreign technology to catch up with industrialised countries? Furthermore, empirical evidence on the productivity gains from trade and FDI is mixed, and the debate on the importance of foreign versus indigenous innovation efforts is inconclusive.[1]

This chapter attempts to explore the drivers of technology upgrading in middle-income developing countries, which often have sizeable domestic markets, considerable human capital and a strong desire for economic independence. It assumes that developing countries, especially middle-income countries, are not only users but also creators of new technology in certain industrial sectors. It also takes into account

---

[1] Görg and Strobl (2001) and Meyer (2004) provide excellent surveys of the relevant literature.

108

the fact that the industry structure of these countries often consists of industries of a variety of technology intensities.[2]

The empirical analysis is carried out using a firm-level panel data set of 56,125 Chinese firms over the 2001–2005 period. China provides a good case for this study given its huge FDI inflows and its emphasis on indigenous innovation and industry upgrading. A non-parametric frontier technique is used to decompose the total factor productivity (TFP) growth of firms into technical change and efficiency improvement. The drivers of these changes are examined with special emphasis on the impact of indigenous and foreign research and development (R&D) efforts. Three types of R&D effort are considered: R&D at the firm level, R&D in all foreign invested firms within the same industry and region in China, and international R&D spillovers facilitated by FDI. To test the effect of the third type of foreign R&D effort, the international industry-specific R&D stock is linked to the Chinese firm-level data in the corresponding industry and adjusted by industry- and firm-level FDI intensity.

This chapter is organised as follows: Section 5.2 presents a theoretical framework for the understanding of the drivers of technological upgrading in a middle-income developing country. Section 5.3 provides a brief overview of FDI and innovation in China. Section 5.4 discusses data, model and methodologies. Section 5.5 presents the empirical results. Section 5.6 concludes with a discussion of policy implications.

5.2 Theoretical framework

Innovation is costly, risky and path dependent. Innovation activities have therefore been largely concentrated amongst a few developed countries. If technologies are costless to diffuse and if the effectiveness of a technology is the same in different local contexts, developing countries can rely on foreign technology transfer and easily catch up with the world technology frontier without indigenous innovation. Foreign direct investment as a bundle of technological and managerial knowledge as well as financial capital has long been regarded as a major vehicle in the transfer of advanced foreign technology to developing

---

[2] Technology intensity is often proxied by the ratio of R&D expenditure to value added.

countries (Dunning, 1993; Lall, 2003). A further reason to expect that FDI will lead to technology transfer derives from the fact that most of the world's R&D investment is concentrated amongst a few large multinational enterprises (MNEs).

FDI may contribute to technological upgrading in the host economy in several ways. Technology spillovers from foreign invested firms may contribute to technical change in indigenous firms. Knowledge spillovers may take place from foreign to local firms in the same industry and region through movement of trained labour, demonstration effects and competition effects when the competitive pressure caused by the foreign presence forces local firms to improve their production technology and management (Caves, 1974; Fosfuri, Motta and Ronde, 2001; Buckley, Clegg and Wang, 2002). There may also be significant knowledge transfer within the supply chain via forward and backward linkages (Javorcik, 2004). Moreover, advanced technologies embedded in imported machinery and equipment in foreign invested enterprises (FIEs) may raise the average technology level of the host economy. Multinational enterprises may also bring in advanced innovation management practices and thus improve the innovation efficiency of the local innovation system (Fu, 2008). On the other hand, the introduction of FDI may make competing domestic firms worse off (Aitken and Harrison, 1999) and reduce the R&D efforts of local firms (OECD, 2002). This could occur if foreign firms exploit their superior technology and marketing power to force local competitors to reduce their outputs or if they attract the most talented researchers, which in particular might threaten local small and medium enterprises (SMEs) (Aitken and Harrison, 1999; Hu and Jefferson, 2002; UNCTAD, 2005).

Moreover, several preconditions are needed for local firms to benefit in an effective manner from FDI spillovers. First, technology transfer via the supply chain requires effective linkages between foreign firms and their local suppliers and customers (Fu, 2004; Javorcik, 2004). Second, significant spillovers from foreign to local firms require sufficient absorptive capacity in the local firms (Cohen and Levinthal, 1989; Fu, 2008). A threshold level of human capital is also necessary (Eaton and Kortum, 1996; Xu, 2000). R&D activities are important as a means of learning and accumulating absorptive capacity (Aghion and Howitt, 1992; Griffith, Redding and Van Reenen, 2003). Third, different types of FDI have markedly different productivity spillover effects (Driffield and Love, 2003). Given these preconditions, it is not surprising that despite the possible benefits from international technology transfer, empirical evidence in this field is mixed.

Moreover, the need for foreign technology to be appropriate to the specific socioeconomic and technical context of a developing country implies that developing countries cannot rely on foreign technology for technological upgrading and that indigenous innovation is of crucial importance. Different technologies are specific to particular combinations of inputs (Basu and Weil, 1998). For a particular country, an appropriate technology is a technology tailored to fit the psychosocial and biophysical context prevailing in a particular location and period (Stewart, 1983; see also Willoughby, 1990). Therefore, technological progress can be seen as localised learning by doing (Atkinson and Stiglitz, 1969).

Acemoglu (2002) suggests that technologies are designed to make optimal use of the conditions and factor supplies in the country where the technology is developed. Most new technologies are invented and developed in industrial countries (e.g., OECD countries), which are abundant in skilled labour. Therefore, these new technologies often make intensive use of skilled labour, for example, engineers, managers and other professionals, and are usually capital augmenting or skilled-labour augmenting. Such advanced technologies might be inappropriate for conditions in developing countries and hence less productive given the different factor endowments that the developing countries have (Acemoglu and Zilibotti, 2001; Acemoglu, 2002). The extent of directed technical change and the difference in factor endowment between creator and user economies will determine how appropriate or inappropriate a technology is with respect to the needs of the importing country.

As endowments in developing countries differ between countries, and the demand for skilled labour varies across industries, the degree of appropriateness of foreign technology for productivity growth in a developing country depends on the characteristics of the country and the industry under study. As demand for unskilled and semi-skilled labour is higher in labour-intensive industries, adoption of unskilled-labour augmenting technology will generate greater returns than the use of skilled-labour augmenting technology. In other words, firms using unskilled-labour augmenting technology will be more efficient than firms using skilled-labour augmenting technology in low-technology industries. For similar reasons, skilled-labour augmenting technology will be more efficient in high-technology industries. Indigenous technology created in a

labour-abundant developing country will be unskilled-labour augmenting, as suggested by the Directed Technical Change theory. Therefore, in
such populous developing countries, indigenous technology might be
more efficient than foreign technology in labour-intensive industries. By
contrast, foreign technology created in developed economies will be more
efficient than indigenous technology in technology-intensive industries. In
sum, technical change and the appropriateness of a technology are sector
specific. This sectoral extension of the analysis is important because in
reality countries often produce a diverse mixture of goods rather than
simply specialising in either labour- or capital-intensive production.

   Middle-income countries have accumulated a pool of knowledge and
skills that distinguishes their factor endowments from those of the least
developed countries as well as those of the industrialised countries.
Therefore, middle-income economies are more likely to generate 'intermediate' innovations with medium-level technology intensity. These
middle-income countries can reap the gains from investment in such
technologies through the sale of patents, payment of royalties or South-
South foreign direct investment between developing countries.
Moreover, for the same relative factor prices, the gain from introducing
new techniques is higher the larger the volume of demand. This also
implies that countries such as China, Brazil and India are more likely to
generate intermediate technology than smaller economies with the same
degree of capital scarcity (Findlay, 1978).

   In sum, while there are potential gains from international technology
transfer, the extent of benefits might be limited given the inappropriateness of foreign technology to local conditions and the preconditions for
effective FDI-assisted technology transfer. The relative importance of
indigenous and foreign innovation varies with the technology intensity
of the industries, the development level of the host country and the
difference in factor endowments between foreign and host countries.

5.3 FDI and innovation in China

Since the start of its economic reforms in 1978, China has received a large
volume of international direct investment and is now the second largest
FDI recipient in the world. In 2008, FDI inflows into China reached a
peak of US$92.40 billion (MOFCOM, 2010). Whereas investments from
overseas Chinese in Hong Kong, Macao and Taiwan were the major
sources of inward FDI in the 1980s, the 1990s saw increasing inward FDI

from the major industrialised countries and other OECD countries. A major objective of China's opening up to FDI is to 'exchange markets for technology' in the 7th Five-Year-Plan (1986–1990). Moreover, the science and technology system reform that began in 1985 has also specified the acquisition of foreign technology as one of the main strategies for technology development. FDI and imports are employed as major channels for foreign technology transfer. In 1995, the Chinese government decided to accelerate science and technology development and pursue a technology- and education-led development strategy. This signalled the transition of the focus of China's technology development from technology transfer to indigenous innovation. The shift was further strengthened in 2006 when the promotion of indigenous innovation was formally listed as one of the country's top priorities. In this process, the total R&D expenditure in China grew from RMB 7.4 billion in 1987 to RMB 35 billion in 1995 and to RMB 300.3 billion in 2006, at an average annual growth rate of 21 per cent (MOST, 2010a).

5.4 Data and methodology

Data

We draw on the Annual Report of Industrial Enterprise Statistics compiled by the National Bureau of Statistics of China, covering all state-owned firms and other types of firms with annual turnover of more than RMB 5 million (US$0.7 million). The data set includes variables such as firm ownership structure, industry affiliation, geographic location, year of establishment, number of employment, gross output, value added, fixed assets, exports, R&D and employee-training expenditures.[3] The data currently available cover 2001 to 2005 and are broadly classified into five ownership categories: (1) state-owned, (2) collectively owned, (3) privately owned, (4) foreign owned and (5) others. Foreign-owned firms are further divided into firms with investments from Hong Kong, Taiwan and Macao (HKTM firms) and firms with investments from other foreign sources (FIEs). 'Other' firms are mainly shareholding enterprises (SHCs). Following Eurostat (2004), we used a fourfold division of technological capabilities: high technology, medium-high

---

[3] Nominal values are deflated using industry-specific ex-factory price indexes obtained from the China Statistical Yearbook 2006.

technology, medium-low technology and low-technology.[4] Details of industries in each category can be found as part of Appendix 5.1. The sectoral pattern of their R&D activities is also reported in Appendix 5.1.

We are interested in the drivers of technological upgrading in indigenous firms. The econometric work is hence confined to domestically owned enterprises only. We nevertheless use the full sample of firms to construct several variables of interest, for example, the share of foreign firms in an industry in each region or the Herfindahl index of market concentration. We include only those firms for which there is a full set of observations during the sample period, as the estimation of TFP growth and its components using data envelopment analysis (DEA) requires balanced data sets. The final data set consists of 269,905 observations from 53,981 firms.

The international industry-specific R&D stock is linked to the Chinese firm-level data. The estimates of international R&D stock are based on R&D expenditure data from the OECD's 'Main Science and Technology Indicators'. Following Coe and Helpman (1995), R&D capital stock (S), which is defined here as the stock at the beginning of a period, is calculated from R&D expenditure (R) based on the perpetual inventory model $S_t = (1 - \delta) S_{t-1} + R_t$, where δ is the depreciation rate, which is assumed to be 5, 10 and 15 per cent, alternatively. The starting value for the stock, S_0, is calculated following the procedure suggested by Griliches (1979) as $S_0 = R_0 / (g + \delta)$, where g is the average annual logarithmic growth of R&D expenditures over the period for which published R&D data were available, and R_0 is the first year for which the data were available. Domestic R&D capital stocks are converted into euros at 2000 constant prices.[5] The R&D stocks of the 22 OECD countries are then summed to proxy the world R&D stock. Table 5.1

---

[4] Technological groups are divided according to the technology intensity (R&D expenditure to value-added ratio) of the industries. We follow the standard used in the Eurostat data set, which is based on the NACE Rev 1.1 Classification at the three-digit level, which is converted into the SIC two-digit level classification.

[5] Real R&D expenditures are nominal expenditures deflated by an R&D price index (PR), which is defined as $PR = 0.5P + 0.5W$, where P is the deflator for industrial output and W is an index of average industry wages. This definition of PR implies that half of R&D expenditures is composed of labour costs, which is broadly consistent with available data on the composition of R&D expenditures.

Table 5.1 *Summary statistics of the variables*

Variable	Definition	Obs.	Mean	Std. Dev.	Min	Max
Technical efficiency	TE based on variable returns to scale	269905	0.3836	0.2106	0	1
TFP growth	Geometric mean of two indexes estimated as the ratios of distance functions of a firm from the frontier	269905	0.8811	0.5825	0	11.391
Efficiency change	Change in efficiency between two periods	269905	0.9924	0.9231	0	16.25
Technical change	Shift in technology between the two periods	269905	1.0258	0.9639	0	7.905
Firm R&D intensity	The ratio of R&D expenditure to total sales	269905	0.0017	0.0118	0	1
SOE R&D	Log of total R&D expenditure of state-owned firms in the same industry and region	269905	8.1727	3.2957	0	14.7872
POE R&D	Log of total R&D expenditure of private firms in the same industry and region	269905	8.3919	1.8876	0	12.6489
COE R&D	Log of total R&D expenditure of collectively owned firms in the same industry and region	269905	6.2982	2.7883	0	11.3304
SHC R&D	Log of total R&D expenditure of shareholding firms in the same industry and region	269905	9.8352	2.2576	0	15.4538
HKTM R&D	Log of total R&D expenditure of Hong Kong, Taiwan and Macau–invested firms in the same industry and region	269905	7.7628	2.6586	0	13.8253
FIE R&D	Log of total R&D expenditure of foreign invested firms in the same industry and region	269905	8.1425	2.7045	0	14.6711
International R&D*firm	International R&D capital stocks*foreign capital share at firm level	268991	1.3270	3.5505	0	13.7443
International R&D*industry	International R&D capital stocks*foreign capital share at industry level	263331	9.2225	1.7379	0	13.0004
Initial technical efficiency	Initial technical efficiency level	269905	0.3965	0.2043	0.013	1
Age	Log of age	269905	2.6242	0.6989	0.6931	5.1874

Table 5.1 (*cont.*)

Variable	Definition	Obs.	Mean	Std. Dev.	Min	Max
Firm size	Log of employment	269905	5.2039	1.1096	0.6931	11.9031
Market concentration	Herfindahl index (three-digit industry)	269905	0.0196	0.0266	0.0017	1
Intangible assets per person	Log of intangible assets per person	269900	0.9052	1.3799	0	9.0027
Training expenditure per person	Log of training expenditure per person	269891	0.0834	0.1734	0	4.0108
Exports	Log of export sales	269905	3.3919	4.7273	0	18.0558
Foreign capital share	Share of foreign capital in a firm	269905	0.0905	0.2610	0	1
HKTM capital share	Share of Hong Kong, Taiwan and Macau capital in a firm	269905	0.1053	0.2841	0	1
Ownership classifications	1 State-owned enterprises (SOEs)	269905	0.1115	0.3147	0	1
	2 Collective-owned firms (COEs)	269905	0.1093	0.3120	0	1
	3 Private-owned firms (POEs)	269905	0.2638	0.4407	0	1
	4 HKTM firms (investors are from Hong Kong, Taiwan, Macau)	269905	0.1449	0.3520	0	1
	5 Foreign invested enterprises (FIEs)	269905	0.1219	0.3271	0	1
	6 Others, mainly shareholding companies (SHCs)	269905	0.2488	0.4323	0	1
High tech	Dummy equalling 1 for SIC 27 40 41	269905	0.0774	0.2672	0	1
Medium-high tech	Dummy equalling 1 for SIC 26 28 36 37 39	269905	0.2343	0.4236	0	1
Medium-low tech	Dummy equalling 1 for SIC 24 25 29 30 31 32 33 34 35 42	269905	0.3404	0.4739	0	1
Low tech	Dummy equalling 1 for SIC 13 14 15 16 17 18 19 20 21 22 23	269905	0.3479	0.4763	0	1

gives the definitions of the variables used in the analysis along with some summary statistics.

Methodology

The empirical study is carried out using the following steps. First, we estimate TFP growth using the Malmquist productivity index and decompose it into technical progress and efficiency change. TFP is estimated for each industry separately allowing for different technology and production functions for different industries. Second, we identify the firms that are located on the technology frontier, as measured by firms' technical efficiency and compare foreign with domestic firms. Third, we use econometric techniques to estimate the drivers of TFP growth, technical change and efficiency improvement for firms in each technology category.

Estimation of TFP growth

The conventional technique for estimating TFP is the Solow residual method. This method, however, suffers from several well-known limitations. For example, the production function is assumed to be known and to be homogenous across industries and firms, and technical change is assumed to be neutral. If these assumptions do not hold, TFP measurements will be biased (Arcelus and Arocena, 2000). Therefore, this chapter estimates TFP growth by using a non-parametric programming method developed by Fare et al. (1994). Following Fare's approach, a production frontier is constructed based on all existing observations. Technical efficiency is defined as the distance of each observation from the frontier. TFP growth is defined as a geometric mean of two Malmquist productivity indexes and is estimated on the basis of the ratios of distance functions of observations at times t and t + 1. This approach is capable of measuring productivity in a multi-input, multi-output setting and does not require the assumptions of the Solow method. It also has another advantage in that it allows for the decomposition of productivity growth into two mutually exclusive and exhaustive components: (1) technical change measured by shifts in the technological frontier and (2) efficiency change measured by movements towards (or away from) the frontier. The latter is a measurement of catching up (Fare et al., 1994).

This decomposition of TFP growth enables us to investigate the different effects of foreign and indigenous innovation on technical progress and efficiency improvement. The main shortcoming of this technique is the lack of a provision for statistical noise or measurement errors in the model (Greene, 1997). Any deviation from the frontier is attributed to inefficiency. The frontier is hence sensitive to outliers in the data. To reduce the possible bias caused by this shortcoming, careful data cleansing has been carried out on an industry-by-industry basis.

The Malmquist TFP growth index of the production point (x^{t+1}, y^{t+1}) relative to the production point (x^t, y^t) is given as follows:

$$M_0(x^{t+1}, y^{t+1}, x^t, y^t) = \left[\left(\frac{D_0^t (x^{t+1}, y^{t+1})}{D_0^t (x^t, y^t)} \right) \left(\frac{D_0^{t+1} (x^{t+1}, y^{t+1})}{D_0^{t+1} (x^t, y^t)} \right) \right]^{\frac{1}{2}}$$

(5.1)

A value greater than 1 indicates positive TFP growth in period $t + 1$. When performance deteriorates over time, the Malmquist index will be less than 1.

Equation (5.1) can be rewritten as

$$M_0(x^{t+1}, y^{t+1}, x^t, y^t) = \frac{D_0^{t+1} (x^{t+1}, y^{t+1})}{D_0^t (x^t, y^t)}$$

$$\times \left[\left(\frac{D_0^t (x^{t+1}, y^{t+1})}{D_0^{t+1} (x^{t+1}, y^{t+1})} \right) \left(\frac{D_0^t (x^t, y^t)}{D_0^{t+1} (x^t, y^t)} \right) \right]^{\frac{1}{2}}$$

(5.2)

where efficiency change $= \dfrac{D_0^{t+1} (x^{t+1}, y^{t+1})}{D_0^t (x^t, y^t)}$ (5.3)

and technical change $= \left[\left(\dfrac{D_0^t (x^{t+1}, y^{t+1})}{D_0^{t+1} (x^{t+1}, y^{t+1})} \right) \left(\dfrac{D_0^t (x^t, y^t)}{D_0^{t+1} (x^t, y^t)} \right) \right]^{\frac{1}{2}}$

(5.4)

Thus, TFP change is decomposed into two components: efficiency change and technical change. Efficiency change measures whether production is getting closer to or further away from the frontier. Technical change captures the shift in technology between the two periods. It indicates whether or not technical progress occurred at the input-output combination of a particular industry. A value greater than 1 indicates technical progress or efficiency improvement correspondingly. A value of less than 1 indicates deterioration in performance. The Malmquist productivity index is estimated by using non-parametric linear programming techniques. Details of the estimation method are given in Appendix 5.2. This chapter follows the basic DEA model, which includes three inputs: labour (number of employees), capital (net fixed assets) and variable costs (intermediate costs); and one output: total firm output. Returns to scale can be variable.

Foreign and indigenous R&D efforts and TFP growth

Having decomposed productivity growth, the next step is to estimate the drivers of TFP growth, technical change and efficiency improvement using regression analysis. Following Findlay (1978), foreign capital and domestic capital are regarded as distinct factors of production in this model, reflecting the fact that capital, management and technology are inextricably combined.

The empirical analysis of the impact of indigenous and foreign innovation on indigenous technology upgrading is based on the following model:

$$\Delta Y_{it} = \chi RD_{it} + \gamma FDI_{it} + \beta X_{it} + \delta D_{it} + \varepsilon_{it} \qquad (5.5)$$

where the dependent variable ΔY represents TFP growth, technical change and efficiency improvement, respectively. RD is a vector of R&D variables. FDI is FDI intensity measured by the ratio of foreign investment to total assets. X is a vector of control variables. D is the full set of time and sector dummies, and ε is a random error term; i and t denote firm and time, respectively.

We are most interested in the set of R&D variables. Our specification contains three types of innovation efforts: innovation at the firm, industry and international levels. We construct the variables as follows: (1) the intensity of a firm's own R&D activities; (2) the industry-level innovation effort in each of the 171 three-digit industries and 31 provinces, which is constructed as the total R&D expenditure of different ownership types in the same industry and region; (3) international R&D spillover, which is constructed as the interaction term of international industry-specific R&D stock and FDI share at both firm and industry levels. The full empirical model is therefore as follows:

$$\Delta Y_{it} = \chi_1 RDF_{it} + \chi_2 RDI_{it} + \chi_3 RDW_{it} * FDIF_{it} \\ + \chi_4 RDW_{it} * FDID_{it} + \gamma FDI_{it} + \beta X_{it} + \delta D_{it} + \varepsilon_{it} \tag{5.6}$$

where *RDF* is firm R&D intensity, *RDI* is a vector of industry-level R&D spillover variables, *RDW* is world R&D stock constructed from the OECD STAN (Structural Analysis Database) database as discussed earlier, and *FDIF* and *FDID* are FDI intensity at firm and industry levels, respectively.

Control variables consist of the initial level of technology efficiency, age, firm size, exports, intangible assets, labour training and market concentration. These variables are chosen on the basis of the existing empirical literature (e.g., Bernard and Jensen, 1999; Aw, Chung and Roberts, 2000; Fu, 2005; Girma, Gong and Görg, 2009). Smaller firms, firms with exports and firms with greater amounts of labour training are more likely to have faster TFP growth, technical change and efficiency improvements. Firms already on the frontier are unlikely to grow as fast as other firms. There is no agreed relationship between firm age, intangible assets and market concentration.[6] For example, the effect of market competition on innovation may be a double-edged sword. Geroski (1990) argues that lack of competition in a market gives rise to inefficiency and sluggish innovative activity. On the other hand, Schumpeterians claim that monopoly power makes it easier for firms to appropriate the returns from innovation and thereby provides the incentive to invest in innovation (Cohen and Levinthal, 1989; Symeonidis, 2001).

In the earlier specification, FDI is represented by two variables, the share of foreign capital and HKTM capital at the firm level. We conjecture that firms might grow faster if they have easier access to advanced foreign technical and managerial knowledge through their foreign or HKTM Chinese partners. We distinguish between foreign and HKTM capital to account for any differences in motivation between foreign and HKTM capital. Foreign investors are more likely to be market oriented, whereas HKTM investors might look for less expensive labour and rent to reduce costs and export their outputs.

---

[6] According to *Accounting System for Business Enterprises*, the costs to develop intangible assets are regarded as the R&D costs of self-created products that are registered for a legal right to the asset, such as a patent (Pacter and Yuen, 2001).

Some independent variables in the earlier specification are arguably determined simultaneously with the dependent variable, TFP growth and its components. In other words, there might be a potential endogeneity problem even after controlling for fixed effects. For example, firms with relatively large R&D activities are more likely to have higher TFP growth and faster technical change. However, it is also possible that firms with higher growth rates might invest more in R&D activities to keep their technology advantages. Another example is the foreign share of a firm. Firms with a higher foreign capital share could have better access to foreign technology and therefore have higher growth rates, but there also might be a 'cherry-picking' effect (Huang, 2003) whereby foreigners choose to invest in faster growing firms. Similar arguments can be made in the case of export and HKTM capital participation.

To deal with the problem of endogeneity, we employ the fixed effects generalised method of moments (GMM) regression technique (see, inter alia, Hansen, 1982 and Arellano and Bond, 1991). The use of industry and region dummies in the regressions is designed to mitigate part of this potential endogeneity problem. Lagged values of the potentially endogenous variables (exports, R&D intensity, foreign capital share and HKTM capital share) are used as instruments. In addition, the shares of foreign and HKTM firms in the industry and region are used as extra instruments. Given the low level of competition from state-owned firms (Girma et al., 2009), we assume that a sector will be more efficient if more foreign or HKTM firms are participating in it. We also formally test whether the assumption of endogeneity is borne out by the data at hand and whether our instruments are relevant in the sense of exhibiting sufficiently strong correlation with the potentially endogenous variables. We also test for the appropriateness of the instrumental variable candidates using Hansen J's test for overidentifying restrictions and the validity of the instruments using the Sargan test. Reassuringly, we find that our instruments are appropriate on all counts.

5.5 Results

Technical efficiency and TFP growth

Figure 5.1 reports the level of technical efficiency of firms by ownership. FIEs have the highest level of average technical efficiency, whereas that

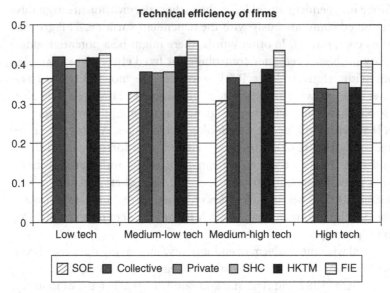

Figure 5.1 Technical efficiency by ownership and technology category

of SOEs is the lowest. The average technical efficiency of HKTM firms ranks second in the medium-technology sectors but is lower than that of SHCs in the high-technology sectors. Across technology groups, FIEs enjoy an advantage in technical efficiency over indigenous firms. The gap is small in low-technology industries but becomes larger in other categories that have higher technology intensity.[7] In the high-technology sector, the estimated technical efficiency of FIEs is about 30 per cent higher than that of SOEs.

Figure 5.2 reports estimated TFP growth by firm ownership. Looking at growth dynamics, it is clear that in all industries Chinese firms have experienced considerable TFP growth during the 2001–2005 period with growth running at an average annual rate of 4.8 per cent. The growth is mainly due to technical change at an average annual growth rate of 5.1 per cent rather than to efficiency improvements: the average

[7] The t-test results suggest that the size of the gap in TE between SOEs and FIEs in the low-technology sector is significantly smaller than that in the other three technology categories. Although the size of this gap also differs between the other three sectors, the magnitude of these differences is negligible.

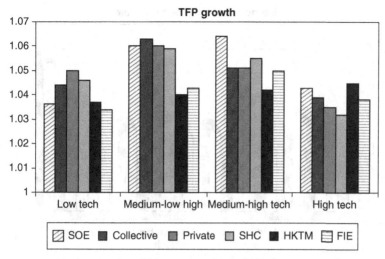

Figure 5.2 TFP growth in Chinese manufacturing firms, 2001–2005

annual growth rate of efficiency improvement was only 0.7 per cent over the sample period. The growth is widely spread across different sectors, and indigenous firms have taken the lead in this growth process in comparison to foreign invested firms.

Drivers of technological upgrading

Despite the lower average technical efficiency of indigenous firms than of foreign-invested firms, a large number of indigenous firms stand on the frontier in the low- to medium-high–technology sectors (Figure 5.3). On the contrary, in the high-technology sector, a larger number of foreign firms stand on the technology frontier.[8] A considerable number of SOEs are also found on the technology frontier. This might be

---

[8] The industries in which foreign firms have obvious dominance include electronics and telecommunications, instruments and measuring equipment, culture, educational and sports goods, as well as garments and leather products for which HKTM firms have a clear lead. Indigenous firms have dominant presence in the low- and low-medium–technology industries such as food processing, papermaking, smelting and processing of ferrous and nonferrous metals. There are also a number of industries in which foreign and domestic firms share the lead and push the frontier upwards together.

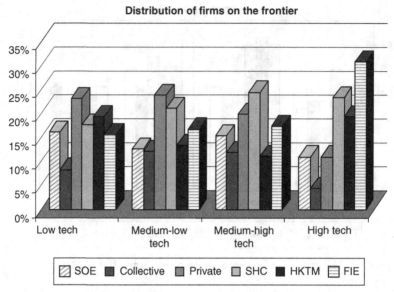

Figure 5.3 Distribution of firms on the frontier
Note: All firms in each category (e.g., low-tech) add up to 100 per cent.

explained by the fact that historically the Chinese science and technology system was influenced by the former Soviet Union model in which the state takes the leading role in R&D. Overall, technological upgrading in the Chinese economy is not dominated by any single sector. Foreign firms have considerable advantages in the high-technology sector and indigenous firms have taken a lead in the low- and medium-technology sectors. Shareholding companies, which are relatively rich in capital and skilled labour, enjoy a lead in the medium-high–technology sector. Privately owned enterprises take a lead in the low- and medium-low–technology sectors.

The greatest amount of technical change in China has taken place in the medium-high–technology industries (Figure 5.4). This change is driven by both indigenous and foreign firms, although indigenous firms have a higher rate of change. In the low-technology industries, again, indigenous firms, especially private firms, are the main drivers of technical change. In contrast, in the high-technology industries, foreign firms are the leading force, with HKTM Chinese firms and FIEs enjoying a growth rate of 7.7 per cent and 7.3 per cent, respectively. However,

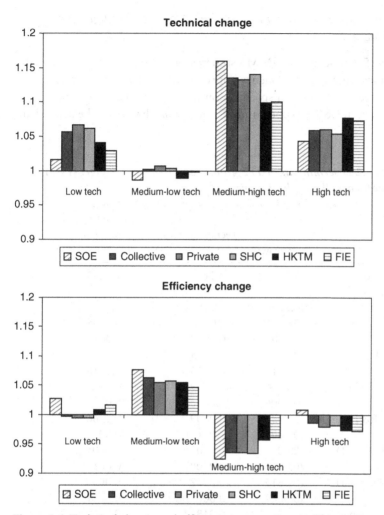

Figure 5.4 Technical change and efficiency improvement in Chinese manufacturing firms, 2001–2005

the average efficiency change indexes in these industries are less than 1, suggesting that most followers have not been able to catch up with the innovation leaders. On the contrary, in the medium-low–technology sector, most progress is made by followers through efficiency changes, while there is a lack of significant technical progress in the sample period.

Indigenous and foreign innovation efforts and indigenous technical change

Table 5.2 reports the GMM estimates of the drivers of TFP growth, technical change and efficiency improvements in domestic firms. Results from the Wu-Hausman specification test suggest significant endogeneity between R&D, exports and FDI on the one hand and the dependent

Table 5.2 *Determinants of TFP growth and technical change: GMM estimates of full sample of domestic firms*

	TFP growth	Technical change (shift of frontier)	Efficiency improvement (catch-up with frontier)
Firm R&D Intensity	0.941***	–0.219	1.388***
	(0.29)	(0.17)	(0.33)
SOE R&D	0.00110*	0.0016**	–0.0006
	(0.0006)	(0.0007)	(0.001)
POE R&D	–0.0045***	0.0125***	–0.0105***
	(0.001)	(0.0013)	(0.0016)
COE R&D	0.0004	–0.0039***	–0.0024***
	(0.0006)	(0.0007)	(0.0009)
SHC R&D	0.0031***	–0.0009	0.0066***
	(0.0009)	(0.0012)	(0.0016)
HKTM R&D	0.0004	–0.0007	–0.0005
	(0.0006)	(0.0008)	(0.0010)
Foreign R&D	–0.0015**	–0.0082***	0.0023**
	(0.0007)	(0.0009)	(0.0011)
International R&D*Firm	–0.0160**	0.0133**	–0.0160*
	(0.0066)	(0.0067)	(0.0094)
International R&D*Industry	–0.0053***	–0.0034*	0.0083***
	(0.0016)	(0.0019)	(0.0027)
Initial Technical Efficiency	–0.194***	–0.186***	–0.483***
	(0.0071)	(0.0077)	(0.011)
Age	0.0008	0.0036*	0.0035
	(0.0018)	(0.002)	(0.0027)

Table 5.2 (*cont.*)

	TFP growth	Technical change (shift of frontier)	Efficiency improvement (catch-up with frontier)
Firm Size	−0.0223***	0.0164***	0.0006
	(0.0013)	(0.0015)	(0.0019)
Market Concentration	0.0851	0.0342	−0.0574
	(0.058)	(0.066)	(0.097)
Intangible Assets	0.0050***	−0.0045***	0.0001
	(0.0009)	(0.001)	(0.0014)
Training Expenditure	0.0722***	−0.0419***	0.0531***
	(0.0084)	(0.0081)	(0.012)
Exports	0.0013***	−0.0002	0.0011**
	(0.0004)	(0.0004)	(0.0006)
Foreign Capital Share	0.559***	−0.361*	0.447
	(0.200)	(0.200)	(0.290)
HKTM Capital Share	0.183**	−0.127*	0.0214
	(0.075)	(0.071)	(0.091)
Constant	1.326***	0.522***	2.294***
	(0.019)	(0.022)	(0.032)
Observations	155885	155,885	155,885
Exogenous Test	0.0000	0.0000	0.0000
Hansen J Test	0.7605	0.5560	0.4743

Note:
1. Robust standard errors in parentheses;
2. *significant at 10 per cent; **significant at 5 per cent;
   ***significant at 1 per cent.
3. All specifications include the full set of time and two-digit industry dummies.

variable on the other hand. The GMM estimation results are therefore preferred to the OLS estimates. As a robustness check, regressions of the basic model with industrial and international R&D spillovers at three alternative depreciation rates (5 per cent, 10 per cent and 15 per cent) were carried out. The estimated coefficients from different model specifications are consistent, underlining the robustness of the estimated results.[9]

Evidence from Table 5.2 indicates that firms' own R&D efforts have a significant and positive impact on their TFP growth. This comes mainly from their substantial positive impact on the catch-up process: the estimated coefficient of 1.388 is much higher than those of all the other explanatory variables. This fact highlights the crucial role of firm-level R&D in the assimilation and adaptation of advanced technology diffused from the frontier. Industry-level R&D spillovers from other SOEs had a significant positive effect on technical change, suggesting positive social returns to the R&D investment made by the state sector. Likewise, the industry-level R&D spillovers from other privately owned firms have a significant positive effect on the technical change of other firms in the same industry. The magnitude and significance level of the estimated coefficient of R&D spillovers for POEs is greater than that of the R&D variable for SOEs, suggesting that R&D investments made by POEs have exerted greater externalities on indigenous technical change than those of SOEs. The overall spillover effect of R&D investment in shareholding companies does not appear to contribute significantly to technical change in the industry; it does, however, appear to contribute significantly to the catch-up process of follower firms in the industry. Unexpectedly, the overall spillover effect of the R&D activities of collectively owned firms appears to be negative. We will explore this later (Table 5.3 and Table 5.4) by looking into its effect in different industries.

Turning to the spillover effects of foreign R&D, spillovers from the R&D activities of FIEs and HKTM Chinese invested firms both appear to have a negative effect on indigenous technical change, and this effect is statistically significant at the 1 per cent level for FIEs. However, R&D efforts in the FIEs have a positive effect on the catch-up process, suggesting that R&D activities in these firms do not influence innovations on the frontier but contribute to the diffusion of existing relatively superior technology. Finally, international R&D spillover through FDI has mixed effects. Greater FDI intensity at the firm level appears

---

[9] Both OLS and GMM estimations were carried out but only results from GMM regressions are reported here. We have only reported the GMM estimates with a 10 per cent R&D depreciation rate because of space limitations. Results of all the estimations are available from the authors on request.

Table 5.3 *Determinants of technical change: GMM estimates by industry group*

	High tech	Medium-high tech	Medium-low tech	Low tech
Firm R&D Intensity	−0.0128	0.166	−0.479	−0.457
	(0.17)	(0.28)	(0.34)	(0.92)
SOE R&D	0.0049**	0.0142***	−0.0020*	0.0012
	(0.0023)	(0.0018)	(0.0012)	(0.001)
POE R&D	0.0071**	0.0172***	0.0045**	0.0137***
	(0.0031)	(0.0029)	(0.002)	(0.0022)
COE R&D	0.0098***	0.0108***	−0.0111***	0.0114***
	(0.0019)	(0.0013)	(0.0012)	(0.0011)
SHC R&D	0.0016	−0.0252	0.0084***	−0.0032
	(0.0044)	(0.0025)	(0.0018)	(0.002)
HKTM R&D	−0.0067**	0.0096***	−0.0028***	−0.0031*
	(0.0035)	(0.0016)	(0.001)	(0.0017)
Foreign R&D	−0.0056	−0.0232***	0.0012	−0.0152***
	(0.004)	(0.0021)	(0.0013)	(0.0017)
International R&D *Firm*	−0.0086	0.0047	0.0267*	0.0040
	(0.0074)	(0.011)	(0.015)	(0.016)
International R&D *Industry*	0.0043	−0.017***	0.0200***	0.0016
	(0.0056)	(0.0032)	(0.0029)	(0.0065)
Initial Technical Efficiency	0.00813	−0.222***	−0.222***	−0.176***
	(0.02)	(0.015)	(0.013)	(0.013)
Age	−0.0008	−0.0057	0.0090***	0.0048
	(0.0052)	(0.004)	(0.0031)	(0.0034)
Firm Size	0.0021	0.0185***	0.0176***	0.0151***
	(0.0041)	(0.0028)	(0.0023)	(0.0025)
Market Concentration	0.303**	−0.0947	0.294***	0.796***
	(0.14)	(0.098)	(0.1)	(0.21)
Intangible Asset	0.0024	−0.0067***	−0.0064***	−0.0001
	(0.0023)	(0.0018)	(0.0017)	(0.0019)
Training Expenditure	−0.0156	−0.0473***	−0.0470***	−0.0486***
	(0.014)	(0.015)	(0.013)	(0.016)

Table 5.3 (*cont.*)

	High tech	Medium-high tech	Medium-low tech	Low tech
Export	0.0007	−0.0011	0.0006	0.0009
	(0.0011)	(0.0009)	(0.0007)	(0.0007)
Foreign Capital Share	0.326	−0.162	−0.737*	−0.0693
	(0.28)	(0.4)	(0.44)	(0.42)
HKTM Capital Share	−0.174*	−0.153	−0.109	−0.0817
	(0.1)	(0.26)	(0.15)	(0.12)
Constant	0.703***	1.503***	0.799***	0.517***
	(0.077)	(0.036)	(0.036)	(0.064)
Observations	9,610	37,377	56,227	51,997
Exogenous Test	0.0000	0.0000	0.0000	0.0000
Hansen J Test	0.0511	0.0708	0.4589	0.5955

Note:
1. Robust standard errors in parentheses;
2. *significant at 10 per cent; **significant at 5 per cent; ***significant at 1 per cent.
3. All specifications include the full set of time and two-digit industry dummies.

Table 5.4 *Determinants of efficiency improvement: GMM estimates by industry group*

	High tech	Medium-high tech	Medium-low tech	Low tech
Firm R&D Intensity	0.666*	1.229**	2.694***	3.404*
	(0.38)	(0.61)	(0.79)	(1.81)
SOE R&D	−0.0055	−0.0001	−0.0036**	0.0025
	(0.0042)	(0.0025)	(0.0016)	(0.0016)
POE R&D	−0.0159**	−0.0122***	−0.0098***	−0.0073***
	(0.0064)	(0.0033)	(0.0029)	(0.0027)
COE R&D	−0.0092***	−0.0044**	0.0031*	−0.0109***
	(0.0035)	(0.0021)	(0.0018)	(0.0014)
SHC R&D	−0.0076	0.0080**	0.0062***	0.0123***
	(0.0073)	(0.0034)	(0.003)	(0.0026)
HKTM R&D	0.0002	−0.0082***	−0.0032***	0.0033
	(0.0054)	(0.0018)	(0.0015)	(0.0022)

Table 5.4 (*cont.*)

	High tech	Medium-high tech	Medium-low tech	Low tech
Foreign R&D	0.0171***	−0.0030	0.0096***	−0.0136***
	(0.0056)	(0.0026)	(0.0018)	(0.002)
International R&D*Firm	0.0002	−0.0287	−0.0468*	−0.0103
	(0.012)	(0.022)	(0.028)	(0.019)
International R&D*Industry	−0.0005	0.0453***	−0.0236***	0.0585***
	(0.0075)	(0.0042)	(0.0051)	(0.0077)
Initial Technical Efficiency	−0.373***	−0.243***	−0.652***	−0.501***
	(0.035)	(0.02)	(0.019)	(0.018)
Age	0.0004	−0.0048	0.0053	0.0128***
	(0.0087)	(0.0047)	(0.0049)	(0.0045)
Firm Size	−0.0148**	−0.0081***	0.0151***	−0.0031
	(0.007)	(0.0034)	(0.0036)	(0.0033)
Market Concentration	−0.528	0.262*	−0.452***	−0.774***
	(0.47)	(0.15)	(0.17)	(0.23)
Intangible Assets	0.0095**	−0.0038*	0.0021	−0.0018
	(0.0039)	(0.0023)	(0.0025)	(0.0025)
Training Expenditure	0.0949***	0.0737***	0.0336	0.0317
	(0.028)	(0.021)	(0.021)	(0.022)
Exports	−0.0001	0.0027***	0.0014	−0.0007
	(0.0017)	(0.001)	(0.0011)	(0.0009)
Foreign Capital Share	0.0234	1.143	1.273	0.275
	(0.44)	(0.88)	(0.84)	(0.5)
HKTM Capital Share	0.3	0.674	−0.186	0.0775
	(0.2)	(0.71)	(0.18)	(0.14)
Constant	1.737***	0.622***	1.959***	1.837***
	(0.12)	(0.051)	(0.058)	(0.074)
Observations	9,610	37,377	56,227	51,997
Exogenous Test	0.0000	0.0000	0.0000	0.0000
Hansen J Test	0.1312	0.2395	0.4646	0.8785

Note:
1. Robust standard errors in parentheses;
2. *significant at 10 per cent; **significant at 5 per cent; ***significant at 1 per cent.
3. All specifications include the full set of time and two-digit industry dummies.

to encourage the diffusion of frontier technologies. Greater FDI intensity in the industry facilitates the diffusion of superior, rather than the most advanced, technology. This suggests that with greater control of firms, MNEs are more likely to bring in more advanced technology. On the other hand, greater openness to FDI in the industry will increase the knowledge flow into the host economy, which will help the majority of followers move closer to the frontier.

As regards the coefficients of the control variables, firms with better initial technical efficiency tend to grow more slowly. Larger and older firms appear to have experienced greater technical change. Firms with high export intensity, high FDI intensity, more training and greater intangible assets have higher TFP growth than those that lack these characteristics. Their effects on the two components (technical change and efficiency change) are, however, different, which we will discuss in greater detail later (Tables 5.2–5.4).

Taking advantage of this rich data set, we examine further the impact of innovation efforts on technical change and efficiency improvements in different technology categories. The results reported in Tables 5.3 and 5.4 indicate different effects of indigenous and foreign innovation efforts in different industry groups. The indigenous R&D of individual firms has no significant impact on technical change. It has, however, contributed significantly to efficiency improvements, which reflects catch-up towards the frontier. The lower the technology intensity of the sector, the larger is the impact of indigenous firm-level innovation. This is not surprising given that the First National Economic Census in 2004 found that about 95 per cent of total business R&D expenditure was spent on development and only 5 per cent was spent on basic scientific research. Interestingly, spillovers from R&D at the industry level appear to be the main drivers of indigenous technological upgrading. In general, industry-level R&D activities in indigenous firms, especially POEs, SOEs and COEs, have shown significant positive spillovers on the technical progress of indigenous firms in most technology groups. This evidence suggests that it is collective indigenous R&D activities, that is, R&D at industry level, that push out the technology frontier and drive the technological upgrading of indigenous firms.

On the other hand, the R&D activities of FIEs and HKTM firms at the industry level show a negative spillover effect on technical change in indigenous firms in most industry groups, with the exception of

HKTM firms in the medium-high–technology sector. This can be explained by several factors. First, foreign technology may not be appropriate in these industries. Local firms are likely to find it difficult to adapt foreign technology to the local context. Second, foreign R&D activities may well intensify competition for the limited domestic talent pool (Chang et al., 2006) and crowd out indigenous firms from local labour, resource and product markets. Moreover, foreign R&D centres may have limited interest in sharing knowledge with domestic firms and R&D labs (Chang et al., 2006; Zhou, 2006. This may also be explained by the strict intellectual property rights protection of these high-end FIEs that aim to protect their intellectual property against indigenous firms. Finally, the findings of recent studies (Narula and Zanfei, 2004) suggest that the core technology development of MNEs is still carried out within the headquarters of a firm, whereas the application and adaptation of research are principally the tasks of its affiliates in foreign countries. Therefore, these R&D activities may not contribute to technical change but might have a positive impact on catching up. This also explains the result in Table 5.4 that industry-level R&D of FIEs has a significant positive effect on the catching-up process of indigenous firms in the high and medium-low technology industries.

As regards international R&D spillovers facilitated by FDI, the spillover effect on indigenous technical change is mostly insignificant or negative except in the medium-low–technology sector, where technical change is negligible over the sample period as Figure 5.4 illustrates. On the other hand, the spillover effect of FDI on catch-up seems to be mixed. In the low- and medium-high–technology sectors where indigenous firms have led technical change in China, industry-wide openness to FDI appears to have facilitated spillovers of second-tier technology that helped follower firms catch up with the frontier. However, in the medium-low–technology sector, since the effect of international R&D spillovers has been significant in pushing out the frontier, albeit to a small extent, the effect of such spillovers on catch-up will be negative given the way in which technical change and efficiency improvement are defined and decomposed.

The differing spillover effects of indigenous as compared with foreign innovation efforts on the technical change of domestic firms suggests that indigenous technologies fit the local technical context better and are therefore more likely than foreign technology to be adopted by domestic firms. Innovation activities in foreign invested firms not only fail to offer sufficient positive externalities for the domestic firms but even exert significant negative pressure on the technical change of local firms. Therefore, although foreign technology transfer may facilitate technology development at an early development stage and may assist the diffusion of second-tier technology, developing countries have to rely on collective indigenous innovation at the industry level in their catch-up with the world technology frontier.

With respect to the control variables, the results show that firms with higher initial technical efficiency grew more slowly in terms of both technical change and efficiency improvement. However, the estimated coefficient in the high-technology sector is positive, suggesting that in this sector firms standing on the frontier tend to move faster than followers. Moreover, larger firms have faster rates of technical change, except in high-technology industries. However, the effect of firm size on efficiency improvements is mixed. Exports do not have a significant effect on technical change, a finding that is consistent with that of Fu (2005), who uses Chinese industry-level panel data. This result suggests that a focus on cost competitiveness based on low-cost unskilled labour and an over-reliance on processing trade provide little effective incentive for firms to innovate.

As expected, training exerts a significant positive impact on efficiency improvement but, surprisingly, has a significant and negative impact on technical change. Training in China is likely to be concerned with the teaching of new or advanced practices but not with the creation of frontier technologies. The estimated coefficients of the intangible assets variable are either negative or statistically insignificant in the technical change equation, possibly because in Chinese accounting practices, intangible assets include R&D investment at the development stage but not at the research stage. For firms in technology-intensive industries, novel research activities may play a more important role in keeping them on the frontier. Moreover, intangible assets are correlated with the fixed assets that are the measure of capital in the TFP estimation, which for accounting reasons generate a negative association between TFP and intangible assets. Finally, market concentration appears to promote technical change and innovation, which is consistent with the Schumpeterian hypothesis. Lack of competition, however, deters efficiency improvements in most sectors.

5.6 Conclusions

This chapter explores the drivers of TFP growth and technological upgrading in a middle-income developing country. In particular, the role of indigenous innovation and foreign technology transfer is analysed. The main findings can be summarised briefly. First, neither foreign nor indigenous firms dominate the technology frontier in China. In low- and medium-technology sectors, more indigenous firms are located on the frontier. Privately owned firms have taken a lead in the low- and medium-low–technology industries, and shareholding companies are the leaders in medium-high–technology industries. In the high-technology sector, foreign firms dominate the frontier. In other words, foreign technology is not always superior to indigenous technology, especially in a middle-income country. In the low-technology sector, indigenous technology is more appropriate and hence more efficient than foreign technology. China has also accumulated the capability to create technology appropriate to the medium-technology sector.

Second, indigenous Chinese firms have experienced considerable TFP growth, at an average annual growth rate of 4.8 per cent from 2001 to 2005. This growth was driven mainly by technical change in all sectors except the medium-low–technology industries. In the low- and medium-high–technology sectors, indigenous firm technical growth is considerably higher than in foreign invested firms. Collective indigenous R&D activities at the industry level are the major driver of the technological upgrading process. R&D investment in POEs, SOEs and COEs has had significant positive externality effects on technical change in indigenous firms.

The effects of R&D activities in FIEs are, however, controversial. Such activities have exerted a significant negative effect on indigenous technical change, whereas their impact on catch-up in follower firms is positive in some industries. International R&D spillovers facilitated by FDI are insignificant for indigenous technical change. In sum, although foreign technology transfer may facilitate technology development at an early development stage and assist in the diffusion of second-tier technology, developing countries have to rely on collective indigenous innovation efforts to catch up with the world technology frontier.

These findings have important implications for technology policy in developing countries. First, the net technological benefits from FDI are often limited. It is collective indigenous innovation efforts that drive indigenous technological upgrading in a developing country. Indigenous technology will be more efficient than foreign technology in sectors that intensively use factors that developing countries have in abundance. Therefore, there is an important role for technology and industrial policies in developing countries to encourage indigenous innovation for technological upgrading and catch-up.

Second, developing countries may not only be users of new technology but also creators of new technologies in some sectors, especially in middle-income countries. Such technologies may be more appropriate for other developing countries with similar factor endowment and at a similar development stage. For countries in the developing world, foreign technology is multi-tiered, rather than solely originating in developed countries. This should be taken into account in strategies for technology choice. International technology transfer through South-South trade and FDI should be the major transmission channels.

Finally, the technology gap between developed and developing countries in certain industries remains remarkable. The Chinese experience of the 'two-leg forward strategy' suggests that in order to maximise the benefits from existing knowledge and accelerate the catch-up process, both indigenous innovation and acquisition of foreign knowledge are needed, but with the optimal mixture differing among sectors and stages of development. An effective technology policy package may thus be country, region and industry specific, but well-focused policies to foster the absorptive capacity and innovation capabilities of indigenous firms are always crucial for success.

Appendix 5.1 *Sectoral pattern of R&D activities (all firms in our sample)*

SIC2	Fraction of R&D investors		R&D expenditure/sales (firm with R&D)	
	2001	2005	2001	2005
High technology				
27-Medical and Pharmaceutical Products	0.4451	0.5016	0.0172	0.0818
40-Electronic and Telecommunications	0.3114	0.3266	0.0183	0.0284
41-Instruments and Meters	0.3159	0.3133	0.0182	0.0248

Appendix 5.1 (*cont.*)

	Fraction of R&D investors		R&D expenditure/sales (firm with R&D)	
Medium-high technology				
36-Special Purposes Equipment	0.3237	0.2856	0.0123	0.0188
39-Electric Equipment and Machinery	0.2476	0.2218	0.0138	0.0128
37-Transport Equipment	0.2738	0.2646	0.0079	0.0123
26-Raw Chemical Materials and Chemical Products	0.2126	0.1848	0.0079	0.0113
28-Chemical Fiber	0.2189	0.1791	0.0049	0.0057
Medium-low technology				
35-Ordinary Machinery	0.2168	0.1950	0.0088	0.0135
42-Artefact and Other Manufacturing	0.0926	0.0775	0.0078	0.0092
34-Metal Products	0.1092	0.0892	0.0071	0.0090
29-Rubber Products	0.1921	0.1746	0.0060	0.0088
31-Nonmetal Mineral Products	0.1131	0.0822	0.0073	0.0085
24-Cultural, Educational and Sports Goods	0.1143	0.1006	0.0067	0.0074
30-Plastic Products	0.0991	0.0832	0.0047	0.0073
33-Smelting and Pressing of Nonferrous Metals	0.1683	0.1599	0.0077	0.0055
25-Petroleum Refining and Coking	0.1818	0.1875	0.0070	0.0053
32-Smelting and Pressing of Ferrous Metals	0.1388	0.0976	0.0031	0.0051
Low-technology				
23-Printing and Record Media Reproduction	0.0654	0.0675	0.0093	0.0100
17-Textile Industry	0.0857	0.0769	0.0050	0.0084
19-Leather, Furs, Down and Related Products	0.1049	0.0841	0.0061	0.0078
18-Garments and Other Fibre Products	0.0494	0.0536	0.0055	0.0071
21-Furniture Manufacturing	0.0930	0.1008	0.0048	0.0071
13-Food Processing	0.1022	0.0786	0.0047	0.0067
15-Beverage Industry	0.1692	0.1645	0.0056	0.0066
14-Food Production	0.1711	0.1680	0.0065	0.0064
22-Papermaking and Paper Products	0.0748	0.0601	0.0046	0.0062
20-Timber Processing	0.0756	0.0628	0.0062	0.0057
16-Tobacco Processing	0.4271	0.4479	0.0019	0.0031

APPENDIX 5.2

Assume a production technology S^t that produces a vector of outputs, $y^t \in R_+^M$, by using a vector of inputs, $x^t \in R_+^N$, for each time period t=1, ..., T. The output-based distance function at t is defined as the reciprocal of the maximum proportional expansion of the output vector y^t, given inputs x^t.

$$D_0^t (x^t, y^t) = \inf \{\theta : (x^t, y^t / \theta) \in S^t\}$$
$$= (\sup \{\theta : (x^t, \theta y^t) \in S^t\})$$

$D_0^t (x^t, y^t) \leq 1$ if and only if $(x^t, y^t) \in S^t$. $D_0^t (x^t, y^t) = 1$ if and only if (x^t, y^t) is on the frontier. The distance to the frontier is estimated by using non-parametric linear programming techniques. Assume $k = 1, \ldots, K$ firms using $n = 1, \ldots, N$ inputs $x_n^{k,t}$ at each time period $t = 1, \ldots T$ to produce $m = 1, \ldots \ldots, M$ outputs $y_m^{k,t}$. To estimate the productivity change of each firm between t and t+1, we need to solve four linear-programming problems for $D_0^t (x^t, y^t)$, $D_0^{t+1} (x^t, y^t)$, $D_0^{t+1} (x^{t+1}, y^{t+1})$ and $D_0^t (x^{t+1}, y^{t+1})$ (Fare et al., 1994). The output-oriented LP problem for estimation of $D_0^t (x^t, y^t)$ under variable returns to scale is as follows:

$$[d_0^t (x_t, y_t)]^{-1} = \max_{\phi, \lambda} \theta,$$

$$st - \theta y_{it} + Y_i \lambda \geq 0,$$

$$x_{it} - X_i \lambda \geq 0,$$

$$\lambda_i \geq 0,$$

$$\sum \lambda_i = 1, \, i = 1, \ldots ., n.$$

where θ is a scalar and λ is a nx1 vector of constants. The linear-programming problems for the estimation of $D_0^{t+1} (x^t, y^t)$, $D_0^{t+1} (x^{t+1}, y^{t+1})$ and $D_0^t (x^{t+1}, y^{t+1})$ are similar to the earlier formulation with corresponding adjustments. For details, see Fare et al. (1994).

PART II

Development of indigenous innovation capacity and catch-up

6 | The role of state policy in shaping innovation practices: The case of open innovation in China

6.1 Introduction

Open innovation (OI) has been an emergent concept in innovation studies and a major trend in practice attracting wider attention from academics, policy makers and practitioners. It refers to 'the use of purposive inflows and outflows of knowledge to accelerate internal innovation and to expand the markets for external use of innovation, respectively' (Chesbrough, Vanhaverbeke and West, 2006). Many firms started to implement open innovation as a necessary organisational adaption to changes in the environment (Chesbrough, 2003). Firms may open up their innovation processes in two dimensions (Lichtenthaler and Ernst, 2007). Inbound open innovation refers to inward knowledge acquisition and to leveraging the discoveries of others because firms need not rely exclusively on their own R&D (Chesbrough and Crowther, 2006). Outbound open innovation refers to outward technology transfer, and it suggests that firms can look for external organisations with business models that are suited to commercialising a technology exclusively or in addition to its internal application (Chesbrough and Crowther, 2006). Generally, firms can combine both technology exploitation (inside-out OI) and technology exploration (outside-in OI) to create maximum value from their technological capabilities or other competencies (Lichtenthaler, 2008).

Is open innovation a new phenomenon in China, or it is 'old' in practice and 'new' in concept? Much of the extant literature indicates that since the reforms, the Chinese government has encouraged firms to source external knowledge by acquisition of foreign technology. More recently, since 2000 it has encouraged Chinese firms to 'go global', to actively search for and acquire relevant foreign technology. Some pioneering Chinese firms have adopted various modes of open-oriented strategy to manage innovation activities (Chen and Chen, 2008). What, therefore, is the current status of open innovation in China? What is the role of open innovation in spurring innovation upgrading in China? What are the possible trends and challenges of Chinese firms while adopting open innovation? Although the era of open innovation has become a reality for most Chinese firms, we still lack a systematic understanding of the context, environment and mechanisms, inside and outside of the organisation, and when and how to fully profit from the new model for latecomer firms in emerging economies. This chapter aims to fill the gap in the literature by providing a systematic review of the evolution of the policies and practices of open innovation in China. It also explores the implications of open innovation strategy for latecomer firms in building indigenous innovation capability and competing in today's global innovation networks. As far as we are aware, this is one of the first systematic review studies on open innovation policies and practices with a focus on the context of emerging economies.

The rest of the chapter is organised as follows: Section 6.2 provides an overview of the current situation in openness in innovation in China. Section 6.3 discusses the theoretical framework, especially the role of government policies in shaping innovation mode and practices in firms. Section 6.4 examines the policies introduced by the Chinese government in the past three decades that affected the development of open innovation in China. Section 6.5 reviews the firm-level practices of open innovation in China. Section 6.6 discusses the trends and challenges of open innovation in China. Section 6.7 presents conclusions.

6.2 Openness in innovation in China: an overview

China has experienced a substantial transformation in the innovation landscape since the economic reforms and opening up in 1978. In the early stage of the reforms, Chinese firms, motivated and facilitated by various policies, relied on foreign technology transfer through imports and foreign direct investment (FDI) for technology upgrading. This contributed to the new – to the firm or country – imitation-type diffusionary innovation. Since the late 1990s, Chinese firms have started to transit from a technology-transfer–focused development strategy to an indigenous innovation-oriented growth strategy (Fu and Gong, 2011). Especially since China's entry into the WTO in 2001, a rapid internationalisation of innovation activities in China by both foreign and indigenous firms has occurred. The latecomer firms in China began to learn how to utilise external R&D resources or technological knowledge via acquisition of foreign technology or equipment; joint venturing; and collaborating with users, suppliers and public or private research institutions (Chen, 2009). In recent years, some domestic firms also set up local and overseas R&D centres and have acquired foreign technology-intensive firms through mergers and acquisitions (M&A) (Bai, 2009). On the other hand, some Chinese firms have also started to use licensing, intellectual property selling, spin-offs as well as corporate venturing to exploit external opportunities in commercialising the inventions they possess.

Although open innovation is a new concept, a firm-level national innovation survey carried out by the National Bureau of Statistics of China and the Research Centre for Technological Innovation at Tsinghua University in 2008 suggests a relatively high degree of adoption of open innovation in Chinese manufacturing firms.[1] Tables 6.1

Table 6.1 *Sources of product innovation*

Source	Number of firms	Proportion (percentage)
Internal	732	75.9
Affiliated group (domestic)	130	13.5
Affiliated group (overseas)	101	10.5
Collaboration with other firms or research institutes	357	37.0
Other firms or research institutes	40	4.1

Note: Firms are allowed to make multiple choices.

[1] This survey covers all industrial sectors in the Chinese economy. The valid sample includes 1,408 firms in 42 cities across the country. The survey asks questions regarding firms' general innovation input and performance in the three years from 2005 to 2007, which contains sufficient items to measure various indexes of innovation activities for those indigenous firms in China. The method and types of questions used in this innovation survey are primarily based on the Oslo Manual (OECD, 1997, 2005) and also the core Eurostat Community Innovation Survey (CIS) (Stockdale, 2002; DTI, 2003), although with some adaptive adjustments because of the different survey context.

Table **6.2** *Sources of process innovation*

Source	Number of firms	Proportion (percentage)
Internal	820	86.8
Affiliated group (domestic)	123	13.0
Affiliated group (overseas)	81	8.6
Collaboration with other firms or research institutes	351	37.1
Other firms or research institutes	46	4.9

Note: Firms are allowed to make multiple choices.

and 6.2 report the sources of product and process innovation in the sample. 'Intra-firm innovation' and 'collaboration with other firms or research institutes' appear to be the major sources of product and process innovation. Taking product innovation as an example, on the one hand, most Chinese firms develop a new product or new process heavily based on their own resources and capability (75.9 per cent of firms innovate by themselves). On the other hand, more than a third of the firms acquire new innovations by co-operation. Although the phenomenon of so-called closed innovation shows a relatively higher proportion, we still cannot ignore some surprising differences. More than one-third of product innovations stem from industrial collaboration or research alliance (projects), which shows collaborative innovations should also be an important part of all types of innovation activities in China. In addition, some firms' innovations are still dependent on their affiliated domestic or overseas groups. This mainly reflects the situation of those joint venture (JV) firms in China. An interesting finding is that a relatively higher proportion of domestic groups' resources have been used than those of overseas groups. This refers to those joint ventures that are beginning to incline to use domestic resources to develop new innovations in the Chinese market. What's more, the condition of process innovation is quite similar to that of product innovation, although the latter relies less on closed innovation.

Table 6.3 reports the importance of different types of information in the sampled firms. Not surprisingly, about 42 per cent of firms regard internal sources (itself or its affiliated groups) as having a relatively higher importance compared to most other sources, which complies

Table 6.3 *The importance of information sources in innovation activities*

Information sources		Proportion of firms that regard the source as being of high importance (percentage)	Mean of importance
Internal	Firm itself or its affiliated group	41.7	3.09
Market information sources	Suppliers of equipment, raw material, component or software	17.9	2.63
	Users or consumers	52.5	3.25
	Competitors or other firms within the same industry	34.3	2.96
	Consultants or private R&D institutes	5.7	1.96
Institution information sources	Universities	8.3	2.06
	Government or public R&D institutes	10.0	2.12
	Government S&T plan	14.4	2.21
Other sources	Trade or sales program, academic conference	22.5	2.61
	S&T journal or literature, trade or patent literature	9.7	2.30
	Professional industry association	18.6	2.52

Note: Firms are allowed to make multiple choices.

with the heavy dependence on internal resources for developing new products or processes as mentioned earlier. Regarding various external sources, the differences among them are very significant. Undoubtedly, users (clients or consumers) are ranked first in importance for innovation research, which accounts for 52.5 per cent in all, together with the highest degree of importance (3.25). In particular, the index of degree of importance suggests more about the depth of one specific information source, whereas the proportion of importance only measures the breadth or popularity of one source adopted by firms. Therefore, we can find that both users and competitors (including other firms within the same industry) can be viewed as the most important sources for research innovation. In addition, another important source can be traced to those trade (or sales) programmes and academic conferences (22.5 per cent), and even industrial associations (18.6 per cent). Furthermore, we find most important external sources are market channels or information (including users, competitors, suppliers etc.), whereas institutional information is regarded as less important. To sum up, external sources play a crucial role in the innovation process and present a relatively high scale of importance for most domestic firms, whereas a large proportion of domestic firms still employ internal channels for sourcing innovation.

6.3 The role of government policy in shaping innovation practices of firms

A government can play an important role in framing and promoting a credible innovation policy. In theory, three major roles for government can be identified: a role as a broker, a role in demand articulation and a role in stimulating innovations (Faber, Kemp and Van der Veen, 2008). In this section, we discuss these three roles in relation to open innovation practice.

First, as a broker, government commits to bringing together different players in the innovation system. Open modes of innovation activities need various players or platforms co-operating and complementing in acquiring mutual benefits. In particular, national framework conditions and the public infrastructure for research cultivated by government policy play a major role. To some extent, this corresponds to the environmental side of public policy, which can greatly influence firm-level behaviours. For example, one particular policy issue, related to intellectual property rights (IPR), may receive much attention. Till now, the immature intellectual property protection regime in China has been subject to long-running criticism by many foreign companies that enter the Chinese market. However, the globalisation of R&D and the emergence of open innovation strategies in firms clearly raise intellectual property issues. The shift towards IPR sharing in open innovation strategies may require different kinds of management tools in universities and public research organisations. While strong IP protection can attract R&D-related FDI, excessively strong protection can act as a barrier towards open innovation strategies that rely on knowledge sharing and access (OECD, 2008). Some scholars suggest that the platforms and repositories for the 'intellectual commons' are greatly required and can be facilitated by government regulations and investment in a strong Information and communication technology (ICT) infrastructure. Another example that needs to be highlighted is the building of efficient technology transaction markets. Most firms source knowledge in various ways, but licensing and purchasing technology and knowledge embodied in patents or other forms of IP are important. Creating rules and conditions that facilitate the development and transfer of technology can facilitate open innovation (OECD, 2008).

Second, government can play a role in demand articulation. This amounts to the creation of markets for open innovations by setting relevant standards. For instance, markets can be created through the use of economic incentives and special agreements with industry. In general, it is possible to pull open innovation in a way that benefits economic and political circumstances; the theory behind this is usually related to the work of Michael Porter, who argued that countries may increase their competitive advantage by setting strict entry or environment standards (Porter, 1990). This idea is of great importance for the market to be competitive and open to innovative newcomers, which actually implies a competition policy towards open innovation. Designing a competition policy that does not preclude cooperation is an important challenge, especially in industries where excessive competition can produce innovation (OECD, 2008). Besides, when government builds more commercialisation channels (such as science parks as incubators and industrial technological strategic alliance), most firms, particularly new entrants in high-tech or emerging industries, would be more inclined to adopt open modes of technological exploitation activities.

The third role of government takes effect on the supply side of the national innovation system. This is embodied in various structural public policies (science and technology [S&T] policy, fiscal policy, capital markets etc.). Most OECD countries' S&T policies are predominantly national in scope, but it is becoming clear that policies designed for geographically circumscribed knowledge-based activities or for vertically integrated value chains of firms need to be reviewed (OECD, 2008). For example, policies to promote networking and clusters can have a great influence on promoting firms to adopt an open mode of technological exploration in their R&D processes. Another prominent example can be seen in government's fiscal policies, which mainly supply a large number of tax incentives, fiscal subsidies, preferential credits and direct capital input to stimulate innovative collaboration activities. Besides, policies related to dynamic capital markets supported by government do matter because a free and flourishing financial environment can greatly stimulate open innovations. Insofar as corporate venturing is one channel through which firms add value internally and externally, capital markets that allow for corporate venturing and exit to secondary markets are important for open strategies (OECD, 2008).

Finally, government policies favouring open innovation can also help many latecomer firms catch up on technological innovation. Whatever the normative or regulatory styles, policies have had a strong influence on the catching-up process (Li and Kozhikode, 2009). Hobday (1995) observed that governments in emerging economies often protected local firms from initial failures and encouraged them to learn from MNEs. Kim (1997) observed that the intellectual property regime in South Korea supported local firms by allowing them to imitate the technologies of global players during the early stages of catching up. However, this support was only available until the Korean firms began to develop their own innovative offerings. Although the initial innovations of the latecomers were not ground breaking, over time and with increased investment in R&D, both internally and in collaboration, these firms gradually were able to develop more innovative offerings (Hobday, 1995). In addition, open innovation practice can sometimes influence the changes in the governance of innovation policies (OECD, 2008). On the one hand, the challenge for government is to help firms adjust their innovation strategies to a changing environment; on the other, many firms, in particular latecomer firms, actively respond and react to the changing of government policies. Hence, understanding the typical patterns of open innovation practices in China would have significant implications for government policies.

In sum, government may have a significant impact on the innovation mode, practices and performances at the firm level through the design and implementation of relevant innovation and industry policies. A systematic examination of such policies and the corresponding innovation practices adopted by firms as a result of such policy influence will enable us to have an in-depth understanding of the evolution of innovation behaviour of Chinese firms, especially the push and pull factors that motivate firms and how they shape the innovation practices in Chinese firms.

6.4 Policies affecting open innovation in China

The governments of a growing number of emerging economies have played an active role in making their respective economies attractive to global R&D investments (UNCTAD, 2005). In the past few decades, Chinese policy makers have attempted to lead the entire innovation environment in being more open and co-operative although open innovation is not regarded as a clear national strategy. It is expected that effective policy support could help most Chinese firms overcome many pressing obstacles in order to cultivate a highly open condition in the era of indigenous innovation in China. For instance, open innovation can be considered a private-collective innovation model. Instead of the private investment model of innovation with Schumpeter's temporary monopolistic profits, the free revealing of inventions, findings, discoveries and knowledge is a defining characteristic of the open innovation model (von Hippel and von Krogh, 2003). This implies the corresponding role of government in stimulating the free and efficient flow of knowledge and technology in the domestic market.

The core development strategy of the Chinese government is to encourage indigenous innovation and to build an innovation-oriented economy in the new century. Many S&T, industrial and macroeconomic policies are given much attention to stimulate technological innovation and improve competitiveness. As we know, the open business model emphasises absorbing external knowledge and exploring external paths to commercialisation (Chesbrough, 2006). Accordingly, Chinese policy makers have continued to make the domestic market and institutional environment more open and favourable to innovation flow. The most recent indigenous innovation policy stemmed from two revolutionary documents: the *Decision on Implementing the Outline of the Scientific and Technological Plan and Enhancing the Independent Innovation Capacity* and the *National Guideline for Medium and Long-term Plan for Science and Technology Development (2006–2020)* (Fang, 2007; Wang and Liu, 2007). The open-oriented innovation ideology has been revealed clearly in the initiating of the national strategy of indigenous innovation within these two policy documents, which regard 'integrated innovation' and 'innovations on the basis of introduction, digestion and absorption' as two basic forms of indigenous innovation. In fact, both these innovation forms emphasise the utilisation and integration of external R&D resources and commercial paths. Regarding the development of relevant public policies for open innovation in China, many significant innovation policies are indeed involved, although they still lack specifics. We classify them into three main policy clusters.

Policies towards inbound open innovation

Inbound open innovation refers to the acquisition of external technology in open exploration processes. In accessing and sourcing external technologies and knowledge, EIRMA (2004) distinguished some modes: purchase of technology, joint venturing and alliances, contract R&D, collaborations with universities, equity in university spin-offs and equity in venture capital investment funds. In fact, some of them, such as international technology transfer and assimilation, are much more common in China because of the many relevant policies stimulating inbound open innovation for indigenous firms. Early in the 1980s, most Chinese firms introduced a large number of foreign technologies and equipment to attempt shortening the huge gap in R&D and also in manufacturing capacity. This open strategy of 'technology introduction, digestion and absorption' was directed and facilitated by trade policies relating to imports of equipment and machinery and the encouragement of inward foreign direct investment. The *Regulations on the Administration of Technology Acquisition Contracts* (1985), *Regulations on Promoting Technology Introduction, Digestion and Absorption (1986)* and *Regulations on Administration of Import and Export of Technologies* (2001) all encouraged the import of advanced and useful technologies. Correspondingly, the *Notice of Taxation on Issuing State Industrial*

Technology Policies (2009) clearly emphasised making extensive efforts in international co-operation and exchange and reinforcing technological introduction, digestion and re-innovation. For instance, introducing key components that make it difficult to achieve localisation could take 50 per cent to 70 per cent of tax incentives when their proportion of introduction is less than 40 per cent. Moreover, enterprises that undertake key scientific and technological projects for the state should be exempted from import duties and import value-added taxes for the domestically unavailable key scientific research apparatus, facilities, raw materials and components imported by them. Those policies helped domestic firms effectively break technology barriers in the early stages and improved manufacturing and technology application capability in a relatively short time.

In addition, to encourage the introduction of advanced technologies and promote industrial restructuring and technological progress, a large number of stimulating policies were issued to attract foreign companies and protect common interests of co-operation between foreign and domestic firms. Early in the 1980s, not only supplying taxation incentives, many relevant policies also strengthened the financial support for foreign-funded enterprises and encouraged foreign investment in the midwestern regions, together with guiding them to invest in key industries and important fields. Admittedly, foreign technology transfer is only one of the measures relating to open innovation, in particular, the inbound aspect of open innovation, which refers to inward technology transfer (Lichtenthaler, 2009). Although solely relying on foreign technology transfer may weaken the incentives and capabilities of indigenous innovation, it has played an indispensable role in helping Chinese firms source external knowledge and produce new – to the country or firm – imitation-type diffusionary innovation in the past three decades. For the vast developing countries that are still at the early stage of takeoff, this channel of open innovation is still an important policy choice.

What's more, policies supporting indigenous firms going global are also on the increase. The Chinese government supports going global not only by promoting technology and product export but also by encouraging overseas investment and acquisition. For instance, the special loans for Chinese overseas investments since 2004 are mainly used for supporting such enterprises as overseas resource development projects (which can make up for the relative insufficiency of domestic resources), overseas productive projects and infrastructure projects (which can give impetus to the export of domestic technologies, products, equipment, and labour services etc.), overseas R&D centres (which may utilise internationally advanced technologies, management experiences and professional talents) and overseas enterprise M&A projects (which can improve the international competitiveness of enterprises and accelerate exploration of international markets). In sum, a long history of favouring inbound open innovation for acquiring knowledge and resources has been the most crucial reality in the evolution of Chinese policies promoting innovation in an open way.

Policies towards outbound open innovation

Another primary innovation policy cluster in China is designed to accelerate outbound open innovation activities. Outbound open innovation describes the outward transfer of technology in open exploitation processes. It also refers to earning profits by bringing ideas to market, selling IP, and multiplying technology by transferring ideas to the outside environment (Enkel, Gassmann and Chesbrough, 2009). Profiting from the high speed of economic development, especially together with domestic market expansion, the Chinese government has enacted various measures to broaden the channels of outbound innovation. After institutional transformation towards building a market economy, the government clearly pointed out the relevant policies for releasing the paths of commercialisation and industrialisation of S&T achievements, which means diversifying the innovation channels. An initiating policy document, the *Decision on Strengthening Technical Innovation, Development of High-tech and Realisation of Its Industrialisation* (1999), constructed the foundation for enriching various business models for developing high-tech products. The *Law of Promoting the Transformation of Scientific and Technological Achievements* (1996) clearly and creatively demonstrated the strategic principles and plentiful modes of commercial and industrial innovation knowledge. It suggested that the holders of S&T achievements may have their knowledge commercialised via investing in it themselves, transferring it to another party with their achievements as the conditions for co-operation or investing their achievements as trade-in or converted shares or as proportions of the contribution to the investment. Besides, to adopt new inventions, an enterprise may publish information on its own or entrust an intermediate institution engaged in the trade of technology to solicit the S&T achievements, and it has the right to conduct the transformation of S&T achievements independently or jointly with domestic or foreign enterprises or institutions or other collaborators.

Moreover, the government also issued a series of policies in support of taxation, finance and infrastructures as well as talent incentive mechanisms to promote processing of those commercial and industrial modes, such as specific or risk funds or preferential tax policy. The primary reason is that such S&T achievements or inventions need substantial investment, involving considerable risks and promising high yields. Furthermore, the state is increasingly exploring diversified investing channels and building multiform business models for profiting from innovation. For instance, the government has greatly developed venture capital markets to finance innovation. It has widely enabled many indigenous firms in recent years to expand financing channels, absorb the social capital, establish and develop the social industrial investment fund aimed at reforming the traditional industries by high technology. In particular, building a venture capital mechanism and developing public venture capital institutions are both emphasised by the existing policy goals. The state also attaches importance to the fostering of talents for management and operation of venture capital, to the establishment of the venture capital system and venture capital funds composed mainly of social investment and for the multi-input structure of venture capital. In sum, the institutional environment supporting external commercialisation of new technologies has been greatly improved in recent years. Both indigenous and foreign firms could benefit from innovation by the utilisation of various channels to capture useful opportunities to commercialise new products or industrialise new inventions. Admittedly, the actual business environment advocating open innovation is still at a relatively low level compared to other developed economies. A more open and more reliable business environment for commercialising innovation would be a long-term focus for policy makers in China.

Policies towards open innovation networks

The global innovation network that links people, institutions (universities, government agencies, etc.) and other companies within and across different countries has developed rapidly (OECD, 2008). In response, the innovation policies in China have tended to be more aggressive and more open to building open innovation networks in China.

The first policy has been to establish production-study-research combination networks that centre on the enterprises and jointly bear the risks and to establish the open technological innovation service systems relying on cities, suggested by the *State Industrial Technology Policies* of 2002. In this document, the government greatly advocates establishing the production-study-research associations of different enterprises, domestic universities and public or private research institutes to form a market-oriented R&D system. And the open production-study-research mechanism based on the comparative advantages and strategic needs of China could select the areas of independent development and advances, explore new technology routes through system integration and mutual absorption and develop new technology with independent intellectual property rights. In addition, regarding global R&D co-operation projects or international strategic alliances starting to emerge in China, many relevant institutional supports have been encouraged to come forth. As the focus shifted from purely internal R&D activities to outside innovation, firms that do not co-operate or do not exchange knowledge would reduce their knowledge base on a long-term basis and lose the ability to enter into exchange relations with other firms (Koschatzky, 2001). This group of policies has been advocated and implemented by the Ministry of Science and Technology more and more often in recent years.

Moreover, the development of the technology transaction market is another important policy arena favouring and reinforcing open innovation networks. This transaction market can greatly facilitate the flow of technological knowledge across firms and other organisations. Generally, it includes technology transfer, technology consultation, technical services, technical training, technology-equity share exchange, technology intermediation and various research-production co-operations. At all times, active technology equity exchange and transaction markets also play a significant role in creating national networks of open innovation in China. China set up its first technology stock exchange market in Shanghai in 1999. Since then, large-scale technology equity platforms have emerged in Beijing, Chengdu, Shenzhen, Wuhan, Tianjin and Shenyang and accelerated the outbound trade of technological innovation as well as corporate venturing in commercialising internal new technology, products and large numbers of patents. These transaction markets were used for immediate innovation service institutions as well as for science parks and incubators and helped indigenous firms broaden their commercialisation channels and external technology resources. However, the role that the technology transaction market has played in China's regional innovation system was not significant over the 1998–2004 period (Fu, 2008).

The lack of protection of intellectual property rights is seen as the major obstacle to innovation networks building (OECD, 2008). The protection of intellectual property has been a part of the reform and openness policy in China and an important institutional factor for promoting scientific, technological and cultural development. To adapt to necessary changes in global innovation networks, China has in recent years speeded up its IP legislation and successively promulgated such laws as the Patent Law of the People's Republic of China, the Law of the People's Republic of China on Technology Contracts, the Copyright Law of the People's Republic of China and the Law of the People's Republic of China for Countering Unfair Competition, which have begun to link up with international standards and have played a positive role in promoting reform and openness in China. As it is only recently that China has established its IP system, a sufficient understanding of the importance of protecting IP is still lacking in certain regions and departments. Specifically, the *Decision on Further Strengthening the Intellectual Property Protection* (1994) has introduced some important regulations on managing IPR but still lacks all-around considerations and effective implementations. Till now, it has been widely realised by policy makers that the IPR regime plays a major role in getting the national framework and business environment right, which not only helps standardise the innovation among local organisations but also increases the possibility of sharing knowledge from foreign entrants. In addition, the IPR regime will be managed in a more open way (OECD, 2008) because many studies have reported that the use of patenting has evolved from a focus on defensive applications as part of business and management strategy (e.g., licensing, building a patent portfolio) to exploitation of a financial asset (i.e., attracting external sources of financing).

In sum, policies affecting open innovation in China have been introduced for a long time. They are, however, not comprehensive. There is a need to build a more comprehensive policy system in China.

Based on a report on the evolution of Chinese S&T, economic and innovation policy from 1979 to 2008 (Wu et al., 2009), Table 6.4 shows selected policies illustrating the evolution of public policy for open innovation.

Table 6.4 *The main public policies for open innovation in China*

Year	Policy document	Policy focus and main measures
1986	*Regulations on Promoting Technology Introduction, Digestion and Absorption*	Technology exploration; tax incentives to import advanced technology and technology learning, localisation.
1986	*Provisions on the Encouragement of Foreign Investment*	Technology exploration; tax incentives for foreign investment firms in the technology-intensive sector.
1993, 2007	*Law on Science and Technology Progress*	Coupled process; overall level of financial input; R&D expenditure as cost, credits and loans; open to domestic foreign organisations or individuals to fund S&T, build information exchange and networks and security systems to protect IP.
1996	*Law on Promoting the Transformation of Scientific and Technological Achievements*	Technology exploitation; support measures including initiation funds, discount loans, subsidy funds, venture capital and other special establishment funds; a preferential tax policy, loans, venture funds; build data bank of S&T achievements.
1999	*Plan for Vitalising Trade by Science and Technology*	Technology exploitation; tax and export preferential support for high-tech products.

Table 6.4 (*cont.*)

Year	Policy document	Policy focus and main measures
1999	*Decision on Strengthening Technical Innovation, Development of High-tech and Realisation of Its Industrialisation*	Technology exploitation; R&T input, tax preference, loans and credits and other direct financial input for commercialisation of S&T; management reform of domestic S&T institutions.
2002	*Measures for the Administration of Technological Innovation Plans of the State*	Coupled process; developing industrial technologies and experiments, the popularised application of new technologies, joint development, technological centres and service system, and the trial production of new products, etc.
2002, 2009	*State Industrial Technology Policies*	Technology exploitation; fiscal, tax, investment; financial and government procurement policies to provide support for enterprises to increase investment in innovation.
2006	*Decision on Implementing the Outline of the Scientific and Technological Plan and Enhancing the Independent Innovation Capacity*	Technology exploitation; encouraging selling IP and multiplying technology by transferring ideas to outside, independent innovation and innovative talent strategy; cultivating a batch of large-size enterprises, enterprise groups and technical alliances.
2006	*National Guideline for Medium and Long-term Plan for Science and Technology Development (2006–2020)*	Coupled process; tax, loans and credit measures to support introducing external R&D and innovation,

Table 6.4 (*cont.*)

Year	Policy document	Policy focus and main measures
		together with government procurement, especially for indigenous innovation products.
2008	*Notice on Printing and Distributing the Outline of the National Intellectual Property Strategy*	Technology exploitation; improving the intellectual property law enforcement and administration systems through finance, investment, government procurement, industry, energy and environmental protection policies.
2009	*Opinions on Encouraging Technology Export*	Technology exploitation; encouraging IP exchange (out-licensing and multiplying technology) and high-tech export.
2008, 2009, 2010	*Notice of Promoting on Industry Technological Innovation Strategic Alliance*	Coupled process; encouraging domestic enterprises to form technical R&D institutions outside China by way of joint venture, co-operation, merger, etc.; set up R&D alliances and utilise overseas superior forces to develop industrial technologies with independent IPR.

6.5 Practices of open innovation in China

The primary modes of open innovation in China represent some basic characteristics of those indigenous firms in opening their innovation processes. The closed and open models of innovation are typically presented as two extremes of a spectrum ranging from doing everything in house (vertical integration) to outsourcing everything to external partners (OECD, 2008). Following Enkel, Gassmann and Chesbrough (2009), we also divide open innovation practices into three categories: outside-in, inside-out and doubled process. According to our review of relevant firm-based cases adopting open innovation, Table 6.5 shows some typical modes of open innovation and their characteristics in practice.

Evidence from these case studies suggests three characteristics of open innovation in China. First, the proportion of firms adopting outside-in process, or technology exploration modes, is high. This fact suggests that most Chinese domestic firms are inclined to acquire advanced technology or knowledge through external sourcing, networking, co-operation or acquisition. Not surprisingly, most Chinese firms, as late-comers in the global innovation network, greatly expect to acquire complementary assets and enhance innovation capability with methods of technology exploration.

Second, the proportion of inside-out process, or technology exploitation, still stays at a lower level. As it broadly weakens technological accumulation and innovation capability, it is difficult for many domestic firms to adopt licensing or corporate venturing such as spin-off whereby a company splits off sections as separate businesses or spins out when members of a company or university set up a new business often based on a new technology. Limited knowledge resources make business models gradually outdated, and the immature venture capital market in China does not facilitate the growth of those new business models.

Third, an interesting pattern relates to differences between sectors and firm size. Generally, companies enjoying fast and medium-level growth use the inside-out process actively, although it is still less than the intensity of outside-in process usage (Gassmann et al., 2010). However, many firms in traditional or low-growth sectors also use inside-out modes of innovation in China. In particular, this phenomenon occurs more often when production-study-research combination programmes are well established or involved. Moreover, it is expected that only large multinationals have an active out-licensing strategy to which they allocate substantial resources (Lichtenthaler and Ernst, 2007; OECD, 2008). In China, however, some start-ups in high-tech or emerging industries would be apt to out-license their new inventions with forms of contractual collaboration to speed up the commercialisation of new technology.

Table 6.5 *Selected cases of open innovation in Chinese firms*

Modes	Main Forms	Company	Industry	Source
Coupled process	Knowledge sourcing from domestic universities, private research institutions and consultancy Co-operation in R&D with overseas partners	ChunLan (in Taizhou, Jiangsu Province)	Electric equipment	Wang (2006)
Coupled process	Absorption of foreign technology Setting up overseas R&D centres Selling IP and spin-off internal know-how Joint-venture with MNEs	FeiYue (in Taizhou, Zhejiang Province)	Electric equipment (sewing machine)	Zhu &Chen (2007)
Outside-in process	Production-study-research combination, in particular with universities External networking with suppliers	Little Swan Co. Ltd (in Wuxi & Hangzhou, Zhejiang Province)	Electric equipment (washing machine)	Li (2007)
Outside-in process	Outsourcing R&D Production-study-research combination, in particular with universities and private research institutions	JiangHuai Auto (JAC) (in AnHui province)	Automobile	Tang & Zhao (2007)

Process	Activities	Company	Industry	Reference
Coupled process	Absorption, digestion and innovation Building globally distributed R&D centres Co-operation with leading giants	International Marine Containers (Group) Ltd. (CIMC) (in Shenzhen)	Equipment manufacturing (Machinery)	Zheng, He and Chen (2008)
Outside-in process	Outsourcing R&D Knowledge sourcing from other industries and leading universities	Neusoft (in Shenyang, Liaoning Province)	Software (medical, service)	Liu (2008)
Coupled process	Co-operation through production-study-research combination Building overseas R&D centre	Shenyang Machine Tool (Group) Co. Ltd	Equipment manufacturing (machinery)	He (2008)
Coupled process	Participating strategic technology alliance Production-study-research combination	Dongbei Special Steel Group Co. Ltd (in Liaoning Province)	Steel	Liu & Hou (2008)
Coupled process	Transnational mergers and acquisitions (M&A)	Nanjing Automobile	Automobile	Yu & Wang (2008)
Coupled process	External networking Outbound commercialization with restructuring industrial value chain Joint venture to market globally	Guizhou Special agriculture, i.e., Yanhuang Shiye Co. Ltd	Agriculture	Zhang & Liu (2008)

Table 6.5 (*cont.*)

Modes	Main Forms	Company	Industry	Source
Outside-in process	Supplier and competitor integration and also user innovation Production-study-research combination Distribute R&D centres globally	BOE Technology Group Co. Ltd (in Beijing)	Supplier of display products	Jiang (2009)
Coupled process	Absorption, digestion and innovation Transnational M&A Strategic alliance R&D outsourcing	Shenhua Group Corporation Limited (Shendong Mine Group, in Neimenggu Province)	Coal	Sun & Xu (2009)
Coupled process	International co-operation for synergic R&D Building overseas R&D centres	Weichai Power Co. Ltd. (in Shandong Province)	Automobile (supplier)	Hou (2009)
Inside-out process	Corporate venturing Spin-off	Lenovo Venturing (Beijing), Tsinghua Ziguang (UNIS, Beijing), B&H Investment (Shenzhen)	Venture capital	Xu et al. (2009)

Source: Classified by the authors and referenced to relevant literatures presented earlier.

'Collaborative innovation' appears to be the most popular innovation mode. Firms may engage in collaboration to acquire missing knowledge, complementary resources or finance; to spread risks; to enlarge their social networks; or to reduce costs (Hoffman and Schlosser, 2001). In addition, a firm's innovation strategies can combine characteristics of both innovation models, and the degree of openness depends on factors such as the importance of the technology, the firm's business strategy and the industry's characteristics. Companies traditionally seek to retain their core capabilities and decide what to outsource or with whom to collaborate on innovation on the basis of the previously discussed benefits and the conditional factors (OECD, 2008). Here, we still use evidence from our survey data set to empirically explain the content of innovation collaboration in China.

Table 6.6 gives us the frequency results of different innovation types. Most innovations, together with their funding and information sources, are developed and sourced internally to a large extent as the previous overview shows; thus, the proportion of internal R&D activities accounts for the majority (those firms that have internal R&D take up nearly half of our sample, whereas fewer than 10 per cent of firms have no internal R&D). Purchasing equipment, machines or software also occupies quite a large proportion (32.7 per cent of firms). What's more, it is necessary to highlight that external R&D activities are not as popular as expected: more than 50 per cent of firms admit that they never conduct external R&D activities. Similarly, effective acquisition of external technological knowledge is quite difficult for many sampled firms, with nearly half expressing that they never conduct innovation by using external technological knowledge. These results can reflect, to some extent, that the innovation types of many domestic firms are still simply independent, and most others are introduction-oriented or learning-oriented innovation. The frequency of using external technological sources generally stays at a low level.

6.6 Trends and challenges of open innovation in China

Trends of open innovation in China

The organisation of innovative activities across firm boundaries is clearly on the increase, with more balance between internal and external sources

Table 6.6 *Types of innovation mode and frequencies*

Types of innovation mode	Never		Sometimes		Very often		Sum total
	No. of firms	Proportion (percentage)	No. of firms	Proportion (percentage)	No. of firms	Proportion (percentage)	
Internal R&D	90	9.1	418	42.4	477	48.4	985
External R&D	465	52.2	356	40.0	70	7.9	891
Purchasing machine, equipment and software	165	17.2	482	50.2	314	32.7	961
Acquiring external technological knowledge	436	48.6	374	41.6	88	9.8	898
Training and marketing activities	302	33.3	454	50.1	150	16.6	906

of innovation (OECD, 2008). To build an inimitable competitive advantage, many multinational companies globally integrate complementary technology, capital, branding, channels and low-cost labour resources. Transnational innovation becomes more popular (Fagerberg, Mowery and Nelson, 2005). The latecomer firms in emerging economies face a rather different situation while adopting open strategies because of their unique policy institutions and innovation practices discussed earlier.

The *World Investment Report 2005* (UNCTAD, 2005a) illustrates that some developing countries have an enhanced position in attracting transnational R&D investment. In such a highly open environment, latecomer firms could integrate globally all the potential resources of technology, manufacturing, raw materials, channels and brand, which means that Chinese firms should acquire the knowledge resources distributed globally (Jiang, 2004; Xiong and Li, 2008). In fact, most Chinese enterprises started to take advantage of R&D resources overseas much earlier. In the 1990s, some Chinese companies in Shanghai were the forerunners of Chinese overseas R&D investment, and since 2000 this phenomenon has become generally more popular, especially in the ICT industry. Nowadays, companies are much more dependent on outside resources. In the Chinese high-tech industry, it is increasingly difficult for firms to acquire core technology from MNEs in China. This forces Chinese firms to go out to look for suitable R&D resources by themselves. At the same time, it will be a new opportunity for Chinese enterprises to benefit from globalisation of innovation and make great use of available international resources. The factors that Gassmann (2006) recognised as driving higher performance of open innovation models are in fact equally prominent in today's China. Hence, 'the era of open innovation' is flourishing in China.

Many Chinese enterprises have not developed their technology in a closed model. On the contrary, they have learned to take advantage of global R&D resources, for example, by introducing and absorbing advanced foreign technology and then further studying it. In addition, they can actively participate in international scientific and technological exchanges and co-operation for the realisation of open innovation. For example, a Chinese leading IT company, ZTE, set up an R&D organisation overseas, does its architectural R&D overseas and its final product innovation at home. This has produced outstanding results.

Challenges of open innovation in China

Latecomer firms that want to benefit from openness face a number of challenges. First, as China's economy becomes highly open and the degree of domestic competition becomes increasingly high, most indigenous firms need to learn how to build up the crucial competence to make good use of open innovation in a highly open environment. Admittedly, companies investing in open innovation activities face risks and barriers that hinder their profiting from their initiatives (Enkel, Gassmann and Chesbrough, 2009). Some Chinese scholars have already criticised the possibly fatal disadvantage of blindly sourcing external knowledge (Chen, 1994; Zhang, 2003). Considering future competition and challenges from those latecomer players, most foreign companies prefer not to spill over their core technologies. Many local firms often complain that those technologies by the time of their introduction were typically out of date. Without absorbing key and advanced technologies, many indigenous firms may always lag behind in technical upgrading.

Moreover, as a result of the weakness of absorptive capacity, many Chinese firms cannot improve their internal R&D and long-term innovation capacity. Latecomer firms are unable to cultivate indigenous innovation capability by only using simple inbound open innovation. For example, international R&D co-operation requires the reorganisation of R&D personnel, R&D expenditure, an R&D facility and R&D information distributed across different countries or regions. Because of the limitations of their low absorptive and integrative capacity, it is difficult for latecomers to share the R&D outcome. Till now, many leading Chinese enterprises chose to use M&A. However, M&A may not be suitable to achieve technology absorption if the acquiring firm lacks technological capability. It is hard to make foreign R&D personnel and cross-national managers stay.

Finally, we need to be cautious about conducting open innovation in different contexts, in particular regarding catching-up economies. Open innovation is not an imperative for every company and every innovator (Gassmann, 2006). Openness is not a choice for the firm but an outcome of capabilities, industrial organisation and wider innovation systems. Existing literature also argues that latecomer enterprises cannot rely too heavily on global R&D resources (Nolan, 2001). The development of the Chinese automobile industry proves this point. Most joint ventures are unwilling to share their core advanced technology know-how and invest too much in developing key technology in China because of their worries about losing a leading advantage. For example, in the past few decades, the vehicle models introduced by joint ventures in their early days of entering the Chinese market have always been outdated models from foreign collaborators. Except for the fact that the overall market demand is relatively low end, the more intrinsic reason is attributed to the fear and unwillingness of those foreign partners. Most Chinese collaborators only make small incremental improvements and then have to follow the old technological path. Therefore, latecomer firms should have clear and rational expectations when choosing appropriate partners.

6.7 Conclusions

Open innovation has been a new innovation paradigm and a future trend widely accepted and adopted by scholars and practitioners in the era of increasing globalisation. This chapter provides the first systematic review of the policies and practices of open innovation in China. In general, open innovation is not a new phenomenon in China. In fact, it has been a long-evolving and ongoing innovation mode adopted by Chinese firms in the past three decades. In other words, open innovation is a 'new' concept towards innovation strategy based on a mix of old and new practices in China. Although OI is a recent concept, both science and technology and economic policies in China have to a great degree incorporated the creation and facilitation of an open market environment and innovation atmosphere and the encouragement of external knowledge sourcing and acquisition as well as the commercialisation of scientific research discoveries and inventions. Although the implementation and execution of policies at national, regional and especially firm levels vary greatly across regions and firms depending on the interpretation of the policies and the capabilities of local government and firms, Chinese firms have no doubt moved in the direction of making good use of external knowledge via inbound or outbound open innovation to build indigenous technological capabilities. As a strong developmental state that is widely accepted in the literature, the Chinese government has played a crucial role in the national innovation system in initiating and coordinating a wide set of institutions and incentives. All the innovation-related financial, tax, industry, trade and S&T

policies have served as effective *linkages* that connect all the relevant players at various levels of the national innovation system and ensure that the national innovation strategy is well communicated from policy makers at the top to firms at the lower levels.

The evolution of the orientation of policies and hence the practices adopted by Chinese firms echo the different stages of economic and technological development in China. From encouraging all-around external sourcing since the 1980s, policy makers have diversified channels of commercialising innovation in the mid-1990s. Since the 2000s, with the increase of globalisation and the growth of technological capabilities of Chinese firms, policy orientation has become more open and aggressive to incentivise indigenous companies to acquire advanced external knowledge through 'going global'. All this reflects the Chinese government's objective of promotion of indigenous innovation in a highly open era. Despite the strong government policy support to open innovation, however, some critical institutional challenges, such as the lack of a strong intellectual property rights regime to protect and facilitate knowledge sharing, still need urgent attention and effective effort to reinforce them. Moreover, innovation policies can no longer be designed solely in a national context. Because of a country's attractiveness as a place for innovation activity becoming a priority, framework conditions that affect the location of production and costs become critical (OECD, 2008). So, structural policies, which include competition and regulations, public infrastructure, S&T base and talent education policies, are all of great importance.

Increasing globalisation and changes in global innovation systems have driven the shift to a more open innovation mode. Our review suggests that selected Chinese domestic firms have adopted a variety of OI practices; for example, Chinese firms in different industries have often used the outside-in mode, the inside-out mode and the coupled mode at different development stages. Therefore, future research should explore systematically why and how latecomer firms can efficiently use open innovation for catching up. In particular, what is the role of OI in emerging economies? How can the emerging economies make the best use of open innovation for indigenous capabilities building? These are important questions for an in-depth understanding of open innovation for latecomer firms in emerging economies.

Technological learning is regarded as a necessary process for late-comers to improve their technological capabilities, skipping the repeated technological manufacturing cycle and thus avoiding the huge investments in technological systems in the initial stages in order to catch up with the developed countries (Hobday, 1995). The ability to use inside-out and outside-in strategies is facilitated by frameworks that allow for the purchase or sale of intellectual assets that can create value and opportunities for firms inside or outside their core businesses. Therefore, both technology transaction markets and IPR protection processes do matter in fostering open innovation. Moreover, firms may differ in their modes of learning. Some learning modes are superior to others in terms of the learning outcome in a particular situation (Li and Kozhikode, 2009). While firms might have a variety of sources to choose from, the path dependency of learning and the learning outcome makes it difficult to gauge the value of a given learning source a priori. Hence, another avenue for future research should be concerned with establishing the best learning strategies for latecomers to deal with various technology or organisation challenges in opening their innovation processes. More in-depth industrial or firm-level case studies or relevant large-scale empirical surveys should be carried out in the future.

7 | *Open innovation as a response to constraints and risks*

7.1 Introduction

In recent years, open innovation has become a new imperative in innovation practice and research. It refers to the use of purposive inflows and outflows of knowledge to accelerate internal innovation and to expand the markets for external use of innovation using outside-in, inside-out or coupled modes (Chesbrough, Vanhaverbeke and West, 2006). However, to date it has mainly been analysed in the context of the industrialised economies, particular with respect to large, high-technology multinational enterprises (MNEs) (Chesbrough, 2003; Chesbrough and Crowther, 2006; Keupp and Gassmann, 2009). The research on open innovation in smaller organisations or developing countries is scarce, with some isolated exceptions (e.g., Vrande et al., 2009; Lee et al., 2010; Fu, 2012a). Given the rising importance of the emerging economies, understanding the determinants of open innovation in latecomer emerging economies is of crucial importance.

Perhaps the two most important questions to address are why and when firms in emerging economies should adopt open innovation. Firms may choose open innovation for different reasons, from tapping into the best talents to keeping a firm's leadership in innovation (Chesbrough, 2003) to overcoming the various impediments that a firm faces (Keupp and Gassmann, 2009). Firms in emerging economies face substantial institutional, resource and capability constraints for innovation. How do firms respond to these constraints and the risks of innovation given their limited resources and capabilities? What role can open innovation play in firms' strategic responses to constraints and risks? How relevant or useful are existing open innovation theories and practices, primarily developed in Western countries, when they are applied to the emerging economies such as China?

This chapter attempts to fill the gap in the literature by providing the first analysis of the drivers of open innovation in emerging economies.

The chapter has a special emphasis on firms' adoption decisions in response to the institutional, financial and capabilities constraints and risks. A national firm-level innovation survey data set of 1,408 firms in the Chinese manufacturing sector is employed in the research. As one of the major emerging economies, China opened up its economy after 1978 and has actively engaged in the acquisition of external knowledge and encouraged university-industry linkages ever since. Chinese firms in most traditional or emerging sectors are still catching up with their foreign rivals, especially in terms of technological innovation capability.

Technological learning will be a long-term task for most latecomer firms (Lee and Lim, 2001; Xie and Wu, 2003). Owing to a lack of adequate resources and capabilities to deal with technological and the market uncertainty of innovation as well as the rising costs of internal R&D risks, most Chinese firms are not able to meet all the challenges of innovation on their own and choose to source external knowledge and resources to be able to accomplish the innovation process in full. Until the late 2000s, firms collaborated with other partners and usage of external information sources for innovation was widely observed in the economy (Fu and Xiong, 2011). Therefore, China provides a good case study.

Findings from this chapter contribute not only to our understanding of open innovation in emerging economies but also contribute to the empirical evidence on the linkage between impediments to innovation and firms' choice of innovation mode. Evidence on this question is not currently available (with the exception of Keupp and Gassmann [2009], based on data from Switzerland).

The rest of this chapter is organised as follows: Section 7.2 discusses the theoretical framework. Section 7.3 describes data and methodology. Section 7.4 presents the empirical results. Section 7.5 discusses the findings in detail and then presents conclusions.

7.2 Theory and hypotheses

Determinants of open innovation

The literature has pointed out various determinants of open innovation. It is well recognised that companies should not innovate in isolation but instead should co-operate with external partners throughout the innovation process (OECD, 2008). Instead of using the usual exploration-exploitation dichotomy to explain firms' decision to adopt open innovation, we deploy the 'push-pull' factor framework.

Most prior contributions have argued that the motivation of open innovation is a result of pull factors external to firms, such as environmental change and pressures; availability of skilled workers, knowledge or venture capital; more intense competition from rivals, suppliers or new entrants (Chesbrough, 2003); technology intensity and fusion (Gassmann, 2006); knowledge transfer and leveraging of spillovers (De Bondt, 1997; Chesbrough et al., 2006); and partner advantages (Hagedoorn, 2002) that drive the externalisation of R&D activities beyond the boundary of the firm.

Many firms have started to implement open innovation as a necessary organisational adaption to changes in the environment (Chesbrough, 2003). As the boundaries of firms become porous (Lichtenthaler and Ernst, 2007), companies interact intensively with their environment; this leads to large volumes of external technology acquisition and external technology exploitation (Chesbrough, 2003). Firms combine both technological *exploitation* and *exploration* to create maximum value from their technological capabilities or other competencies (Lichtenthaler, 2008).

On the other hand, a series of internal constraints that firms face may also push them to open up the innovation process. Keupp and Gassmann (2009) explain the externalisation of R&D as a result of weaknesses internal to the firm. They examine empirically how impediments to innovation spur openness at the firm-level based on the *Swiss Innovation Survey* and show that information-/capability-related impediments and risk-related impediments will increase both the breadth and depth of open innovation.

Moreover, much of the literature emphasises the direct effect of internal factors on open innovation activities. EIRMA (2003) shows that R&D managers of large corporations engage in technological venturing not just for market-related motives such as meeting customer demands but also to acquire new knowledge. Vrande et al. (2009) in particular claim that small and medium enterprises (SMEs) pursue open innovation primarily for sustainable growth or to keep up with competitors. In addition, innovation collaboration studies suggest that enterprises may engage in collaboration to acquire missing knowledge, complementary resources or finance; achieve abundant revenue (i.e., sale of intellectual property [IP] and leveraging); spread risks; enlarge social networks; or reduce costs (Mohr and Spekman, 1994; Hoffmann and Schlosser, 2001; Gassmann, 2006). Koruna (2004) identified some further motivations, including specific industry standards, attempts to profit from infringements, realisation of learning effects and guarantees of freedom to operate by establishing cross-licensing agreements with other organisations.

In sum, there has been an important shift from a focus purely on internal R&D towards emphasising external resources and partnership for innovation (e.g., Rigby and Zook, 2002; Christensen, Olesen and Kjar, 2005). With globally dispersed specialised knowledge, highly mobile skilled workers, abundant venture capital, greatly reduced product life cycles, external options for ideas currently sitting on the shelf as well as an ever increasing number of emerging and effective competitors, most enterprises can no longer afford to innovate on their own. Firms have therefore begun to think of new ways to harness external ideas while leveraging their in-house R&D outside their current operations (Chesbrough, 2003; Gassmann, 2006; Vrande, et al., 2009). Our analysis of the determinants of open innovation in the context of an emerging economy, China, focuses on the push factors while recognising the effects of the pull factors arising in the dynamic environment.

Innovation and open innovation: constraints and risks

Generally, obstacles to innovation include economic risk, costs, financing constraints, rigidities of an organisation, lack of skilled personnel, lack of information on technology and markets, lack of customer responsiveness to innovation and institutions (Galia and Legros, 2004). In fact, these obstacles can vary among different types of firm. A number of prior studies have reconstructed these obstacles into specific sets or groups, such as finance-/risk-related obstacles, market-/ institution-related obstacles and information-/skill-related obstacles (Baldwin and Lin, 2002; Keupp and Gassmann, 2009). Some of these erosion factors, such as the increasing costs and risks of innovation, greater competition or the increased complexity of new technologies, may stimulate open innovation (Chesbrough, 2003).

If firms experience these constraints and risks to innovation, they are often more likely to open up the innovation process to overcome internal rigidities caused by constraints and risks. For example, many firms have to look for partners with complementary expertise to secure rapid access to new leading knowledge or to learn by networking. In particular, for indigenous firms in the emerging economies, the finance-/risk-related obstacles, market-/institution-related obstacles or information-/skill-related obstacles of this group of firms could be quite distinct because their context is that of catch-up in global innovation networks (OECD, 2008). Firms are prone to miss many opportunities because a significant number of these will fall outside the organisation's current business or need to be combined with external technologies to unlock their potential (Chesbrough, 2003).

Hence, we argue that open innovation is an active response for late-comer firms in emerging economies as a means to overcome internal rigidities and reinforce their innovation resources and capabilities. This perspective has already been supported by some case-based illustrations (Rigby and Zook, 2002; Xie and Wu, 2003; Chen and Chen, 2008; OECD, 2008). To our knowledge, this hypothesised relationship has not yet been systematically tested in the context of developing countries or specifically in the case of China.

Our first proposition is that weaknesses external to the firm, partic-ularly environmental innovation pressure, spur open innovation in China. Here, environmental innovation pressure refers to intense and low-end market competition; uncertainty of customer needs or lack of responsiveness to innovation; and institutional challenges such as a weak IP protection regime, immature industrial standards, norms, legislation or regulations. We term these issues *market- and institution-related constraints to innovation*. The intensity of market competition or monopolisation in some sectors may affect the out-come of innovation strategies (Fosfuri, 2006), promoting open inno-vation activities in particular. Many Chinese firms are still stuck in the low value-added element of the global value chain, and some have to face increasingly intense competition in local markets. Accordingly, these firms are extremely keen to find partners who possess advanced R&D capacity or strong branding to help them get away from the low-end value chain and extremely intense competition. In addition, in light of the large but layered and dynamic market in China, the high level of uncertainty with respect to customer needs leads most local firms to be hesitant in decision making with respect to innovation, in both the short and long term. Having realised that dependence on quick imitation or introduction of simple products cannot provide a sustainable benefit, many local firms are more likely to adopt networking with suppliers, users or even potential rivals or to build or participate in strategic alliances to reduce the uncertainty of market needs and increase customer responsiveness to new products or process innovation.

Furthermore, the existence of relatively weak institutions forces some local firms to try their best to build linkages with government or universities to be first to learn of market opportunities and knowledge. For instance, the quality of any relationship with central or local governments is widely regarded to be one of the most important forms of social capital in China. Networking with regional governments to access inside information may have a great influence on a firm's future business strategy or its acquisition of government funding and/or preferential tax rates. Thus, it is proposed that indigenous firms that suffer from more market- and institution-related constraints to innovation will be inclined to increase their openness to innovation via relationships with various external organisations or public institutions. We therefore posit the following hypothesis:

H7–1:   Firms that face greater market- and institution-related constraints to innovation are more likely to adopt greater openness in innovation.

Our second proposition is that financial constraints and risk-related impediments to innovation could also stimulate a model based on an open style of innovation. In this case, such an impediment is related to certain input or cost considerations, including a lack of input capital or appropriate sources of finance, excessively high innovation costs and excessive perceived economic risk. In fact, investing and financing capabilities do matter in industrial development for latecomers (Malerba, 2002). For example, notwithstanding the lack of venture capital to commercialise new inventions or sustain investment in industrialisation, many Chinese biotech firms remain stuck at the laboratory stage or fail because of a long R&D cycle and the fact that no further capital is then available at the necessary time. Thus, some of these firms try to source external strategic partners, whether leading firms or venture capitalists, to achieve technological exploitation.

In addition, technological innovation always requires significant capital input, which places innovators under high cost pressure, especially in the case of those emerging latecomers whose profit margins or revenue-making competences are quite unstable. Hence, they have to co-innovate with external sources (such as lead users, suppliers or universities) to share R&D costs and reduce failure risks. In some cases, once the notion of inter-organisational innovation collaboration has entered an industry, any firm that does not participate will experience serious competitive disadvantages (Enkel, Gassmann and Chesbrough, 2009).

In addition, excessive economic risks in innovation activities have been widely recognised and confirmed (OECD, 2005). Studies on domestic R&D co-operation show that risks associated with innovation should promote R&D collaboration or inter-firm partnerships (Bayona, García-Marco and Huerta, 2001; Hagedoorn, 2002; Tether, 2002). Evidence based on the *Swiss Community Innovation Survey* also finds that the existence of risk-related impediments leads to greater openness amongst Swedish firms (Keupp and Gassmann, 2009). All these arguments suggest that firms that suffer from greater financial constraints and risk-related impediments to innovation are more likely to make use of open innovation to obtain access to external finance or share R&D risks. This leads to the following hypothesis:

H7–2: Firms that experience financial constraints and risk-related impediments to innovation are likely to have greater openness in innovation.

In our third proposition, we tentatively argue that knowledge-/skill-related constraints can promote Chinese firms' willingness to deploy open innovation. In the Chinese case, a greater number of internal constraints exist, such as a lack of skilled personnel, a lack of information on technologies, a lack of information on markets, a lack of innovation collaborators, a lack of a technological basis, too large a technological gap or even resistance towards change in the firm. Knowledge-based assets are the primary resources latecomers lack as compared to leading firms in the global market (Amsden, 1992). However, knowledge and learning are key strategic levers because knowledge development is cumulative (Tushman and Anderson, 1986).

In terms of their weak accumulation of knowledge, most Chinese firms tend to partner with foreign entrants in order to learn. Indeed, exploratory tasks such as external sourcing are typically associated with the need for skills that transcend the current capabilities of the organisation (Katila and Ahuja, 2002). Inter-organisational collaboration has proven to be an effective strategy to learn and manage intellectual capital (Powell, Koput and Smith-Doerr, 1996). Moreover, global modularisation has provided a valuable opportunity for many Chinese firms, especially those firms that produce complex products, to enter into the global production chain. The decomposability of technology and reduced external transaction costs as a result of the increased availability of international R&D resources have made open innovation appealing and useful within Chinese manufacturing innovation. Hence, Chinese firms that face more knowledge-/skill-related constraints to innovation may tend to be more open in sourcing external knowledge and skills for innovation. Therefore, we have the following hypothesis:

H3:· Firms that experience knowledge and skill constraints to innovation are likely to have greater openness in innovation.

Most firms in emerging economies are still at a transitional phase of catch-up and innovation capability building. It is often argued that it is difficult for latecomers to skip stages in the evolutionary process of learning. Hence, tapping into external resources and knowledge forms the foundation of cultivating indigenous innovation capability (Kim, 1997a, 1997b). Opening up the innovation process is likely to be a natural choice for latecomers in emerging economies to mitigate R&D pressure, overcome various constraints, diversify risks and share uncertainties.

7.3 Data and Methodology

Data

The research principally uses the 2008 Chinese national innovation survey of 1,408 manufacturing firms, which includes information regarding firms' innovation activities from 2005 to 2007. The National Statistical Bureau carried out the survey. It covers 42 cities in China in both the coastal and inland regions. A total of 1,408 valid responses were received, with a response rate of 83.6 per cent. The questionnaire is designed to have high consistency and comparability with the European Community Innovation Survey (CIS). The sample includes firms of all major ownership types that exist in China, and the sample is composed of 9 per cent state or collectively owned enterprises, 7 per cent privately owned firms, 53 per cent publicly owned and limited liability companies, and 30 per cent foreign invested companies that are wholly owned subsidiaries of MNEs or joint ventures in which foreign investment accounted for more than 25 per cent of total investment. Larger innovative firms are over-represented in the sample. About 50 per cent and 17.5 per cent of the firms in the sample represent medium- and large-sized firms, respectively.[1] The total reported R&D investment in the sampled firms was RMB 53,350 million, accounting for 18.2 per cent of China's total R&D investment in the manufacturing sector in 2007. After careful data cleansing to exclude observations with missing values for the necessary variables, the final data set used in the estimation contains 626 firms, of which 95 per cent have innovated in their products or processes. Therefore, the results of this study reflect the decision to engage in open innovation made by innovative Chinese firms rather than by Chinese firms generally. This is a limitation of the research that we should bear in mind when drawing conclusions.

Measurement

Dependent variables

The operational practice of openness is nuanced; therefore, different measures are deployed to measure a firm's openness in innovation. Laursen and Salter (2006) develop two measurements of openness involving the breadth (range of external sources) and depth (importance of sources) of the innovation process:

- The breadth of openness refers to the number of search channels a company draws on in its innovative activities.

---

[1] The term medium- and large-sized enterprises (MLEs) refers to firms with between 300 and 2,000 employees and more than 2,000 employees, respectively. The total number of MLEs in the sample is 950, accounting for 2.4 per cent of China's total MLEs in the manufacturing sector in 2007, according to the 2008 National Economic Census Yearbook.

- The depth of innovation refers to the extent to which companies draw intensively on different search channels or sources of innovative ideas.

Following this perspective, in this chapter we measure the breadth of open innovation by calculating how many of the 10 major external knowledge sources are integrated into a firm's innovation processes; we measure the depth of open innovation by the number of these sources being deeply integrated into a firm's innovation processes. The 10 external sources include those from within the firm or the company group: supplier; customer; competitors; consultancy companies and private R&D institutions; universities; public research institutions; government science and technology programs; trade fair and professional conferences; journals, magazines and patent documents; and industrial associations.

Specifically, our questionnaire asks the interviewed firms to confirm the degree of importance of each source on a scale from 1 to 4, based on the extent of usage by them ('1' means that this source has not been used by the firm; '4' means the highest level of usage). Breadth is calculated as the number of external sources and is rated from 1 to 4. Depth is calculated as the number of external sources that are rated as important with a score of 4.

Independent variables

This survey questionnaire contains 21 Likert-scale items used to question firms regarding the extent to which a specific impediment had significant negative consequences for innovation activities. More specifically, the 21 items involve economic risks, cost, financing channels as well as items on talents, knowledge accumulation, technical information, market information and collaborators, monopoly, competition, profitability, innovation of other firms in same sector and uncertainty of market demand. The items are rated from 1 (no negative consequence) to 4 (very strong negative consequence). We use these items to construct scales intended to measure different kinds of constraints and risks to innovation. We classify the 21 items into three kinds of constraints to innovation: finance- and risk-related impediments, market- and institution-related constraints and knowledge- and skills-related constraints. The market- and institution-related constraints to innovation section includes nine questions, the financial constraints and risk-related impediments to innovation five questions and the knowledge- and skill-related constraints to innovation seven questions. Each constraint/risk variable is estimated as the average of the scores of all the relevant questions. Details of the constraints and risks are given in Appendix 7.1.

Some of the obstacles are likely to have greater impact than others. Hence, ideally we would know the different weights of each of the obstacles and estimate a weighted index instead of giving equal weight to the individual indicators. However, each firm may perceive a different constraining effect as a result of its capabilities and other firm-specific characteristics. It would be difficult to create a reasonable weighting pattern that suits all firms. Moreover, we have experimented with using factor analysis to generate the constraints and found that the outcome in fact is highly consistent with the three impediment indexes that we generated according to theory. Therefore, the indexes that we use here are broadly consistent with theory and the actual variation in the data. In light of the high correlation between the knowledge- and skills-related constraints and the other two constraints and risks, we enter the three impediment variables into the regression alternatively to avoid any multi-collinearity problem.

Control variables

Following the literature on determinants of open innovation, we include firm size, age, ownership, industry effects, regional effects, R&D intensity and collaboration experiences as control variables.

Firm size and *firm age* may affect open innovation strategies and performance because larger or older firms usually have larger technology portfolios (Lichtenthaler and Lichtenthaler, 2009). We measure firm size based on the number of employees. Therefore, a discrete variable that equals 1 for firms of fewer than 300 employees, 2 for firms that have 300 to 2,000 employees, and 3 for large firms with more than 2,000 employees is included as an explanatory variable.[2] *Ownership* may also influence a firm's openness in innovation. We include two dummies to represent the primary types of firm ownership

---

[2] Here we use the firm size classification defined by the National Bureau of Statistics of China.

in China: a state-owned dummy that equals 1 for state-owned enterprises and 0 otherwise, and a private-ownership dummy that equals 1 for privately owned enterprises and zero otherwise.[3] The foreign-owned enterprises are used as the base group.

As there are potentially obvious differences in motives and frequency of open innovation between medium- and high-tech industries and other low-tech industries (Chesbrough and Crowther, 2006; OECD, 2008), we control for the *industry* specific effects at the SIC two-digit level by using a vector of industry dummies. In total, 29 industry dummies are included in the regression. In a large country with significant regional disparities, *regional*-specific effects may also significantly influence a firm's decision to adopt open innovation. For example, firms in eastern regions are more inclined to have an open attitude towards their innovation processes. We therefore likewise control for region by dummy variables that are coded 1 if the firm is based in a city in the eastern region (including four municipalities, Yangtze River Delta and Pearl River Delta) and 0 otherwise.

Absorptive capacity is an important factor when firms choose to learn from outside. To measure this, we use a question that directly asks firms to evaluate the extent of both internal and external R&D input (or participation), scaled from 1 (low input) to 2 (medium input) and 3 (extensive input) to proxy a firm's R&D intensity. Finally, we also control for a firm's *collaboration experience*: this can greatly influence a firm's capacity and experience in open innovation. A dummy variable that equals 1 if a firm reports that collaboration is prevalent in its industry and 0 otherwise is included in the regression.

To ensure that all the observations in all items drawn from the questionnaire are statistically reliable, we use reliability analysis to test for the reliability of the data (with *Alpha* = 0.8975 and 1,408 cases). Given that the dependent variables are count values that range between 0 and 10, standard OLS estimates will be biased. We therefore use ordered Logit for the estimation. Nevertheless, we report both the ordered Logit and OLS estimates as a robustness check.

---

[3] Companies with shareholders are classified as POEs (privately owned enterprises) in the research. Admittedly, some state-controlled shareholding companies are included in this group as a result. This may mask the true behaviour and performance of the POEs, but we believe the proportion and influence are limited.

7.4 Results

Table 7.1 reports the descriptive statistics of the major variables and the correlation coefficients amongst them. The three impediments to innovation – the market- and institution-related constraints, the financial constraints and risk-related impediments and the knowledge- and skill-related constraints to innovation – all appear to be positive and significantly correlated to the degree of openness in terms of both breadth and depth. There are, however, also significant correlations amongst the three impediments variables: this may cause a potential multicollinearity in the regression models. Therefore, we enter the three impediments alternatively into the regression to avoid this problem.

Table 7.2 reports the ordered logistic model estimates of the determinants of the breadth of openness in Chinese manufacturing firms. All three constraints and risks appear to have a significant positive association with firms' breadth of openness in innovation when we enter the constraints into the regression alternatively. When the three constraints are entered into the regression at the same time, institutional- and market-related constraints and financial constraints both show a robust and consistent positive and significant association with the breadth of openness. For a one-unit increase in the financial constraints and risk-related impediments, we expect to see an approximately 35 per cent increase in the odds of having one level higher breadth of openness.[4] Similarly, the odds ratio for institution- and market-related constraints is about 92 per cent, which is the highest impact among the three impediments. In other words, firms are most likely to open up their innovation process when there are institutional and market constraints. However, the estimated coefficient of the knowledge- and skills-related constraints variable becomes insignificant when all three constraints variables are included in the regression at the same time.

Intramural R&D and extramural R&D appear to be positively associated with a firm's breadth of openness and are statistically significant. For each category increase of intramural R&D, the odds of one level of greater breadth of openness is about 74 per cent. Similarly, for each category increase of extramural R&D, we expect to see about a 50 per cent increase in the odds of having one level higher breadth of openness.

---

[4] The odds ratio is calculated as exp(beta).

Table 7.1 Descriptive statistics and correlations

Variable	Obs	Mean	Std. Dev.	breadth	depth	size	age	soe	poe	region	inrd	exrd	collab2	risk2	skill2	makt2
breadth	626	8.527	2.230	1.00												
depth	626	2.404	2.102	0.34	1.00											
size	626	2.377	0.595	0.20	0.07	1.00										
age	626	17.142	19.224	0.10	0.10	0.12	1.00									
soe	626	0.096	0.295	0.02	0.00	0.03	0.34	1.00								
poe	626	0.658	0.475	0.07	0.10	-0.08	-0.05	-0.45	1.00							
region	626	0.610	0.488	0.00	0.03	0.04	-0.12	-0.18	-0.12	1.00						
inrd	626	2.486	0.615	0.29	0.21	0.21	0.09	0.03	0.08	-0.05	1.00					
exrd	626	1.649	0.641	0.22	0.15	0.16	0.05	-0.02	0.07	0.04	0.35	1.00				
collab2	626	2.965	1.014	0.05	0.10	-0.02	0.00	-0.02	0.02	-0.05	-0.02	0.02	1.00			
risk2	626	2.606	0.761	0.16	0.11	-0.02	0.09	0.04	0.13	-0.09	0.06	0.09	0.10	1.00		
skill2	626	2.509	0.703	0.11	0.13	0.00	0.04	-0.02	0.08	0.03	0.02	0.12	0.08	0.49	1.00	
makt2	626	2.366	0.624	0.19	0.14	-0.03	0.02	-0.06	0.10	0.05	0.07	0.12	0.09	0.51	0.69	1.00

Table 7.2 *Determinants of breadth of openness: ordered-Logit model estimates*

	1	2	3	4	Odds ratio (4)
Firm size	0.531***	0.489***	0.528***	0.559***	1.748***
	(0.170)	(0.170)	(0.168)	(0.168)	
Firm age	0.004	0.005	0.005	0.005	1.005
	(0.005)	(0.005)	(0.005)	(0.005)	
SOE	0.136	0.203	0.197	0.162	1.176
	(0.373)	(0.362)	(0.370)	(0.378)	
POE	0.278	0.341	0.296	0.258	1.295
	(0.214)	(0.213)	(0.211)	(0.212)	
Coastal region	0.347*	0.272	0.230	0.290	1.336
	(0.201)	(0.197)	(0.198)	(0.202)	
Intramural R&D	0.551***	0.523***	0.492***	0.520***	1.682***
	(0.160)	(0.161)	(0.161)	(0.161)	
Extramural R&D	0.399***	0.419***	0.409***	0.397***	1.487***
	(0.151)	(0.152)	(0.151)	(0.150)	
Collaboration experience	0.173**	0.193**	0.167*	0.153*	1.166*
	(0.086)	(0.088)	(0.089)	(0.087)	
Finance/risk constraints	0.459***			0.298**	1.347**
	(0.115)			(0.137)	
Knowledge/skills constraints		0.286**		–0.238	0.788
		(0.123)		(0.173)	
Institute/market constraints			0.639***	0.652***	1.920***
			(0.143)	(0.199)	
Industry	Yes	Yes	Yes	Yes	Yes
Observations	627	628	628	626	
Pseudo-R^2	0.076	0.069	0.078	0.082	

***significant at 1 per cent level; **significant at 5 per cent level; *significant at 10 per cent level. Robust standard errors in parentheses; BREADTH, breadth of openness.
Note: Foreign-invested firms are the base ownership group.

All this suggests that firms with greater absorptive capacity are more open in innovation and engage a greater range of external sources.

Firm size also seems to have a positive impact on a firm's breadth of openness. Larger firms tend to have a greater degree of openness in terms of breadth of tapping into external knowledge sources. Firms with previous collaboration experiences are also more likely to increase their openness in innovation. However, we do not see significant differences across ownership types and geographical location with regards to breadth of openness when other firm-specific characteristics are controlled for. In other words, ownership does not seem to have an impact on whether firms have used/integrated external information sources for innovation, but firms are more likely to differ in the extent to which they do so.

Table 7.3 reports the Ordered-Logistic model estimates of the determinants of the depth of openness in Chinese manufacturing firms. Again, all three constraints and risks including institutional- and market-related constraints, knowledge- and skills-related constraints and financial constraints and risks appear to have a significant positive association with firms' breadth of openness in innovation. The estimated results are robust to different model specifications. For a one-unit increase in the financial constraints and risk-related impediments, we expect to see about a 9 per cent increase in the odds of having one level higher breadth of openness. Similarly, the odds ratio for knowledge- and skills-related constraints is 14 per cent and that for institution- and market-related constraints is about 30 per cent, which is again the highest impact amongst the three impediments. In other words, firms are most likely to use deep openness in innovation when there are institutional and market constraints. However, unlike in the case of breadth of openness, the constraints in knowledge and skills for innovation seem to have greater impact on the depth of openness than those involving financial constraints and risk-related impediments. The association between impediments and depth of innovation openness is strong; even in column (4), when all the three impediments are entered into the regression at the same time, the estimated coefficients of the impediments variables are statistically significant at the 1 per cent level.

Intramural and extramural R&D as well as firm size have a significant and positive impact on a firm's depth in openness innovation. In other words, firms that have high levels of in-house R&D, higher levels of extramural R&D and large size are more likely to have greater depth

Table 7.3 *Determinants of depth of openness: ordered-Logit model estimates*

	1	2	3	4	Odds ratio (4)
Firm size	0.082***	0.057***	0.077***	0.080***	1.084***
	(0.021)	(0.021)	(0.021)	(0.022)	
Firm age	0.009***	0.009***	0.010***	0.009***	1.009***
	(0.001)	(0.001)	(0.001)	(0.001)	
SOE	0.018	0.063	0.065	0.052	1.054
	(0.042)	(0.042)	(0.041)	(0.043)	
POE	0.238***	0.244***	0.218***	0.220***	1.246***
	(0.044)	(0.044)	(0.044)	(0.047)	
Coastal region	0.390***	0.363***	0.338***	0.347***	1.415***
	(0.042)	(0.042)	(0.042)	(0.044)	
Intramural R&D	0.529***	0.545***	0.518***	0.522***	1.685***
	(0.020)	(0.020)	(0.020)	(0.021)	
Extramural R&D	0.166***	0.149***	0.154***	0.136***	1.146***
	(0.027)	(0.027)	(0.027)	(0.028)	
Collaboration experience	0.129***	0.121***	0.115***	0.111***	1.118***
	(0.015)	(0.015)	(0.015)	(0.016)	
Finance/risk constraints	0.236***			0.084***	1.088***
	(0.018)			(0.020)	
Knowledge/skills constraints		0.328***		0.130***	1.138***
		(0.019)		(0.021)	
Institute/market constraints			0.418***	0.265***	1.303***
			(0.020)	(0.022)	
Industry	Yes	Yes	Yes	Yes	Yes
Observations	627	628	628	626	
Pseudo-R^2	0.048	0.049	0.050	0.051	

***significant at 1 per cent level; **significant at 5 per cent level; *significant at 10 per cent level. Robust standard errors in parentheses; BREADTH, breadth of openness. Note: Foreign-invested firms are the base ownership group.

in open innovation. Interestingly (and unlike the case of breadth), firm age, ownership, geographical location and previous collaboration experience all have a positive impact on firms' depth of open innovation, and these variables are statistically significant. For every one-year increase in firm age, the odds ratio that a firm will increase its depth of innovation increases by 1 per cent.

Furthermore, while SOEs do not appear to be significantly different from foreign invested firms (FIEs) in terms of depth of open innovation (OI), privately owned firms (POEs) have a significantly higher propensity to engage with deeper open innovation. Finally, firms in coastal regions also have a significantly higher propensity to engage in deeper open innovation than firms in the inland region. Given that their other characteristics are the same, the likelihood of engaging in a higher level of depth of innovation for a POE is 24 per cent greater than for an FIE and 41 per cent for a firm in coastal as opposed to inland regions. The lower openness in innovation in the FIEs than the POEs is likely the result of concerns regarding weak IPR protection in China and the potential to lose technology know-how in the open innovation process of FIEs. FIEs may also face fewer constraints (push factors). The greater depth of open innovation of firms in coastal regions is likely the result of the greater overall economic openness in the coastal region and hence the easier access to external knowledge sources and greater openness in management practice, business models and strategic thinking amongst the entrepreneurs and management in the coastal region. Moreover, the greater technological capacity and hence greater absorptive capacity of firms in the coastal regions may also be an attribute of the significantly greater openness in innovation amongst firms in the coastal region.

Table 7.4 reports robustness check estimates using OLS. The size, sign and significance of the estimated coefficients of the three impediment variables are broadly consistent with those of the Ordered-Logistic model estimates, although the statistical significance of the OLS estimates of the impediments variables is a level lower than that of the Ordered-Logistic estimates in the depth table. Regarding the control variables, in respect to the breadth of openness, the estimated results are robust with regard to the impact of firm size and intramural and extramural R&D intensity. However, the statistical significance of firm size, ownership and collaboration experience changes slightly. In respect to the depth of openness, the estimated results are robust for

Table 7.4 Robustness check using OLS

	Breadth			Depth		
	1	2	3	5	6	7
Firm size	0.531***	0.489***	0.528***	0.061	0.037	0.054
	(0.170)	(0.170)	(0.168)	(0.150)	(0.149)	(0.149)
Firm age	0.004	0.005	0.005	0.010*	0.009	0.010*
	(0.005)	(0.005)	(0.005)	(0.005)	(0.006)	(0.005)
SOE	0.136	0.203	0.197	0.124	0.164	0.190
	(0.373)	(0.362)	(0.370)	(0.340)	(0.334)	(0.337)
POE	0.278	0.341	0.296	0.426**	0.427**	0.420**
	(0.214)	(0.213)	(0.211)	(0.176)	(0.172)	(0.174)
Coastal region	0.347*	0.272	0.230	0.369**	0.316*	0.303*
	(0.201)	(0.197)	(0.198)	(0.185)	(0.181)	(0.182)
Intramural R&D	0.551***	0.523***	0.492***	0.507***	0.515***	0.488***
	(0.160)	(0.161)	(0.161)	(0.142)	(0.142)	(0.142)
Extramural R&D	0.399***	0.419***	0.409***	0.211	0.195	0.202
	(0.151)	(0.152)	(0.151)	(0.143)	(0.145)	(0.142)
Collaboration experience	0.173**	0.193**	0.167*	0.172**	0.168**	0.165*
	(0.086)	(0.088)	(0.089)	(0.085)	(0.086)	(0.086)

	(1)	(2)	(3)	(4)	(5)
Finance/risk constraints	0.459***			0.253**	
	(0.115)			(0.119)	
Knowledge/skills constraints		0.286**			0.323**
		(0.123)			(0.136)
Institute/market constraints			0.639***		0.364**
			(0.143		(0.148)
Industry	Yes	Yes	Yes	Yes	Yes
Observations	627	628	628	627	628
Pseudo-R²	0.076	0.069	0.078	0.157	0.160

***significant at 1 per cent level; **significant at 5 per cent level; *significant at 10 per cent level. Robust standard errors in parentheses; Breadth, breadth of openness; Depth, depth of openness

Note: Foreign invested firms are the base ownership group.

ownership, regional, intramural R&D and collaboration experience. However, the OLS estimates lose statistical significance with regard to firm size, age and extramural R&D intensity probably because the real distribution of the population violates the assumption of normal distribution involved in the OLS model. In general, the OLS estimates have also confirmed the significant link between the constraints and risks that firms face and the degree of openness in innovation that firms may choose.

The ownership effect

Table 7.5 reports the estimated results of firms' responses to constraints and risks in subsamples of firms with different types of ownership. Firms in the sample are classified into three subsamples based on their ownership: state-owned firms (SOEs), privately owned firms (POEs) and foreign invested firms (FIEs).[5] The evidence shown in the table suggests that firms' responses to constraints and risks vary across ownership types. The breadth of innovation openness in the SOEs, the estimated coefficients of the finance and risks-related impediments and the knowledge- and skills-related constraints have positive and statistically significant relationships at the 1 per cent level, indicating that SOEs will utilise more partnerships and a wider information search when they have constraints in their knowledge for innovation. They will also use more partnerships to share the risks when they face excess risks or finance constraints in innovation. However, institution- and market-related constraints do not appear to have a significant impact on the degree of openness in SOEs. It may be that the ownership and political ties that the state-owned firms have had in a half-marketised

---

[5] Another similar approach is to use an interaction term for ownership and constraints to test the statistical significance of the difference in the coefficients (slopes) of the constraint variables as between firms with different types of ownership. However, as the focus of this chapter is the behaviour of firms with different ownership types in the face of the concerned constraints, the statistical significance of the estimated constraints variables is the primary concern, and this can only be revealed by estimating the model in each subsample of firms with different ownership types. Nevertheless, we have also estimated models with interaction terms that confirm that the estimated coefficients in the depth models are significantly different from each other. However, this is not the case for the breadth models.

Table 7.5 *Firms' responses to constraints and risks by ownership*

	SOE						POE						FIE					
	Breadth			Depth			Breadth			Depth			Breadth			Depth		
	1	2	3	4	5	6	7	8	9	10	11	12	13	14	15	16	17	18
Size	1.11*** (0.08)	1.29*** (0.08)	1.17*** (0.08)	1.32* (0.73)	1.52** (0.76)	1.25 (0.82)	0.40* (0.21)	0.38* (0.21)	0.42*** (0.03)	0.06 (0.17)	0.08 (0.17)	0.05 (0.17)	1.25*** (0.44)	1.11** (0.47)	1.00** (0.46)	0.49*** (0.04)	0.45*** (0.04)	0.39*** (0.04)
Age	0.01** (0.00)	0.01** (0.00)	0.01*** (0.00)	-0.01 (0.01)	-0.01 (0.01)	-0.01 (0.01)	0.00 (0.01)	0.00 (0.01)	0.00 (0.00)	0.01 (0.01)	0.01 (0.01)	0.01 (0.01)	-0.01 (0.02)	-0.01 (0.02)	-0.01 (0.02)	0.00 (0.00)	-0.01 (0.00)	0.00 (0.00)
Region	1.62*** (0.15)	1.46*** (0.16)	1.50*** (0.16)	-0.05 (0.87)	-0.16 (0.90)	-0.05 (0.84)	0.40* (0.23)	0.33 (0.23)	0.26*** (0.06)	0.49** (0.20)	0.4** (0.20)	0.38* (0.20)	-0.07 (0.86)	-0.38 (0.80)	-0.35 (0.85)	0.72*** (0.10)	0.61*** (0.10)	0.62*** (0.10)
Intramural R&D	1.36*** (0.08)	1.32*** (0.08)	1.38*** (0.08)	0.69 (0.76)	0.53 (0.83)	0.81 (0.88)	0.63*** (0.21)	0.56*** (0.21)	0.52*** (0.03)	0.58*** (0.18)	0.58*** (0.18)	0.55*** (0.18)	0.27 (0.36)	0.43 (0.40)	0.45 (0.39)	0.32*** (0.04)	0.41*** (0.04)	0.37*** (0.04)
Extramural R&D	0.73*** (0.10)	0.76*** (0.11)	0.83*** (0.11)	0.87 (0.96)	0.85 (0.95)	1.01 (0.87)	0.46** (0.19)	0.50*** (0.19)	0.49*** (0.04)	0.15 (0.16)	0.14 (0.17)	0.16 (0.16)	0.44 (0.37)	0.41 (0.37)	0.38 (0.37)	-0.07 (0.05)	-0.03 (0.05)	-0.07 (0.05)
Collaboration	0.58*** (0.06)	0.49*** (0.07)	0.51*** (0.07)	0.18 (0.44)	0.14 (0.48)	0.13 (0.43)	0.20 (0.11)	0.22** (0.11)	0.17*** (0.02)	0.11 (0.09)	0.11 (0.09)	0.08 (0.10)	0.26 (0.23)	0.18 (0.25)	0.11 (0.23)	0.25*** (0.03)	0.22*** (0.03)	0.26*** (0.03)
Finance/risks	0.51*** (0.07)			0.44 (0.42)			0.39*** (0.14)			0.29** (0.14)			1.07*** (0.36)			0.35*** (0.04)		
Knowledge/skills		0.35*** (0.08)			0.51 (0.45)			0.17 (0.15)			0.27 (0.16)			0.579* (0.34)			0.51*** (0.04)	
Institute/Market			0.13 (0.08)			0.27 (0.56)			0.58*** (0.03)			0.49*** (0.18)			0.82* (0.43)			0.35*** (0.04)
Industry	Yes	Yes	Yes	Yes	Yes	Yes	Yes	Yes	Yes	Yes	Yes	Yes	Yes	Yes	Yes	Yes	Yes	Yes
Observations	60	60	60	60	60	60	413	414	414	413	414	414	154	154	154	154	154	154
r2_p	0.183	0.177	0.175	0.167	0.167	0.162	0.080	0.075	0.087	0.048	0.047	0.051	0.154	0.132	0.136	0.106	0.11	0.104

***significant at 1 per cent level; **significant at 5 per cent level; *significant at 10 per cent level. Robust standard errors in parentheses; Breadth: breadth of openness; Depth: depth of openness.

Note: Foreign invested firms are the base ownership group. Estimated using Ordered-Logit model.

transition economy such as China face fewer institution-related constraints or have other alternatives to overcome such constraints in innovation.

With respect to the depth of openness, none of the estimated coefficients of the impediments variables are statistically significant, which suggests that the depth of openness in innovation in the SOEs is not determined by the constraints or risks that these companies face. Our results also do not support arguments based on the major determinants traditionally suggested by the literature. In fact, other estimation results (not reported in the table because of space limitations) suggest that industry-specific effects have played a significant role in explaining the variations in depth of openness in the state-owned sector.

Interestingly, firms that are not SOEs appear to be more responsive to open innovation as a means to overcome the constraints and risks that they face in innovation. In privately owned firms, the estimated coefficients of the institution- and market-related constraints and the finance- and risks-related constraints are both positive and statistically significant with regard to their impact on the breadth and depth of openness. For a one-unit increase in the institution- and market-related constraints, we expect to see about a 78 per cent increase in the odds of having a one-level higher breadth of openness. The impact on the odds ratio of the depth of openness is 63 per cent for a one-unit increase in institution- and market-related constraints.

The POEs also appear to choose to open up their innovation process to different degrees of depth relative to the financial and risk-related constraints. Unexpectedly, they seem not to widen or deepen openness in innovation to respond to the constraints in knowledge- and skills-related issues that they face. This may be because they can directly hire the talented staff they need and so do not need to rely on any information search or collaboration. This may also be because the POEs do not have the capacity to use open innovation effectively to overcome the skills and knowledge constraints.

FIEs appear to be the most responsive to widening and deepening their openness to overcoming the various constraints they have encountered in the innovation process. In particular, FIEs have used open innovation to share the risks they have in the host country. The estimated coefficients of the financial- and risks-related constraints are positive and both statistically significant at the 1 per cent level. Moreover, they have also deepened their openness of innovation in response to all three types of constraints they encounter. The estimated coefficients of the three impediments variables are positive and statistically significant at the 1 per cent level. The significant and all-around responsiveness in the FIEs that is revealed in the table is consistent with the pattern observed in industrialised countries (e.g., Keupp and Gassmann, 2009). This indicates that the subsidiaries of the multinationals not only have to be responsive to internal constraints and the external environment when innovating but also that they have the knowledge and capability to use this new mode of innovation effectively to overcome obstacles.

The moderating effect of firm size and industry

As the results reported in Tables 7.2 and 7.3 indicate that firm size and industry-specific effects have significant effects on the depth and breadth of openness in innovation, it is also interesting to understand the types of firms that are mostly affected by constraints: for example, firms of different size and in different industries. Table 7.6 reports the estimated results concerning the moderating effects of firm size and the technology intensity of the industry.

With respect to the breadth of the openness in innovation, only the estimated coefficient of the interaction term of financial constraints and high-technology industry dummy is positive and statistically significant at the 5 per cent level. This suggests that firms in high-technology industries are more likely to adopt open innovation when they face financial constraints.

With respect to the depth of openness in innovation, the size and technology intensity of the industry both appear to have significant moderating effects on the association between the various constraints and the depth of openness. Smaller firms are more likely to undertake deep engagement in open innovation to overcome the financial constraints and risks in innovation, whereas larger firms are more likely to do so to overcome constraints in knowledge and skills. However, in the face of institutional constraints, there is no significant difference in firms' response to open innovation. Firms in a high-technology industry are more affected by constraints in finance and skills and are more likely to respond to these constraints by engaging in deeper open innovation. However, in the face of institutional constraints, firms in medium- and low-technology industries are more likely to use open

Table 7.6 *Effects of constraints and risks by size and industry*

	1	2
	Breadth	Depth
Finance C * Size	−0.181	−0.157***
	(0.222)	(0.008)
Skill C * Size	0.364	0.299***
	(0.283)	(0.009)
Institution C * Size	−0.339	−0.010
	(0.351)	(0.009)
Finance C * High-tech	0.794**	0.388***
	(0.331)	(0.037)
Skill C * High-tech	−0.416	0.193***
	(0.391)	(0.039)
Institution C * High-tech	−0.529	−0.420***
	(0.473)	(0.041)
Finance/risks constraints	0.537	0.360***
	(0.509)	(0.021)
Knowledge/skills constraints	−0.966	−0.589***
	(0.673)	(0.022)
Market/institute constraints	1.545*	0.364***
	(0.838)	(0.024)
Other control variables	Yes	Yes
Observations	626	626
Pseudo-R^2	0.087	0.053

***significant at 1 per cent level; **significant at 5 per cent level; *significant at 10 per cent level. Robust standard errors in parentheses; Breadth: breadth of openness; Depth: depth of openness.

Note: Other control variables are the same as those included in Tables 7.2 and 7.3.

innovation to overcome this constraint than firms in a high-technology industry.

7.5 Discussion and conclusions

This chapter examines firms' responses to the external and internal constraints and risks to innovation, with special emphasis on firms' adjustment in their openness in the innovation process. It provides the first empirical evidence concerning drivers of open innovation in emerging economies based on large-scale survey data. Evidence from the research suggests that Chinese firms that suffer from greater market- and institution-related, capability- and skills-related or finance- and risks-related constraints are more likely to engage with open innovation in greater depth and breadth to overcome these impediments. The strength of such responses, however, varies across firms of different ownership types, firm size and technology intensity. Foreign invested firms appear to respond the most by widening and deepening their openness in innovation. Privately owned firms have made significant responses to market- and institution- and finance- and risk-related impediments but not to knowledge- and skills-related impediments, whereas state-owned firms appear to be least responsive in using open innovation to overcome the constraints and risks they face. These insights complement our existing understanding of the determinants of open innovation that are derived mostly from experiences in developed countries.

The first major finding of the research is the direct link between the constraints and risks to innovation and openness in innovation. External impediments such as market- and institution-related constraints to innovation have affected Chinese firms in the past several decades. The market and industry environment in China has been evolving rapidly. A large number of Chinese firms attempt to upgrade their technological capabilities to move away from low value-added manufacturing and price competition in local markets by sourcing external innovation ideas or networking with external partners. Moreover, uncertainty in market demand and the lack of customer responsiveness are widely existing phenomena in emerging economies such as China. Although the Chinese market is large, its structure appears highly segmented and unpredictable (Chen, Liu and Chumlin, 2007). The creation of alliances with complementary partners has been shown to be effective in reducing market uncertainty, in particular during the development of emerging technologies (Li and Xiong, 2009). Moreover, the lagged development of a favourable institutional environment for innovation in China has also significantly hindered the growth of innovation activity. Setting up strategic innovation alliances with other firms or engaging with government departments or firms with political ties may help overcome the negative effect of institutional constraints.

Regarding finance- and risk-related impediments to innovation, technological innovation is an exploratory task where the returns, if any, are distant and uncertain (Levinthal and March, 1993). Existing financial markets or channels in China are not sufficient for most domestic firms to utilise. This pressures Chinese firms to engage with partners in sharing the high costs of innovation. Many prior findings derived from innovation collaboration studies have clearly indicated that the primary motives of pursuing cooperation in innovation are to acquire complementary finance or resources and to spread risks or reduce costs (Mohr and Spekman, 1994; Hoffmann and Schlosser, 2001). Local firms in China, especially SMEs, are lacking in adequate and sustainable capital to carry out internal innovation. They are incapable of acquiring enough funds to support innovation. Therefore, they have to perform innovation searches as widely and deeply as possible to make up for any funding shortage and to share high R&D costs. Such situations exist widely in China, especially in science-based sectors (Li et al., 2010). Increasing openness of innovation could also help latecomers save a large amount of early investment on basic research and better focus on the commercialisation of development (Kim, 1997).

Firms that suffer from more knowledge- and skill-related impediments to innovation also increase the degree of openness in their innovation process. The lack of adequate knowledge and resources has been widely regarded as one of the primary obstacles to Chinese indigenous innovation. As an example, the 'brain drain' and 'crowding-out effect' phenomena caused by the entry of multinational companies (Gao et al., 2007) in the past decades in China has been argued to create obstacles. Hence, it is assumed that learning from external partners or sources appears to be an inevitable choice for Chinese firms wishing to acquire knowledge and build their own capabilities. Despite this logic, more knowledge-/skill-related impediments to innovation do not automatically facilitate or even spur open innovation because of the many specific challenges in open innovation. Our finding is consistent with those in the existing literature that argue that most challenges to open innovation stem from internal firm (or organisational) weakness, in particular knowledge- and skill-related obstacles (Chesbrough and Crowther, 2006; Vrande et al., 2009), together with the potential costs and risks of open innovation activities (Keupp and Gassmann, 2009).

The second major finding of this study is that there is considerable variation in firms' responses to constraints and risks across different types of ownership. Foreign invested firms appear to be the most responsive to impediments by widening and deepening their openness in innovation. Privately owned firms have made significant efforts to respond to market- and institution- and finance- and risk-related constraints but not to knowledge- and skills-related constraints, whereas state-owned firms appear to be least responsive in terms of using open innovation to overcome the constraints and risks they face. This is consistent with the feature of a half-marketised transitional economy such as China and the characteristics of a developmental state. SOEs have privileges in access to financial resources and access to the market. They can obtain loans more easily from the large banks that are state owned. As a result of restrictions on market entry in some key industries, they can also enjoy monopoly power. This financial and status advantage also enables SOEs to attract and accumulate substantial human capital. As a result, this type of firm may face fewer constraints and may have other alternative methods to overcome constraints and risks.

On the other hand, this may also reflect the fact that SOEs are more rigid and closed to embracing external linkages and new modes of innovation management. Moreover, SOEs may be less likely to be chosen as a partner in open innovation because of the bureaucratic image of the SOEs and the state-owned or controlled nature of their ownership. The foreign invested firms are responsive to all the constraints by deepening and widening the openness of innovation. This suggests that they are driven by market forces and make necessary responses to maximise profits; however, they are also confident and capable of employing open innovation to overcome the impediments. Of course, we need to note that the average degree of openness of the FIEs is not significantly different from that of the SOEs, suggesting that the FIEs have not become fully embedded in the local innovation system. This can be explained by the fact that most of the R&D function of MNEs is located at the company headquarters rather than at the subsidiaries and that many FIEs in China are not interacting with potential local research partners because of their concerns regarding weak intellectual property protection in China.

Privately owned firms are more responsive than SOEs. They use open innovation to overcome the constraints to innovation, especially institution- and market-related constraints and finance- and risks-related impediments. This is consistent with the current weak political status of POEs and the lack of financial support to them in China. Interestingly, POEs do not appear to be responsive to knowledge- and skills-related constraints through adoption of open innovation. This may be explained by the fact that, despite requiring external innovation sources, it is difficult to broaden or deepen openness in a genuine way if the firm does not possess adequate absorptive capacity and previous collaboration experiences. In other words, when absorptive capacity is not enough to make innovators confident of 'going outside', some firms may not choose an open strategy and become more conservative instead. Our statistical results also show that absorptive capacity (proxied using R&D intensity) has significant effects on openness, which suggests that absorptive capacity is essential to launching openness in innovation. This may explain why privately owned firms do not appear to be responsive to knowledge- and skills-related constraints using open innovation.

Third, firms' responses to the various constraints appear to vary by firm size and industry, especially in terms of the depth of openness. Smaller firms are more likely to undertake deep engagement in open innovation to overcome financial constraints and share risks in innovation, whereas larger firms are more likely to do so to overcome constraints in knowledge and skills. Firms in high-technology industries are more likely to respond to constraints in finance and skills by engaging in deeper open innovation. However, in the light of institutional constraints, firms in medium- and low-technology industries are more likely to use open innovation to overcome this constraint than firms in a high-technology industry.

Finally, our findings reveal some essential differences with the existing conclusions in the literature developed in the context of Western countries. Innovation leaders, mainly from developed countries, adopt open innovation as a new innovation model as a result of the strong capacity and resources they enjoy. In contrast, latecomers, especially in developing countries, do their best to increase openness in innovation, but they have to overcome additional constraints in their capability and resources if they are to learn and catch up.

Admittedly, this research has some limitations. First, the determinants of openness in emerging economies are diverse and variable because of different types and processes of open innovation (outside-in, inside-out, coupled, etc.), which should be examined more deeply and comprehensively. Future research will benefit from more comprehensive analyses based on a purposefully designed survey to understand the drivers of open innovation. Moreover, future studies should employ panel data sets to capture the dynamics in firms' responses to the various constraints and risks and the evolution over time. Finally, opening up within and outside the country will present different challenges and also different effects on a firm's innovation performance. Future research should explore these differences in the determinants and impact of openness along these two dimensions.

APPENDIX 7.1

Detailed questions used as basis of the estimation of the constraints and risks scores

1. Market- and institution-related constraints:
   (1) Market is dominated or controlled by major competitors (M1)
   (2) Over-competition in the industry (M2)
   (3) Profit rate in the industry is too low (M3)
   (4) Peer firms in the same industry rarely engage in innovation (M4)
   (5) Technological gap between the firm and main competitors is too large (M5)
   (6) There is uncertainty about the demand of the new product (M6)
   (7) No innovation due to: the market lacks demand for technology innovation
   (8) No innovation due to: lack of IPR protection to innovation outcome
   (9) No innovation due to: uncertainty or restriction of the standards in the industry
2. Financial constraints and risk-related impediments
   (1) Economic risks are too large in relation to technological innovation (C1)
   (2) Innovation requires too high an investment (C2)
   (3) Financing costs for innovation are too high (C3)
   (4) Existing financing channels cannot support large innovation (C4)
   (5) No innovation due to: lack of the necessary funds for innovation

3. Knowledge- and skill-related impediments:
   (1) Lack of science and technology personnel (K1)
   (2) Lack of accumulated technological capacity (K2)
   (3) Lack of relevant technology information (K3)
   (4) Lack of relevant market information (K4)
   (5) Lack of partners for innovation (K5)
   (6) No innovation due to: lack of necessary human resources for innovation
   (7) No innovation due to: existing technology available

8 The dual role of universities in industrial innovation
Comparing China and the UK

8.1 Introduction

As an important player in national and regional innovation systems, universities have received increasing attention with respect to their role in innovation, competitiveness and wider social and economic development. Universities are widely regarded as a major contributor to advances in basic scientific research and the creation of innovation of great novelty. Moreover, recent research also suggests that the role of universities is multi-faceted, covering educating, knowledge creation in the form of scholarly publications and patents, problem-solving activities and public space provision (Hughes, 2010). However, most of the received wisdom on the role of universities is based on experiences and evidences from the developed countries. The role of universities in innovation in developing countries, especially the middle-income emerging economies, has received much less attention.

This chapter attempts to examine the role of universities in the emerging developing economies using comparative firm-level analysis of the innovation effects of universities in China and the UK. It argues that universities have two roles in industrial innovation in emerging countries in addition to their educational contribution. One is that they serve the traditional role of knowledge creation in the fields of basic and applied scientific research and hence the generation of innovation of great novelty. The other is that they decipher and adapt advanced foreign technology that is transferred to the developing countries. Their collaboration with industry facilitates the birth of many forms of innovation that are new to the country and/or particular firms in the emerging economies. The importance of the latter role is likely to be greater than the former in the emerging economies. China provides a good case for research given its quickly improving performance in innovation in recent years and the great effort made by the government in encouraging university-based research and technology transfer (Wu, 2007; Fu and Soete, 2010). The UK provides a classical benchmark for the analysis as one of the major developed economies in the world and a country with an excellent university sector.

The remainder of the chapter is organised as follows: Section 8.2 discusses the literature and the theoretical framework. Section 8.3 presents a brief overview of the university sector and its role in the national innovation system in China. Section 8.4 discusses the methodology and data. Section 8.5 presents the results. Section 8.6 presents conclusions.

8.2 The literature and theoretical framework

The literature on national and regional innovation systems has highlighted the role of universities in the innovation systems, not only in training and education but also as active players in knowledge creation and transfer (Nelson, 1986; Porter and Stern, 1999; Fu and Yang, 2009). Universities may contribute to an economy in a multi-faceted manner through education, knowledge creation in the form of scholarly publications and patents, problem-solving activities and public space provision (Cosh, Hughes and Lester, 2006; Kitson et al., 2009; Hughes, 2010). They disseminate knowledge to the real economy by producing qualified students and by interacting with firms through a number of channels such as consulting, licensing, and co-operative research programmes (Eom and Lee, 2010). In the era of the knowledge economy, the importance of universities in contributing to economic growth has become an increasing focus of research (Etzkowitz and Leydesdorff, 2000; Sainsbury, 2007). Fast-paced global competition and technological change also link firms to universities not only through the discovery of knowledge but also by aiding industrialisation (Etzkowitz and Leydesdorff, 1997; Hwang et al., 2003).

Two contrasting views exist regarding the role of a university. The *Triple Helix thesis* argues that universities should form direct links with industry to maximise capitalisation of knowledge and hence serve the need for economic development (Etzkowitz and Leydesdorff, 1997, 2000). In contrast, the so-called *New Economics of Science* states that too close a relationship between science and industry and short-run policies that move resources into commercial applications of scientific knowledge would jeopardise scientific advancement over the long run (e.g., Dasgupta and David, 1994). Criticising any application of both theories to developing countries, Eun, Lee and Wu (2006) suggest a 'contingent or context-specific' perspective on industry-university relationships and that the question as to whether a university should take part in the functioning of an industry should be answered by considering the internal resources of the university, the absorptive capacity of the industries and the existence of intermediate institutions.

The emergence of open innovation as a new mode of innovation suggests that universities may play an increasingly significant role in industrial innovation (Chesbrough, 2003). Technological convergence, declining transaction costs of acquiring external R&D inputs and the shortening of product development cycle times have accelerated the trend of utilising external sources of knowledge (Grandstrand et al., 1992). Collaborations with various partners, both public and private, are important sources of knowledge that directly strengthen firms' technological competences and may thus increase their capacity to innovate (Freeman and Soete, 1997; Kitson et al., 2009. Collaborations among organisations facilitate the attainment of complementary assets related to innovative labour and allow firms to achieve the goals that they cannot pursue alone (Mowery, Oxley and Silverman, 1996; Powell and Grodal, 2005). Moreover, collaborations in innovation are found to be complementary to in-house R&D and facilitate inter-organisational, or international knowledge transfer. Collaborations with customers, suppliers, higher education institutions, and even competitors allow firms to expand their range of expertise, develop specialised products and achieve various other corporate objectives (Porter and Stern, 1999). With sector and size variations, networking is found to be positively associated with innovation (Goes and Park, 1997; Tsai, 2001). Firms embedded in benefit-rich networks are likely to have greater innovative performance (Powell, Koput and Smith-Doerr, 1996). By sharing complementary knowledge and skills, firms can break through the bottleneck that constrains their innovation activities and enable the innovation creation process to be more efficient (Fu et al., 2011). UK Community Innovation Survey data suggest that global engagement in UK firms' innovation is also found to be associated with a higher propensity to innovate (Criscuolo, Haskel and Slaughter, 2005). Yet, as argued by Laursen and Salter (2006), the benefits from openness to external knowledge and resources are subject to decreasing returns as 'over-searching' and working with too many partners will have negative consequences for innovation efficiency.

Given the widely recognised role of universities in the national innovation system, university-firm collaboration is argued to be crucial for the promotion of technological change (Mansfield and Lee, 1996). A growing number of developed and developing countries are seeking to use universities as important drivers of knowledge-based economic development and change (Mowery and Sampat, 2005). Through interaction with the science base, firms are able to access a diversified range of knowledge sources in comparison to intra-firm collaboration (Kaufmann and Todtling, 2001). University participation in research programmes is also found to have a positive impact on firm patenting (Darby, Zucker and Wang, 2003). Public research is also found to have not only initiated new R&D projects but also to have contributed to the completion of existing projects in the U.S. manufacturing sector (Cohen, Nelson and Walsh, 2002). In sum, contracting out research, entering into university-industry alliances and collaborating with university researchers formally or informally can confer substantial advantages.

However, the role of universities in innovation is multi-faceted (Hughes, 2010). Universities may struggle in terms of reconciling the creation of new knowledge regardless of its commercial or innovative value and their role as promoters of technological development (Mowery and Sampat, 2005). The extent of development of an economy will influence the role of its universities in several ways. First, the extent of development of an economy will determine the level of its indigenous technological and innovation capabilities and the major source of technology upgrading. Owing to the lack of sufficient absorptive capacity in the local industry, there is a need to tap into the expertise of science and engineering experts in the universities. Second, the extent of development of an economy is often in line with the level of research capabilities of its universities and hence the type of innovation they are to create. Finally, the extent of development of an economy determines the type of industrial and technology policies the government will adopt to promote economic growth, which in turn affects the type of demand for university research.

In the middle-income emerging economies, given the level of development and the research capabilities of the economy, universities are likely to have a dual role in the innovation of firms in addition to their educational contribution. First, innovation is costly, risky and path dependent. This provides a rationale for developing countries to use foreign technology acquisition as a major source of technological development. Foreign sources of technology account for a large part of productivity growth in most countries. In fact, most innovation activities are largely concentrated in a few developed countries: the United States, Japan and a number of European countries. International technology diffusion will therefore be an important driver in economic growth. Hence, in the middle-income emerging economies, which are at an intermediate stage of development, the assimilation of foreign technology has been a major source of technology upgrading, and innovation. The innovation that is groundbreaking at the national or firm level will be the major type of innovation in these economies. Moreover, most of the firms in these economies are lacking an absorptive capacity (Eun et al., 2006). Therefore, there is a real demand from the industrial sector for external technological experts to help with the assimilation and adaptation of foreign technology. Linkages with universities will help accelerate the adoption of foreign technology.

Furthermore, the middle-income emerging economies have a higher education sector that is relatively stronger than that of the rest of the developing countries. Therefore, universities and especially elite universities in the middle-income emerging economies are capable of collaborating with the industrial sector to assimilate the transferred foreign technology and make the adaptations necessary for the foreign technology to fit within the local technical, economic and social context. Some of the industry-university alliances are not only capable of shallow assimilation (which facilitates the normal operation of the imported equipment in recipient firms) but also deep assimilation of foreign technology through reverse engineering and R&D to make modifications to the transferred foreign technology. This may lead to the transition from imitation to innovation and the creation of innovations that are groundbreaking at the world level. Moreover, knowledge transfer from universities, which is often embodied in codified forms (e.g., publications, patents, contract R&D projects) and which also often contains tacit knowledge (e.g., collaborative research, informal consultation), becomes in this way an important asset in creating learning organisations. Of course, we should not be overly optimistic about the role of universities in this respect in the middle-income emerging economies. Admittedly, there is a gap between the universities in these economies and those of the major developed economies, especially in terms of research quality and impact. Even in one of the fields of emergent technologies, where the emerging economies might claim a lead based on the number of scientific publications, further analysis of the citation share as well as surrogate indicators show the need for China to improve its research impact (Guan and Ma, 2007).

Finally, the level of development of an economy determines the type of industrial and technology policies the government will adopt to promote economic growth, which in turn affects the type of demand for university research. For example, in the United States and the United Kingdom (UK), research universities are simultaneously centres of learning, the foci of basic and applied research and the source of entrepreneurship. In Asian countries such as China, Korea and Singapore, universities have been geared towards training and only recently have begun to pay more attention to research. Elite universities, prompted by government incentives, have started to contribute to technology deepening (Hershberg, Nabeshima and Yusuf, 2007). Unlike the many Western countries that have experienced a transition in science policy from one driven by curiosity to one driven by practical needs and uses, the Chinese government has been advocating from the start a use-driven science policy, requiring universities to serve the national economy by solving practical problems for industry (Hong, 2006). Universities were encouraged to collaborate closely with industry, for example, in solving production problems for factories (Ministry of Education, 1999; Yuan, 2002). Reflections lead to the following hypothesis:

H8-1:   Universities have two roles in industrial innovation in emerging countries in addition to their educational role.

They serve the traditional role of knowledge creation in the field of basic and applied sciences and hence the generation of novel innovations. They also decipher and adapt advanced foreign technology that is transferred to the developing countries. Their collaboration with industries facilitated the diffusion of innovation that can be considered new at the country or firm level in the emerging economies. The importance of the latter role is likely to be greater than the former in the emerging economies.

8.3 Universities and industrial innovation in China

The swift rise of the Chinese economy has been accompanied by the rapid development of its technological capabilities. While acquisition of foreign technology has been a major strategy in the first two decades since the reforms of 1978, the decade since then has witnessed rapid growth in domestic R&D investment. The expenditure on R&D has increased exponentially. In 2010, the total R&D expenditure in China was greater than that of Germany, the UK and France and ranked third in the world, after the United States and Japan. In terms of its gross R&D expenditure to GDP ratio, China is now moving close to the EU average and aims to reach 2.5 per cent by 2020. Moreover, since 2000, China has experienced a rapid surge in patent applications. The number of patent applications from Chinese researchers to the authorities of the so-called Triadic Patent Families has increased more than seven times from 2000 to 2007.[1] China's share in science and engineering articles has risen sixfold since the mid-1990s, from 9,000 to nearly 57,000 each year, accounting for 7 per cent of the global research output in 2007 (Fu, Pietrobelli and Soete, 2010; Gilman, 2010).

Transiting from a centrally planned to a market economy, universities in China have historically played an important role in its national innovation system, similar to that of the science and technology system in the former Soviet Union (Liu and White, 2001). In terms of R&D expenditure and patents, universities and research institutes played a leading role in China (Li, 2009). Reforms started in 1985 to render the science and innovation system more relevant to the market and signalled a departure from the Soviet model whereby scientific research at public research institutions and production at state-owned enterprises were completely separated (Xue, 1997).

The mid-1980s witnessed several reforms in science policy in China. The most significant change was the cutting of government research funding in order to push research organisations into the market (Hong, 2008). From 1986 to 1993, government research funding decreased at an annual rate of 5 per cent (Zhou et al., 2003). Hence, universities began to establish their own enterprises at that time, a practice officially approved by the central government in 1991. Another wave of reform of Chinese universities began in December 1994 when a national forum

---

[1] These are patents applied for/granted in the United States, Europe and Japan.

encouraged institutional mergers and decentralisation in jurisdiction for efficiency purposes. This decentralisation reform has had the effect of promoting collaborations between universities and local industries (Hong, 2008). In addition, the introduction of a Chinese version of the Bayh-Dole Act allowed universities to retain titles to inventions derived from government funding. Due to this act as well as an act of promoting commercialisation of innovation and development of high-tech industry in 1999, Chinese universities have become even more enthusiastic about transferring knowledge to industry (Hong, 2008).

The Chinese government has been advocating a use-driven science policy since its establishment, encouraging universities to serve the national economy by solving practical problems for industry (Hong, 2006). On the one hand, university-industry linkages in China are built through licensing, consulting, joint or contract R&D and technology services, closely resembling how universities in the West interact with industry. On the other hand, a second form of use-driven innovation occurs as a result of university-affiliated or university-run enterprises (Zhang, 2003; Ma, 2004), a system that is uniquely Chinese. Chinese universities since the market-oriented reforms have had strong incentives to pursue economic gains and strong internal (R&D and other) resources to launch start-ups and thus established their own firms, given the low absorptive capacity of industrial firms and underdeveloped intermediary institutions (Eun et al., 2006). Government-driven spin-off formation has proved an appropriate solution for technology transfer at Chinese universities (Kroll and Liefner, 2008). Economy-wise, the economic reforms have led to a gradual evolution of major players in the national and regional innovation system. The importance of the industrial sector in the innovation system has been increasing over the years, which, combined with a varied performance in the reform of enterprises and opening up to foreign direct investment, has led to increased disparities in innovation across Chinese regions (Fu, 2008; Li, 2009).

8.4 Methodology and data

The empirical test of Hypothesis 8–1 is carried out in two stages. First, a statistical test is used to examine the impact of the university linkage on firms' innovation with differing degrees of novelty, that is, innovations that are groundbreaking at world, country or firm levels.

Second, we compare the pattern observed from Chinese data with that contained in UK data. To explore the effect of the technological and cultural gap on the knowledge transfer through innovation collaboration, we distinguish universities located in a firm's own country, the newly industrialised economies, the EU, the United States, Japan and other countries.

To assess the impact of university collaboration on the innovation performance of industrial firms, we regress a firm's innovation output on its collaboration with universities while controlling for a vector of firm- and industry-specific characteristics.

Measurement of the dependent variable

Here, we measure innovation output by the percentage of innovative sales in total turnover. Innovation could be measured in different ways. One way is to use a dummy variable that equals 1 for innovation and 0 for no innovation. This method, however, would omit detailed information with regard to the extent of innovation. A second widely used measure is R&D expenditure. R&D expenditure itself is, however, in fact one of the *inputs* to innovation. A third widely used indicator of innovation output is the number of patents (Jaffe, 1989; Acs, Luc and Varga, 2002). Although an indicator based on the number of patents has its advantages, it also suffers from the validity problem that patents might not adequately reflect the commercial success and value of new and adapted products (Acs et al., 2002). Some studies use innovation counts (Acs, Luc and Varga, 2002; Feldman, 1999). These also have limitations, however, in terms of reflecting the depth and breadth of innovation success.

For these reasons, we use the sales of new or improved products as a measure of innovation output, as this information is available in the survey data set. In the survey, firms are asked whether, besides being new to their firm, the innovation was also new to the market. This allows a distinction between innovations of the latter kind – which may be termed 'novel' — and innovations of the former kind – which may be considered as 'diffusionary' innovations. As we are interested in the different roles of universities in the creation of groundbreaking novel innovation and in translating, deciphering and adapting transferred foreign technology, we use two dependent variables: the proportion of sales accounted for by products that were groundbreaking at the world level and, second, were new to the country or firm.

Measurement of direct university contribution

We consider a number of variables to capture the direct university contribution to firm innovation through innovation collaboration. We include an indicator of the extent to which the firm co-operates with other organisations and institutions in the course of its innovation activity. This is proxied by a co-operation dummy that equals 1 if firms co-operated in any innovation activities with other enterprises or institutions, such as universities and public research institutions, suppliers of equipment/services/software, clients, competitors, consultants and commercial labs, and 0 otherwise. This allows for a direct test of the question as to whether collaboration significantly influences firm innovation performance. To highlight the role of domestic universities in emerging economies, we distinguish universities located in a firm's own country, the newly industrialised economies, the EU, the United States, Japan and other countries. This also allows us to examine the effects of the technological and cultural gap and hence the appropriateness of foreign knowledge on the strength of benefits from collaborations with universities internationally.

The control variables

The control variables include a group of variables that focus on the extent to which the output of product innovations by a firm is a function of the resources committed to innovative activity. These resources are, first, intramural R&D expenditure and extramural R&D expenditure of the firm. Investment in research and development is often found to be a significant determinant of innovation. Firms engaged in R&D are more likely to innovate because R&D directly creates new products and processes and also because these firms are more receptive to new external ideas. However, some economists (e.g., Baldwin 1997) argue that R&D is neither a necessary nor a sufficient condition for innovation. Moreover, control of the size of extramural R&D is also important as a control over the effects of other types of collaborations, for example, collaboration with suppliers, customers, other firms in the same industry and other firms within the company group. Labour force skills, particularly qualified scientists and engineers, is another widely recognised critical factor that contributes to firm innovation performance (Hoffman et al., 1998; Porter and Stern, 1999). To capture this important element and the extent to which the lack of qualified R&D

personnel can constrain innovative activity, a dummy variable that equals 1 for firms reporting a lack of qualified personnel as being of medium and high importance and 0 for others is also included as a control variable. These inputs not only directly contribute to innovation but also enhance the firms' capacity to recognise and absorb relevant external resources for innovation (Cohen and Levinthal, 1990).

We also include other variables to capture size and age effects as well as industry sector-specific effects. The extent to which a firm may be able to exploit its innovative activity may depend on its size per se and on the degree of competition in its final product markets. Larger firms have a greater range of market opportunities through which to exploit innovative opportunities. The size of the firm can therefore act as a proxy for this enhanced incentive to innovate. From the point of view of smaller firms, the existence of a dominant market position by large firms may inhibit their access to the market and hence their ability to translate innovative activity into a significant proportion of new products in their final sales. However, large firms face conflicting possibilities that may arise from the presence of dominant positions. Moreover, firm age is likely to be associated with firms' innovation activity: older firms may have accumulated more experience and knowledge and be more capable in innovation. Alternatively, older firms may be constrained by organisational rigidity and hence are less active in innovation. Finally, because technological and innovation opportunities may occur unevenly across sectors, we include industry dummy variables to proxy for these effects. The full list of variables is summarised in Table 8.1. The correlation coefficients of the variables in the China and UK samples are shown in Appendixes 8.1 and 8.2.

Two estimation problems arise in this model. The first is that the dependent variable, the percentage of innovative sales, is constrained to a value between 0 and 100 and takes a value of zero in a large proportion of sample. The ordinary least squares (OLS) estimates would thus be biased. Therefore, a Tobit model should be introduced to reduce the problem (Tobin, 1958). Second, a number of firms have not undertaken any R&D activity at all and therefore have no sales of new or significantly improved products. So, there is a selection effect based on the decision to innovate or not. A Hurdle model that was originally suggested by Cragg (1971) as a generalised form of the Tobit model needs to be employed to allow for the fact that firms decide whether or not to innovate and, with respect to those that are innovative, the extent to

Table 8.1 *Definition of variables*

Variable	Definition	Mean
newsal	Percentage of new sales	46.796
newsaln	Percentage of sales of products that are groundbreaking in world terms ('novel')	6.798
newsald	Percentage of sales of products that are new to China or the firm or are significantly improved ('diffusionary')	40.719
lrdin	Ln(intramural R&D expenditure)	5.105
lrdex	Ln(extramural R&D expenditure)	0.906
age	Firm age	16.890
Size4	Firm size dummy equalling 1 for large firm and 0 for small firm	0.714
lack_hc1	Human capital constraints dummy variable, 1 = the importance of lack of qualified personnel to innovation is medium and high; and 0 = low or unimportant	0.797
co	Innovation co-operation dummy variable, 1 = yes, 0 = no	0.634
cogd	Dummy variable, 1 = co-operate with other firms within an enterprise group; 0 = no	0.392
cosd	Dummy variable, 1 = co-operate with suppliers; 0 = no	0.407
cocd	Dummy variable, 1 = co-operate with customers; 0 = no	0.396
copd	Dummy variable, 1 = co-operate with competitors or other firms in the same industry; 0 = no	0.291
coprid	Dummy variable, 1 = co-operate with private R&D institutions; 0 = no	0.243
counid	Dummy variable, 1 = co-operate with universities and public research institutions (PRIs); 0 = no	0.482
couni1	Dummy variable, 1 = co-operate with universities and PRIs in China; 0 = no. Dummy variable, 1 = co-operate with universities and PRIs in the same country; 0 = no	0.476
couni2	Dummy variable, 1 = co-operate with universities and PRIs in newly industrialised countries in East Asia (Hong Kong, Taiwan, Singapore, Korea); 0 = no	0.012
couni3	Dummy variable, 1 = co-operate with universities and PRIs in Europe, the United States and Japan; 0 = no	0.019
couni4	Dummy variable, 1 = co-operate with universities and PRIs in other countries not listed above; 0 = no	0.006
counid_2	Dummy variable (UK), 1 = co-operate with universities and public research institutions (PRIs); 0 = no	0.228
couni1_2	Dummy variable (UK), 1 = co-operate with universities and PRIs in the UK; 0 = no	0.219

Table 8.1 (*cont.*)

Variable	Definition	Mean
couni2_2	Dummy variable (UK), 1 = co-operate with universities and PRIs in Europe; 0 = no	0.029
couni3_2	Dummy variable (UK), 1 = co-operate with universities and PRIs in other countries not listed above; 0 = no	0.016

which they will do so (Mairesse and Monhen, 2002). The significance of the presence of the selection effects is indicated by Rho statistics, which reflect the correlation between the error terms of the two equations. If there are significant selection effects, the Generalised Tobit model (selection in censored data) is preferred. Otherwise, we utilise the standard Tobit model. However, in this study, as innovative firms dominate the China data set (about 95 per cent of firms reported having innovated in terms of their products) and the UK data set has similar characteristics, selection bias is not a significant problem.[2] Nevertheless, we also report the results from the Generalised Tobit model as a robustness check.

Data

The research principally uses the 2008 Chinese national innovation survey of 1,408 manufacturing firms in China: this contains data on firms' innovation activities from 2005 to 2007. The survey was carried out by the National Statistical Bureau. It covers 42 cities in China in both the coastal and inland regions. A total of 1,408 valid responses were received, with a response rate of 83.6 per cent. The questionnaire in the Chinese innovation survey was designed by Tsinghua University and demonstrates high consistency and comparability with the design of the European Community Innovation Survey (CIS). The large and innovative firms that are responsible for most of the R&D activities that take place in China dominate the survey. After careful data cleansing to exclude observations with missing values of the necessary variables, the final data set used in the estimation contains 802 firms, of which 95 per cent have innovated in their products. Therefore, the

[2] This is also attested to by the estimated rho statistics of the selection model. Results are available from the authors subject to request.

results of this study reflect the role of universities in innovative Chinese firms rather than in Chinese firms generally. This is a limitation of the research that we bear in mind when drawing conclusions.

We then benchmark the innovation effects of universities in China against those in the UK. Our sample of UK firms is drawn from the 2005 *Fourth UK Community Innovation Survey* carried out by the Office for National Statistics on behalf of the Department for Innovation, Universities and Skills.[3] The UK survey covered all enterprises with 10 or more employees in almost all industries. The survey received valid responses from 13,986 UK enterprises, including 4,296 firms in the manufacturing sector. The response rate of the survey is 58 per cent. It covers nine regions in England plus Scotland, Wales and Northern Ireland. A postal questionnaire was used and responses were voluntary. The survey provides information on UK innovation during 2002, 2003 and 2004. Admittedly, there is a three-year gap between the UK and the Chinese innovation surveys. However, it is reasonable to assume that the pattern of innovation and the role of universities are unlikely to have experienced big changes in a mature developed economy such as the UK over a short period of three years. Hence, the pattern of the role of universities in firms' innovation from the survey is likely to be equivalent to that experienced from 2005 to 2007: this can in fact be proven by detailed comparison of the persistence and changes in UK innovation within UK CIS4 and CIS5 from 2002 to 2006 (DTI, 2008).

These two national surveys cover firms in the whole economy. Such data cannot be used to make straightforward comparisons because countries differ in the distribution of activity across industries and the distribution of innovative firms by size and sector. These factors have an impact on the requirements for, and likelihood of, access to the universities. Therefore, we match the cleansed smaller Chinese survey data set to the UK survey data set by size of firm, by industry and by product innovation in the prior three years. The last criterion is important in the current study because innovative firms dominate

[3] A copy of the questionnaire can be found at http://www.berr.gov.uk/dius/innova tion/innovation-statistics/cis/cis4-qst/page11578.html. Department for Innovation, Universities and Skills was formerly the Department of Trade and Industry or DTI. In 2007, its functions were transferred to the Department for Business, Enterprise and Regulatory Reform (BERR) and the Department for Innovation, Universities and Skills (DIUS).

the Chinese data and it is important to make the data set comparable in this aspect. By this mechanism, we are able to compare the role of universities in the intensity of producing innovation of different degrees of novelty amongst innovative firms of the same sizes and industry technologies in the UK and China. Because of structural differences between the two surveys, we achieved a comparable UK sample of 793 firms.

8.5 Results

Figures 8.1 and 8.2 report the extent of utilisation of external resources in innovative Chinese firms in terms of the percentage of firms that engaged in innovation collaboration with various types of partners.[4] On average, nearly half of the surveyed Chinese firms report that they collaborated with listed external organisations. Interestingly, universities are the most popular collaborator for Chinese firms, which is not surprising given that, as discussed earlier, historically universities and public research institutions (PRIs) dominated the innovation system in China and a strong government policy pushed the development of university-industry linkages. Most of the universities collaborate with Chinese universities and around 10 per cent of the firms that collaborate with universities collaborate with foreign universities. In comparison, about 40 per cent of the British firms in the matched sample reported cooperation with other organisations, at least in some of their innovation activities. Customers and suppliers appeared to be the most frequently used collaborators of British firms: around 30 per cent of firms have collaborated with customers or suppliers in innovation activities. Universities and PRIs ranked as the fourth most frequently used collaborators, ahead of competitors and private R&D institutions. Domestic universities remain the main university collaborator, but a higher proportion (18 per cent) of collaborative British firms collaborated with

---

[4] The wording in the UK survey on this question is 'co-operation'. Although there is subtle difference in English between collaboration and co-operation, the Chinese wording used in the survey (*he zuo*) does not imply this subtle difference. Firms may regard both arms-length close co-operation and collaboration as being *he zuo*. We therefore translate the wording into 'collaboration', which may include recursive and sustained interactions in addition to arm-length co-operation. This may explain the difference in the China and UK samples in which more Chinese firms report having collaborated with external organisations for innovation.

Figure 8.1 Percentage of innovative Chinese firms reporting R&D collaboration with various types of partners

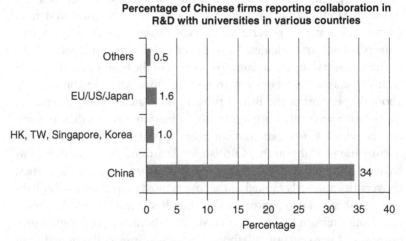

Figure 8.2 Percentage of Chinese firms reporting R&D collaboration with
universities in various countries

foreign universities. In view of the language and cultural differences
between the two economies, direct comparisons of absolute percentages
may not produce rigorous results. However, the pattern of collaboration and the relative importance of various collaborators in the two
economies still provide plausible insights.

Universities and industrial innovation in China

The estimated results of the role of universities in firm innovation in China using the standard Tobit model are reported in Table 8.2. Columns (1) to (3) report the regression results using the percentage of sales of products that are groundbreaking innovations in world terms as the dependent variable; columns (4) to (6) report the results of regressions using innovations that are new to the country or firm and significantly improved products as the dependent variable. The results in columns (1) and (4) suggest that collaborations with other firms or institutions have a positive impact and are significantly associated with the creation of innovations that are new to the world and new to the country/firm. The magnitude of the estimated coefficients is of similar size, but those in the diffusionary innovation regression are of higher significance. However, as shown in columns (2) and (5), collaboration with universities does not appear to have contributed significantly to the process in the country on average. This suggests that although there are individual cases of successful university-industry collaboration induced innovation in China, on average, the contribution of universities to firm innovation is not significant nationwide. Although universities have formed an effective linkage and become a critical source for the industrial innovations in some regions in China, such as Beijing, the fast growth of high-technology industries in many other regions is driven mainly by other sources (Chen and Kenney, 2006).

Breaking down universities according to their country of origin, the estimated results exhibit some interesting findings in columns (3) and (6). Collaboration with domestic universities exhibits a positive but insignificant effect on novel new sales, which can probably be explained by the level of quality and impact of domestic universities in comparison to the world innovation frontier during the sample period (Guan and Ma, 2007). However, the effect regarding diffusion of sales of innovations that are new to the country or firm or significantly improved products is positive and statistically significant. Interestingly, international innovation collaboration between Chinese firms and universities in the newly industrialised economies, namely Hong Kong, Taiwan, Singapore and Korea, appears to have a significant and positive effect on the generation of innovations by Chinese manufacturing firms. Moreover, firms that have collaboration in innovation with universities in countries other than the NIEs and Europe, the United States and

Table 8.2 Universities and firm innovation in China: Tobit model estimates

VARIABLES	Novel innovation			Diffusion innovation		
	1 model	2 model	3 model	4 model	5 model	6 model
co with other organisations	10.40**			9.828***		
	(5.111)			(3.321)		
co with universities		5.344			4.276	
		(5.205)			(3.513)	
co with domestic universities			1.345			5.954*
			(5.094)			(3.532)
co with universities in NIEs			35.67***			-5.64
			(11.25)			(17.1)
co with universities in US/EU/Japan			17.29			-13.58
			(10.72)			(11.04)
co with universities in other countries			35.32**			-8.254
			(15.97)			(16.5)
lrdin	2.106**	1.299	1.203	2.949***	3.007***	2.929***
	(0.865)	(0.937)	(0.921)	(0.544)	(0.589)	(0.595)
lrdex	1.623**	1.623**	1.690***		0.0666	0.0009
	(0.649)	(0.649)	(0.647)		(0.46)	(0.461)
size4	5.967	4.837	3.428	-3.446	-5.144	-5.629
	(5.553)	(5.673)	(5.642)	(3.728)	(3.932)	(3.912)

age	-0.257	-0.244	-0.202	-0.0266	-0.024	-0.0467
	(0.159)	(0.168)	(0.161)	(0.0575)	(0.0603)	(0.0622)
lack_hc1	-1.933	-2.811	-2.645	-2.605	-6.097	-6.154
	(5.134)	(5.171)	(5.067)	(3.63)	(3.874)	(3.869)
Industry dummies	yes	yes	yes	yes	yes	yes
Constant	yes	yes	yes	yes	yes	yes
Observations	928	817	817	910	802	802
F statistics	6.293	5.218	5.73	7.746	5.116	3.445
Log Likelihood	-1454	-1298	-1291	-3741	-3320	-3314

Note: Robust standard errors in parentheses; ***p<0.01, **p<0.05, *p<0.1.

Japan, such as Russia, Israel, India and Brazil, have a significantly higher proportion of sales on accounted for by products that are new to the world. Surprisingly, linkages with universities in the major industrialised economies (i.e., the United States, Japan and Europe), although showing a positive effect, involve an estimated coefficient that is not statistically significant. This may be explained by the technology and culture gap between China and these industrialised economies and the appropriateness of the foreign knowledge of the receiving economy. Further research is needed to investigate why collaboration with this group of highly regarded universities is less fruitful for Chinese industrial enterprises.

Firms' intramural R&D appears to be insignificantly associated with their sales intensity of novel products after controlling for extramural R&D spending but is positive and significantly associated with their diffusion of new sales. This result is consistent with the work of Fu and Gong (2010), which examines the effect of indigenous R&D activities on technology upgrading in China using a large firm-level panel data set produced by the National Statistical Bureau. In contrast, firms' spending on extramural R&D activities exerts a positive and significant effect on firms' novelty of new sales but not on the diffusion of innovation. This highlights the importance of the utilisation of external innovation resources and extramural R&D activities for the creation of innovation involving products that are groundbreaking in world terms by middle-income emerging economies. Firm size and age do not appear to affect the percentage of innovative sales of firms significantly. Although the estimated coefficient of the constraints in the R&D personnel dummy bears the expected negative sign, it is not statistically significant either.

Table 8.3 reports the results of a robustness check using the Generalised Tobit model to correct for potential selection bias. The estimated results are broadly consistent with the standard Tobit model estimates, especially in respect of the effect of university-industry collaboration. The estimated coefficient of the university collaboration variable remains positive and statistically insignificant, whereas the pattern of the influence of universities by country of origin remains highly similar to that in Table 8.2. The effect of collaboration with domestic universities remains significant for the diffusion of new sales but not of novel new sales. International innovation collaboration with foreign universities in the NIEs, major industrialised economies and other countries all demonstrate a positive and significant effect. The

Table 8.3 *Robustness check: Generalised Tobit model estimates*

	Novel innovation			Diffusion innovation		
	1	2	3	4	5	6
co with other organisations	2.3			6.250**		
	(1.442)			(2.824)		
co with universities		2.111			3.967	
		(1.414)			(2.786)	
co with domestic universities			1.045			5.239*
			(1.402)			(2.779)
co with universities in NIEs			12.09**			-0.693
			(5.914)			(11.99)
co with universities in US/EU/Japan			8.429*			-8.014
			(4.696)			(9.338)
co with universities in other countries			17.08**			-5.956
			(8.088)			(15.87)
lrdin	0.409*	0.357	0.267	2.308***	2.331***	2.329***
	(0.213)	(0.224)	(0.227)	(0.427)	(0.453)	(0.45)
lrdex	0.105	0.105	0.119		0.197	0.108
	(0.185)	(0.185)	(0.184)		(0.363)	(0.363)
size4	0.729	0.856	0.397	-5.874**	-5.220*	-5.732*
	(1.502)	(1.498)	(1.501)	(2.962)	(2.968)	(2.979)
age	-0.0534*	-0.0563*	-0.0479	-0.0213	-0.0237	-0.0403
	(0.030)	(0.030)	(0.030)	(0.058)	(0.059)	(0.059)

Table 8.3 (*cont.*)

	Novel innovation			Diffusion innovation		
	1	2	3	4	5	6
lack_hc1	-0.205	-0.468	-0.484	-4.728	-5.600*	-6.201**
	(1.613)	(1.573)	(1.557)	(3.171)	(3.104)	(3.112)
Industry dummies	yes	yes	yes	yes	yes	yes
Constant	yes	yes	yes	yes	yes	yes
Observations	817	817	817	802	802	802
Log Likelihood	-3366	-3367	-3354	-3815	-3819	-3813

Note: Robust standard errors in parentheses; ***p<0.01, **p<0.05, *p<0.1.

level of significance of the estimated coefficients of the NIE and other university collaboration dummies is greater than that of the US/Japan/EU university collaboration dummy, indicating the effectiveness of the former two types of international university linkage. This is, to a certain extent, consistent with the findings from Table 8.2. As regards the control variables, smaller firms appear to have greater diffusion of new sales, and younger firms appear to create more novel innovations. In sum, the results on the role of universities in firm innovation are robust in the main, having allowed for any possible selection bias.

The collaboration variable is arguably determined simultaneously with the dependent variable of innovation. In other words, there might be a potential endogeneity problem. For example, firms that collaborate with other firms and universities are more likely to have more innovative sales. However, it is also possible that more innovative firms might collaborate to a greater extent with other firms and universities. Moreover, they are also more likely to be invited into any innovation collaboration by other organisations. To deal with the potential problem of endogeneity, we employ an instrumental variable regression technique. The instrumental variables used are all the exogenous variables in the model with the addition of four extra exogenous variables, including a firm location dummy that indicates whether a firm is located in the six university-concentrated cities, a group dummy that equals 1 for firms belonging to a corporation group, the importance of information from universities for firm innovation and competition in the industry. Moreover, the use of industry dummies in the regressions is also designed to mitigate part of this potential endogeneity problem. We test whether the assumption of endogeneity is borne out by the data at hand. The Wald tests of exogeneity of the collaboration variables suggest no significant endogeneity problem. Therefore, the standard Tobit model estimates are preferred to the instrumental variable model estimates. Nevertheless, we report the estimated results in Table 8.4 as a robustness check. Consistent with the picture revealed in Tables 8.2 and 8.3, the effect of university collaboration remains insignificant for firm innovation, of both novel and diffusionary types. However, the impact of the general collaboration variable also becomes insignificant using the instrumental variable estimates. Note, however, that because the Wald test of exogeneity indicates no significant endogeneity problem, the standard Tobit model estimates should be used as the valid empirical results for the research.

Table 8.4 *Robustness check: instrumental variable model estimates*

	Novel innovation		Diffusion innovation	
	1	2	3	4
co with other organisations	18.68		−13.28	
	(16.23)		(12.53)	
co with universities		7.868		−0.775
		(11.86)		(8.565)
lrdin	0.665	0.998	3.637***	3.172***
	(1.085)	(1.012)	(0.744)	(0.66)
lrdex	1.308*	1.523**	0.466	0.164
	(0.763)	(0.751)	(0.545)	(0.518)
age	−0.24	−0.24	−0.00426	−0.0181
	(0.164)	(0.169)	(0.0657)	(0.0661)
size4	3.417	4.733	−4.457	−5.526
	(5.762)	(5.675)	(4.129)	(3.923)
lack_hc1	1.606	−2.302	−10.05*	−6.408
	(6.547)	(5.323)	(5.407)	(4.136)
Industry dummies	Yes	yes	yes	yes
Constant	Yes	yes	yes	yes
Observations	816	816	801	801
Log Likelihood	−1691	−1679	−3693	−3680
Wald test of exogeneity (p-value)	0.424	0.768	0.077	0.473

Note: Robust standard errors in parentheses; ***p<0.01, **p<0.05, *p<0.1.
Instrumental variables used are all the exogenous variables in the model and four extra exogenous variables including a firm location dummy indicating whether a firm is located in the six university-concentrated cities, a group dummy that equals 1 for firms belonging to a corporation group, the importance of information from universities for firm innovation and competition in the industry.

Universities and industrial innovation in university-concentrated Chinese cities

Chen and Kenney (2007) found that each Chinese region reacted differently to the government policy of promotion of university-industry linkage. In Beijing, universities and research institutions are a critical source of knowledge. However, in Shenzhen, the rapid growth of high-technology firms did not rely on direct linkages with universities. Moreover, geographical proximity to universities facilitates greater industry-university collaboration. As the geographical distribution of research universities in China is uneven, the impact of universities may be greater in these cities but weak in the remaining cities and regions. Table 8.5 reports estimated results of the contribution of universities to firm innovation in selected university-concentrated cities, namely Beijing, Shanghai, Nanjing, Xian, Wuhan and Chongqing. Consistent with the pattern shown in Tables 8.2 and 8.3,

Table 8.5 *Universities and firm innovation in selected university-concentrated cities in China*

	Novel innovation	Diffusion innovation
	1	2
co with domestic universities	1.297	15.31*
	(14.14)	(8.044)
co with universities in NIEs	5.047	3.239
	(28.14)	(11.00)
co with universities in US/EU/Japan	26.98	4.418
	(25.52)	(8.481)
co with universities in other countries	50.65***	30.68***
	(12.52)	(6.164)
lrdin	0.429	2.076
	(2.307)	(1.375)
lrdex	0.372	−1.184
	(1.603)	(1.078)
age	−0.673*	0.121
	(0.385)	(0.157)
size4	23.57	−38.92***
	(20.84)	(11.02)
lack_hc1	13.99	−6.06
	(16.87)	(11.10)
Industry dummies	Yes	yes
Constant	Yes	yes
Observations	123	117
Log Likelihood	−175.6	−498.8

Note: Robust standard errors in parentheses; ***p<0.01, **p<0.05, *p<0.1.
The six selected university-concentrated cities are Beijing, Shanghai, Nanjin, Wuhan, Xian and Chongqing.

domestic Chinese universities again appear to have a significant effect on the creation of diffusionary innovations in Chinese firms, whereas their effect on novel innovation is insignificant. However, the size of the estimated coefficient of the domestic universities variable is almost three times that in Table 8.2, suggesting a greater innovation effect by universities in these major cities than in the economy as a whole. The effect of international collaboration with universities in other countries also appears to be much larger in these major cities than in the whole economy. However, the impact of collaboration with universities in NIEs loses its statistical significance in the six-city small sample. This is probably because universities in the NIEs collaborate more with firms in some cities in the coastal medium- or small-sized cities, such as Shenzhen, Guangzhou, Zhejiang and Fujian, rather than those six domestic university-concentrated major cities.

Universities and industrial innovation in the UK

Figures 8.3 and 8.4 report the proportions of firms that collaborate in R&D with external partners and with universities in particular from 2002 to 2004. On average, 39 per cent of British firms have engaged

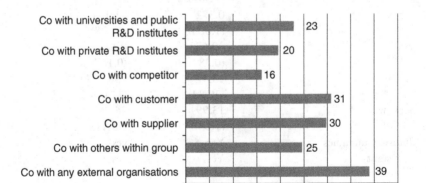

Figure 8.3 Percentage of UK firms reporting R&D collaboration with various types of partners
Note: For matched UK sample.

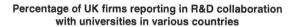

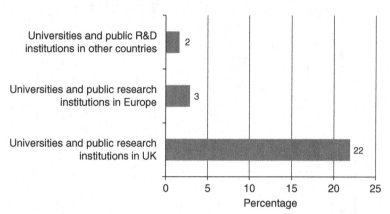

Figure 8.4 Percentage of UK firms reporting R&D collaboration with universities in various countries
Note: For matched UK sample.

with external organisations for collaborative innovation. The most popular partners for collaborative innovation in the UK are customers and suppliers. On average, about 31 per cent of firms report that they have collaborated with customers for innovation, and 30 per cent of firms report collaboration with suppliers. The proportion of firms that have collaborated with universities is 23 per cent, which is 12 per cent lower than that in the China sample. This may be partly the result of the strong government encouragement of university-industry linkage in China. But it may also be because the China sample is biased towards innovative large firms and hence not a representative sample of all the firms in China, whereas that of the UK survey is. Most of the British firms collaborated with domestic universities. About 3 per cent of the firms collaborated with universities and research institutions in Europe, and only about 2 per cent collaborated with such academic partners in other countries.

Table 8.6 reports the Tobit model estimates of the UK sample match by size, sector and product innovation status. We also report the estimates of the full UK manufacturing sample to examine any differences between the matched sample and the UK firm population that may be caused by structural differences in industry, size and innovativeness

Table 8.6 Universities and firm innovation in the UK: standard Tobit model estimates

	Matched sample						Manufacturing full sample					
	Novel innovation			Diffusion innovation			Novel innovation			Diffusion innovation		
	1	2	3	4	5	6	7	8	9	10	11	12
co with other organisations	4.514** (1.820)			1.687 (1.831)			12.92*** (1.351)			13.37*** (1.367)		
co with universities		1.641 (2.128)			0.650 (2.392)			9.834*** (1.685)			7.353*** (1.803)	
co with domestic universities			4.754** (2.222)			1.326 (2.337)			9.613*** (1.733)			6.727*** (1.850)
co with universities in Europe			-4.584 (4.061)			6.345 (6.681)			0.993 (5.001)			4.638 (5.559)
co with universities in other countries			-4.08 (5.586)			-3.866 (8.057)			-6.479 (5.432)			-2.601 (6.643)
lrdin	1.238*** (0.275)	1.060*** (0.284)	1.036*** (0.281)	0.138 (0.261)	0.116 (0.275)	0.13 (0.2770)	3.130*** (0.214)	3.121*** (0.222)	3.152*** (0.222)	2.691*** (0.202)	2.814*** (0.207)	2.827*** (0.207)
lrdex	0.864*** (0.32)	0.873*** (0.318)			0.179 (0.298)			0.880*** (0.256)	0.904*** (0.258)		0.711*** (0.268)	0.709*** (0.268)

Size4	-0.511	-0.838	-1.346	-4.283**	-4.272**	-5.184***	-3.525**	-3.807***	-3.804***	-2.550*	-2.419	-2.411
	(1.859)	(1.884)	(1.917)	(1.76)	(1.821)	(1.849)	(1.411)	(1.457)	(1.46)	(1.484)	(1.539)	(1.539)
age	3.535	3.057	2.924	-13.21***	-13.29***	-13.01***	-1.078	-0.893	-1.005	-6.524***	-6.290***	-6.391***
	(3.136)	(3.172)	(3.105)	(4.193)	(4.186)	(4.003)	(1.919)	(1.92)	(1.916)	(2.247)	(2.248)	(2.246)
lack_hc1	0.0986	-0.219	0.19	1.295	1.249	2.222	4.551***	4.298***	4.383***	5.216***	5.143***	5.145***
	(1.737)	(1.734)	(1.725)	(1.685)	(1.689)	(1.676)	(1.139)	(1.14)	(1.143)	(1.175)	(1.18)	(1.185)
Industry dummies	yes	yes	Yes	yes	yes	yes	yes	yes	yes	yes	yes	yes
Constant	yes	yes	Yes	yes	yes	yes	yes	yes	yes	yes	yes	yes
Observations	793	793	793	793	793	793	4,296	4,297	4,297	4,296	4,297	4,297
F	4.665	4.38	2.157	2.242	1.816	1.699	17.35	16.35	15.23	19.03	16.45	15.21
Log Likelihood	(2146	(2144	-2132	-2741	-2741	-2725	-5886	-5907	-5908	-7619	-7652	-7652

Note: Robust standard errors in parentheses; ***p<0.01, **p<0.05, *p<0.1.

distribution. Co-operation with other firms and institutions in general has a positive and significant effect on novel innovation in the matched sample. Its impact is positive but insignificant for diffusionary innovation. This pattern is somewhat different from that in the matched Chinese sample where the effect of collaboration is stronger for diffusionary innovation. In line with the results in China, the estimated coefficients of the university variable are positive and insignificant. Breaking down the universities by their country of origin, collaboration with domestic British universities shows a significant and positive effect on novel innovations reported in British enterprises, whereas its effect is insignificant for diffusionary innovations. This is the opposite of the pattern we observed from the matched Chinese sample. In contrast to the results from China, international collaboration with universities, both in Europe and in other countries, does not appear to have any significant effect on either novel or diffusionary innovation in the British firms. Consistent with the case in China, extramural R&D contributes significantly to novel innovation only. The effects of intramural R&D expenditure also contribute significantly to novel innovation, which is in contrast to the finding that firm-level R&D in Chinese firms is used mainly for assimilation and development and hence contributes less significantly to diffusion innovation. Larger and older firms also appear to have produced less diffusionary innovation. Constraints in R&D personnel do not appear to have any significant effect.

However, in the case of the UK manufacturing sector as a whole, the role of collaboration, especially collaboration with universities generally and with domestic British universities in particular, demonstrates a positive and significant effect on both novel and diffusionary innovations. The contribution of universities is stronger regarding novel innovations than for diffusionary innovations created in British firms. Consistent with the results obtained from the matched UK sample, international innovation collaboration with foreign universities does not show any significant effect for either novel or diffusionary innovations, which raises an interesting question for future research as to why such international collaborations are set up and why they are not effective.

In summary, the results from Table 8.6 suggest that the role of universities in firm innovation in the UK is consistent with the current received wisdom that they contribute to both novel and diffusionary innovation, but their contribution to the creation of innovations that are groundbreaking at the world level is greater than that in relation to diffusionary innovation. However, the role of universities in the emerging economies is different. Collaboration between domestic universities and industries contributes significantly to diffusionary activities in China but less so to innovation that is groundbreaking in world terms. On the other hand, international innovation collaboration with foreign universities, especially those in the NIEs, contributes significantly to the creation of innovation that is novel at the world level in China.

8.6 Conclusions

This chapter attempts to investigate the role of universities in industrial innovation in emerging economies using a firm-level innovation survey database from China. It then benchmarks the Chinese pattern with that from the UK, a classical industrialised economy from which a significant amount of the received wisdom on the role of universities and their role in innovation has developed. One of the key findings of this chapter is that collaboration with domestic universities has played a significant role in the promotion of the diffusion of frontier technology and the creation of innovation outcomes that are groundbreaking at country or firm levels. In contrast to the traditional view that collaboration with universities will lead to greater innovation, a view that is supported by our evidence from the UK, the contribution of domestic universities to the creation of innovation that is groundbreaking in world terms is limited in China.

International innovation collaboration with foreign universities appears to be fruitful in enhancing Chinese firms' capabilities in the creation of innovation outcomes that are groundbreaking in world terms. In particular, innovation collaboration with universities in the NIEs in East Asia, such as Hong Kong, Taiwan, Singapore and Korea, and in countries other than the Western industrialised economies, for example, Russia, Brazil, India and Australia, has proven to be beneficial and effective in promoting novel innovation in Chinese firms. In comparison, collaboration with universities in the Western industrialised economies (the most frequently used innovation partners among foreign universities) does not appear to be as effective and fruitful as expected. The overall pattern of the effectiveness of international university innovation collaboration attests to the argument regarding the importance of technological and cultural gaps and hence the importance of the appropriateness of technology for effective international technology transfer. This is consistent with the theory of directly technical change (Acemoglu, 2002) and the findings from Fu and Gong (2010) that the transfer of Western technology is not effective in promoting indigenous technological capabilities in many Chinese industrial sectors. In contrast, knowledge from universities in the NIEs and the emerging South appears to be more compatible to the Chinese firms. In summary, international universities from compatible economic and technology backgrounds have played a role as a global source of knowledge, contributing to the creation of innovation that is groundbreaking at the world level in the emerging economies. However, this is not the case in the UK, where collaborative linkage with domestic universities is the only form that contributes significantly to industrial innovations in British firms. Nevertheless, future research should investigate in depth, in both China and the UK, the reasons why international innovation collaboration with universities in the most advanced economies functions ineffectively in nurturing novel industrial innovations.

Findings from this research also indicate that when we focus on innovative firms and control for size and industry, universities appear to be the most popular innovation partner for Chinese firms. There is a possible language issue in the definition and interpretation of *he zuo* ('collaboration') and the concept in English of 'co-operation' that may prevent us from a direct comparison of the levels of collaboration/co-operation between countries. Language issues notwithstanding, high percentage of Chinese firms that report having collaborated with universities in innovation activities suggests that the strong government policy push and the marketisation reform of the science and technology system have effectively promoted a strong university-industry linkage in China.

Findings from the current research have important policy and practical implications for firms in both emerging and developing countries with regard to the processes involved in tapping into knowledge and resources from universities to promote innovation. Domestic universities are best positioned to help firms in developing countries assimilate, grasp, adapt and decipher transferred foreign technology. First, given the importance of technology transfer in developing countries, especially in the early stage of industrialisation, policies in the developing countries should greatly promote university-industry collaboration as a means of enhancing the absorptive capacity of the indigenous economy. Second, geographical, technological and cultural proximity have led to a closer relationship between Chinese firms and the NIEs. In these cases, the synergy, compatibility, level of advanced technology and technological gap between the two partners form a creative and knowledge-enriching basis to create innovative ideas, products and processes. Moreover, collaboration with universities from the emerging South also appears to make a robust positive contribution to the production of novel innovations. In recent years, Chinese firms have increasingly established processes of international innovation collaboration with foreign universities following the increasing internationalisation of Chinese firms. For example, Huawei extended investment on technological alliances to a number of foreign universities such as Stanford (US), University of California, Berkeley (US), Imperial College London (UK), University of Surrey (UK), and Poznan University of Technology (Poland) (Fu, 2014). Such efforts also proved to be rewarding. Moreover, China's technology leadership in the solar PV industry is also obtained through collaboration with an Australian university. Therefore, firms in the developing countries seeking international collaboration should not constrain themselves by considering only universities in the Western countries such as the United States, Europe and Japan: universities in the NIEs and the emerging South will provide a more compatible and effective innovation partner in the creation of novel innovation outcomes.

Appendix 8.1 Correlation coefficient in the Chinese sample

China	newsal	newsaln	newsald	lrdin	lrdex	co	cogd	cosd	cocd	copd	coprid	counid	couni1	couni2	couni3	couni4
newsal	1															
newsaln	0.2644	1														
newsald	0.877	−0.2169	1													
lrdin	0.2833	0.1081	0.2292	1												
lrdex	0.1475	0.0611	0.1115	0.4035	1											
co	0.1839	0.0558	0.1618	0.3681	0.3194	1										
cogd	0.1504	0.0199	0.1461	0.2651	0.2141	0.5965	1									
cosd	0.1207	0.0409	0.1099	0.2364	0.222	0.6167	0.5988	1								
cocd	0.1444	0.027	0.1409	0.2093	0.1984	0.6033	0.5267	0.6705	1							
copd	0.1089	0.035	0.1041	0.2228	0.2055	0.4852	0.5151	0.635	0.6112	1						
coprid	0.1145	0.0572	0.0834	0.2041	0.2645	0.433	0.4592	0.5493	0.5227	0.557	1					
counid	0.1616	0.0407	0.1352	0.4018	0.3737	0.7315	0.4151	0.4584	0.4669	0.4329	0.4476	1				
couni1	0.1643	0.0325	0.1421	0.397	0.3645	0.7224	0.4047	0.4537	0.462	0.4302	0.4319	0.9876	1			
couni2	0.0388	0.0763	−0.0005	0.0386	0.0817	0.08	0.0855	0.0804	0.0819	0.1389	0.13	0.1094	0.0633	1		
couni3	0.0389	0.0895	−0.0074	0.0922	0.1019	0.1037	0.1549	0.1292	0.1313	0.1329	0.0904	0.1417	0.0882	0.2474	1	
couni4	0.0655	0.1267	0.0011	0.0725	−0.0419	0.0595	0.0671	0.0633	0.0645	0.053	0.0641	0.0813	0.0506	0.1419	0.2229	1

Appendix 8.2 Correlation coefficient in the matched UK sample

UK	newsal	newsaln	newsald	lrdin	lrdex	co	cogd	cosd	cocd	copd	coprid	counid_2	couni1_2	couni2_2	couni3_2
newsal	1														
newsaln	0.4687	1													
newsald	0.5989	-0.0564	1												
lrdin	0.1323	0.1699	0.0552	1											
lrdex	0.1024	0.146	0.0347	0.3939	1										
co	0.0492	0.075	0.014	0.252	0.3145	1									
cogd	0.0573	0.0433	0.0407	0.2423	0.2978	0.7147	1								
cosd	0.0719	0.0772	0.0384	0.2217	0.2766	0.8147	0.6723	1							
cocd	0.054	0.0632	0.0259	0.2066	0.2658	0.8344	0.7233	0.7433	1						
copd	0.0428	0.0277	0.033	0.1275	0.2364	0.5465	0.5731	0.5505	0.5805	1					
coprid	0.0673	0.0155	0.0675	0.2518	0.3782	0.6169	0.5604	0.5973	0.5947	0.5391	1				
counid_2	0.0414	0.0682	0.009	0.2656	0.3031	0.6806	0.5198	0.5923	0.5879	0.4589	0.6336	1			
couni1_2	0.0518	0.0774	0.0156	0.2564	0.295	0.6635	0.4968	0.5879	0.5708	0.4581	0.6223	0.9749	1		
couni2_2	0.0109	-0.0183	0.0226	0.1026	0.1812	0.2163	0.2503	0.2326	0.2267	0.1909	0.2938	0.3178	0.2352	1	
couni3_2	0.0128	0.01	0.0089	0.158	0.1658	0.1616	0.18	0.1766	0.1721	0.1602	0.2369	0.2374	0.1955	0.4511	1
UK manufacturing full sample															
counid_2	0.1982	0.1631	0.1585	0.3204	0.2874	0.675	0.5251	0.5969	0.6049	0.5036	0.634	1			
couni1_2	0.1918	0.1564	0.1541	0.3119	0.2862	0.6609	0.5079	0.5857	0.5891	0.4943	0.6177	0.9792	1		
couni2_2	0.0755	0.0575	0.0626	0.1417	0.149	0.2196	0.2215	0.2237	0.2203	0.2142	0.2611	0.3254	0.2367	1	
couni3_2	0.0708	0.0539	0.0588	0.1436	0.1438	0.1485	0.1599	0.158	0.16	0.153	0.2052	0.22	0.1922	0.3489	1

9 | Technological learning, tacit knowledge acquisition and industrial upgrading: The Chinese optical fibre and cable industry

9.1 Introduction

Although definitions of technological progress and technological learning may differ, it is clear that technological learning – broadly, the process of accumulation of technological capability to improve competitiveness – can have significant effects on profits and growth (Lee and Lim, 2001; Geroski and Mazzucato, 2002), productivity (Keesing and Lall, 1992), exports (Zahra, Ireland and Hitt, 2000; Ernst, 2004) and innovation (Leonard-Barton, 1995, Zahra, 1996, Padilla and Tunzelman, 2008). The aim of this chapter is to contribute to our understanding of how 'tacit' knowledge – the knowledge embodied in the experience and know-how of workers and researchers – can be acquired through various internal and external knowledge sources as part of the technological learning process.

Technological learning plays a particularly important role in industrialisation: it is vital to understand the processes by which less developed countries can acquire the necessary technologies from developed countries, manage the learning process, move up the value chain and ultimately narrow the currently wide gaps in technology and living standards. Empirically, the experience of the newly industrialised economies (NIEs) of South Korea, Taiwan, Singapore and Hong Kong provides the best examples of the impact of technological learning in practice. The latecomer studies of Pack and Westphal (1986), Lall (1987) and Amsden (1989), as well as the industry-specific studies of the NIEs of Hobday (1995), Kim (1997) and Lee and Lim (2001), clearly demonstrate the impact of technological improvements that transformed poor and technologically backwards countries into modern, affluent and world-leading economies within the space of a generation. As Freeman (1994) states, the study of technological learning is an important building block in economic catch-up, which brings unique transformative value both to the economy and human society.

The literature has thus identified an indisputable and essential role for technological learning in development. However, the existing literature on technological learning so far has tended to treat knowledge as homogenous and has not distinguished knowledge of different natures. The definition of knowledge should include tacit knowledge and explicit, codified knowledge. Expanding the definition in this way raises interesting research questions. For example, are the sources of tacit knowledge the same as those of codified knowledge? Which sources are more effective for tacit knowledge learning than for codified knowledge?

As there has been no systematic research on these questions to date, this chapter is an attempt to study the effective sources of tacit knowledge to understand how such knowledge can be acquired and promoted. To date, this concept has been recognised to be an important element of the internal processes involved in the acquisition of technological knowledge, capabilities and competitive advantage, but there is currently a lack of empirical data and reliable methodologies relating to the investigation of this elusive but essential component of technical learning.[1] This chapter is an attempt to improve our understanding in these areas.

The aim of this chapter is to examine the sources of the acquisition of the tacit form of knowledge through a case study of the Chinese optical fibre and cable industry. The chapter uses an econometric estimation process to determine the impact, if any, of tacit forms of knowledge in the technological learning process via a firm-level survey of 95 optical fibre and cable manufacturers located in China. This Chinese optical fibre and cable industry provides a useful case study for our purposes because the batch process structure of the supply chain separates the industry as a whole into three sub-industries that involve different balances between tacit and explicit knowledge. This allows us to test which of the potential forms of knowledge is more significant in the case of tacit knowledge–intensive sub-industries, and vice versa.

The chapter is organised as follows: Section 9.2 discusses the literature and the theoretical framework. Section 9.3 provides a brief

---

[1] See Kessler, Bierly and Gopalakrishnan (2000) and discussion in Section 9.2.

overview of the Chinese optical fibre and cable industry. Section 9.4 discusses data and methodology. Section 9.5 presents the results, and Section 9.6 provides conclusions.

9.2 External and internal sources of tacit knowledge

The precise meaning of 'technological learning', like many definitions, is subject to dispute and complications. We can distinguish between at least two senses of the term. In the first, 'technological learning' is a description of the trajectory or path that firms or an economy takes to accumulate technological capability. These paths can change over time, becoming shorter or longer as technological capability is accumulated at different rates. This macroeconomic definition adopts a high-level perspective of the learning process. Alternatively, technological learning can be studied in a much more microeconomic sense whereby attention is paid to the processes themselves though which individuals acquire technical knowledge that firms convert into technological capability. In this sense, technological learning is a process itself. This chapter contributes to our understanding of the ways in which tacit knowledge can be acquired. We examine various possible channels of tacit knowledge and, based on the characteristics of tacit knowledge and the relatively sparse literature on this concept, we formulate four hypotheses regarding the relative importance of the different channels to the specific case of the optical fibre and cable industry. The hypotheses are presented at the end of this section and are based on the definitional considerations that we next review.

Within the process-related meaning of the term, certain distinctions can be made. Some authors define technological learning in broad terms,[2] whereas others suggest that it involves more specific processes.[3] A rich literature has developed regarding the internal processes and linkages involved in the technological learning process. Kessler, Bierly and Shanthi (2000) examine the various merits of internal versus

---

[2] Bell and Pavitt (1992) define technological learning (or technological accumulation) as 'any process by which the resources for generating and managing technical changes (technological capabilities) are increased or strengthened'.

[3] A common theme within the works of Amsden (1989), Hobday (1995) and Xie (2004) is that technological learning requires the acquisition (copying or borrowing) of foreign technologies, possibly followed by adaptation and improvement.

external knowledge acquisition and development, finding that internal forms offer advantages in terms of speed of innovation and lasting competitive advantage. Figueiredo (2003) shows how the key features underlying learning processes can influence inter-firm differences in their accumulation of technological capabilities and improve operational performance in a latecomer context.[4] Lokshin, Belderbos and Carree (2007) show that internal and external knowledge forms must be combined in an optimum manner that does not involve the maximisation of either type of approach on its own: in other words, there must be sufficient internal absorptive capacity and in-house R&D must be of the correct standard and type if external technical knowledge is to be used optimally.[5] Similarly, Cassiman and Veugelers (2006) call for further research on complementarities and internal research processes after finding that high-quality internal R&D processes are required to complement external knowledge.[6] A heavy emphasis on examination of internal processes brings the investigation of effective management techniques (e.g., Chen and Qu, 2003) within the scope of research on technological learning.

The extensive literature on technological learning reviewed here has treated tacit and codified knowledge in a bundle. In fact, they are different in the nature of knowledge each of them relates, the way that such knowledge is generated and stored and the transferability of each. Codified knowledge is knowledge that is articulated into formal language, including grammatical statements, mathematical expressions, specifications, manuals and so on. This articulation means that explicit knowledge can be readily transmitted and shared with others. Codified knowledge can also be given a physical form via publications, patents and textbooks. In principle, and allowing for sufficient ability in the learner and sufficiently clear instruction, codified knowledge can be transmitted at a distance in an impersonal manner. The speed with which the recipient assimilates codified knowledge is more a function

---

[4] Figueiredo concludes that rates of technological capability accumulation and improvement in operational performance can be accelerated through the knowledge processes within a company, through devotion of attention to the variety, intensity, functioning and interaction of four identified processes: external knowledge acquisition, internal knowledge acquisition, knowledge socialisation and knowledge codification.

[5] Based on a six-year panel data set covering 304 Dutch manufacturing firms from 1996 to 2001.

[6] Based on a data set covering 1,335 Belgian manufacturing firms in 1993.

of the recipient's intellectual capacity and less a matter of the time spent gaining experience with the subject matter.

Tacit knowledge is personal knowledge embedded in individual experience. It is a type of knowledge that is used by all people, but people do not necessarily find it easy to articulate. Most tacit knowledge can never actually be articulated for 'much of it is not introspectable or verbally articulable (relevant examples of the latter would include our tacit knowledge of grammatical or logical rules, or even of most social conventions)' (Pylyshyn, 1981:603). Tacit knowledge is thus difficult to codify or detach from individual researchers, employees or managers. Therefore, it does not submit to easy transfer by written or other verbalisation (Polanyi, 1967). The transfer of tacit knowledge requires close, personal and ongoing interaction between instructor and learner as well as strong efforts at assimilation. Although tacit knowledge is difficult to define, it exists and is important: the value to a firm of staff with tacit knowledge (experience and know-how) is obvious to all business leaders as a key determinant of a firm's success. Tacit knowledge is harder to copy and is therefore likely to lead to more lasting forms of competitive advantage than external, codified knowledge that is bought in. Therefore, firms that have significant tacit knowledge resources have a competitive advantage over others because tacit knowledge is less susceptible to copying or imitation (Kessler et al., 2000). When applied to the research and technological learning process, such forms of knowledge are correspondingly key to our understanding of success in technological learning and catch-up.

Regardless of the abilities of the learner, tacit knowledge requires significant time to acquire through experience and learning by doing. Once it is acquired, a skilled worker intuitively knows the adjustment to be made to a production process through a slight variance in materials, efforts or technique in a way that an inexperienced new starter would not know and would not be able to glean from an entirely rules-based approach. Learning by being told and learning by observation are two key ways in which to capture tacit knowledge from groups and individuals (Parsaye, 1989). The so-called soft technologies, such as the 'way things are done' in the firm, management practices and learning can be included within characteristics of a tacit nature (Nelson and Winter, 1982).

In sum, tacit knowledge has a few distinctive characteristics. First, it has strong embeddedness in that tacit knowledge is often embedded in the person who owns it and takes a long time to acquire through learning-by-doing. Second, tacit knowledge is difficult to transfer and imperfectly imitable. These defining characteristics of tacit knowledge suggest that it is difficult to transfer from one person (firm) to another person (firm). Given the differences in the nature of the two types of knowledge, the sources and mechanisms for learning and acquisition of them are different. The acquisition of tacit knowledge requires strong self-study, learning-by-doing and sustained interpersonal interaction over time. Therefore, in-house R&D is a crucial source of tacit knowledge because of the strong learning function of R&D (Cohen and Leventhal, 1989). The demand for sustained interpersonal interaction in the transfer of tacit knowledge also suggests that imports of machineries and equipment are not an effective channel for the acquisition of foreign tacit knowledge. Therefore, we have the following hypotheses:

H9–1:   In industries where tacit knowledge is relatively more important, R&D activities are a more important source of tacit knowledge.

H9–2:   In industries where tacit knowledge is relatively more important, imports of foreign equipment/technology are a less important source of tacit knowledge.

Tacit technological knowledge, for example, experiences and know-how, can have considerable industry specificity. Technological know-how accumulated in peer firms can have great relevance to firms in that industry. Such know-how can be diffused through movement of labour, industry association conferences and meetings, social networks and other formal or informal interpersonal interactions. Therefore, we have the following hypothesis:

H9–3:   In industries where tacit knowledge is relatively more important, peer firms in the same industry are a more important source of tacit knowledge.

Compared to the other three sources (R&D, imports and linkages with firms in the same industry), universities are likely to be sources of *both* tacit and codified knowledge. Tacit knowledge can be gained via collaborative research with universities and informal and formal consulting initiatives, whereas publications, patents, R&D project outputs and licensing are important forms of codified university knowledge (Etzkowitz and Leydesdorff, 1997; Hong, 2008; Eom and Lee, 2010).

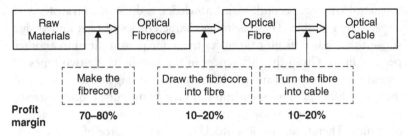

Figure 9.1 The production chain in the optical fibre and cable industry

In the process of transfer of tacit knowledge from universities, collaborative research and informal consultation play more of a role than publications and patents (Hong, 2008). These insights suggest the following hypotheses:

H9–4a: Universities are effective sources for the transfer of both codified and tacit knowledge.

H9–4b: The importance of universities is likely to be similar in industries in which tacit knowledge is relatively more important and those in which it is not.

9.3 The Chinese optical fibre and cable industry: an overview

The optical fibre and cable industry is neither an assembly industry such as automobiles nor a continuous process industry such as steel. Instead, it is a batch process industry that consists of three independent continuous processes in the (1) fibrecore, (2) fibre and (3) cable sub-industries as shown in Figure 9.1. Although the Chinese optical fibre and cable industry originated in the late 1970s at the Wuhan Research Institute of Post and Telecommunication, large-scale operations only began in 1984. From 1984 to 1986, seven optical fibre manufacturers, all state owned, including Beijing Glass Factory, Shanghai Quartz Glass Factory and Shanxi Taiyuan Mine Wool Factory, introduced 34 forms of fibrecore manufacturing equipment and 17 draw-benches from British Special Gas Control (SGC) at an average expense of US$20 million. However, all seven pioneers left the market before 1991 mainly because of the high cost of absorbing technical know-how and the lack of complementary industries.

From 1991 onwards, the industry experienced large-scale growth and expansion when technological learning became market driven and started from the basis of the least technologically sophisticated sub-industry of cable production rather than the most technology-intensive fibrecore manufacturing sub-industry. Indigenous capabilities upgraded gradually from cable manufacturing to fibre manufacturing and then to fibrecore manufacturing. Up to 2006, the market supply exceeded 20 million kilometres of core and total sales achieved were US$600 million, meaning that the Chinese optical fibre and cable industry underwent a boom and became the second largest in the world.

The fibrecore is crucial to the performance and quality of both fibre and cable. The technical barrier and process requirements are high in the manufacture of fibrecore. Initially, most indigenous SOEs attempted to adopt a relevant learning path involving digestion and absorption of the technology at the upstream fibrecore stage but were unsuccessful. After this tremendous failure at the first stage, most indigenous firms, especially those private firms without government support, started to operate at the downstream stage of the industry, importing fibre and producing cable from fibre. The relatively low technological requirements of this process enabled indigenous firms to expand their production capacity and achieve economies of scale. At the same time, some firms also attempted to set up joint ventures with foreign companies to promote in-depth technological co-operation. From 2000 on, market opportunities, technological learning and various collaborations allowed indigenous enterprises to engage successfully in fibrecore production.

9.4 Data and methodology

Data

This chapter uses firm-level survey data relating to all firms in the optical fibre and cable industries in China. Questionnaires were sent to the presidents, vice-presidents or chief engineers of each enterprise asking them to provide self-assessments on a list of questions regarding their sources and experiences of technological learning. The answers to these questions were scored using a Likert scale with labels of 'strongly disagree' assigned a numeric value of 1 and 'strongly agree' assigned a numeric value of 7.

In total, 103 questionnaires were returned representing a response rate of 95 per cent. After data cleansing, the final data set included

Table 9.1 *Perception of the technological characteristics of the optical fibre and cable industry*

Statements	Mean	Std. Dev.
Tacit knowledge (operating techniques and know-how) in fibrecore manufacturing is significant	5.81	1.075
Tacit knowledge (operating techniques and know-how) in fibre manufacturing is significant	5.54	1.114
Tacit knowledge (operating techniques and know-how) in cable manufacturing is significant	4.49	1.015

95 firms representing 87 per cent of the population. Most of the respondents agreed that the production of cable helps a firm master fibre technology and that the production of fibre has similar benefits in terms of the fibrecore technology. The scores on intensity of tacit knowledge show that it rises consistently as we move upstream in the production chain of the optical fibre industry; that is, tacit knowledge is most intensive in the fibre core industry but relatively less significant as we move to consider production of fibre and cable, respectively (Table 9.1). Table 9.2 summarises the definition and the descriptive statistics of the variables. The survey covers the whole population of firms in this industry; therefore, we can expect the results to be consistent and representative. However, as the data capture results at a single point in time, the study does not provide any analysis of causal relationships.

Methodology

We test the effectiveness of different sources of tacit knowledge by testing the importance of these sources in firms' competitiveness in industries of low and high intensity of tacit knowledge. The literature has found a robust linkage between technological learning and firm performance in the areas of profits and growth (Lee and Lim, 2001; Geroski and Mazzucato, 2002), productivity (Keesing and Lall, 1992), exports (Zahra et al., 2000; Ernst, 2004) and innovation (Zahra, 1996, Padilla and Tunzelman, 2008). Therefore, we estimate the following regression equation using an Ordered Logit model:

Table 9.2 *Definition of variables*

Variables	Definition	Mean	Std. Dev.
comp	Competitiveness of firms proxied by firms' market leadership	2.5	0.9
tacit1	Tacit knowledge: foreign	3.9	2.1
tacit2	Tacit knowledge: other firms in the industry	1.1	1.4
tacit3	Tacit knowledge: universities	1.2	1.2
tacit4	Tacit knowledge: in-house R&D	3.7	1.4
codified1	Explicit knowledge: foreign	3.8	2.1
codified2	Explicit knowledge: other firms in the industry	1.2	1.4
codified3	Explicit knowledge: universities	1.2	1.3
codified4	Explicit knowledge: in-house R&D	3.8	1.4
lnlab	Ln (no of employees)	6.2	0.8
lnass	Ln (total assets)	8.3	1.5
hc	Level of human capital	0.3	0.2
intechl	Initial level of technology	2.8	1.5
rd2	Relative R&D strength score	2.7	1.1
te	Industry dummy, 1 = firms producing fibrecore, 0 = others	0.19	0.4

$$C_i = B_0 + B_1 TL_i^{in} + B_2 TL_i^{ex} + B_3 X_i + u_i \qquad (9.1)$$

where C represents the competitiveness of a firm, TL^{in} represents sources of internal technological learning, TL^{ex} is a vector of sources of external technological learning, and X is a vector of firm-specific control variables.

The dependent variable, competitiveness, is a polytomous response variable that is based on the market leadership of each firm. It is measured by firms' self-assessment of market leadership, ranked on a scale of five values ranging from minimum to maximum levels of market leadership in each sub-industry. For firms producing in more than one sub-industry, we take the average of the rank scores. Admittedly, firms' competitiveness revealed in their market leadership is not the only outcome of technological learning. Competitiveness can also be an outcome of other factors. Therefore, it is important to control for other important firm characteristics. Although we have tried to control for other factors affecting competitiveness, as a result of data availability, the test may still have an omitted variable issue, and we should therefore be cautious when drawing conclusions.

The independent variable TL_i^{in} measures technological learning from internal sources, composed of knowledge acquisition from internal sources such as in-house R&D. Similarly the independent variable TL_i^{ex} measures technological learning from external sources, composed of knowledge acquisition from (1) foreign sources through imports and licensing, (2) other firms in the industry and (3) universities. The equation also includes a vector of control variables represented by X_i, which includes a firm's size (measured as the log of asset holding), the firm's age (measured in years), ownership dummies (which includes the following categories: state-owned enterprises, shareholding, joint ventures, foreign-owned enterprises, collectively owned enterprises, privately owned enterprises and others), level of human capital (measured as the percentage of technicians in total employees) and dummy variables for sub-industry type.

In this chapter, we found an Ordered Logit model to be appropriate for the analysis as the dependent variable is the self-assessment response of market leadership of each firm, restricted to ordered values of 1 to 5. Ordered Logit models are used to model relationships between a polytomous response variable and a set of repressor variables. These polytomous response models can be classified into two distinct types, depending on whether the response variable has an ordered or unordered structure.

The measurement of learning and knowledge acquisition is not straightforward. In this research, we use firms' assessment of the importance of various sources for technological learning to proxy the importance of different knowledge sources. A total of eight self-assessment factors regarding the importance of different sources of technology were used, relating to the codified and tacit knowledge acquired from foreign sources, other firms in the industry, universities and in-house R&D. It is worth mentioning that the independent variables exhibit a high degree of multicollinearity, and this may result in an imprecise point estimate. Following Adler and Golany (2001), we use factor analysis to summarise the variations in the eight variables into a few principal components. This approach explains the variance structure of a matrix of data through linear combinations of variables that capture a large proportion of the variance in the data but, at the same time, reduce the data to a few principal components. If most of the population variance can be attributed to the first few components, they can replace the original

Table 9.3 *Factor analysis*

Variable	Factor 1: acquire from other domestic firms in the industry	Factor 2: in-house R&D	Factor 3: acquire from universities and research institutions
Tacit knowledge: foreign	**-0.647**	-0.538	-0.520
Tacit knowledge: other firms in the industry	**0.980**	-0.039	0.073
Tacit knowledge: universities	0.062	-0.111	**0.962**
Tacit knowledge: in-house R&D	-0.047	**0.947**	-0.140
Codified knowledge: foreign	**-0.715**	-0.437	-0.510
Codified knowledge: other firms in the industry	**0.956**	-0.088	0.058
Codified knowledge: universities	.201	-0.183	**0.868**
Codified knowledge: in-house R&D	.047	**0.922**	-0.111

Note: Figures highlighted in bold are the highest values obtained in the estimation and therefore the main variables captured by each factor.

variables without much loss of information. The factor analysis results are summarised in Table 9.3. We found that 96.3 per cent of the variation in the eight tangible and intangible knowledge acquisition variables is explained by three factors: (1) knowledge acquired from other domestic firms in the same industry, (2) knowledge acquired via in-house R&D and (3) knowledge acquired from universities and research institutions. The factor analysis results indicate a consistent pattern in one aspect: firms that use any of the domestic knowledge sources, either internal or external, do not appear to use direct foreign knowledge sources. In other words, firms do not appear to use foreign and domestic knowledge sources in a complementary way.

Given the nature of tacit knowledge, direct measurement is challenging. In this chapter, we therefore use indirect measurement of tacit knowledge. As discussed earlier, the three sub-industries in the optical fibre and cable industry represent three sectors with increasing intensity of tacit knowledge. The fibrecore sector is the most intensive in tacit knowledge and the cable sector is the least intensive in using tacit knowledge. This is proven by the basic survey evidence. Moreover, the firms in the sample are divided into two blocks: about 70 firms produce cable and/or fibre but do not have the technology to produce fibrecore and more than 20 firms produce fibrecore with some also producing fibre.[7] Therefore, the firms can be divided as follows: the first group of firms operates in the low tacit knowledge–intensive cable/fibre sector, and the second group has mastered the tacit knowledge–intensive fibercore production technology. Therefore, we use a dummy variable that equals 1 for firms in the more tacit knowledge–intensive sector, and 0 for firms in the less tacit knowledge–intensive sector. We use interaction terms to examine the effectiveness of different knowledge sources of tacit and codified knowledge.

9.5 Results

Table 9.4 reports the Ordered Logit estimation of the model. Column (1) reports the estimated results of the full model where the three knowledge source factors are entered into the model together. Columns (2) to (4) report the results of the regressions where the three factors are entered into the regression separately. The point estimate on the university factor is found to be positive and statistically significant in the regression that has a full set of controls (column [1]) as well as in the regression where the university factor is estimated separately (reported in column [4]). This result suggests that firms that have universities as an important knowledge source are more competitive in the market. To note, given the cross-sectional nature of the data, claims regarding any causal relationship would not be warranted. Knowledge sources from other firms in the industry do not appear to have a significant effect on the competitiveness of firms in general. The estimated coefficient of

---

[7] Three of them also produce cable.

Table 9.4 *Knowledge sources and technological learning*

	Dependent variable: competitiveness			
Factor 1 (other firms in the industry)	−0.003	−0.008		
	(0.013)	(0.012)		
Factor 2 (in-house R&D)	0.007		0.009	
	(0.013)		(0.014)	
Factor 3 (universities)	0.0214*			0.0227**
	(0.012)			(0.011)
rd2	0.794***	0.791***	0.795***	0.787***
	(0.071)	(0.069)	(0.069)	(0.07)
intechl	−0.002	−0.008	−0.007	−0.001
	(0.012)	(0.011)	(0.011)	(0.011)
lnass	−0.001	−0.002	0.001	0
	(0.013)	(0.014)	(0.013)	(0.012)
hc	0.099	0.112*	0.106*	0.106
	(0.061)	(0.065)	(0.06)	(0.065)
Industry dummy	y	y	y	y
ownership dummy	y	y	y	y
Constant	y	y	y	y
Log likelihood	−105.7	−109	−108.8	−105.9
Chi2	56.53	53.23	53.46	53.18

Note: 1. Robust standard errors in parentheses;
2. *significant at 10 per cent; **significant at 5 per cent; ***significant at 1 per cent.

in-house R&D bears the expected positive sign but is not statistically significant. However, the relative R&D strength variable that indicates a firm's R&D activity relative to the rest of the firms in the industry shows a positive effect on firms' competitiveness and is statistically significant at the 1 per cent level. The size of the estimated coefficient is much larger than the rest of the control variables, indicating an important contribution of R&D to a firm's competitiveness. This variable is likely to correlate with the internal knowledge source variable and explain the insignificance of the internal knowledge source variable. As regards the rest of the control variables, human capital has a positive and significant effect on competitiveness as expected. Firm size and the initial technology level variable do not appear to have a significant effect on a firm's competitiveness.

To test whether or not the embeddedness of tacit knowledge in the industry matters, we estimate the Ordered Logit model using the three factors as explanatory variables and also interact the factors with an industry dummy (dummy = 1 if tacit knowledge is perceived to be important for the industry and 0 otherwise). The results are reported in Table 9.5. The regression result with a full set of controls (column [1]) finds that the point estimate on the interaction term on the industry peers factor is 0.10 and is statistically significant. In industries where tacit knowledge is crucial, industry peers appear to be an important source of knowledge accumulation. The point estimates on the other interaction term and the factors are not found to be statistically significant. We also estimate the model for each factor and the corresponding interaction term separately (reported in columns [2] to [4]). The point estimate on the interaction term on the industry peer factor declines marginally to 0.09 but continues to be statistically significant (column [2]). Similarly in column (3), the point estimate on the interaction term on the in-house R&D factor is positive (0.06) and statistically significant. On the other hand, results in column (4) show that while the point estimate university factor is positive (0.03) and statistically significant, the interaction term on the university factor is not statistically significantly different from zero. This may indicate that universities are an important actor in tacit knowledge accumulation irrespective of which industry the firm belongs to. These findings also support our initial hypothesis on the relative effectiveness of different tacit knowledge acquisition channels.

Although summarising the knowledge sources into principal factors offers useful advantages, analysis of the effect of the individual original knowledge source indicators also provides rich in-depth information about the effect of each source of the different types of knowledge. Table 9.6 reports the estimated results of the regressions using the original scores of individual tacit knowledge sources. We interact the four tacit knowledge acquisition variables with an industry dummy that equals 1 if tacit knowledge is perceived to be important for the industry, and 0 otherwise. To avoid the problem of multicollinearity, which may give rise to imprecise point estimates, we estimate the model for each tacit knowledge variable and the corresponding interaction term separately (reported in columns [1] to [4]).

The regression results in columns (2) and (4) report statistically significant and positive point estimate on the interaction term on tacit

Table 9.5 *Does the embeddedness of tacit knowledge in the industry matter?*

	(1)	(2)	(3)	(4)
	Dependent variable: competitiveness			
Factor 1 (other firms in the industry)	−0.0104	−0.0114		
	(0.0119)	(0.0108)		
Factor 2 (in-house R&D)	−0.0016		−0.0045	
	(0.0159)		(0.0153)	
Factor 3 (universities)	0.0235			0.0258**
	(0.0147)			(0.0126)
te*fac1	0.101***	0.0909***		
	(0.0365)	(0.0325)		
te*fac2	0.0574		0.0595*	
	(0.0346)		(0.0355)	
te*fac3	−0.02			−0.0107
	(0.0304)			(0.038)
te (industry dummy)	0.0803**	0.0396	0.0267	0.0138
	(0.0332)	(0.0359)	(0.0385)	(0.0448)
intechl	−0.01	−0.0058	−0.013	−0.0036
	(0.0149)	(0.0121)	(0.0133)	(0.0115)
lnass	0.0027	0.0020	0.0006	0.0008
	(0.0141)	(0.0134)	(0.0127)	(0.012)
hc	0.0488	0.110*	0.0604*	0.105
	(0.0608)	(0.0607)	(0.0636)	(0.066)
rd2	0.757***	0.764***	0.774***	0.791***
	(0.0819)	(0.0702)	(0.0729)	(0.0735)
ownership dummy	y	y	y	y
Constant	y	y	y	y
Log likelihood	73.7	52.92	65.15	53.76
Chi2	−104	−108.5	−107.5	−105.7

Note: Robust standard errors in parentheses; *significant at 10 per cent; **significant at 5 per cent; ***significant at 1 per cent.

knowledge from industry peer sources and the in-house R&D source (0.057 and 0.056, respectively) indicating positive association. This suggests that in industries where domestic knowledge is important, domestic peers and R&D activities are important sources of

Table 9.6 *Does the embeddedness of tacit knowledge in the industry matter?*

	(1)	(2)	(3)	(4)
	Dependent variable: competitiveness			
tacit1	−0.0020			
	(0.0077)			
te*tacit1	−0.0314**			
	(0.0146)			
tacit2		−0.0066		
		(0.0081)		
te*tacit2		0.0573*		
		(0.0302)		
tacit3			0.0087	
			(0.0094)	
te*tacit3			−0.0096	
			(0.0342)	
tacit4				−0.0042
				(0.0101)
te*tacit4				0.0560*
				(0.0306)
rd2	0.766***	0.755***	0.788**	0.771***
	(0.0761)	(0.0686)	(0.0712)	(0.0736)
te	0.168**	−0.0358	0.012	−0.191*
	(0.0719)	(0.0472)	(0.0442)	(0.112)
intechl	−0.0052	−0.0044	−0.0055	−0.0144
	(0.0121)	(0.0127)	(0.0122)	(0.014)
lnass	0.0034	0.0015	0.0011	0.0023
	(0.0132)	(0.0137)	(0.0123)	(0.013)
hc	0.0886	0.125*	0.113*	0.0558
		(0.0645)	(0.0645)	(0.0601)
ownership dummy	y	y	y	y
Constant	y	y	y	y
Log likelihood	69.87	53.46	54.21	64.6
Chi2	−108.7	−109	−107.9	−107.4

Note: Robust standard errors in parentheses; *significant at 10 per cent; **significant at 5 per cent; ***significant at 1 per cent.

technological learning. On the other hand, regression results in column (1) report a statistically significant but negative point estimate on the interaction term on tacit knowledge from foreign sources (−0.03) indicating negative association. This finding supports our hypothesis that foreign sources of technology are less likely to be effective learning channels. The point estimate on the interaction term on tacit knowledge from the university source is found to be statistically insignificant (column [3]). As hypothesised earlier, empirical estimates show that universities are effective in transferring both tacit and codified knowledge.

9.6 Conclusions

This chapter analyses the effectiveness of various sources of technological learning in transferring and assimilating tacit knowledge using firm-level data from the Chinese optical fibre and cable industry. Evidence from the research suggests that in industries where tacit knowledge is a more important component of technological learning, internal R&D activities and domestic peers are important knowledge sources for technological learning. Moreover, universities have been an important asset in creating learning organisations and effective knowledge sources for technological learning. They play the same important role in transferring both tacit and explicit knowledge. However, imports of equipment and licensing are a less effective learning channel in the acquisition of tacit foreign technology.

Moreover, our results show that the difficulty in acquisition of tacit knowledge has been a significant barrier to technological learning, which may be the reason that motivates firms to start in the cable sub-industry, the sub-industry that requires the least tacit knowledge. As firms gain technological knowledge and expertise, both tacit and explicit, from producing less sophisticated products, they move up the technology ladder to produce more technologically advanced and sophisticated products. In the case of China, firms are finally capable of producing the fibrecore that has the highest tacit knowledge requirement. In other words, the requirements of tacit knowledge and the process of technological learning and accumulation have had a significant impact on the evolution and trajectory of the Chinese optical fibre and cable industry.

Results from the research also indicate that firms that use any of the domestic knowledge sources, either internal or external, do not appear to use direct foreign knowledge sources. In other words, firms do not appear to use foreign and domestic knowledge sources in a complementary way. Note, however, that in this survey and hence this study, foreign knowledge sources refer to foreign knowledge acquisition through imports and licensing. Foreign joint ventures or foreign subsidiaries in China are regarded as domestic peers in the same industry. These foreign invested firms provide better proximity and greater likelihood for the transfer of tacit knowledge (e.g., better managerial practice, technological know-how). Therefore, future research is needed to explore fully the role of foreign direct investment in the learning process, and caution should be exercised in offering any conclusion as regards the role of foreign knowledge sources.

Although this chapter has brought to light some interesting and important insights on the relative effectiveness of different knowledge sources/channels in technological learning in the Chinese optical fibre and cable industry, there are two caveats in the data. First, future research should focus on analysis with panel data. Second, such work should include objective measures of variables that allow us to control for firm heterogeneity and dynamics in the learning process.

Appendix 9.1 Correlation coefficients

	comp	codified1	codified2	codified3	codified4	Tacit 1	Tacit 2	Tacit 3	Tacit 4	intechl	lnass	hc	fibrecore	fie
comp	1													
codified1	-0.039	1												
codified2	0.060	-0.657	1											
codified3	0.090	-0.483	0.114	1										
codified4	-0.082	-0.432	-0.099	-0.266	1									
tacit1	-0.032	0.939	-0.710	-0.491	-0.282	1								
tacit2	0.076	-0.601	0.921	0.147	-0.127	-0.689	1							
tacit3	0.099	-0.484	0.291	0.817	-0.276	-0.511	0.224	1						
tacit4	-0.150	-0.443	0.008	-0.188	0.819	-0.418	-0.064	-0.284	1					
intechl	-0.063	0.404	-0.433	-0.360	0.140	0.442	-0.462	-0.346	0.098	1				
lnass	0.114	0.318	-0.348	-0.172	0.012	0.430	-0.356	-0.144	-0.185	0.295	1			
hc	0.090	-0.024	-0.138	-0.020	0.209	-0.031	-0.121	-0.074	0.217	0.201	-0.323	1		
fibrecore	-0.117	0.399	-0.249	-0.291	-0.101	0.307	-0.242	-0.248	-0.012	0.501	-0.107	0.289	1	
fie	0.026	0.141	-0.196	-0.291	0.224	0.203	-0.189	-0.248	0.075	-0.016	0.117	-0.073	-0.174	1

10 | Leapfrogging in green technology: The solar-PV industry in China and India

10.1 Introduction

Building a global green economy will require technology transition in both developed and developing countries. Among the developing countries, some emerging economies have quickly established significant technological capabilities in fields related to the green economy. The growth of production capacity and the diffusion of green technology in these emerging economies have been dramatic. China and India, in particular, have become global leaders in some of the emergent green technology sectors such as solar photovoltaic (PV) panels, wind turbines and electric and hybrid electric vehicles. Given the rapid eminence of these green sectors, what are the respective contributions to technological progress from learning by doing; indigenous research and development; and technology transfer through FDI, trade and other channels? What is the role of national innovation systems in promoting more effective technology acquisition, adaptation and development? What lessons can other developing countries learn from the development of green sectors in China and India? Drawing on an analysis and comparison of technology progress strategy in the solar-PV industry in China and India, and considering the different role of technology transfer and indigenous innovation as well as the national innovation system in the development, diffusion, application and adaptation of green technologies, this chapter addresses the key determinants of green technological capability in emerging economies. The major contributions of this chapter are twofold. First, it illustrates that the 'two-leg forward' strategy, that is, adopting both technology transfer and indigenous innovation simultaneously, is suitable for the technological progress and development of green technology sectors in developing countries. It provides the right mix and sequence of technological progress that can be applied to green technology industries in developing countries, showing the importance of each mechanism during different stages of development. Second, it finds that national environmental innovation systems are important in assisting sustainable technological progress and 'leapfrogging' development towards a competitive green economy.

The chapter is organised as follows: Section 10.2 reviews the mechanisms of technology progress in developing countries, including conventional and unconventional mechanisms of technology transfer and indigenous innovation and catching up. Section 10.3 provides an overview of the science and technology sector and solar-PV industries in China and India, using case studies of leading solar-PV companies. Section 10.4 analyses the technology progress strategies that have been adopted in both countries. Section 10.5 discusses the role of public policies and institutions as well as private actors in the innovation systems with special reference to the environmental innovation system. Section 10.6 presents conclusions and outlines policy implications for developing countries seeking to enhance their technological capabilities for a green economy.

10.2 Technology transfer, indigenous R&D and technological progress in emerging economies

Innovation is costly, risky and path dependent. This may provide a rationale for poor countries to rely on foreign technology acquisition for technological development. In fact, most innovation activities are largely concentrated in a few developed countries. International technology diffusion is therefore an important condition for the economic growth of developing countries. If foreign technologies are easy to diffuse and adopt, a technologically backward country can catch up rapidly through the acquisition and more rapid deployment of the most advanced technologies (Grossman and Helpman, 1991, 1994; Romer, 1994; Eaton and Kortum, 1995).

Technology can be diffused between firms and across regions and countries through various transmission mechanisms, including (1) licensing; (2) movement of goods through international trade; (3) movement of capital through inward and outward foreign direct investment (FDI and OFDI); (4) movement of people through migration, travel and foreign education of students and workers; (5) international research collaboration; (6) diffusion through media and the Internet of disembodied knowledge; and (7) integration of benefits into global value chains from foreign technology transferred within the supply chain (Fu, Pietrobelli and Soete, 2011). Some knowledge is transferred intentionally from the knowledge owner to the recipient, but a large proportion of knowledge spillovers take place as unintended knowledge leakage. In recent years, the mode of innovation is becoming more and more open and is making good use of external resources. International knowledge diffusion can therefore benefit a country's or firm's innovation at every stage of the innovation process.

FDI and technology transfer

Inward FDI has long been regarded as a major vehicle for the transfer of advanced technology to developing countries (Lall, 1992; Dunning, 1994). Multinational enterprises (MNEs) have internal incentives encouraging the transfer of technology across borders to share technology between parent companies and subsidiaries (Markusen, 2002). Therefore, it is expected that in the medium to long run, local firms will benefit from MNEs via (1) technology transfer within the foreign invested joint ventures through imported machinery and equipment and the training of labour, (2) horizontal technology spillovers to other firms in the same industry/region through demonstration effects and labour turnover, (3) vertical technology spillovers within the value chain through forwards and backwards linkages; and (4) the competition effect of pushing inefficient firms to exit from the market and force others to innovate to maintain a competitive edge (Caves, 1974; Fosfuri, Motta and Ronde, 2001; Javorcik, 2004). As one of the largest recipients of inward FDI in the world, China has introduced a set of policies to enhance linkages and knowledge transfer from foreign to indigenous firms. However, FDI may also have a detrimental impact on the technological upgrading of local firms. First, FDI may make the competing domestic firms worse off and even crowd them out from the market (Aitken and Harrison, 1999; Hu and Jefferson, 2002). Second, strong competition from foreign subsidiaries may reduce local firms' R&D efforts (OECD, 2002). Moreover, foreign subsidiaries may remain as enclaves in a developing country with a lack of effective linkages with the local economy. As a result, empirical evidence on the effect of inward FDI on the productivity and innovation capabilities of indigenous firms is mixed, for instance, the positive impact in Buckley, Clegg and Wang

(2002) and the depressive effects in Hu and Jefferson (2002) and Fu and Gong (2011) using Chinese industry–/firm-level data, as well as the negative impact in Sasidharan and Kathuria (2008) using Indian firm-level data.

Licensing and technology transfer

The second conventional method of technology transfer is licensing, which is an important source of international technology transfer for developing countries (Correa, 2005). Licensing is particularly useful in terms of transferring patented and codified knowledge. From the aspect of the licensee, licensing is less costly than in-house R&D and less risky and shortens the time required to bring new products to the market. For the licensor, licensing is less risky than FDI and highly profitable but may lead to the risk of technology leakage in the host country through copying or movement of labour (Darcy et al., 2009). Therefore, some MNEs may prefer FDI (avoiding engagement in licensing) or may transfer only lagging technologies (Maskus, 2000). In addition, a successful transfer also depends on the capability of licensees to learn, develop and market the technology (Hoekman, Maskus and Saggi, 2005; Kamiyama, Sheehan and Martinez, 2006).

Imports and technology transfer

Imports of machinery and equipment are another important channel for countries to acquire advanced technology and enhance competitiveness (Fagerberg, 1994; Coe and Helpman, 1995). However, using such machines to produce high-quality products does not mean that developing countries necessarily master the skills required to design and produce advanced machinery. Substantial technological learning and reverse engineering are required to grasp the technologies embedded in the imported machinery. In the case of China's high-technology industries, Li (2011) finds that investing in foreign technology alone does not enhance innovation in domestic firms, unless it is coupled with an industry's own in-house R&D effort. On the contrary, the inverse is true; he finds that domestic technology purchases alone are found to contribute to innovation, suggesting that domestic firms much more easily absorb indigenous technology.

Outward FDI and technology transfer

For multinationals from emerging economies, one of the major motivations to directly invest in developed economies is knowledge sourcing through the setting up of joint ventures with foreign firms, R&D labs, research institutions and universities and greenfield new production facilities with R&D functions. Mergers and acquisitions of local firms and institutions that own the needed technology know-how or simply the research personnel or potential also serve this function. Asset exploration has become a major type of OFDI from the emerging economies (Dunning, Kim and Park, 2007). The mode of innovation becomes increasingly open. Active knowledge sourcing through such OFDI will serve as an effective mechanism for enhancing firms' innovation capabilities, especially for firms with the necessary absorptive capacity.

Indigenous innovations and catching up

The diffusion and adoption of technology is costly, requires certain preconditions and is often difficult. First, technology producers are usually reluctant to share the underlying capabilities, and MNEs also try to control knowledge leakage because these are the core competencies needed to maintain their competitiveness (Mallett et al., 2009, Fu et al., 2011). Second, many technologies are tacit and difficult to transfer; thus, in-house R&D is crucial for the acquisition of tacit knowledge and universities may provide some assistance. Third, knowledge is cumulative and path dependent, suggesting that indigenous R&D is an important and necessary element for the effective assimilation and adaptation of transferred foreign technology and the development of indigenous technological capabilities for catching up. Finally, foreign technologies created in developed countries can sometimes be unsuitable for developing countries if we consider the notion that technological change is a 'localised learning by doing' process (Atkinson and Stiglitz, 1969). Therefore, effective technological capability building in developing countries should make use of both the indigenous innovation efforts and foreign technology transfer (i.e., a two-leg forward strategy), although the relative importance of each driver varies according to the stage of industrialisation and development in the concerned developing country (Fu and Gong, 2011; Fu et al., 2011).

Foreign technology transfer and indigenous innovation, in fact, reinforce each other: localised innovation is a prerequisite for developing domestic absorptive and creative capabilities to ultimately benefit from transfer mechanisms. Unconventional technology transfer mechanisms, such as international R&D collaboration and outward direct investment, are only possible once local industries have developed world-class firms with international recognition and possess the resources and clout to collaborate with, or acquire, foreign firms. Such emerging MNEs are dubbed 'national champions' and play an active role in the acquisition of new technology and know-how by leveraging global value chains to innovate within their network (Fu et al., 2011).

Another role of indigenous innovation is that it has the dual function of creating knowledge and promoting learning and absorptive capacity (Cohen and Levinthal, 1989; Aghion and Howitt, 1998). An important component of absorptive capacity is the R&D activities carried out by local firms. Li (2009), Fu (2008) and Fu and Gong (2011) all support this hypothesis based on experiences from China. Foreign technology will generate a positive effect on local firms' technological change and upgrading only insofar as sufficient indigenous R&D activities and human capital are present.

The two-leg forward strategy is also suitable for the technological progress of a green economy. Foreign technology transfer remains an important driver and has been a crucial part of the global solution for reducing greenhouse gas emissions under the United Nations Framework Convention on Climate Change (UNFCCC) framework. Nevertheless, Bell (1990) argues that low-carbon innovation capabilities are likely to depend on indigenous investment in training, R&D and reverse engineering. Based on the experience of the wind power, solar energy and electric and hybrid vehicles sectors in India and China, Lema and Lema (2012) find that conventional technology transfer mechanisms such as patent licensing, inward FDI and imports were important for industry formation and takeoff. However, other mechanisms such as indigenous R&D, global R&D networks and acquisition of firms in the West become more important after these sectors have taken off and start catching up with global leaders.

10.3 Science and technology development and growth in the solar-PV industry in China and India

Over the past three decades, tremendous economic growth in China has been accompanied with significant growth in R&D expenditure. When compared to peers such as India and Brazil, China has had the largest increase in R&D expenditure, at an annual rate of 19 per cent since 1995, and draws the largest number of its youth towards research and science careers (OECD, 2008).[1] In addition, foreign firms had established more than 1200 R&D centres in China by 2008 (Zhu, 2010). Although there is still a gap between China's technological capabilities and those of OECD countries, China's science and technology (S&T) sector has produced considerable innovative accomplishments during the 11th Five-Year Plan period (2006–2010). The R&D intensity in China has increased from 0.6 per cent in 1995 to 1.7 per cent in 2009. In 2009, the number of higher education graduates (in science, engineering, agriculture and medicine only) was about 8 times the 1995 level, granted patents about 13 times higher, and high-technology exports more than 28 times higher (OECD, 2008; China National Bureau of Statistics[2]).

Considerable breakthroughs in research on renewable energy have also taken place. For example, the range of notable milestones in 2009 include substantial progress on several adjustable-speed wind energy power plants including two 1.5 megawatt (MW) in early stages of production as well as a 2.5MW and 3MW in later stages of installation; notable progress in solar energy and battery technologies including 21 cities using solar for illumination; collaboration with Japanese technology companies to develop small generators for wind-powered irrigation in arid areas; and collaboration with the leading U.S. solar company First Solar to develop a 2GW solar power station in Inner Mongolia. Substantial ongoing resource allocations supported these efforts for 2009–2010, such as RMB 20 billion budgeted for the development of solar power plants, RMB 200 million for the public electric cars project in 13 cities, RMB 2 billion to boost related parts for electric cars and ¥6 billion to support innovation in battery technology (MOST, 2010).

China's production capacity for renewable technologies has grown rapidly in the since 2003. In the solar-PV industry, China's global share increased from less than 1 per cent in 2003 to that of the world's largest producer in 2008 (Climate Group, 2009; Strangway, Liu and Feng,

---

[1] As of 2006, China is only second to the United States with 1.2 million full-time researchers (OECD, 2008).

[2] http://www.stats.gov.cn/english/statisticaldata/yearlydata

Table 10.1 *Renewable technology targets for 2020 in China*

Type of power generation	2006 actual	2010 estimates	2020 target
Total water (MW)	130,000	180,000	300,000
Small-scale water (MW)	47,000	60,000	85,000
Wind (MW)	2,600	5,000	30,000
Biomass (MW)	2,000	5,500	30,000
Feed-in solar (MW)	80	300	2,000
Solar-powered water heaters (m^2)	100	150	300
Ethanol for fuel (million tons)	1	2	10
Bio-diesel (million tons)	0.05	0.2	2
Biomass pellets (million tons)	0	1	50
Gas from biomass (million tons)	8	19	44

Source: Martinot and Li (2007).

2009). According to Solarbuzz, China produced 2570 MW of solar cells in 2009, accounting for 37 per cent of worldwide production. China's global market share of on-grid building-mounted segments rose from 33 per cent in 2008 to 88 per cent in 2009.[3] However, around 95 per cent of China's PV products have been exported. The domestic demand of PV installation in China was only 228 MW in 2009, although an impressive 552 per cent increase over 2008. Moreover, China has set ambitious national goals for 2020 (Table 10.1). These targets translate to a level of renewable energy generation by 2020 that is three times that of 2006 and an increase in renewable energy as a percentage of all power generation to 21 per cent from 16 per cent in 2005. Finally, these forecasts envisage that solar-powered water heaters will be installed in one-third of all households by 2020.

Following strong economic reforms, Indian growth has also occurred at a fast pace, as has expenditure on education and R&D. During the first decade of the twenty-first century, Indian public expenditure on education increased by 126 per cent from 2000 to 2009 according to the Indian Ministry of Statistics and Programme Implementation (MOSPI).[4] From 2001 to 2008, there was an 80 per

---

[3] www.solarbuzz.com
[4] http://mospi.nic.in/Mospi_New/site/India_Statistics.aspx?status=1&menu_id=14

cent increase in the number of universities; a 90 per cent increase in the training of research doctors; and a 48 per cent increase in higher education graduates in science, engineering, agriculture and medicine. During its 11th Five-year Plan (2007–2012), the Indian central government raised its expenditure on science, technology and environment by 194 per cent, and local governments raised such expenditure by 539 per cent compared with the 10th Five-year Plan period (2002–2007) (MOSPI). Support has also increased for indigenous research, design and development of new and renewable energy in India. In its 11th Plan Proposal, the Ministry of New and Renewable Energy (MNRE) highlighted how important it is that 'domestic industry is in a position to provide the market with cost-effective state of the art quality and reliable products and services without excessive reliance on imports' (MNRE 2006, p. 8). An up to 100 per cent subsidy is given to public R&D institutions and universities for achieving well-defined outputs and 50 per cent is available to industry. More subsidies are provided to industry in the initial stage if the time horizon for maturation of technology is relatively high, and R&D effort is encouraged in production upgrading, introduction of standards and so on. R&D collaboration with foreign companies is also supported if a larger national interest is visible and is served. India has realised that R&D is critical in the energy sector and has considered R&D as a public good to be financed by the government, particularly for R&D in solar, bio-energy, alternate fuel and storage technologies (MNRE, 2006).

India is also a key emerging country in terms of solar power. MNRE estimated that overall production was more than 175 MW for solar cells and 240 MW for PV modules during 2008 and 2009 (India Semiconductor Association, 2010). Different from the rest of world, Indian PV applications mainly focus on off-grid (rather than on-grid) connectivity and small capacity applications, used mostly for public lighting and domestic power back up in cities and small electrification systems and solar lanterns in the rural areas. Similar to China, India has relatively limited domestic PV demand and exported 75 per cent of PV cells to international markets (India Semiconductor Association, 2010; Lema and Lema, 2012). India also has set national goals for 2022 (Table 10.2), which in total are about five times that of the 2007 level. However, these targets are much lower than those set by China.

Table 10.2 *Renewable technology targets for 2022 (end of 13th Plan) in India (in MW)*

Type of power generation	2007 actual	2012 estimates	2022 target
Wind power	5,333	10,500	22,500
Small hydro power	522	1,400	3,140
Bio power	669	2,100	4,363
Solar power (grid/off-grid)	1*	50	N/A
Distributed/decentralised renewable power system	N/A	950	N/A

Note: *Grid only.
Source: MNRE (2006).

10.4 Technology transfer and indigenous innovation in the solar-PV industry in China and India

A phenomenal feature of the development model of the solar-PV industry in China is a strong emphasis on indigenous R&D. All the major firms are R&D intensive, although they are also engaged in licensing agreements to access PV technologies (Lema and Lema, 2012). Up to 2009, than 500 solar-PV firms and R&D labs in China actively pushed the frontiers of related technologies (Climate Group, 2009). In general, the industry has not only invested greatly in R&D but has also invested upstream and downstream in the value chain including the processing of silicon materials.

Based on total shipments of megawatts in 2010, national champions Suntech, Yingli Solar and Trina Solar are ranked as global top-10 companies in the industry (Lema and Lema, 2012). Detailed information on these firms appears in Table 10.3. Suntech has the world's largest solar power plants. It develops, manufactures and delivers solar modules to more than 80 countries in the world. Suntech's creed is that 'technology is the core competency and innovation is the soul'. Suntech adopts a mix of mechanisms of technology transfer and indigenous innovation. Different from other high-tech companies that usually introduce the whole set of foreign equipment and machines, Suntech only licensed the core equipment and then internalised foreign technology through integrating with domestically produced equipment.

Table 10.3 *Details of leading solar-PV companies in China and India*

	China[a]			India		
	Suntech	Yingli Solar	Trina Solar	Moser Baer Solar	TATA BP Sola[b]	HHV Solar
Year founded	2001	1998	1997	2005	1989	2007
No. of employees	20, 231	11, 435	12, 863	>7000	>600	100–500
Turnover (million)	$2901.9	$1893.9	$1857.7	> $500	$250	$35[c]
Total assets (million)	$ 5217.1	$3664.9	$2132.1	>$1000	N/A	N/A
Sales in MW	1572	1061.6	1057	300[d]	67.4	40
Exports (percentage) of sales	94.7	94.00	96.20	90	79.20	81–90

Note: [a]all data for Chinese companies are as of the end of 2010; [b]turnover, sales, and exports for TATA BP solar are as of 2008–2009 fiscal year; [c]the 2010 goal set by HHV Solar; [d]production capacity by 2010.
Source: Company websites, annual reports and various press news.

Besides this conventional technology transfer strategy, Suntech has focused more on in-house innovation since it was established. It put 5 per cent of its annual revenue to R&D activities every year at the takeoff stage (Jiang, 2009). It now has a world-class research team including more than 450 experts and has collaborated closely with universities and research institutions in China and abroad. It has developed and commercialised its own core silicon and cell technologies, solar module designs and encapsulation methods, which resulted in a great number of patents.[5] Suntech has set up vertical strategic alliances with upstream and downstream companies and gained financial and

---

[5] As of December 31, 2010, Suntech Power Holdings had a total of 87 issued patents, 216 pending patent applications in China, and 4 issued patents and 44 pending patent applications outside China through Suntech China, and 52 issued patents and 46 pending patent applications in Japan, 8 pending patent applications outside Japan through Suntech Japan and 2 issued patents in

non-financial support from local and central governments. In terms of unconventional technology transfer mechanisms, Suntech has carried out OFDI and overseas acquisitions. For example, in 2006 it took over Japan's largest PV module producer MSK, which at that time held 98 patents and had more than 20 years experience in designing and implementing building-integrated PV (Jiang, 2009). Since 2009, it has set up several subsidiaries in the United States and Europe. The benefits are twofold: it is closer to the suppliers of high-standard immediate products and the main consumers of Suntech's final products, and it is easier for Suntech to grasp the latest technologies of solar cells in these technologically advanced countries.

Similar to Suntech, Yingli Solar and Trina Solar are both innovation focused. Moreover, they both have adopted vertical integration business models and so have established more strategic technological collaborations with downstream suppliers. Yingli Solar has also engaged in overseas investment. In addition, Suntech, Yingli Solar and Trina Solar have successfully listed on the New York Stock Exchange, allowing these companies to make use of global resources. As a result, at the macro level, China has become a global leading location in solar-PV research and production, which has attracted major MNEs to set up R&D labs or joint R&D labs in China (Lema and Lema, 2012).

Therefore, the model of technological capability building in the Chinese solar-PV industry is an advanced indigenous R&D-led model with close links from industry to universities and research institutions, and with increasing national and international R&D collaborations. The Indian solar-PV sector is a mix of three major approaches including patent licensing, joint ventures and acquisitions and in-house R&D (Mallett et al., 2009), which matches the current development level of the technology and production capacity in the Indian solar-PV sector. The biggest solar manufacturers in India are Moser Baer Solar, Tata Power and HHV Solar (see Table 10.3 for more details). Moser Baer Solar has long-term R&D plans, focusing on improving efficiencies and reducing cost through innovations. It has set strategic alliances with American solar technology companies focusing on distribution and production of solar technologies. It has its own R&D facilities across

Germany through KSL-Kuttler. In addition, it has 5 pending patent applications filed under the Patent Cooperation Treaty, which provides a unified procedure for filing patent applications to protect inventions internationally (Suntech Annual Report 2010).

India and collaborative research programmes with internationally reputed research institutions and industrial players in India and abroad. HHV Solar also has a mature R&D centre and overseas partnerships; Tata power employed a conventional technology transfer mechanism by setting up a joint venture, Tata BP Solar, with BP Solar, one of the leading solar companies in the world.

Figure 10.1 summarises the main technology transfer and creation mechanisms used in China and India in the solar-PV industry. It shows that companies in both countries have used a mix of technology transfer and indigenous innovation mechanisms and these mechanisms change across the sequence stages of development in companies. At the early stages or 'takeoff phase', these companies have mainly adopted licensing, joint venture, joint R&D and in-house R&D. The importance of these mechanisms is the same in China and India. At the later stages – the 'catch-up phase', in-house R&D, local technology linkages, overseas R&D labs, and mergers and acquisitions have played increasingly important roles, although joint ventures, R&D collaboration and licensing have remained essential. Comparing China with India, the evidence suggests that China has taken a more home-based outside-in technology transfer and indigenous innovation model, whereas India has taken a more go-global active technology acquisition model.

To sum up, Figure 10.2 provides a general path of development for the solar-PV industries of China and India, although their paths are not absolutely identical. The comparison between targets of India and China (Figure 10.1 and Figure 10.2) may have implications for the green technology sectors of emerging economies.

10.5 National innovation systems and technology acquisition, adaptation and development

Indigenous innovation and technology transfer are both important for the development of the solar-PV industries of China and India. Private firms are the major force in undertaking R&D and transforming scientific inventions into production technologies and ultimately commercialising them for the market. However, this cannot be sustained without a favourable external environment. Therefore, it is necessary to have a supportive national innovation system (NIS), formed by market-driven private firms, all levels of government agencies, research and training

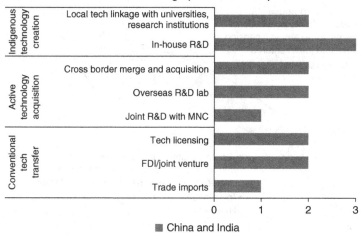

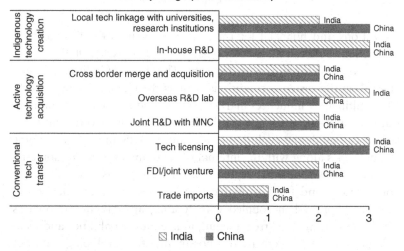

Figure 10.1 Technology transfer and indigenous knowledge-creation mechanisms adopted by solar-PV industry in China and India

Note: Top Chinese national firms: Suntech, Yingli Solar and Trina Solar; top Indian national firms: Moser Baer Solar, TATA BP Solar and HHV Solar. 1 denotes low importance; 2 denotes medium importance; 3 denotes high importance.

Source: Company websites, annual reports, Lema and Lema (2012), Strangway et al., Lewis.

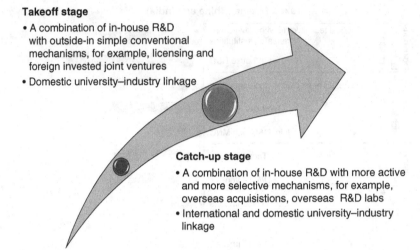

Takeoff stage

• A combination of in-house R&D with outside-in simple conventional mechanisms, for example, licensing and foreign invested joint ventures
• Domestic university–industry linkage

Catch-up stage

• A combination of in-house R&D with more active and more selective mechanisms, for example, overseas acquisistions, overseas R&D labs
• International and domestic university–industry linkage

Figure 10.2 Mixing and sequencing of technology creation and acquisition mechanisms in solar-PV industry in China and India

institutions and financial intermediaries, as well as the linkages and interactions between these actors (Balzat and Hanusch, 2004).

The NIS is sector and context specific. The effects of individual actors depend on the system's conditions such as the regulatory framework, which ultimately influences market demand and underlying technological push-and-pull dynamics (Walz, 2008). As such, government regulations can guide the evolution of a country's NIS and help determine competencies along with the international competitiveness of domestic industries. Environmental regulation, for example, is a key driver of domestic demand for sustainable technologies in water, energy and transportation. When coupled with funding and favourable policies aimed at creating and strengthening indigenous capabilities and technological expertise, there are real possibilities for developing countries to take alternative paths towards development and leapfrogging into an internationally competitive low-carbon economy.

Therefore, an important feature of the NIS, including the environmental innovation system, is collaboration and coordination between the relevant government departments and the introduction of a comprehensive set of complementary innovation policies that can effectively guide and incentivise firms to innovate. Policies may include increasing investment in science and technology and public research institutions, targeted tax incentives, increasing R&D financial support, specific government technology procurement to support innovation and strengthening intellectual property rights.

The second important feature of the NIS is university-industry linkage. Universities are widely regarded as a major contributor to advances in basic scientific research and innovation. However, scientific research in universities should not be separated from industrial production. It is important to build linkage between the two. The leading solar-PV companies in both China and India have adopted this strategy. In the case of China, universities are historically important in its NIS and have played a leading role in terms of R&D expenditure and patents of inventions (Liu and White, 2001; Li, 2009). The Chinese government has been advocating a use-driven science policy, encouraging universities to serve the national economy by solving practical problems for industry (Hong, 2006). University-industry linkages are built through licensing, consulting, joint or contract R&D and technology services. A second form of use-driven innovation occurs as a result of university-affiliated or university-run enterprises, given the market-oriented reforms and the low absorptive capacity of industrial firms and underdeveloped intermediary institutions (Ma, 2004; Eun, Lee and Wu, 2006). Chinese universities have played a significant role in the promotion of the diffusion of frontier technology and the creation of new country- or firm-level innovation outcomes. However, their contribution to the creation of groundbreaking innovations is still limited (Fu and Li, 2010).

Foreign firms can be active players in the NIS through knowledge transfer, knowledge creation (sometimes) and the effects of competition. On average, MNEs use relatively cleaner technology than domestic firms in developing countries so that there is a possibility of clean technology transfer from foreign to domestic firms. This is especially the case in joint ventures in green energy sectors such as solar power, wind power and hybrid/electric vehicles. However, there is also a possibility that MNEs are looking for institutional voids where they can effectively relocate to 'pollution heaven'. Zhang and Fu (2008) find that as a result of its lower pollution standards and lack of enforcement, China has selectively attracted more heavily polluting industries. FDI in such industries tends to target regions with relatively weak environmental regulations. Therefore, the role of FDI in the national environmental innovation system is two sided.

In terms of the national environmental innovation systems in China and India, Walz (2008) found that from 2000 to 2004, neither country specifically aimed at decoupling environment and resource consumption from economic development. Moreover, he found that India had been experiencing an increasing shortage of young scientists, representing a large barrier for capacity development in sustainability research and public research in general. However, looking at both countries now, growth in green technology and the development of a green economy have been dramatic.

Table 10.4 compares the environmental innovation systems in China and India. In China, it is a state-led innovation system. Since 2006, China has made sustainable technology a primary component of

Table 10.4 *Sustainability-oriented innovation systems of China and India*

	China	India
Technological specialisation	Solar-PV, wind turbines, electric cars and other renewable energies.	Wind turbines, solar-PV, biopolymers and electric cars.
Framework conditions	State-led innovation system, strong university-industry link, strong general manufacturing and trade.	Resilient private sector; functional overall framework conditions for general innovation.
Government policy	Strong policy U-turn now emphasising development of sustainable technologies since 2006 whereby a set of fiscal, financial, technology, trade and industry policies have been introduced and public procurement used.	Increasing government support, increasing R&D investment, but the private sector plays a leading role.
Sustainable R&D	Rapid increase in R&D investment in this sector since 2005/6. Strong encouragement of international R&D collaboration in green technology.	Material efficiency and water technologies. Wind turbine industries started in 1990s. Strong R&D in the private sector in this area.

Table 10.4 (*cont.*)

	China	India
Sustainable IP	Largest number of transnational patents in absolute numbers. Major breakthroughs in this area since 2003.	Low number of patents in contrast to high capabilities and IP in other sectors.
FDI attractiveness (trade policy)	Most attractive and far ahead in magnitude. FDI strong in manufacturing sector.	Lowest inflows. Relative strength of FDI in services sector.
Exports of sustainability technology products	Highest exports in solar (PV) panels. Electric cars catching up. Leader in wind turbine exports.	High exports in solar-PV sector, but exports of minor international importance in the rest of green sector.
Summary and implications	A rapidly growing role of sustainable technologies since mid-2000s. Strong demand and strong government policy support for green technology. Acquisition of foreign technology through licensing and joint venture at the takeoff stage, followed by heavy indigenous R&D activities. FDI strength implies China possesses most absorptive capacity for technology.	Increasing role of sustainable technologies since 1998. Possesses well-functioning overall framework conditions for innovation and a vivid private sector. Legacy of weak environmental protection.

Source: Authors' summary and Walz (2008).

national policy and has made strides in many fields including wind turbine and solar-PV technologies. As a result, it has been the export leader in wind turbines and solar-PV products. In contrast, the private sector plays a leading role in India. The overall framework conditions are functional for innovation, with increasing government support.

India's solar-PV exports and intellectual protection, for instance, have increased dramatically. Nowadays, both China and India stand at the forefront of many environment-related industries, and both countries have formed a clear innovation strategy for the development of environment-related industries and the transition to a green economy. This is accompanied by strong government policies and funding for green technology innovation, especially in China. A rapid catch-up in environment technology-related innovation systems has taken place in these two countries that lagged behind even as recently as the start of the twenty-first century. This evidence demonstrates the possibility that developing countries could take an alternative path of development with green technology industries growing with leaps and bounds and hence leapfrogging into an internationally competitive low-carbon economy.

10.6 Conclusions

This chapter analyses the strategy of mixing and sequencing different technology transfer and indigenous innovation mechanisms in the solar-PV industry in China and India and discusses the role national innovation systems play in sustaining technology acquisition, adaptation and development. Both China and India have grown dramatically in the solar-PV industry in a short time period. Their successful leapfrogging in this industry has significant implications for the growth of developing countries. It suggests that developing countries have opportunities to catch up with developed countries in the emergent green industries.

The development of the solar-PV industry in both China and India has made good use of mixed and sequenced mechanisms of indigenous innovation and international technology transfers. The importance of different transfer mechanisms varies across the different levels of technology and production capabilities that the domestic industries have at a given development stage. Most leading solar-PV companies in both countries started from international technology transfer through licensing and joint venture with MNEs. At the same time, all of them have put increasingly substantial effort into in-house R&D for the assimilation and adaptation of transferred technologies and the development of indigenous technological capabilities. However, once the basic production and technological capabilities were built up, they started more active knowledge acquisition and creation through indigenous innovation, international R&D collaboration and cross-border mergers and acquisitions. Such experiences suggest that accomplishing such catch-up processes requires a combination of international technology transfer and indigenous innovation. Technology transfer will be a feasible and evidence-proven entry point for developing countries, although this should be accompanied with substantial indigenous efforts in assimilation and learning. In this respect, attractive bundles of trade, investment and technology policies are important to leverage technology transfer mechanisms.

The experience of China suggests that the state has a crucial role in initiating the transition and maintaining the momentum of the catch-up process. Given the nature of technology as well as that of the environment as a public good, government-funding support through focused R&D programmes has been crucial in promoting technological breakthroughs – and hence indigenous technological capabilities – as well as the acquisition of foreign green technology. The experience from China also demonstrates that the development of a green economy requires a set of complementary and coherent policies covering regulatory, finance, technology and industrial policies to motivate and reinforce the transition and ensure a substantial change. In addition, the connection between industry and universities and public research institutions is important in transforming outputs of scientific research into applied technologies and assisting firms to move closer to the technology frontier.

Despite the rapid progress of solar-PV along with other green technology industries in China and India, substantial challenges remain. First, in China, for example, although there is strong government support for green technology, the lack of core indigenous technological capability still lingers in a wide range of sectors. Industry-academic joint research is not strong despite the substantial government push for greater research-industry linkage. Many research outputs from the universities either do not meet the needs of industry or are put on the shelf and not commercialised (Strangway et al., 2009). Thus, there is a demand for increased investment in science and technology and in education, along with improvement in government policy and services to push research organisations into the market.

Second, in both China and India, environmental regulations are relatively weak, as is the enforcement of these regulations, in general, and with considerable variations across regions. A 'new' problem that emerged in the development of industrial capabilities in the green technology sector is the heavy pollution generated in the production process of renewable energy or the manufacturing process of related green energy equipment. For example, the production processes for some important material used for making solar panels, especially the purification of polisilicon, is high in energy consumption and heavy in environmental pollution. Only six or seven firms in developed countries have developed a cleaner production technology. Chinese and Indian firms still use old and dirty technologies. Other waste products from solar-PV systems also pollute earth and water (Du and Cao, 2010). While China and India are, respectively, exporting more than 90 per cent and 70 per cent of their solar-PV panels to international markets, the waste is left behind. Therefore, significant attention to these ethical issues, adequate strategic planning and continued technological innovation to reduce the negative externalities in the production of the clean energies should be emphasised. Developing countries need to avoid the trap of becoming the new world manufacturing workshop of environmentally damaging industries for green products.

Finally, the transition from a traditional to a green economy requires not only technology and financial input but also involves considerable transition cost. The availability of cheap coal and the significant switching cost suggests that the transition will not come naturally. Indeed, the current reliance on coal in both developed and developing countries indicates there is a long way to go. Middle-income countries, which have already taken the traditional industrialisation route without sufficient technological and financial capabilities, will face the biggest challenge in comparison to the high- and low-income countries. In low-income countries, the sunk cost of transitioning from existing systems of production to a green economy is low. Combining this advantage with appropriate technology and financial resources, the low-income and some middle-income countries will be able to carry out the transition at a relatively low cost.

PART III

Towards a global innovation leader

11 Internationalisation, reverse learning and capabilities upgrading: The case of Huawei and ZTE[*]

XIAOLAN FU AND ZHONGJUAN SUN

11.1 Introduction

In recent years, a significant number of technology-intensive firms have not only operated successfully inside China but also moved quickly offshore, penetrating the market previously dominated by established Western multinational companies (Zheng, 2014). While such internationalisation plays a disproportionately large role in the telecommunication industry of China as the locus of both technology development and its corporate capability upgrading, few studies elucidate the learning process by which these internationalisation activities developed. Related studies address China's internationalisation strategies (Prange, 2012), innovation capability development (Fan, 2006; Zhou and Li, 2008), telecommunication market and industry (Chang, Fang and Yen, 2005; He and Mu, 2012), innovative capability and export performance (Guan and Ma, 2003), technology learning and development (Jin and von Zedtwitz, 2008) and the interaction between R&D and marketing in these firms (Li and Atuahene-Gima, 2001). However, our understanding of the nature and the process of the learning in this process and its impact on strategic capabilities of firms is still limited.

A substantial literature addresses learning and capabilities development as a critical challenge for latecomer multinational firms in developing countries, dislocated from centres of technological development (Gassmann and von Zedtwitz, 1998; Boutellier, Gassmann and von Zedtwitz, 2002). Over the past three decades, a significant number of

* The research on which this chapter is based was supported by the British Academy Grant No: SG122404. We would like to thank Jizhen Li and Jiangang Victor Zhang for helpful discussions and Huawei Technologies Ltd. and Zhongxing Telecommunications Equipment Corporation for their support for the fieldwork.

279

studies have examined this issue at the project, firm, industry and national levels of analysis in a developing country context, South Korea in particular. These studies identify different modes and processes of technological capabilities upgrading based on development motivation and source of initiation (Kim and Lee, 2003) and argue that the technology capabilities development process in newly industrialised economies follows three steps of transfer, absorb and diffuse and finally move to innovate and develop (Kim, 1997; Kim and Nelson, 2000).

For China, a small number of studies describe learning activities in Chinese organisations. Firms that have been studied include Lenovo (Xie and White, 2004; Liu, 2007; Sun et al., 2014), Huawei (Nakai and Tanaka, 2010) and Datang (Mu and Lee, 2005; Fan, 2006; Jin and von Zedtwitz, 2008). Studies of China's telecommunication industry have either focused on the firms' entry modes for international markets and technology catch-up strategy (e.g., Fan, 2006) or the role of the government (Mu and Lee, 2005) and capability accumulation based on a single case study (e.g., Xie and White, 2004; Sun et al., 2014 on Lenova) that finds stage-wise development from initial sales, distribution and service activities to manufacturing, product and process design and finally developmental R&D. Huawei has been a classical case for study, but most of the existing studies focus on its general experiences of catch-up (Fan, 2006; Liu, 2010) or its IPR strategy (e.g., Nakai and Tanaka, 2010). None of the existing studies has specifically examined the channel, mode and impact of reverse learning in firms' internationalisation process, especially for MNEs originating from developing countries.

The objective of this chapter is to shed light on the reverse learning and capability upgrading in the process of internationalisation of Chinese multinational enterprises through an in-depth study of multiple cases, specifically, Huawei and Zhongxing Telecommunications Equipment Corporation (ZTE), both leading global information and communication technology (ICT) solutions providers. These two cases provide a basis for conceptualising the process by which corporate capability upgrading evolved from internationalisation of business activities to become successful, global firms based on proprietary technology and capability. We focus on the evolving nature of learning by which the firms were able to realise such a transition and the implications for both research and practice. This chapter contributes to the literature by providing the first study of reverse learning through internationalisation and capability upgrading of emerging market MNEs based on multiple case studies. In particular, we focus on the channels of reverse learning and their impact on the upgrading of firms' overall corporate capabilities, which include both technological and non-technological capabilities.

This chapter is structured as follows: Section 11.2 reviews the literature on internationalisation and knowledge sourcing. Section 11.3 provides an overview of internationalisation of Chinese firms. Section 11.4 discusses methodology. Section 11.5 presents background information of the firms under study. Section 11.6 discusses the reverse learning and capability upgrading in the internationalisation process based on a comparative analysis of two cases. Section 11.7 offers conclusions and discussions.

11.2 Internationalisation and knowledge sourcing: received wisdom

The extant literature related to internationalisation and technology mostly focuses on the internationalisation of R&D/technology/innovation systems at the firm level (e.g., Granstrand, Håkanson and Sjölander, 1993; Granstrand, 1999; Carlsson, 2006; Beersa, Berghäll and Poot, 2008; Dunning and Lundan, 2009) and the internationalisation of technology-based firms (e.g., Yli-Renko, Autio and Tontti, 2002; Johnson, 2004; Evangelista, 2005; Blomqvis et al., 2008; Andersson, Curley and Formica, 2010). The research focusing on how the process of internationalisation contributes to the accumulation of organisational capabilities of the investing firms focuses mainly on the impact of organisations' networks on the internationalisation market expansion.

Network relationships are an effective tool for international market expansion because firms not only can access indirect network relationships from other members in the network but can also learn from network partners, such as customers, collaborators and competitors. Network relationships, particularly alliances with partners in the foreign market, constitute an effective strategy to overcome deficiencies, such as a lack of resources or foreign market knowledge, on entering international markets (Lu and Beamish, 2001). They also act as a strategic tool for overcoming the negative perceptions held by foreign investors (Zain and Imm Ng, 2006). In addition, networks can help entrepreneurs identify international opportunities and establish credibility and often lead to strategic alliances and other co-operative strategies (McDougall and Oviatt, 2005), which may provide information about business opportunities, foreign market characteristics, obstacles and problems involved in the process, resulting in decreased risk (Barney and Hansen, 1994; Gulati, 1999; Iyer, 2002). Moreover, according to the Uppsala model (e.g., Johanson and Vahlne, 1977) and the network model (e.g., Johanson and Mattsson, 1988), internationalisation is an incremental process to accumulate knowledge via learning by doing international operations, with firms' increasing propensity to commit to international operations.

Knowledge of international markets is another type of knowledge that firms acquire through internationalisation (Johanson and Vahlne, 1977). Market knowledge is important because it makes it easier to cope with both opportunities and problems that might arise when conducting operations abroad (Bördin and Längnér, 2012). Firms can acquire objective knowledge and experiential knowledge through internationalisation. The objective knowledge can be taught, whereas experiential knowledge can only been learned through personal experience (Johanson and Vahlne, 1977).

Some research investigates the relationship between internationalisation and technological capabilities (e.g., Elango and Pattnaik, 2007; Kafouros et al., 2008; Filatotchev and Piesse, 2009; Lowe, George and Alexy, 2012). As an effective channel to form the direct linkages with foreign partners, internationalisation has facilitated cross-border technology learning and assimilation. Enterprises are able to build capabilities in international operations through networks, learning, transfer of knowledge and transfer of capabilities (Kogut and Zander, 1993; Tsang, 1999; Elango and Pattnaik, 2007).

FDI has been recognised as an effective mechanism to facilitate cross-border knowledge flows. It not only brings technology from parent companies to the host country through training, imported machinery and equipment, demonstration effects and knowledge spillovers (Driffield and Love, 2007; Fu, 2012b), but it is also argued that direct investment abroad directly can be used for strategic asset seeking. For example, technological and managerial knowledge absorbed by subsidiaries in the host countries would reverse flow back to the home country (Singh, 2007; Fu, 2012b). Investment abroad has been found to help firms build up R&D and organisational capabilities through organisational learning (Kuemmerle, 1997; Steensma et al., 2004). The productivity of the subsidiaries is found to be associated with the performance of the parent company, which may, to a certain extent, reflect the impact of knowledge flow from subsidiaries on the performance of the parent company, although the causality may go the other way (Harzing and Noorderhaven, 2006; Driffield et al., 2010; Marin and Giuliai, 2011). The productivity of firms in the UK is linked with their investment levels in the United States (Griffith et al., 2006). The authors suggest that an underlying desire in the internationalisation of production is not to exploit existing technology within the firm but to acquire the leading-edge technology within a host economy.

In the context of developing countries, increasing research has found evidence of reverse technology transfer impelled by MNEs from emerging economies (Child and Rodrigues, 2005; Liu and Buck, 2007; Lima and Barros, 2009). Not all multinationals land in foreign markets with ownership advantages that are traditionally possessed by MNEs from industrialised economies (Fosfuri and Motta, 1999; Siotis, 1999). This is likely the case for many Chinese MNEs, which, therefore, may not only seek market expansion through direct investment in foreign countries but also see acquisition of strategic assets that are not available in their home markets for the upgrading of their technological capabilities.

11.3 Internationalisation of Chinese firms: an overview

Since the introduction of the 'go global' strategy in the late 1990s, internationalisation of Chinese firms through outward foreign direct investment (OFDI) has increased rapidly. The total stock of Chinese OFDI has increased from near zero in 1990 to around US$300 billion in 2010 (Figure 11.1). The growth of Chinese overseas investment is consistent with its economic development according to the investment development path theory developed by Dunning and Narula (1996). After more than 30 years of rapid economic growth, China has become the world's second largest economy, the world's largest exporter and a major driving force for global economic growth. In parallel with its continuous expansion in economic growth, Chinese firms' OFDI has also increased rapidly.

Although mining has been an important destination of Chinese overseas direct investment, it only accounted for 14 per cent of total Chinese OFDI stock and 6 per cent of total overseas firms by 2010. In fact,

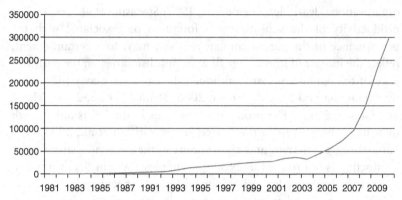

Figure 11.1 Stock of China's outward direct investment, mil$
Source: MOFCOM.

manufacturing has been the largest sector in terms of total number of overseas firms, accounting for 29 per cent of total Chinese invested overseas firms by 2010. Wholesale and retail trades as well as leasing and business services are the top two and three destination sectors of Chinese OFDI. Four per cent of the overseas firms were in scientific research by 2010 (Table 11.1).

Amongst the firms invested in the manufacturing sector, as Figure 11.2 shows, evidence from a firm-level survey carried out in Guangdong province in 2010 suggests that the industry dispersion of the Chinese overseas investment is wide, ranging from textiles and apparel to metal processing, automobile and electronic industries (Fu, Liu and Li, 2013).

These Chinese firms going abroad are for a variety of motivations. Fu et al. (2013) examine the overseas investment strategies of firms in Guangdong Province of China based on a firm-level survey conducted in 2010. They focused on the characteristics of firms that undertake OFDI, the incentives for and the main obstacles of overseas investment, the destination of OFDI from Guangdong, the strategies to conduct OFDI and the impact of overseas investment on company performance and future development. According to their findings, firms in Guangdong Province invested overseas for a wide range of motivations, including to exploit international markets and to acquire advanced technological and managerial knowledge. Figures 11.3 and 11.4 demonstrate some major objectives for surveyed firms investing in

Table 11.1 *Industry distribution of China's OFDI: by FDI stock and number of subsidiaries, 2010*

Industry	OFDI stock, percentage of total	Industry	Number of overseas subsidiaries, percentage of total
Leasing and business service	31	Manufacturing	29
Banking	17	Wholesale and retail trade	23
Mining	14	Leasing and business service	13
Wholesale and retail trade	13	Construction	7
Transport, storage and post	7	Mining	6
Manufacturing	6	Agriculture	5
Computer services	3	Scientific research	4
Real estate	2	Transport, storage and post	4
Construction	2	Services to households	3
Scientific research	1	Computer services	2
Public utility	1	Real estate	1
Services to households	1	Lodging & catering	1
Agriculture	1	Banking	1
Environment management	0.4	Culture & entertainment	1
Lodging & catering	0.1	Public utility	1
Culture & entertainment	0.1	Others	0.5
Public services	0.02		
Total	317210.59	Total	16107

Source: Ministry of Commerce (MOC) statistics, People's Republic of China. http://english.mofcom.gov.cn/article/statistic

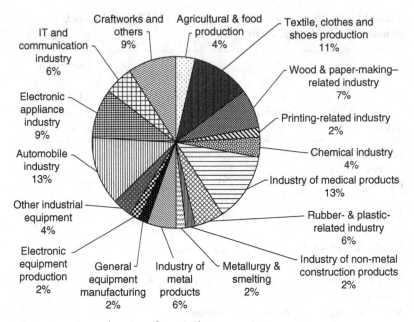

Figure 11.2 Manufacturing firms with overseas investment
Source: Fu et al. (2013).

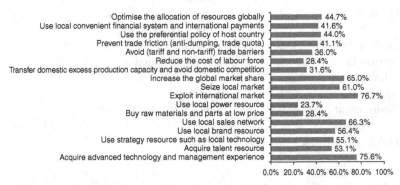

Figure 11.3 Main incentives for investing in developed countries
Source: Fu et al. (2013).

developed and developing countries, respectively. For firms that
invested in developed countries, 'to explore international markets' and
'to acquire advanced technology and management knowledge' are the
top two objectives. About 77 per cent and 76 per cent of the surveyed

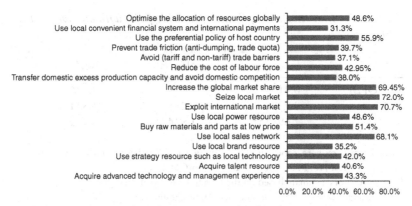

Figure 11.4 Main incentives for investing in developing countries
Source: Fu et al. (2013).

firms regarded these two as their objectives to invest in developed countries, respectively. However, firms that invest in developing countries appear to have wider and somewhat different objectives than those that invest in developed countries. For example, only 43 per cent of the firms regard 'to acquire advance technology and management experience' as an important objective for investing in developing countries. Instead, market expansion appears to be the most important objective to invest in developing countries, with about 72 per cent of the surveyed firms regarding 'to seize the local market' as an important motivation.

In the survey, the proportion of income from new products/technologies is positively related to the percentage of firms with overseas investment. New products/technologies contribute more than half of the income of 64 per cent of firms with overseas investment. We can see that for firms that have more than 50 per cent of their revenues generated from new products/technologies, 55 per cent have overseas investments. This figure drops to less than 30 per cent among firms in which new products/technologies contribute less than 10 per cent of their revenues.

On average, firms that go global through OFDI appear to have significantly higher innovation frequency and more investment in R&D and have achieved a higher percentage of sales accounted for by new or significantly improved products. As Table 11.2 shows, the proportion of innovators in the firms with OFDI was 94 per cent, which is significantly higher than that in the firms without OFDI at 82

Table 11.2 *Innovativeness of firms: comparing firms with and without OFDI*

	Innovation	New sales	R&D
Non OFDI	0.819	0.219	3.076
OFDI	0.938	0.295	4.624
t-test	2.698***	1.944*	3.972***

Note: Innovation here is measured by dummy, value 1 indicates innovator and 0 otherwise; t-test Ho: Mean(Non OFDI)–Mean(OFDI) = 0.
Source: Authors' estimate based on the Guangdong OFDI survey.
*** 1% significance; ** 5% significance; 10% significance.

per cent. The average percentage of new product sales in total sales is 30 per cent, also significantly higher than that in the firms without OFDI. The comparison of R&D spending also reinforced the message. The average R&D spending-to-sales ratio is 4.6 per cent in firms with OFDI, which is significantly higher than that in firms without OFDI. The t-test statistics indicate that the differences between the two groups are statistically significant at the 1 per cent or 10 per cent level.

This result indicates that internationalisation through OFDI is positively associated with the higher innovation capacity of the investing firms. What is the direction of the causality? In what follows, this chapter examines learning and capability upgrading in the process of internationalisation of Chinese multinational enterprises based on case studies of Chinese MNEs in the information and telecommunications industry so as to shed light on the causality of the impact of internationalisation on capabilities upgrading in the Chinese MNEs and the transmission mechanisms.

11.4 Methodology

Research Method

We constructed a multiple-case exploratory design to develop the existing theory. The case studies focus on individuals and analyse dynamic issues and are particularly suitable for in-depth study of one problem. First, exploratory case studies allow researchers to construct theories in a relatively new research area with rather limited literature; the study on the learning mechanism and corporate capability upgrading in the process of internationalisation of Chinese multinational enterprises is appropriate for this method.

Second, the characteristics of the learning mechanism, corporate capability upgrading and the process of internationalisation are comprehensive, complex and dynamic; hence, the case study is necessary for comprehensive and in-depth analysis of the phenomenon. We attempt to study the learning mechanism and corporate capability upgrading focusing on the experience of two cases by exploring their internationalisation process.

Third, the interviews with key decision makers can enhance our understanding of the problems and issues occurring in daily operations, so as to apply the theories and framework that could interpret the valuable experiences that occurred during the process of internationalisation, even to produce new theories on the learning mechanism and corporate capability upgrading.

Research Design

Eisenhardt (1989) studied building theories from case studies and its roadmap, which is constituted by several main steps including the definition of research questions, selecting cases, collecting and analysing data, shaping hypotheses, comparison with the literature and finally drawing conclusions. This roadmap synthesised previous work on qualitative methods (e.g., Miles and Huberman, 1984). In this study, we will follow Eisenhardt (1989)'s design of case study research.

We introduce the research target in the introduction section and then introduce the way to select and collect cases in the methodology section. The introduction to cases analyses the case history of internationalisation, along with learning and corporations' capability upgrading. Our discussion on the comparable analysis between two case practices and between the practice and the literature appears in the section on shaping hypotheses.

Case selection

Over the past three decades, the telecommunication industry has sprung up (Yu and Wang., 2008), and it plays a pivotal role in national growth and firm competitiveness in the current knowledge economy (OECD, 2004; Takahashi et al., 2004; Ollo-López and Aramendía-Muneta, 2012). Meanwhile, many Chinese multinational enterprises in telecommunications are classic examples of Chinese firms 'going out' because they have achieved great success in internationalisation. These firms not only have rich experience to enter foreign markets but also learn relevant technology, obtain management knowledge and achieve upgrading of their corporate capability. Therefore, the communication industry is our research field.

In this study, the following qualification criteria were applied to explore the learning mechanism and corporate capability upgrading in the process of internationalisation of Chinese multinational enterprises. First, from the perspective of time, decades of internationalisation experience allow historical analysis of successes and failures, and these are classic examples because of their growth, performance and contribution to the world. Second, the depth and breadth of academic analyses based on these firms and the archival data are available. Third, because of their comparability, we can identify the relevant conclusions including internationalisation practices, learning activities and corporate capability upgrading. Fourth, they are appropriate for building the theory. Therefore, Huawei and ZTE are the two cases selected for our study.

Both Huawei and ZTE are representative firms for at least three reasons. First, the tremendous successes achieved by these two companies in fewer than 30 years provide a rich research field and also are well worth learning from for companies that are striving for internationalisation. They were built up after the Chinese economic reform and opening up to the outside world. Starting their internationalisation in the 1990s, they have become two of the leading multinational firms in the ICT industry in China and in the world. All of these achievements are good examples for other Chinese firms undertaking internationalisation. Second, they also have, to a degree, similar internationalisation paths but also slightly different ones in the past few decades; hence, their experiences have strong comparability. Accordingly, a comparison between them can lead to some interesting results. Third, they employ good management practices with documented savings and file arrangements, so we can easily collect data from them. Finally, Huawei's and ZTE's internationalisation in both market expansion and corporations' capability upgrading are also an interesting area for researchers.

Data Collection

We collected extensive archival data on our two cases and the communication industry from 2011 to 2014. Most of these data are interviews of the key project's president and senior-level officers or managers from newspapers and business magazines. We believe that the interview documentation is the most reliable public resource for our research purpose. First, the interviews from mainstream conferences, newspapers and business magazines are in general credible. Second, the interview topics with senior-level managers or officers between the two cases covered different angles and are representative of the research target. Third, the senior-level managers or officers understand better the corporate strategy and corporations' capability upgrading and internationalisation process, which ensures the efficiency of our research.

To study the learning mechanism and corporate capability upgrading in the process of internationalisation of Chinese multinational enterprises, we picked 17 interview documentations that satisfy two conditions: (1) the interview topics relate to the research problem and (2) the interviews were conducted between 2011 and 2014 with the project's president, senior-level officers or managers. The date, interviewer and topics discussed are listed in Appendix 11.1.

11.5 Overview of the cases

Huawei and its internationalisation

Huawei Technologies P/L was founded in 1987, is the second largest telecommunications equipment company in the world by revenue and is poised to become the largest (Ahrens, 2013). It is an entirely employee-owned private company that provides customised network solutions for telecom carriers around the world with a vision to enrich life through communication. Huawei provides competitive solutions and services via end-to-end capabilities across the carrier networks, enterprise and consumer markets that have been deployed in more than 140 countries, serving more than one-third of the world's population.

Huawei's internationalisation takes the path of 'using the countryside to surround the cities'. In this case, it was developing countries instead of the countryside and developed markets instead of the cities. It is the first internationalisation push to occupy developing countries' markets from 1996 to 2004, and surrounding developed countries has been its second step since 2001.

The first phase of internationalisation – occupying developing markets
While business was booming in China in the 1990s, competition in advanced technologies from international competitors was still fierce, and Huawei looked abroad for continued growth. The builder of Huawei, Zhengfei Ren, likened Huawei's situation to that of a mountain goat needing to run faster and climb higher than a lion so as to avoid being eaten. Subsequently, Ren said that Huawei needed to be a wolf, a metaphor he used for years.

Huawei's first international customer was Hutchison Telecommunications (owned by Li Ka-shing) in Hong Kong in 1996, which purchased switches and related equipment for its fixed-line network. Hong Kong was a well-developed telecom market, yet it was close to Shenzhen, providing Huawei with an excellent first test case.

Then, the following year, Huawei formed a joint venture in Russia with the Beto Corporation to produce switching equipment, essentially assembling Huawei switches in Russia. Huawei was able to undercut international prices by around 12 per cent, but its after-sales service was what really impressed the Russians. Its first sale amounted to only US$12 million, but by 2001 its sales had reached US$100 million.

Soon after entering Russia, Huawei made sales in Thailand, Brazil, and South Africa. Its pricing became more aggressive, often undercutting rivals by 30 per cent. With its status as a national champion, Huawei's international marketing strategy is oriented to winning many international friends, like China's diplomatic route, and Huawei became an active partner under this strategy, which resulted in a large increase in profits. In November 2000, China's vice-premier, Wu Bangguo, travelled together with Ren Zhengfei during a trip to Africa, laying the foundation for future business deals, including a US$20 million contract in Ethiopia in 2003, and a US$200 million code division multiple access (CDMA) project in Nigeria in 2005 (Kuo, 2006). Ghana, Mauritius, Morocco, Congo and Kenya followed in 2006, along with another large Nigerian contract.

In the internationalisation process of occupying developing countries, Huawei's lower price for affordable technology is its biggest advantage. This push for internationalisation led to growth such that by 2004, its international revenues were higher than its domestic revenues.

The second phase – penetrating into the advanced markets
Following successes in Russia and a number of developing markets, Huawei started to turn its attention to developed markets. In 2001, Huawei made its first major sales in Europe, to the Netherlands and Germany. The wireless station product sold to the Dutch enabled multiple communications standards to be run, and upgrades were done by software rather than hardware (Pomfret, 2010). The product was a good example of 'cost innovation', in that it provided advanced features at low cost, while saving the carrier money on hardware (Zeng and Williamson, 2007). The Germans purchased optical network (SDH) products.

Soon after, Huawei made a sale to Neuf, the French operator, not only offering rock-bottom prices but also actually building part of it free of charge and allowing the operator to run it for three months to test it before purchase (Farhoomand and Ho, 2006). A subsequent sale to the United Arab Emirates made that country the first Arab state with 3G technology.

In 2004, Huawei made sales to a Danish company (in Portugal) and then made a major sale to the Netherlands for building out the 3G network. In 2005, British Telecom (BT) included Huawei as a preferred supplier for its massive next-generation network. Some analysts believe that this was a crucial factor in raising Huawei's international profile, because soon after it signed a global supplier agreement with Vodafone (Conti, 2007).

On Valentine's Day in 2001, Huawei entered the U.S. market, setting up an office in Plano, Texas. Three years later, Huawei was still without a single American customer (Prasso, 2011). Huawei has since had success, however, and its Plano office is now its U.S. headquarters, overseeing its 12 other offices and 7 R&D centres. In the United States, it has 1,100 employees, of whom 900 or so are Americans. It has yet to get a tier-one customer, but it is gaining traction in middle markets. Its North American sales were US$765 million in 2010, with customers including Leap (equipment and devices); Best Buy; and, purportedly, Level3 Communications.

Meanwhile, Huawei was also entering the emerging Internet data communications market. The giant in this area had been Cisco Systems, with 80 per cent of the Chinese router market. Three years later, Huawei had chipped away at Cisco's share and had captured 12 per cent to Cisco's 69 per cent. While lower prices certainly helped, Cisco claimed that Huawei had stolen its software (as well as user interface and manuals), and parts of Cisco's code were found in Huawei's products. By the time Huawei settled with Cisco, Huawei had about a third of the market (Ahrens, 2013).

By 2002, Huawei had also overtaken Shanghai Bell, the dominant China-based international joint venture (IJV) at the time. In 2004, Huawei amped up its second major international push, with extensive credit backing from the China Development Bank (CDB), which provided a credit line of US$10 billion, and the Export-Import Bank of China, which provided an additional US$600 million. With this robust backing, Huawei started to make a major global push. It slashed prices well below those of its competitors, purportedly sometimes by as much as 70 per cent, and provided vendor-financed loans to the customers. Sales in the first half of 2005 skyrocketed to more than US$4 billion, an 85 per cent increase over the previous year. More than 50 per cent of this value came from abroad. Sales growth in 2007 was more than 50 per cent; in 2008, when most suppliers saw negative sales growth, Huawei's sales still grew more than 40 per cent. In 2011, Huawei and Ericsson recorded approximate net revenues of US$32.9 billion and US$32.4 billion, respectively. By July 2012, Huawei's sales had bested those of Ericsson by US$500 million (based on half-year sales).

Huawei currently has around 110,000 employees worldwide, with 30 per cent or so in Shenzhen. Approximately two-thirds of its revenues come from international markets, and, according to Huawei, it works with 45 of the 50 largest carriers globally. Huawei has also filed more than 49,000 patents, as its focus on R&D continues. It has also played a leading role in standards development, both in China and abroad. It is the leading contributor to LTE core specifications, and it holds 83 positions in various standards bodies (Huawei press release, 2011).

According to Huawei's website, it participates in The 3rd Generation Partnership Project (3GPP), APT (Asia-Pacific Telecommunity), ARIB (Association of Radio Industries and Businesses), ETSI (European

Telecommunication Standards Institute), IEEE (Institute of Electrical and Electronics Engineers), IETF (Internet Engineering Task Force), ITU (International Telecommunication Union), TIA (Telecommunication Industry Association) and WWRF (Wireless World Research Forum). Aside from allegations of intellectual property impropriety, Huawei has undoubtedly become a technology leader.

ZTE and its internationalisation

The ZTE Corporation is a Chinese multinational telecommunications equipment and systems manufacturer, headquartered in Shenzhen, China. It was founded in 1985 in Shenzhen by a group of state-owned enterprises associated with China's Ministry of Aerospace. Listed on the Shenzhen Stock Exchange in 1997, since 2004 ZTE can also be found on the Hong Kong Stock Exchange. Today, general investors hold 67 per cent of stock shares, with overseas investors holding 18.3 per cent – a number that continues to increase every year; the company has 107 offices worldwide and subsidiaries in more than 100 countries.

With a market share of 4.3 per cent in 2012, ZTE is the world's fourth largest mobile phone manufacturer measured by unit sales. Furthermore, it is the world's fifth largest telecom equipment manufacturer measured by 2011 revenues. In 2012, ZTE became the fourth largest smart phone manufacturer in the world.

ZTE started its internationalisation by selling its products in developing and threshold countries. It took its first steps towards globalisation when it established branches in Indonesia in 1996. In 1998, ZTE signed a US$95 million contract, its first big overseas project in Pakistan. The first engagement in Africa was in 1999, when the company deployed a video conferencing system in Kenya. In 2001, ZTE considered its internationalisation strategy as a formal one and completely entered the overseas market. The first marketing sector was built in 2002, and the foreign marketing strategy has become one of intensive cultivation rather than extensive cultivation.

In 2003, ZTE became the largest code division multiple access (CDMA) system provider to BSNL, India's largest telecom services company. The internationalisation strategy of the following years was characterised by strategic partnerships especially in Europe and North America. Better still, years of endeavours in the overseas market started to pay back. The three growing product series and the overseas expansion worked together to push the company to a higher level in 2003. On January 8, 2004, a board announcement showed a record of new contract sales of RMB 25.19 billion in 2003, which represented a yearly growth of 50 per cent. This included RMB 4.82 billion from the mobile phone sales and represented a yearly increase of 66.3 per cent. It also included US$610 million from the overseas market, which represented a yearly increase of more than 100 per cent.

In 2004, the overseas market for mobile phone and 3G was pointed out as two principal growth sources of the company. Specifically, the company generated revenue of RMB 34 billion, of which RMB 13.6 billion (US$1.644 billion) was contributed by overseas contract sales, up 169.5 per cent from the previous year, thus ushering in a new era in the history of the company in building its international name. Over the whole year, more than 10 million sets of mobile phones were sold, up 100 per cent from 2003. This year witnessed the tremendous growth of the company in both international and domestic markets, proving that it was the fastest growing and most robust telecom equipment manufacturer in China.

In 2005 ZTE began its internationalisation The company started collaborations with Alcatel, Ericsson, France Telecom and Portugal Telecom in 2005. Two years later, the company announced a strategic long-term partnership with France Telecom and signed a long-term contract with Canada's second largest telecommunications operator Telus. To broaden the market abroad, ZTE considers developing countries as its main market target, and Pakistan is the first localisation market after occupied domestic market position. Then, ZTE entered Russia and the European market. In 2007, it formed strategic partnerships with Vodafone, Telefonica and Hutchison. The result of this continuous internationalisation strategy is reflected in ZTE's revenue stream, wherein international operations accounted for 60 per cent of the company's total revenue in 2011.

Moreover, ZTE rose to be the fourth largest smart phone manufacturer in the world during the third quarter of 2012. The overseas market has become ZTE's strategic market. ZTE has already started partnerships with more than 150 operators in more than 60 countries around the world. ZTE has definitely become the leader in Chinese multinational communication firms entering the international market.

11.6 Reverse learning and capability upgrading

Huawei and ZTE are now two leading multinational corporations in the communication industry. When they started internationalisation and going global, they had accumulated some technological capabilities in the domestic market, but they were far from being industry leaders at that time. Therefore, instead of beginning with core proprietary technologies and exploiting them in the process of internationalisation, our study reveals that they followed a technology and capability upgrading and development process driven by reverse learning from foreign customers, collaborators and subsidiaries. This section describes these processes.

Reverse learning from customers

Because information technology develops quickly, and customers expect more choices and better services, any operations mechanisms must make corresponding adjustments to improve operational efficiency and remain competitive. Therefore, customer-centric thinking has become the necessary method in the process of the reverse learning path.

Reverse learning
Huawei and ZTE represent the way in which a new entrant may challenge incumbents, especially foreign competitors, by developing resources and capabilities that are especially adapted to the local market. On the one hand, the payoffs from innovation activities are determined by market processes that involve not only the activities of the innovator but also the reactions of customers and competitors (Koellinge, 2007). Huawei and ZTE strive to maintain their market-focused product innovations that proved hard for domestic competitors to replicate. Huawei and ZTE have kept this strategy as they have extended their capabilities into manufacturing and R&D; namely, a major objective of Huawei's and ZTE's ongoing activities is to develop products that target specific customer segments. This case clearly illustrates how the nature and direction of business activities evolves in a firm's accumulation of relevant resources and capabilities. For example, every Huawei innovation stems from close interaction with its customers to understand their needs and market demands. Huawei annually invests an average of 10 per cent of its annual revenue to R&D. In 2011, Huawei increased its R&D investment to RMB 0.09 billion, equivalent to 13.7 per cent of sales in that year.

Currently, Huawei has 14 regional headquarters, 16 R&D centres, 28 joint innovation centres and 45 training centres worldwide. Customers want more from Huawei; Huawei is a huge company, and customers tell it what they want to buy, so what happens next is 4G, 5G, 6G. Therefore, Huawei naturally progresses from being a fast follower to becoming the leader and innovator.

The picky customer is an important motive to improve the standards for the appearance, material and technical aspects of the product. Because customers are both demanding and picky, Huawei has engaged in more technology and process testing as it has searched for better solutions to customer needs. For example, Huawei has produced a high-end water-proof phone, the Huawei Ascend D2. Through such a process, Huawei has continuously pushed the frontiers of technological development.

Similarly, one of advantages of ZTE is satisfying customer needs quickly. Through ZTE's 3G road show, it shows its customers ZTE's latest R&D results and its capability in building up commercial 3G networks in Turkey. It is estimated that 250 customers attended the Turkish leg of ZTE's road show on 22 and 23 March 2005 at the Crown Hotel, Istanbul, including senior executives from the Turkish Transportation Ministry, the Turkish Telecom Authority, Turk Telekom, Turk Cell, Telsim and Avea. ZTE has established 14 offices in Europe and has made significant steps into the European market.

Capability upgrading

The traditional value chain begins with the company's core competencies, its assets. It then moves to inputs and other raw materials, to an offering, to the distribution channels, and then finally to the customer. But the customer is the first source of Huawei's and ZTE's learning, with whom they have direct contact and provide their extensive solutions. The entire thought process has been reversed. Figure 11.5 shows the process of capability upgrading beginning with the customer.

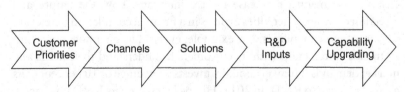

Figure 11.5 The reverse learning chain from customers

In this reverse process of capability upgrading, understanding customers' demands and prioritising them underlies basic capability learning. Next, according to customer demands, the firm builds capability by selecting and testing innovative ideas, product concepts and product prototypes through improved channels, solutions and R&D investment. In addition, in this process, management capability, especially in controlling and managing the distribution network, and some intangible assets including the brand name and firm reputation have also been improved.

First, understanding what customers value can be quite complex and is the first demand on firms because customers select products, services and providers of those products and services based in large part on how well they create value for them. Managers or firms can gain some understanding of customers through indirect means such as analysing sales data and sales call reports or can gain the deepest insights from direct interaction with customers from a research perspective, observing their operations and meetings and listening openly to their views, their market environment interpretations and their strategic discussions through open-ended in-depth interviews. When Huawei UK and ZTE entered the European market, their first challenge was to establish long-term customer relationships to understand subdivided markets and diverse customer requirements and to monitor the market and customer preferences. They were especially concerned with the package of combining functional, service, and relationship benefits as they relate to market entry and market share. This kind of understanding of the customer is based on direct and indirect communication with customers and is the first accumulated capability.

Second, selecting and testing innovative ideas, product concepts and product prototypes make up the second capability accumulated by multinational firms. For example, in China, people do not use a technology product with point-point connection, but this is popular in Europe; hence, Huawei developed and provided differentiated new products for the European market that followed customers' habits. People in many countries such as in Africa like mobile Internet and do not use fixed telephony. When Huawei began to enter the African market, it did not provide services very quickly. Instead, Huawei built infrastructure because that was the real need in these countries. After several years, Huawei became the dominant player in the communication industry market in Africa. This kind of capability of selecting innovative product concepts is a form of capability learning through totally understanding customers.

In addition, learning from the customer improves management capability, especially the capability of controlling and managing distribution networks. Long-term customer relationships for understanding subdivided markets and diverse customer requirements and monitoring the situation in a market and customer preferences according to customer requirements and competitive goals can lead to enhanced ability to control and manage a distribution network.

Finally, firms' intangible assets can obviously be improved after providing good service and technological assistance, such as improving the brand name and firm reputation, shortening the time from trial manufacturing to commercialising and formatting the virtuous circle in communication with dominant customers and suppliers.

Reverse learning from co-operation

In recent years, even the largest innovative organisations have not been able to rely solely on internal resources; they also acquire knowledge and capability from external sources. Therefore, in the innovation and global deployment phase, Huawei and ZTE gained external markets and technology capability through alliances, collaboration and joint R&D centres as external sources can facilitate the building of innovation capability.

Reverse learning

Huawei has focused on expanding its mobile technology and networking solutions through a number of partnerships while it has engaged in internationalisation (see Table 11.3).

In 1993, Huawei achieved its primary threshold of knowledge accumulation on PBX and successfully made the first breakthrough in C&C08 digital telephone switch by effectively taking advantage of the technology diffusions from Shanghai Bell (the first Sino-foreign joint venture in China). Huawei thereafter successfully monopolised the Chinese rural market and small cities within China. Afterwards, with higher product quality and improved product development, Huawei started to compete with foreign enterprises in the Chinese urban market.

From 1998 to 2003, Huawei's management style evolved through the influence of IBM, especially in the field of R&D and supply-chain

Table 11.3 *Huawei's history of alliances*

Date	Partners	Country
1989–1994	Shanghai Bell Telephone Manufacturing Company Sino-foreign joint venture	U.S. JV
20 Feb. 97	Texas Instruments	U.S.
9 Apr. 97	BETO TELEKOM	Russia
26 Aug. 99	Fujian Provincial Mobile	China
8 Jun. 00	Qualcomm	U.S.
27 Nov. 01	NEC, Matsushita Communications	Japan
21 Oct. 02	Agere System	U.S.
21 Oct. 02	Microsoft	U.S.
23 Oct. 02	NEC, Matsushita Communications	Japan
19 Mar. 03	3Com	U.S.
4 Jun. 03	Avici Systems	U.S.
29 Aug.03	Siemens Info& Common Mobile	Germany
16 Sep. 03	Infineon	Germany
12 Feb. 04	Nokia Siemens Networks	Germany
25 Apr. 05	Intel	U.S.
2 Mar. 06	HP	U.S.
31 May. 06	Freescale Semiconductor	U.S.
25 Jul. 06	Motorola	U.S.
13 Feb. 07	Qualcomm	U.S.
14 May. 07	Global Marine Systems	UK
21 May. 07	Symantec	U.S.
31 Oct. 07	International Telecommunication Union	Organisation
1998–2003	IBM	U.S.
12 Dec. 08	Microsoft	U.S.
20 Mar. 09	Infineon	Germany
9 Aug. 09	Sun Microsystems	U.S.

Source: Zhang (2009); Nakai and Tanaka (2010); Huawei interviews in Shenzhen and Reading (UK); http://www.huawei.com/en

management. It reorganised as an IT solution vendor from a mere hardware wholesale company. It survived the collapse of the IT bubble at the beginning of the 2000s, with advice from IBM consultants, increasing profits through better supply-chain management, stronger R&D and a more integrated corporate structure (Nakai and Tanaka, 2010).

In March 2003, Huawei and 3 Com Corporation formed a joint venture company, 3Com-Huawei (H3C), which focused on the R&D, production and sales of data-networking products. The company later divested a 49 per cent stake in H3C for US$880 million in 2006.

In 2005, Huawei began a joint venture with Siemens, called TD Tech, for developing 3G/TD-SCDMA mobile communication technology products, and Huawei established a Shanghai-based joint R&D centre with Motorola to develop UMTS technologies and a joint venture with Telecom Venezuela, called Industria Electronica Orinoquia, for research and development and the sale of telecommunications terminals after 2006 (Orinoco, 2010). In 2008, Huawei launched a joint venture with a UK-based marine engineering company, Global Marine Systems, to deliver undersea network equipment and related services (Wang, 2008).

Similarly, ZTE's internationalisation strategy was characterised by strategic partnerships especially in Europe and North America. ZTE started collaborations with Alcatel, Ericsson, France Telecom and Portugal Telecom in 2005. Two years later, the company announced a strategic long-term partnership with France Telecom and signed a long-term contract with Canada's second largest telecommunications operator Telus. In 2007, ZTE formed strategic partnerships with Vodafone, Telefonica and Hutchison. The result of this continuous internationalisation strategy is reflected in ZTE's revenue stream – international operations accounted for 60 per cent of the company's total revenue in 2011.

Capability upgrading

As a latecomer in the global knowledge economy, China can obtain the critical resources and capabilities to move from the position of late-follower to that of rapid-follower, or even leader through different internationalisation routes (Child and Rodrigues, 2005; Deng, 2007). One important route is the contract manufacturer/JVs (Child and Rodrigues, 2005): many mainland Chinese companies, such as Huawei and ZTE, choose to co-operate with foreign MNCs through JVs, contract manufacturing or technology licensing. They gradually learn the technologies or capabilities they need and move up the value chain.

First, building the global brand via collaborations with local famous firms is a shortcut to upgrade firms' reputations and competitive power. As we discussed, Huawei set up many joint R&D labs with renowned firms such as Texas Instruments and IBM, and created strategic alliances with multinational giants such as Siemens and 3COM. In the joint venture with 3COM, it learned about innovative marketing strategies and branding, for example, by selling under the Huawei-3COM name to improve and diffuse its own brand. Huawei has already moved well up the value chain of a typical original equipment manufacturer, but to achieve the pricing power and profits of a Sony or a Nike, the missing part of the jigsaw is the brand. Building a global brand takes time and is expensive. Thus, collaborative branding proved successful; in 2005, Huawei's contract sales were already US$8.2 billion, of which nearly 58 per cent came from foreign markets.

Before 1991, ZTE only developed low-end systems based on traditional chip production methods. The specialised chips that supported large capacity and complex systems were almost inaccessible to the firm. For a long time, this low-price route was successful in the Chinese market – when local brands experienced their most prosperous period, with local mobile phone manufacturers Ningbo Bird, Amoi, TCL, China Kejian and Konka evenly matching their foreign counterparts, including Nokia and Motorola. At that time, almost all top-selling mobile phones were made by contract manufacturers of low-end products. These brands, however, could only resort to low-price strategies to gain a share of the Chinese cell phone market. When foreign mobile phone producers also adopted medium- and low-price strategies, local mobile phone brands lost large numbers of manufacturing contracts. Facing a tough price war between 1995 and 1998, ZTE experienced difficult times. For comparable products, ZTE prices were estimated to be around 25 per cent lower than those of Western rivals, but lacking in innovation to distinguish themselves from other companies. However, continuous effort on the technical innovation front has proved to be extremely fruitful. The strategic alliance with international communication leaders Alcatel and Nortel laid a firm foundation for ZTE's goal to strive to build-up CDMA as a number one global brand. ZTE now has 14 wholly owned R&D centres across the United States, Europe and Asia.

Second, firms build up competence through taking advantage of technological complementarity among different collaborators. Zhengfei Ren, the president of Huawei, said that the goal of co-operation is to explore new technology and corporate capability. Targets include quickly transferring technology into products and sharing high-end technologies when Huawei collaborates with other firms in the communication industry that have some advantages in the specific aspects, such as firms providing retail services that are more familiar with markets, as well as with companies that operate in network development layers and are more powerful in regulation and infrastructure. Both Huawei and ZTE have regular exchange meetings with their collaborative institutions, through which R&D input, data transferring, product exploration and exploitation and appearance design capability have been improved the most.

Third, collaboration is helpful to firms' growth, in both technology and managements. For example, UK companies have a long history of strong product demand and rigorous quality and health-safety requirements. This has enabled ZTE to develop in these areas when it entered the UK market through continuous contact with local firms. ZTE UK not only learned how to regulate its operation management but also received feedbacks that are related to the headquarters. Therefore, technology and management capability for subsidiaries and headquarters is the third channel of capability upgrading.

Project management is also an important capability for firms to learn from the collaborative experiences. Huawei and ZTE came to the consistent conclusion that establishing project targets, phases' standards and project managing regulations and adjusting organisation structure flexibly in the new innovation projects are important capabilities accumulated from previous collaborations.

Other corporate capabilities have been accumulated from collaboration practices, such as facilitating communication among R&D personnel, harmonising basic research, developing and commercialising, promoting information flow and interconnection between different function departments and perfecting production regulations and systems.

Learning from subsidiaries

Learning from subsidiaries is the third characteristic for both Huawei and ZTE. International marketing involves recognising that people all over the world have different needs. Huawei and ZTE have brands that are now recognised across the globe. While many of the products that these businesses sell are targeted at a global audience using a consistent marketing mix, it is also necessary to understand regional differences, hence the importance of international marketing. They must accept that differences in values, culture, languages and currencies will mean that some products will suit only certain countries even within global markets. For example, there are important regional differences in cell phone colour, wire colour and infrastructure fix trial criteria for different countries. Huawei produced the high-end waterproof phone Huawei Ascend D2 within the European market environment where stringent standards for the appearance of the product, material and technical aspects; more technology and process testing; and picky customers ensured that Huawei had to find a better solution. Managers at ZTE also point out that document management in UK firms is an important aspect of the ZTE learning process.

What's more, learning from each other through different subsidiaries is another interesting learning activity. For Huawei, the UK is the first country (in Europe) that it entered; it also learned a great deal from developing countries and about technology by establishing a relationship between Africa and the UK.

The UK is the first developed country in which ZTE developed its brand and enhanced its reputation to be able to respond to customer needs. ZTE provides an interesting case about learning among different subsidiaries. It met huge obstacles when it sold 3G phones to Africa because of lack of charging power. To solve this question, it developed new energy resources such as a storage battery utilising solar energy, and this technology provides huge market profit not only in the African market but also worldwide.

Third, learning a new operating vision in developed markets, such as social responsibility, is an obvious advantage. Huawei met significant barriers in the United States; the U.S. government considered it untrustworthy. As a consequence, Huawei is extremely careful to obey local laws in the country it is operating in, to accept social responsibility for its actions and to promote good collaboration with local partners. All of this will be good for Huawei in its future business activities. Similarly, in the case of ZTE, advanced operational thinking is regarded as a shortcut for operating its business in the future.

The headquarters and knowledge integration and diffusion

In the process of learning from subsidiaries, the headquarters serve as a knowledge gatekeeper, integrator and mediator between subsidiaries. The subsidiaries are the first unit that creates or acquires a new technology. The parent company then acts as the mediating unit that collects and selects knowledge transferred back to the headquarter, integrates it with the company's existing capabilities and then disseminates the new or integrated knowledge to other subsidiaries of the company group. Finally, other subsidiaries adopt the new knowledge and technology diffused from the headquarters and sometimes from regional headquarters. In this process, technology- or the knowledge-providing unit (a subsidiary) is a point, and the headquarters is the hub. Huawei has a capabilities centre in its headquarters in Shenzhen. This centre is responsible for (1) assessing the capabilities of the company and identifying areas to improve; 2) collecting knowledge and information from its subsidiaries all over the world, identifying the relevant knowledge that is needed by the company and integrating it with the company's existing technologies; and (3) diffusing the newly acquired or integrated knowledge to the departments or subsidiaries that are in need of it. The regional headquarters of Huawei also serves to collect and diffuse relevant new technologies or other non-technological knowledge to other subsidiaries in the region directly. This function of the regional headquarters also allows the reverse transfer and re-diffusion to be faster and more efficient.

Capability upgrading

Most Chinese firms are deeply embedded in their institutional context. Huawei and ZTE also have a deep understanding of their local markets, including knowledge about customer preferences, adaptation requirements and price sensitivity. Changing rules of global competition require Huawei and ZTE to constantly update their resource base and explore new market space. Overseas markets are there to be acquired, new technology and capability have to be absorbed and upgraded and subsidiaries are the units that first acquire technology; hence, communication among subsidiaries is helpful to capability improvement.

A firm's long-term development strategy and management philosophy will obviously be improved based on learning from subsidiaries in developed areas. Strategic capability normally includes connections between technological strategy and business strategy, advanced decision systems, entrepreneurial spirit and intense innovation environment, adjusting innovation strategy accordingly and so on.

Developed markets look for something different from developing countries; in the process, they become the market leader. Developing countries look for solutions and provide services into their respective countries. Both Huawei and ZTE said that they have learned some advanced management ideas from the European market, such as health-safety issues and corporate social responsibility, and this is a developing trend for the Chinese headquarters and other subsidiaries. An investment philosophy exists amongst most firms in Europe, whereas few firms in China seem to adopt such an outlook. Therefore, the firm's long-term development strategy regarding management capability will be improved when the subsidiaries in developed countries have absorbed and shared this investment philosophy with other subsidiaries.

Both Huawei and ZTE also illustrate a firm's accumulation of relevant resources and capabilities in business operations because the subsidiary in a new market is a new project or a wholly new entrepreneurship. Comparing developed countries to developing countries, different subsidiaries in different countries have different production lines, which does not imply that one is better than the other; it is just different. The African market, which researches technology, presents a different problem; a company needs to try solutions and then get differentiated products. It is worthwhile to note that most of this behaviour is learned from other subsidiaries in developed countries, sometimes just a kind of imitation; hence, the ability of the China mainland to re-innovate when facing the international market was obviously improved. Huawei and ZTE also learned that subsidiaries will feed back accumulated experiences and capabilities to headquarters, such as establishing project targets, phases' standards and project managing regulations and adjusting organisation structure flexibly. Therefore, this is the second contribution to learning among subsidiaries to accumulate business operation abilities.

Cultivating learning consciousness and investing in learning comprise a kind of learning path combining unconscious absorption and planned learning behaviours in the connection with subsidiaries in different sub-markets. On the one hand, as we have already discussed, subsidiaries provide technology or knowledge in the process of learning. They transfer their information back to headquarters and achieve information exchange via the network of branches and subsidiaries led by the headquarters. These are planned learning behaviours. On the other hand, some informal information flow and interconnection between different functional departments create opportunities for unconscious learning, absorption and capability upgrading.

Besides the previously discussed aspects of capability upgrading, companies' management capability in human resource management, total quality management and organisational capability of benchmark system are also upgraded. Interviews with subsidiary managers of both Huawei and ZTE also highlighted the gains in these aspects.

11.7 Conclusions

This study of Huawei and ZTE has several important findings regarding the relationship between a latecomer firm's internationalisation strategy and market expansion on the one hand, and its capability upgrading on a particular learning path on the other. First, reverse learning generates revenues from foreign customers, collaborators and subsidiaries. Learning from these sources improves an MNE's capability in several areas such as understanding customers' needs, selecting and testing innovation ideas, transforming customer needs and innovative ideas into product concepts and product prototypes, controlling and managing the distribution network, business operations management, building global brand via collaboration, building competence based on complementarities amongst collaborators and management philosophy and cultivating learning consciousness. It also has significant effect on a firm's long-term development strategy and the growth of its technology and management capabilities. Therefore, the gains from internationalisation are the upgrading of the overall capabilities of these firms in addition to technology upgrading as normally expected.

In addition, these two cases clearly illustrate that learning may have its root in a project or in a collaboration, whereas capability upgrading based on it may take place in the headquarters and through it also in other subsidiaries of the company group. For example, in the case of ZTE, the obstacle of lack of pricing power in the African market induced the development of new energy resources such as a storage battery using solar energy. This innovative technology provides ZTE significant profit not only in the African market but also worldwide. For Huawei, the breakthrough in the Netherlands has contributed significantly to the company's success in the continental European market. Experiences from the Netherlands served as a model for the European market, and the company learned and built up the capability to communicate with government, operators and customers and how to price their products and services.

The two case studies illustrate an alternative path, namely reverse learning, for a new entrant to build corporate capability. This learning path includes several branches, including learning from customer-related activities in marketing, sales and service; learning through collaboration with other firms, institutions and R&D centres; and also learning from headquarters and other subsidiaries in the company group. In each learning branch, specific learning activities lead to upgrading in relevant capability areas.

Finally, the two cases examined also represent the way in which a new entrant may challenge incumbents by developing resources and capabilities that are especially adapted to the local market. Huawei and ZTE accumulated customer knowledge and created the strong customer-priority solution department that is very difficult for their Western competitors to achieve because often in-house R&D leads the direction of production and operation in these companies instead of customer needs. They have continued with this customer-priority solution strategy even when their competitive advantage has moved from marketing to manufacturing and R&D. A major objective of their ongoing activities is to develop products that are even more finely attuned to increasingly more specific customer segments. This consistent focus and deepening capability in this regard have also emerged as a significant competitive advantage for them in the domestic and foreign markets.

Findings from the ZTE and Huawei cases have clear implications for management. The two companies' experiences in capability building through reverse learning suggest to managers that they can build up technological and overall capabilities of firms through operation in foreign countries and acquire knowledge and capabilities through subsidiaries abroad. They should clearly link their existing set of resources and capabilities in headquarters and subsidiaries to desired changes in those features that they see as necessary to enhance competitiveness.

Furthermore, the customers are the primary source of Huawei's and ZTE's learning. It is with the customers that Huawei and ZTE had direct contact through their extensive distribution network. Innovating and upgrading in response to highly demanding customers have become major drivers of capabilities upgrading in these firms. Huawei's and ZTE's first success can arguably be attributed to their efforts to master and understand customer needs before investing significantly in R&D.

The case also shows how a firm's development of new capabilities requires different structures for learning. A firm can acquire different capabilities through different means, for example, through communicating with customers, collaborating with a partner and learning among subsidiaries. Furthermore, as a firm develops capabilities in new functional areas or sub-markets or broadens the range of capabilities in a particular function, the organisation must be restructured to support effective and efficient coordination of increasingly diverse activities and improve capability to ensure new activities.

To note, although the research shed important insights on the benefits in learning alongside firms' internationalisation process, considering the exploratory nature of this study based on two cases, one needs to be cautious in generalising the research findings of this study. The conclusions need to be validated with further research.

Appendix 11.1 *Interviews coverage*

Date	Name and Title	Topics	Resources
23 June 2014	Chao Ai, VP Technology collaboration Haibo Lin, head of technology collaboration	Huawei's global technology collaboration and knowledge integration	Case interview in Shenzhen sponsored by the British Academy project
24 October 2013	Don Kelly, deputy COO at Huawei Technologies	Huawei UK's strategy and product solution paths and strategy	Case interview sponsored by the project
24 Oct. 2013	Elton Yuxuan Huang, service director, UK&I	Market entry strategy, technology-upgrading strategy	Case interview sponsored by the project
25 Feb. 2013	Yang Shao, CMO at Huawei Technologies	Stand out with the Samsung/Apple competition	http://phone-news-today.com/archives/1239
17 Jan. 2014	Jack Guo, senior product manager at ZTE (UK) Limited	ZTE's strategy, production solutions, technology-upgrading strategies	Case interview sponsored by the project
16 Oct. 2013	Stefano Cantarelli, CFO for network and carrier business units	Channels of building technological capability	Case interview sponsored by the project
7 Feb. 2013	CEO of Huawei Technologies UK	Huawei story	Oxford Department of International Development (ODID) and the TMD Centre co-hosted the Distinguished Guest Lecture, the lecture organised by a professor of this project
7 Feb. 2013	CEO of Huawei Technologies UK	Internationalisation and innovation	An informal discussion between professors of this project and Victor Zhang

Appendix 11.1 (*cont.*)

Date	Name and Title	Topics	Resources
20 Nov. 2011	Richard Ye Lihe, ZTE's senior director of wireless product operation, product R&D system	Internationalisation distribution and firm strategy	Interview from the Mobile Asia Congress 2011. The video can be accessed from http://www.youtube.com/watch?v=96htGIAbqs4
12 Jan. 2012	Lixin Cheng, CEO of ZTE (USA) Inc.	Technology preference, development strategy in the coming year	2012 International Consumer Electronics Show (CES). The video can be accessed from http://www.youtube.com/watch?v=yGCz_rf1UxQ
15 July 2011	Edward Zhou, CMO, Huawei Technologies	The introduction about Huawei UK, products, localisation and so on	Cambridge Wireless, 2011. The video can be accessed from http://www.youtube.com/watch?v=tTFghIAo5o4
2 Oct. 2013	James Lockett, vice-president, Huawei Technologies Co., Ltd.	Does innovation foster trade or does trade foster innovation?	WTO Public Forum TV 2013. The video can be accessed from http://www.tvballa.com/video-gallery/Huawei-Technology#erfl2g9IDemIKmrd.99
1 Aug. 2011	Zhu Shi, president	The background behind Exotic story of ZTE's growth	ZTE Malaysia GSMA Board Meeting interview. The video can be accessed from http://www.youtube.com/watch?v=dUjkdInrvY0#t=36

Date	Person	Topic	Source
7 March 2012	Javier López, sales manager	New technologies and new productions	Mobile World Congress 2012. Interview by Total Television. The video can be accessed from http://www.youtube.com/watch?v=3KAJS2KKItY
15 Oct. 2012	Hu Xue Mei, CMO, ZTE, MEA	Industry change, opportunities and challenges	ITU TELECOM WORLD 2012, Dubai. The video can be accessed from http://www.youtube.com/watch?v=Uo_iuqSaEiQ
14 May 2013	Zhengfei, Ren	Huawei founder gives first media interview	Microblog Buzz, China. The video can be accessed from http://www.youtube.com/watch?v=jBgYTw8mU68
27 May 2013	Lixin Cheng, CEO of ZTE USA	Lixin Cheng on ZTE's U.S. future at CTIA 2013	The Engadget Interview. The video can be accessed from http://www.engadget.com/2013/05/27/the-engadget-interview-lixin-cheng-on-ztes-us-future-at-ctia-2

12 | *International collaboration and radical innovation*

12.1 Introduction

For latecomer economies, the acquisition of advanced knowledge through imports, licensing and attraction of inward foreign direct investment is the most frequently used conventional channel for international knowledge acquisition (Fu, Pietrobelli and Soete, 2011). China is no exception in this regard. All these knowledge diffusion mechanisms are followed by acquisition, assimilation and adaptation and hence are closely linked to imitative innovation in terms of producing products or using processes that are new to the country but not new to the world. In recent years, in its pursuit of the transition from imitator to innovator, China has increasingly employed various 'unconventional' international knowledge-sourcing mechanisms. These include the attraction of highly skilled returning migrants, outward direct investment in advanced economies and international innovation collaboration to create or co-create new knowledge. Will China become a frontier innovator through unconventional international knowledge sourcing? With internationalisation of innovation and changes in the innovation mode from closed to open, innovation is increasingly a collaborative and global undertaking. Therefore, in this chapter we explore the role of international innovation collaboration in China's transformation from imitator to innovator.

The rest of the chapter is organised as follows: Section 12.2 briefly overviews the patterns and trends in innovation collaboration amongst Chinese firms. Section 12.4 presents the empirical results. Section 12.5 provides conclusions.

12.2 International collaboration and radical innovation: the literature

The transformation from imitation to innovation requires increasing novel or radical innovation that has greater novelty than the diffusionary, imitative innovations that China mainly engaged with in the takeoff and catch-up stages. Radical innovations represent major departures from existing practices and involve the disruptive creation of new insights (Ettlie, 1983). Accordingly, the launch of radical innovation requires an extension of both the depth and breadth of knowledge (Zhou and Li, 2012). The high requirements to launch radical innovation lead firms to acquire knowledge not only from internal R&D but also from external learning and collaboration (Birkinshaw, Bessant and Delbridge, 2007; Bao, Chen and Zhou, 2012).

One of the mechanisms to tap into external innovation resources and capacities is collaboration. External linkages, both public (including universities) and private, benefit firms' innovation (Freeman and Soete, 1997). Through collaboration, firms can expand the range of expertise, strengthen R&D capacities, acquire complementary resources and enhance commercialisation capacities. Collaborating with other firms may not only help a firm acquire knowledge from outside its boundary but also combine different sources of knowledge that could be useful in exploring uncertain worlds (Belderbos, Carree and Lokshin, 2004). By being involved in collaborative relationships, a firm could 'open up gateways to new knowledge that departs from existing organizational memory' (Bao et al., 2012) and obtain the opportunity to synergistically integrate partners' capabilities and resources. Moreover, heterogeneity in technological knowledge and difference in market domains between partners ensure diversity of inter-firm knowledge portfolios (Prabhu, Chandy and Ellis, 2005), increasing the possibility of the development of new architecture or functions. Collaborative innovation is of particular importance for radical innovation because it requires acquisition of knowledge not only from internal R&D but also from external learning and collaboration (Birkinshaw et al., 2007; Bao et al., 2012). Therefore, companies should not innovate in isolation but cooperate with external partners throughout the innovation process (OECD, 2008).

Innovation has increasingly become internationalised. Firms go across the border for either exploitation or exploration of knowledge (Archibugi and Iammarino, 2002). The globalisation of innovation has three components: (1) the international exploitation of nationally generated innovation, (2) the global generation of innovations by MNEs and (3) global techno-scientific collaboration (Archibugi and Iammarino, 2002). These activities can be either asset-exploiting R&D or asset-augmenting activity (Dunning and Narula, 1995). In addition to MNE-led global innovation generation, strategic technology partnering (STP) is argued to be a key strategy complementary to internal R&D-based innovation (Narula and Zanfei, 2004). This stream of literature finds that large firms tend to enter into STP because of their strong technological capabilities and absorptive capacity. This enables these firms to keep up with the technological frontier (Cantwell, 1995). On the other hand, Narula (2002) finds that small firms rely on non-internal sources because of their limitations in managerial, financial and knowledge resources. Hence, international technology collaboration has changed from technology transfer to organisational learning (Niosi, 1999). Non-equity STPs can be a useful tool as they are more flexible and more suitable for knowledge development and learning.

The wave of innovation internationalisation and the rise of the emerging economies have induced a large number of R&D outsourcing activities from the United States and EU in the emerging economies (EEs) – in particular, China and India. This encourages innovation collaboration between the developed countries such as the UK and the EEs. Moreover, the emerging economies, especially China and India, have invested heavily in R&D and both have reservoirs of low-cost but skilled labour (Fu et al., 2011). This also makes them attractive partners for international innovation collaboration.

Despite the heavy investment in R&D and the large pool of educated scientists and engineers, studies on middle-income country firms in South East Asia engaging in radical innovation at the technology frontier suggest that firms from developing and emerging economies are normally constrained by their level of technological capabilities and human resources to achieve world-leading innovation performance (e.g., Hobday, Rush and Bessant, 2004; Dantas and Bell, 2009). Innovation through international collaboration is likely to break these constraints. Evidence from Chapter 8 suggests that Chinese firms engaged in innovation collaboration with universities in the newly industrialised economies are more likely to produce novel innovations. Therefore, international innovation collaboration may nurture more radical innovation and change the technology trajectory in China.

12.3 Collaborative innovation in China: an overview

Using the national innovation survey carried out in 2008 by the National Bureau of Statistics of China and Tsinghua University, we

Table 12.1 *Collaborative innovation activities*

Firm ownership	Firms that have joined collaborative innovation		Firms that have not joined collaborative innovation	
	No. of firms	Proportion (percentage)	No. of firms	Proportion (percentage)
State-owned	64	4.6	58	4.2
Private	443	32.0	399	28.8
Foreign invested	161	11.6	260	18.8
Total	668	48.2	717	51.8

Source: 2008 China National Innovation Survey by Tsinghua University and NBS.

have an overview of the pattern of innovation collaboration in Chinese firms. As explained in Chapter 8, this sample is biased towards innovative firms. Therefore, the results may overestimate the actual breadth and depth of innovation in the population of Chinese firms.

As Table 12.1 indicates, around 48 per cent of sampled Chinese firms have engaged in collaborative innovation; 52 per cent have not. This is on par with the share of firms engaged in collaborative innovation in the United Kingdom from 2008 to 2010 (BIS, 2013). Interestingly, in the domestic sector, a majority of state-owned (SOEs) and privately owned firms (POEs) engaged in collaborative innovation: 64 SOEs versus 58 SOEs, and 443 POEs versus 399 POEs. In contrast, with respect to foreign invested firms, a majority have not taken part in collaboration, which could be indicative of their relative reluctance towards networking with local firms.

Firms do collaborate with various partners including other firms within their company group; suppliers of equipment, raw material or software; customers; competitors; consultants or private R&D institutes; and universities or public R&D research institutions. As Table 12.2 reports, universities and public research institutions are the sector that registered the largest number of collaborations, mainly because of the high number of collaborations with domestic universities and research institutions. Suppliers and customers also have seen a large number of innovation collaborations. In particular, collaboration with foreign customers is the most popular pattern of international collaboration with 187 cases registered in this category, followed by foreign

Table 12.2 *Types of collaborators and regional distribution*

Types of collaborators	Collaboration with domestic partners	Collaboration with international partners	Total number of collaborations	Do not collaborate
Other firms within affiliated group	315	119	434	223
Suppliers of equipment, raw material or software	316	162	478	204
Users or consumers	291	187	478	217
Competitors or other firms within the same industry	222	106	328	318
Consultants or private R&D institutes	223	48	271	362
Universities or public R&D institutes	473	35	508	157

Note: Firms are allowed to make multiple choices.
Source: 2008 China National Innovation Survey by Tsinghua University and NBS.

suppliers, which also reported 162 cases of international collaboration. With regard to collaboration with other partners, we still see a relatively high proportion in comparison to internationally leading innovative nations such as the UK in the same collaborative category.

12.4 Collaborative innovation and China's transformation from imitator to innovator: empirical evidence

Using the China 2008 National Innovation Survey and similar methods used in the analysis of the role of universities in China's industrial

Table 12.3 *The impact of collaboration on innovation performance in Chinese firms: Tobit model estimation results*

	1	2
	Novel new sales	Imitative new sales
Co_international	16.13***	1.819
	(5.178)	(3.610)
Co_domestic	−1.277	7.565*
	(5.728)	(3.921)
Ln(inhouse R&D)	1.326	2.776***
	(0.903)	(0.590)
Ln(extramural R&D)	1.515**	−0.074
	(0.642)	(0.462)
Age	−0.132	−0.066
	(0.157)	(0.062)
Size4	1.019	−5.425
	(5.57)	(3.868)
Constraints in human capital	−2.361	−4.431
	(5.13)	(3.913)
Coastal region	2.644	−6.406*
	(4.892)	(3.533)
Foreign invested firm	15.24***	−5.787
	(5.158)	(3.934)
Industry dummies	yes	yes
Constant	yes	Yes
Observations	819	804
F statistics	4.476	4.358
LogLikelihood	−1291	−3320

Note: Robust standard errors in parentheses; *** $p<0.01$, ** $p<0.05$, * $p<0.1$.

innovation (details discussed in Chapter 8), this section presents the empirical test results on the impact of international innovation collaboration on industrial innovation in China. As Table 12.3 reveals, innovation collaboration with foreign partners has had a positive and significant effect on novel innovation in firms. On average, the percentage of sales of products that are new to the world in firms that have collaborated with international partners is 16 per cent higher than that of those firms that have not. The estimated coefficient is statistically significant at the 1 per cent level. Not surprisingly, collaboration with domestic partners does not exert a significant effect on novel innovation in Chinese manufacturing firms. The estimated coefficient of the extramural R&D variable is positive and statistically significant at the 5 per cent level, suggesting engaging with extramural R&D contributes to the creation of radical innovation in China. Foreign firms are more creative than domestic firms. The average share of sales on account of novel innovation in foreign invested firms is 15 per cent higher than that of domestic firms.

In contrast, collaboration with domestic partners appears to have a positive impact on the generation of imitative diffusionary innovation in China, although the estimated coefficient is only marginally significant at the 10 per cent level. The main contributor to imitative innovation in China is in-house R&D activities. The estimated coefficient is positive and statistically significant at the 1 per cent level, suggesting that a 1 per cent increase in in-house R&D spending increases the percentage of new sales by 0.12 per cent. Firms in coastal regions appear to have less imitative innovation than that of the firms in the inland region. But the estimated coefficient is only marginally significant at the 10 per cent level. The difference between the foreign and domestically owned firms does not appear to be significant in this regard.

Distinguishing the collaborative partners according to the type of their external partners, Table 12.4 reports the estimated results of their impact on novel innovation. We have controlled for collaboration with domestic partners and other foreign partners to single out the effect of the particular type of collaboration under concern. Except for collaboration with partners within the company group, collaboration with all other types of foreign partners appears to have a significant positive effect on the creation of novel innovation in Chinese firms. Collaboration with foreign customers appears to have the largest impact on novel innovation. The average share of sales on account of novel products in firms that collaborated with foreign customers appears to be 33 per cent higher than for those that did not. Collaboration with the suppliers also appears to have a significant contribution to novel innovation. But the size of the effect and the significance of the effect are considerably smaller than those of collaboration with customers. Collaboration with foreign universities appears to have the second largest benefits. The average sales of novel products in firms that collaborate with foreign universities are

Table 12.4 *The impact of international collaboration on novel innovation in China: Tobit model estimation results*

	1	2	3	4	5	6	7
	Dep Var: Novel new sales percentage						
Co_within company group_int'l	0.0731	6.114					
	(7.715)	(7.305)					
Co_supplier_international	4.225		11.74*				
	(6.483)		(7.116)				
Co_customer_international	25.28***			33.34***			
	(5.618)			(7.215)			
Co_competitor_international	4.499				15.47**		
	(6.56)				(7.004)		
Co_private res. institute_int'l	8.297					19.32**	
	(8.693)					(8.372)	
Co_University&Pub res. inst_int'l	14.49						23.54**
	(9.926)						(9.212)
Co_international		16.02***	11.89*	−2.714	12.19**	15.60***	15.60***
		(5.614)	(6.733)	(7.326)	(6.026)	(5.479)	(5.37)
Co_domestic	−7.037	−4.806	−5.451	−5.332	−4.723	−4.75	−4.525
	(5.344)	(5.639)	(5.595)	(5.511)	(5.601)	(5.631)	(5.603)
Ln(inhouse R&D)	1.083	1.129	1.17	1.118	1.06	1.132	1.11
	(0.883)	(0.91)	(0.908)	(0.892)	(0.908)	(0.917)	(0.904)
Ln(extramural R&D)	1.509**	1.569**	1.541**	1.640**	1.470**	1.508**	1.504**
	(0.646)	(0.649)	(0.648)	(0.636)	(0.653)	(0.646)	(0.646)

Table 12.4 (*cont.*)

	1	2	3	4	5	6	7
			Dep Var: Novel new sales percentage				
Age	-0.148	-0.178	-0.176	-0.167	-0.188	-0.176	-0.169
	(0.158)	(0.166)	(0.164)	(0.162)	(0.168)	(0.165)	(0.163)
Size4	1.317	2.762	2.726	2.178	2.81	2.558	2.307
	(5.586)	(5.63)	(5.665)	(5.569)	(5.663)	(5.617)	(5.627)
Lack human capital	-2.256	-2.056	-2.100	-2.924	-1.769	-2.253	-1.011
	(5.014)	(5.174)	(5.166)	(5.025)	(5.157)	(5.136)	(5.174)
Sector dummies	Yes	Yes	Yes	Yes	Yes	Yes	Yes
Constant	Yes	Yes	Yes	Yes	Yes	Yes	Yes
Observations	819	819	819	819	819	819	819
F statistics	5.362	4.274	4.376	5.836	4.71	4.816	4.936
Loglikelihood	-1278	-1291	-1290	-1280	-1289	-1289	-1289

Note: Robust standard errors in parentheses; *** p<0.01, ** p<0.05, * p<0.1.

Dependant variable: percentage of sales that are new to the world.

23.5 per cent higher than for those that did not. Collaborations with foreign private research institutions and foreign firms in the same industry all appear to have brought considerable gains to the firms. The estimated coefficients are all statistically significant at the 5 per cent level.

12.5 Conclusions

Given the fact that innovation is increasingly a collaborative task and that more and more firms are adopting international collaboration in today's globalisation era, this chapter analyses the contribution of international collaboration to China's transformation from imitator to (radical) innovator. Whereas collaboration between domestic partners only appears to be marginally beneficial to the production of diffusionary innovation in China, collaborations with foreign partners are found to have made a significant positive impact on the creation of novel innovation in Chinese firms. The type of foreign partners that Chinese firms may benefit collaborating with covers a wide range, including foreign customers, suppliers, universities, private research institutions and firms in the same industry. Collaboration with foreign customers generates the largest benefits for the creation of novel innovation. Collaboration with foreign universities also proves to be fruitful for the generation of innovations that are new to the world.

Findings from this research have profound policy implications. To achieve the important second-stage catch-up and move the economy to the high-income group is the main development objective of China and many other middle-income countries. This movement to the world frontier requires high-level creative ideas and talents that are quantitatively and qualitatively different from those that are required for imitative innovation. It requires an open mind and a strategy for path-breaking innovation instead of path-following incremental innovation. It requires vision in identifying strategic direction, heavy investment for such long-term R&D activities, partners to share the risks and the high-level and complex skills that are required to carry out such groundbreaking innovations. International collaborative innovation is therefore an effective mechanism to address the challenges for the path-breaking radical innovations that are necessary to achieve and maintain international innovation leadership. This is, in fact, a widely observed trend among the OECD countries, which have introduced a series of programmes to encourage and support international collaboration. Results from this chapter confirm that it is an effective channel that will bring significant gains to Chinese firms for the creation of novel radical innovation.

13 | *Innovation efficiency and the cross-country gap in innovation*

13.1 Introduction

The gap in innovation between European Union (EU) countries and the United States has been well documented. Publications by the European Commission and the UK Department of Trade and Industry on international research and development (R&D) expenditure show that Europe lags behind the United States and some Asian economies in R&D investment (DTI, 2005; EC, 2005). Hall (2004) and other studies have also suggested an increasing gap between Europe and the United States. Numerous academic and government studies investigating the factors affecting national innovation performance and quantifying national innovative capacity have identified gaps between the OECD economies and the United States as the lead economy in this respect (e.g., Porter and Stern, 1999; EC, 2002, 2005; Furman, Porter and Stern, 2002; Mairesse and Mohnen, 2002; DTI, 2003a, 2003b, 2003c, 2005; Faber and Hesen, 2004; Furman and Hayes, 2004; Jaumotte and Pain, 2005).

One of the most influential contributions to this literature has been based on a particular notion of innovation capacity. This is defined as 'the ability of a country – as both a political and economic entity – to produce and commercialise the flow of new-to-the-world technologies over the long term' (Furman et al., 2002, p. 900). This notion of innovative capacity is 'not the realised level of innovative output per se, but reflects more fundamental determinants of the innovation process' (ibid.). This notion, operationalised by the authors as a 'production function' for international patents, is – they argue – readily captured by a small number of observable factors that describe a country's national innovative capacity. These are the (1) *common innovation infrastructure*, including overall science and technology policy, basic research support mechanisms, higher education and the stock of cumulative technological knowledge; (2) *specific innovation environments*, such as industrial clusters of the kind identified by Porter (1985) in his work on the sources of national competitive advantage; and (3) *linkages* between the common innovation infrastructure and the clusters influenced, amongst other things, by the nature of the university system and the nature of funding sources for new ventures linked to the particular industrial clusters.

In most developments of this approach, innovation output is proxied by USPTO patenting per capita. The contribution or 'weight' of each of the potential drivers is then derived from a regression analysis. This analysis attempts to explain the cross-country patterns of patenting in terms of proxy variables designed to capture infrastructure, cluster and linkage variables. On the basis of these estimated weights and the value of the underlying innovation drivers, countries may then be ranked in terms of per capita national innovation capacity (for a review of developments using this approach see Gans and Hayes, 2008).

Other multivariate regression approaches to the analysis of cross-country patterns of innovation outputs have used different estimation procedures and have augmented or moved away from patents as a proxy for innovation output. Jaumotte and Pain (2005), for example, model the determinants of business sector R&D and then separately model the determinants of patenting. They then model the determinants of R&D employment and real wages in an attempt to assess the potentially adverse impacts that an increased demand for R&D employees might have on the cost of R&D to the private sector. Faber and Hesen (2004) and Mairesse and Mohnen (2002) replace or augment patents as an indicator of innovation with more direct measures arising from the European Community Harmonised Innovation Surveys. These more direct variables include measures of the share of innovative products in final sales. Unfortunately there are no comparable data for the United States or Japan or other non-EU countries that can use these more direct measures of innovation, so broader OECD comparisons continue to be primarily based on patenting data (Gans and Hayes, 2008).

Each of these approaches has provided important insights into cross-country patenting and innovation performance differences. However, they fail to distinguish explicitly between the extent to which innovation output differences across countries result from the lack of innovation input per se, and the efficiency with which those inputs are converted into innovation outputs. The innovation performance of an economy depends not only on how much it invests in innovation (e.g., R&D

investment and personnel) but also on how efficiently it manages the innovation process and successfully transforms the innovation inputs into useful innovation outputs, such as patents. With low innovation efficiency, an increase in investment in, say, R&D or the science base may not produce the expected increase in outputs. The importance of such inefficiency is implicit in many policy discussions. The EC (1995) *Green Paper on Innovation*, for instance, states that

Europe suffers from a paradox. Compared with the scientific performance of its principal competitors, that of the EU is excellent, but . . . its technological and commercial performance in high-technology sectors such as electronics and information technologies has deteriorated. One of Europe's major weaknesses lies in its inferiority in terms of transforming the results of technological research and skills into innovations and competitive advantages.

Although the innovation capacity approach includes innovation system variables that one might expect to influence the translation of inputs into innovation outputs, it is not able to systematically distinguish and account for the relative contribution of these system effects that influence efficiency compared to inputs per se. In this chapter, we attempt to do this by decomposing each country's gap in patenting compared to an estimated world-patenting frontier into basic patenting capacity based on innovative inputs and the efficiency with which those inputs are used. We employ the stochastic frontier analysis (SFA) approach to estimate the world patenting frontier. SFA is a widely used standard efficiency estimation approach in productivity analysis, which we apply in the new context of knowledge production.[1] The advantage of the SFA approach lies in that it explicitly decomposes the observed patent performance into two components: the patenting potential of a country given the best practice use of inputs and an 'efficiency gap' relative to the best practice patenting frontier. This is different from the traditional total factor productivity (TFP) approach that defines productivity as the residual of the patenting production function. In contrast, SFA takes account of measurement error and decomposes a country's deviation from the frontier into inefficiency and a random error.

An alternative approach to SFA in the evaluation of cross-country patenting efficiency would be to apply data envelopment analysis

---

[1] For examples of the application in traditional productivity analysis, see Banker, Datar and Rajan, 1987; Hofler and Payne, 1993; Lovell, 1996; and Hiebert, 2002.

(DEA). Using this approach, and with R&D capital stock and personnel as inputs and patents and academic publications as innovation outputs, Wang and Huang (2007) evaluate the relative efficiency of the R&D activities of 30 countries. They find that fewer than one-half of the countries are fully efficient in R&D activities. Similarly, Hollanders and Esser (2007) carry out a DEA analysis using scores from the European Innovation Scoreboard (EIS) for 2007. Their model includes three categories of innovation inputs, namely innovation drivers, knowledge creation and innovation and entrepreneurship, and two broad categories of outputs that they term applications and intellectual property. Applications include, *inter alia*, the CIS-based direct innovation measures and indirect measures based on high-tech activity. Their study also shows a variety of efficiency in innovation across countries. Both studies focus on the estimation of innovation efficiency and report relatively little on innovation capacity. Moreover, the DEA method attributes all the deviation from the frontier to inefficiency (see, e.g., the discussions in Fu, 2012 and Fritsch and Slavtchev, 2007), whereas SFA has the advantage of controlling for statistical noise in the estimation of innovative efficiency.

Using USPTO patenting as our innovation output proxy, we define a country's patenting capacity as its predicted patent output if it were located on the estimated patenting frontier. We define patenting efficiency as the ratio of observed patenting value to estimated patenting at the frontier. The use of patents allows direct comparability with the previously cited major studies of comparative international patent performance. We recognise that the use of the USPTO imparts a country bias when comparing any one country's performance relative to that of the United States, but there is no reason for this bias to vary across countries when comparing each to the United States.

This chapter contributes to the literature as the first attempt to apply the SFA approach to the analysis of cross-country innovation activity provided by patents. In addition, we attempt to allow for structural differences between economies that may affect the incidence of patenting. As patenting varies significantly across industries, we include industry structure as one of the explanatory variables affecting observed patenting gaps. Given the pressure of home country patent data bias, we focus relatively more on the comparison of non-U.S. economies with each other relative to the United States. However, given the fact that the United States is widely regarded as one of the leading economies in innovation, we include it in the construction of the world patenting frontier.

The rest of the chapter is organised as follows: Section 13.2 discusses the theoretical framework. Section 13.3 presents some stylised facts. Section 13.4 discusses the model, data and methodology. Section 13.5 reports the estimated results. Section 13.6 benchmarks China against the world innovation frontier using data covering the 2005 to 2011 period, and Section 13.7 presents conclusions.

13.2 Determinants of national innovation performance

In this chapter, we seek to identify sources of differences in national innovation performance as proxied by patenting, in terms of differences in countries' innovation systems. Following existing work in this field, we define a national innovation system as a set of agents, the institutional framework within which they operate and the networks and interrelationships among them. The national systems approach argues that taken together, these system elements determine national innovation performance. The institutional framework and patterns of relationships condition, and co-evolve with, the motivation and abilities of firms to invest in R&D and human capital and to develop and commercialise product designs and service activities and manufacturing and service production processes that are new to them (Freeman, 1987; Lundvall, 1992; Nelson, 1993). The innovation performance of a nation is determined not only by the quantity of human and capital factor inputs into innovation but also by institutional and other system factors. These factors constitute constraints and/or incentives for innovation (Pavitt, 1980; Furman et al., 2002; Faber and Hasen, 2004). They also influence the direction and nature of innovation decisions taken by firms and hence determine the efficiency of the national innovation system (Mairesse and Mohnen, 2002).

Within an innovation system perspective, we seek to estimate the innovation capacity of a country based on its basic innovation inputs of overall R&D expenditure, the stock of research workers and educational expenditure. We then seek to explain distance from the frontier (or innovation inefficiency) in terms of system variables such as the scale of the economy, the IPR regime, the availability of venture finance, the breakdown of R&D between the public and private sectors and economic openness. Our approach as summarised in Figure 13.1 is similar in spirit to the approach of Furman et al. (2002) and subsequent papers.

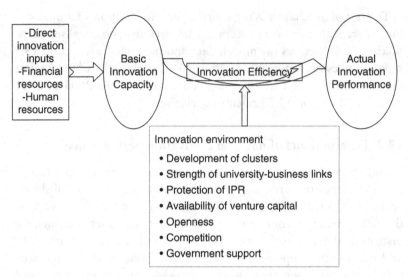

Figure 13.1 National innovation system: a system theoretic framework

However, here we associate innovation capacity with the basic inputs and attempt to distinguish and quantify the impact of system effects explicitly, in translating those inputs into performance.

Determinants of basic innovation capacity

We consider R&D inputs and human capital resources as key input factors affecting patent production. Investment in R&D is often found to be a significant determinant of innovation performance. Countries that invest more in R&D are more likely to produce more patents and/ or new products and processes. This is of particular importance at the country level, although R&D is neither a necessary nor a sufficient condition for innovation in a firm (Baldwin, 1997). Labour force skills and the availability of qualified scientists and engineers, particularly qualified research staff directly involved in R&D activities, are widely recognised critical factors that also contribute to a firm's innovation performance (Hoffman et al., 1998; Porter and Stern, 1999).

In addition to input factors per se, we also allow for variations in sectoral structures that may affect the role that each may play at an aggregate level. The particular technological or input requirements of sectors and patterns of supplier or customer behaviour and innovation strategy may lead to variations in the requirements for particular combinations of inputs and outputs. This leads to variations in the incidence of patenting across sectors but also in underlying rates of R&D activity and other measures of innovation input and output (Malerba, 2006). Variations across countries in the sectoral distribution of activity may therefore affect innovation performance of a country, especially its patenting performance. For example, it has been argued that the EU-U.S. innovation gap is the result of such differences: 'compared to the United States and Asia, Europe as a whole is under-represented in fast-growing R&D-intensive sectors such as IT hardware, software and electronics, and over-represented in profitable but less innovative areas such as food manufacturing, oil and utilities' (Cookson, 2005, pp. 30–2).

Determinants of innovation efficiency

The actual innovation performance of nations is determined not just by factor inputs but also by the efficiency of the inherently recursive process by which innovation opportunities are recognised, and the necessary capabilities and inputs to commercialise new ideas and appropriate market value put into practice. Innovation efficiency thus reflects a nation's intangible capability for transforming direct, tangible innovation inputs into final commercially successful innovation outputs. It explains the difference between actual outcomes and expected innovation outcomes based on inputs alone. Innovation efficiency is affected by the institutional and networking aspects of an economy that encourage, cultivate and facilitate the creation and exploration of new ideas (Furman et al., 2002; OECD, 2003b). Government policy and support for innovation, openness of the economy, the relative involvement of the business and public sectors in R&D, the linkages between the science base and industries, the information infrastructure of the economy and the strength of protection for intellectual property are all important factors affecting the innovative efficiency of nations.

The participation of the private sector in innovation is one of the most important factors in a national innovation system. The private sector is not only a financier and creator of innovative ideas but also the place where the commercialisation takes place. As Porter and Stern (1999) argue, therefore, the extent of R&D funded by private firms is a reflection of whether or not wider system conditions are conducive to commercialisation. As innovation has become more open and more global, there has been an increasing emphasis on universities as partners for business. The nature of that contribution must, however, be seen in the context of the much more intensive use of commercial partners as innovation knowledge sources and in the wider set of contributions through human capital and public space functions that universities perform (HM Treasury, 2003; Hughes, 2008). Given that caveat, universities – as major producers of knowledge – are a significant element in determining the innovative efficiency of a national innovation system.

In addition to funding from government and the private sector, venture capital is frequently attributed an increasingly important role in financing innovation activities and in affecting innovation performance, particularly in the high-technology sector (Porter and Stern, 1999; Lerner, Sorensen and Stromberg, 2008). The success of the Silicon Valley model is often cited as evidence of the important role played by informal venture capital. However, the role of government defence expenditure and the labour market in that respect cannot be underestimated (Lécuyer, 2006). Moreover, venture capital does not appear to systematically change patent quantity (Lerner et al., 2008) and tends to focus on relatively few industries, such as biotechnology, the Internet, and telecommunication firms in the late 1990s (Gompers, 2006). Moreover, in the case of the United States and the UK, little formal venture capital goes to early-stage high-technology businesses (Hughes, 2008). Therefore, we might expect that the share of venture capital per se may play a nuanced role in overall innovation performance and perhaps more through large business and later-stage developments than through early-stage high-tech developments.

The degree of openness to international trade and investment is another institutional factor that it is argued may affect national innovative efficiency. On the one hand, greater openness may increase competitive pressure on domestic firms and compel them to innovate (e.g., Geroski, 1994; Nickell, 1996; Blundell, Griffith and Van Reenen, 1999). Market augmentation through exporting may also increase the returns to R&D investment and thereby provide the incentive for innovation. Moreover, the diffusion of knowledge through foreign contacts and foreign direct investment may contribute to domestic innovation activities via knowledge spillovers. On the other hand, openness to imports and foreign direct investment (FDI) may crowd out local small and medium enterprises, create certain degrees of brain drain of skilled scientists and engineers to foreign firms or to foreign countries and result in some dependence on foreign technology transfer (Jaumotte and Pain, 2005; Fu and Gong, 2008). The ability to appropriate returns to innovation-related investment is therefore important. Strong protection of intellectual property will, it is argued, encourage firms to invest in innovative activities and signal the attractiveness of the country as a site in which to locate innovative activity.

13.3 Cross-country differences in innovation activity: the stylised facts

R&D investment, patent counts, and sales of new or significantly improved products are the most frequently used indicators in attempts to shed light on the innovation activities of nations. In Figures 13.2 and 13.3, we present data on R&D and patenting respectively.

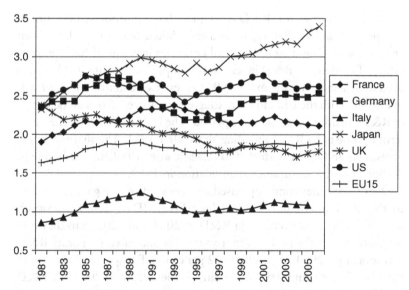

Figure 13.2 Total national R&D as percentage of GDP for major industrial countries
Source: OECD (2008).

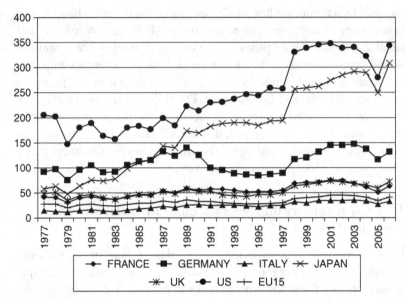

Figure 13.3 Patents granted by USPTO, 1982–2006
Source: EUROSTAT.

As a key input factor, R&D investment has a harmonised definition. Figure 13.2 shows that Japan and the United States have long been among the leading major industrial countries in terms of R&D expenditure. The share of R&D investment as a proportion of GDP has also been increasing since the mid-1990s in these two countries. In contrast, in Europe, both the UK and France have experienced drops in the shares of R&D spending over the same period. The UK experienced a medium-term decline in its R&D spending share after 1981. The share of R&D investment in Germany started to increase after 1999, after a decade of decline and stagnation since reunification in 1989.

Data from other company-based sources confirm the gap. According to the 2005 International R&D Scoreboard (DTI, 2005), European companies invested no more in R&D in 2004 and 2005 than they had on average over the previous four years. The increased corporate R&D investment for 2004 and 2005 was 2 per cent in Europe but 7 per cent in the United States and Asia. According to the 2002 and 2003 UK R&D Scoreboard (DTI, 2002c, 2003c), the average R&D intensity of European top firms in 2003 was 3.7 per cent, which was significantly lower than that of top U.S. or Japanese companies at 5.2 and 4.3 per cent, respectively.[2] The figure for the UK top 700 companies was only 2.2 per cent, which was low even compared to the rest of Europe. In contrast, many smaller European economies have significantly increased spending on R&D. For example, Sweden, Finland, Denmark and Ireland have all accelerated spending as a share of output in the past 20 years by 72 per cent, 172 per cent, 88 per cent and 104 per cent, respectively (DTI 2005).

A basic problem in relying on R&D investment as an innovation performance indicator is that it is basically a measure of innovation inputs, which could be used inefficiently (Jensen, 1993), and says little directly about innovation outputs. An alternative is to use the share of innovative/new sales in a firm's total sales, based on firm-level survey data grossed up to the national level. This is a direct measure of successful innovation. However, for present purposes, this measure is effectively restricted to European comparisons because it is most widely available on a consistent basis as a result of the regular Community Innovation Surveys (CIS) and cannot be used to compare all countries with either Japan or the United States.[3]

Patent counts are another widely used innovation measure suitable for international comparison and are widely available for countries outside Europe. They are a measure of non-trivial inventive technologies with commercial promise (Smith, 2004). They are available over time and across countries so that cross-country performance can be compared over time. But patent count data, too, have well-known limitations: they represent only a portion of innovative activity, and they do not reflect the economic value of different patents (Griliches, 1990). While recognising these limitations, it has been argued that the patent count is nonetheless a useful measure for international innovation comparison given the alternatives (Trajtenberg, 1990; Furman et al., 2002), and that the 'analysis of patent data has proven very fruitful' (Smith, 2004 page 160). For this reason, we will use patent count in this chapter as a proxy of innovation output, albeit imperfect.

---

[2] The DTI R&D Scoreboard compares the innovation activities by the top 700 UK and top 700 international R&D investing companies. Detailed comparison of large-firm R&D activities based on DTI (2002 and 2003) is summarised in Appendix 13.1.

[3] A notable exception is Cosh, Hughes and Lester (2004), who provide a comparison using this class of measures for the UK and the United States. The comparison is for manufacturing and business services. There is no economy-wide comparison.

On this basis, it is clear that Europe has long lagged behind the United States and Japan in the number of patents granted by USPTO per million population. Since the mid-1990s, while the number of patents granted by USPTO per million population has increased significantly for the United States and Japan, the growth of patents in Europe has instead been rather modest (with the exception of Germany). This has led to a widening gap in patenting between Europe and the United States (see Figure 13.2). The data on European patent applications also confirm this trend. Although the predominance of U.S. firms holding U.S. patents reflects a home advantage, the United States records a relatively strong performance in the EU market as well. With regard to the UK, its record on patent numbers is only a third of that of Germany, and less than those of France, Japan and the United States.

13.4 Estimating the patenting frontier and patenting efficiency: model, data and methodology

Model and method

We use stochastic frontier analysis to construct an international patenting frontier. We then use distance from the frontier and the factors affecting that distance to estimate the patenting efficiency of national innovation systems and the determinants of that efficiency. In the spirit of Jones (1995), we thus emphasise the distinction between efficiency in the use of inputs from the magnitude of the inputs themselves. Following Griliches (1979), Jaffe (1989), and Eaton and Kortum (1999), we start from a patenting (innovation) production function as follows:

$$Y_{it} = A_{it}(X_{it})\varphi \qquad\qquad (13.1)$$

where Y_{it} denotes innovative/patenting output of a nation, X_{it} is a vector of basic innovation inputs, and $A_{it} = \alpha e^{v_{it}-u_{it}}$ is an efficiency parameter, with α as a constant; v_{it} is a random disturbance that captures the effects of statistical noise and is distributed as $N(0, \sigma_v^2)$; u_{it} is a one-sided error term representing a variety of features that reflect efficiency and is interpreted as patenting efficiency by the definition stated earlier; u is independent of v; and $u \geq 0$, distributed as truncations at zero of the $N(\mu_{it}, \sigma_u^2)$ distribution.

Based on empirical data, SFA constructs a patent production frontier, which maximises patent production given the inputs. In applying SFA to estimate national patenting efficiency, we rewrite Equation (13.1) in the following functional form:

$$y_{it} = f(X_{it})\exp(v_{it} - u_{it}) \qquad (13.2)$$

The deterministic production frontier $f(X_{it})$ represents patenting production possibilities, that is, the estimated maximum innovative capacity with given innovative inputs. The stochastic production frontier is $f(X_{it})\exp(v_{it} - \mu_{it})$. Patenting efficiency is calculated as the ratio of the observed patent output to its maximum potential at the deterministic frontier as follows:

$$\text{Patenting efficiency } (iE_{it}) = \frac{y_{it}}{f(X_{it})\exp(v_{it})} = \exp(-u_{it}) \qquad (13.3)$$

The determinants of patenting efficiency can then be analysed using the following equation:

$$IE_{it} = \alpha_{it} + \delta' z_{it} \qquad (13.4)$$

where IE is patenting efficiency; z_{it} in our study is a vector of factors, other than basic innovation inputs, that affect the innovative efficiency of nations, that is, the innovation environment and the quality of linkages; δ' is a vector of parameters to be estimated; α_i is a vector of nation- or time-specific effects. In this study, because the institutional and structural effects are likely to be captured by country-specific effects, we exclude the country dummies from the model so that the significance of the impact of the institutional and structural factors can be maintained. We experiment with both a traditional two-stage approach and a simultaneous approach for the SFA estimation as a robustness check.[4] It is important to note that while the level of innovative inputs affects innovation outputs, it may itself depend on innovation output and the broader institutional environment. Although the use of SFA allows new

[4] Stochastic frontier analysis is normally conducted in a two-stage procedure. However, this procedure suffers from a contradiction (Battese and Coelli, 1995). The Battese and Coelli (1995) model overcomes this contradiction and allows the simultaneous estimation of the parameters of the stochastic frontier and efficiency determinants. However, the estimation of the simultaneous model is extremely problematic in all but the most favourable of cases (Greene, 2003). Therefore, we experiment with both the traditional two-stage approach and the simultaneous model while bearing in mind the limitations of both.

analytical insights into the relative role of inputs versus efficiency, the method has its limitations, in that it cannot take into account this possible endogeneity problem.

Data and measurement

We focus this study on OECD countries and have constructed the data set from OECD *Main Science and Technology Indicators* (MSTI), the *World Bank Development Indicators* (WBDI) and the Institute for Management Development (IMD) *World Competitiveness Yearbook* (WCY). As some of the data are not available for some countries, especially the transition economies and developing countries, we have included 21 countries in the dataset from 1990 to 2002, for which publicly accessible data are available. The countries included are Austria, Belgium, Denmark, Finland, France, Germany, Greece, Iceland, Ireland, Italy, Netherlands, Norway, Portugal, Spain, Sweden, United Kingdom, Australia, Canada, Japan, New Zealand and United States.

The dependent variable

Following Jaffe (1989) and Furman et al. (2002), we proxy innovation output by the number of granted U.S. patents. The country origin of a patent is determined by the residence of the first-named inventor. In keeping with Furman et al. (2002), we take patents in country j in year $(t+3)$, $PATENTS_{j,t+3}$, as the dependent variable. In other words, we assume that ideas production in a given year is reflected in the patents that are granted three years in the future. We also employ U.S. patents to provide a comparable measure of innovations with substantial commercial importance across the 21 OECD countries in our sample. Given the potential home bias effect of using the number of U.S. patents, we focus our analysis and discussion of the results on the non-U.S. countries.

Explanatory variables for the knowledge production function

The first innovation input to be considered is human capital resources devoted to the ideas-producing sector. We measure these inputs by the number of full-time equivalent scientists and engineers working in R&D in an economy (FTE S&E). Substantial heterogeneity exists among countries and over time in terms of underlying international patenting efficiency (PATENTS / FTE S&E), ranging from more than

70 patents per 1,000 R&D workers for the United States during the 1990s to less than 1 patent per 1,000 R&D workers for Greece and Portugal. Innovation expenditure is another important input to the ideas-producing sector. We measure it by aggregating R&D expenditure. Including both R&D expenditure and personnel in the regression may involve some double counting because a proportion of R&D expenditure is on wages and salaries. This should not affect the relative rankings of countries based on the SFA estimates, but it will affect the interpretation of each variable as the estimated coefficients and their statistical significance are affected. We also include the share of GDP spent on education as an indicator of a nation's commitment to human capital investment.

As discussed earlier, the industry structure in an economy may affect its aggregate innovation performance at the country level, and policy debate has focused on the share of high-technology activity in particular. We therefore attempt to capture these effects by the value-added share of high-technology industries in the total economy.[5] This does vary across countries. For example, Ireland had the highest average value-added share of high-technology industries in the whole economy at 9 per cent from 1990 to 1999. The figures for the UK, the United States, Japan, Germany, Sweden and Finland varied between 6 to 7 per cent in these industries over the same period.

Explanatory variables for the patenting efficiency equation

To account for a nation's patenting efficiency, we included the percentage of R&D funded by private industry and the percentage of R&D performed by higher education institutions as two of the explanatory variables. Porter and Stern (1999) suggested the former as an indicator of the cluster environment for innovation; the latter is an indicator of the involvement of universities in the national innovation system. As discussed earlier, openness is also an important factor affecting innovative efficiency of nations. We measure the degree of openness of an economy by the volume and intensity of its exports and FDI alternately.

---

[5] The high-technology industries include pharmaceuticals; office, accounting and computing machinery; electrical machinery and apparatus; radio, television and communication equipment; medical, precision and optical instruments; aircraft and spacecraft; and post and telecommunications. Note, however, that this figure for 'industry output' may not be a good indicator of high-technology activities or inputs in the economy (von Tunzelmann and Acha, 2005).

In keeping with previous literature, the level of GDP per capita is also included to capture the development level of the economy as a proxy for the overall level of institutional and infrastructural development. The strength of IPR protection and the availability of venture capital in the economy, measured by expert ratings collected in surveys, are also included as explanatory variables.

The empirical model for innovation capacity as proxied by patents is therefore as follows:

$$LnPat_{i,t+3} = \theta LnRD_{it} + \vartheta LnRDP_{it} + \rho LnEDU_{it} + \delta LnHITEC$$
$$+ v_{it} - \mu_{it} \tag{13.5}$$

The empirical model for patenting efficiency is therefore as follows:

$$LnIE_{it} = \alpha_{it} + \phi LnBERD_{it} + \phi LnRDHE_{it} + \gamma IP + \lambda VC$$
$$+ \chi LnOPEN_{it} + \beta LnGDPPC_{it} + \varepsilon_{it} \tag{13.6}$$

where Pat = number of patents, RD = gross R&D expenditure, RDP = R&D personnel, EDU = education expenditure, $HITEC$ = value-added share of high-technology industries in the whole economy, $\mu = IE$ = patenting/innovative efficiency, $GDPPC$ = GDP per capita, $OPEN$ = openness, $BERD$ = business R&D expenditure, $RDHE$ = R&D performed by higher education, IP = strength of intellectual property protection, VC = availability of venture capital. Definitions of variables and sources of the data are listed in Table 13.1. Appendix 13.1 reports the average values of the key variables of the 21 countries.

13.5 Results

The estimated results from the SFA are presented in Table 13.2. R&D personnel exert a significant positive contribution to the basic patenting capacity of nations. The magnitude and the statistical significance are robust across specifications. A 1 per cent increase in R&D personnel increases patenting output by nearly 1 per cent. Aggregate R&D expenditure also exerts a significant positive impact on basic patenting capacity. The estimated coefficient of the education variable is positive but not statistically significant, probably because of the high correlation between education expenditure and R&D personnel.

We also estimated the SFA using the simultaneous model approach suggested by Battese and Coelli (1995). The estimated results are

Table 13.1 *Definition and sources of variables*

Variable	Definition	Sources
Pat	Patents granted in USPTO 3 years later	MSTI
IE	Innovative/patenting efficiency resulting from SFA analysis	
RD	Gross expenditure on R&D in GDP	MSTI
RDP	Number of full-time equivalent researchers	MSTI
BERD	Percentage of R&D funded by private sector	MSTI
RDHE	Percentage of R&D performed by higher education institutions	MSTI
EDU	Total expenditure on education	WBDI
GDPPC	GDP per capita in 1995 constant prices (US$)	WBDI
EXP	Value of total exports (US$m)	WBDI
EXPS	Ratio of exports to GDP	WBDI
FDI	Value of inward FDI stock (US$m)	UNCTAD
FDIS	Ratio of FDI to GDP	UNCTAD
IP	How adequately IPRs are protected (except for 1990, when it is the extent to which protection by IPRs encourages corporate R&D) (scale 0 least, 10 greatest)	WCY
VC	How readily venture capital is available for business development (scale 0 least, 10 greatest)	WCY
HITEC	Value-added shares of high-tech industries relative to the total economy	OECD

Note: We have included 21 countries in the data set, from 1990 to 2002, for which publicly accessible data are available. Detailed list of the countries included is given in the text of the paper.

broadly consistent with the two-step estimates. The estimated coefficient of the R&D variable marginally probably loses statistical significance in the simultaneous model because of the double-counting problem between R&D expenditure and R&D personnel. The practical difficulty of the simultaneous approach as discussed earlier may also be a factor responsible for this change. With regard to industrial structure, the value-added share of high-technology industry in the total economy exerts a significant positive impact on its basic patenting capacity. This result suggests that industrial structure does matter in shaping overall national innovation capacity in patent production. Economies with a greater proportion of industries in the high-technology sector are more

Table 13.2 *Stochastic frontier analysis of basic patenting capacity*

	Dependent variable: number of patents granted 3 years later							
	2-step estimation				Simultaneous estimator			
	(1)		(2)		(3)		(4)	
	Coeff	p-value	Coeff	p-value	Coeff	p-value	Coeff	p-value
Constant	−12.174***	0.000	−11.197***	0.000	−9.925***	0.000	−9.898***	0.000
Log(RD)	0.356***	0.002	0.294***	0.009	0.254	0.122	0.249	0.129
Log(RDP)	0.821***	0.000	0.881***	0.000	1.005***	0.000	1.005***	0.000
Log(EDU)	0.093	0.438	0.069	0.558	−0.001	0.994	0.001	0.994
Log(HITECH)			0.236**	0.032	0.279**	0.040	0.293**	0.036
N	210		205		205		205	
Year dummies	Yes		Yes		Yes		Yes	
Log Likelihood	−87.005		−84.657					

Note: ***significant at the 1 per cent level. **significant at the 5 per cent level. *significant at the 10 per cent level.
Independent variables of the inefficiency equations in models (3) and (4) include *LNRDHE, LNBERD, LNGDPPC, IP* and *LNOPEN*.

likely to have a greater number of granted patents. Whether this is simply an artefact of choosing industries such as pharmaceuticals that are known to have exceptionally high propensities to patent must be left to further research to assess.

Table 13.3 reports the estimated results of the determinants of patenting efficiency. As a robustness check, we report both the Tobit and the OLS estimates, which are consistent in general. The estimated coefficients of the GDP per capita variable are positive, large and statistically significant. The result is robust across specifications and equations. This suggests that the development level of an economy, such as the technology and institution advancement level and infrastructure development, exerts a significant effect on the patenting efficiency of nations.

The share of R&D funded by the private sector also exerts a positive impact on patenting efficiency and is statistically significant in most of the specifications. If the share of R&D funded by the private sector is taken as a proxy for system-wide innovation environment effects (Porter and Stern, 1999), then a higher share of R&D funded by the private sector reflects a more favourable innovation system environment and therefore increases the patenting efficiency of nations. R&D performed by higher education institutions also has a robust significant positive impact on national patenting efficiency. The magnitude of the estimated coefficients is of similar scale as those for the business R&D expenditure variable. This evidence confirms that universities have played a significant role in patenting. Thus, the higher the share of universities in total R&D, the higher the patenting efficiency of a nation will be.

As expected, the degree of intellectual property rights protection has a significant positive impact on patenting efficiency. The higher degrees of intellectual property rights protection motivate greater efforts in innovation and effective commercialisation of patenting inventions. However, the availability of venture capital is negatively associated with patenting efficiency. This may be explained by the fact that, as the OECD data and other work suggest, much or all of the formal venture capital in the UK and the United States is largely focused on the activity of large firms and management buyouts and related restructuring rather than on technology-intensive sectors or early-stage innovative firms (Hughes, 2008). Our result is also consistent with the findings by Lerner et al. (2008) that venture capital does not appear to systematically change patent quantity. The significant negative coefficient remains of concern because it implies that the size of the formal

Table 13.3 Determinants of patenting efficiency

	Tobit				OLS			
	(1)	(2)	(3)	(4)	(5)	(6)	(7)	(8)
Log(RDHE)	0.084***	0.085***	0.074**	0.073**	0.083***	0.084***	0.073**	0.073**
	0.006	0.006	0.018	0.019	0.005	0.005	0.011	0.011
Log(BERD)	0.121**	0.123**	0.105**	0.105**	0.092*	0.092*	0.082	0.082
	0.019	0.019	0.041	0.041	0.091	0.096	0.108	0.108
Log(GDPPC)	0.215***	0.280***	0.204***	0.197***	0.198***	0.241***	0.200***	0.194***
	0.000	0.000	0.002	0.001	0.000	0.002	0.002	0.001
IP	0.012**	0.012**	0.008*	0.008	0.010*	0.010*	0.008*	0.007*
	0.021	0.021	0.099	0.102	0.056	0.060	0.096	0.098
VC	-0.012***	-0.012***	-0.010***	-0.010***	-0.011***	-0.011***	-0.010**	-0.010**
	0.002	0.003	0.008	0.008	0.004	0.006	0.011	0.011
Log(EXPS)	-0.070**				-0.054*			
	0.026				0.091			
Log(EXP)		-0.063**				-0.045		
		0.046				0.134		
Log(FDI)			-0.008				-0.007	
			0.25				0.264	
Log(FDIS)				-0.008				-0.007
				0.231				0.248

Constant	-2.140***	-1.150***	-1.920***	-2.051***	-1.904***	-1.158***	-1.811***	-1.934***
	0.000	-0.008	0.000	0.000	0.001	0.004	0.001	0.002
Country dummies	Yes	Yes	Yes	Yes	Yes	Yes	Yes	Yes
N	205	205	205	205	205	205	205	205
Log likelihood	348.107	347.619	346.278	346.332				
R-squared					0.978	0.978	0.977	0.977

Note: ***significant at the 1 per cent level. **significant at the 5 per cent level. *significant at the 10 per cent level.
Dependent variable: estimated patenting efficiency of nations.

venture capital relative to GDP hinders rather than helps patenting efficiency. This may reflect the extent to which formal venture capital has been focused on the reorganisation of existing assets through buy-outs and cost efficiency drivers rather than investment in high-risk R&D expenditures and/or enhanced patenting performance. This is an issue that requires careful further analysis.

In keeping with the results from Jaumotte and Pain (2005), we find that the impact on patenting of openness to FDI is not significant. Openness to exports even shows a negative impact on patenting efficiency. This result may be partly the result of the fact that, as far as innovation is concerned, the openness of an economy serves as a two-edged sword. While competitive pressure may compel the local firms to innovate to be competitive and foreign contacts may facilitate international knowledge transfer, the competitive pressure may also crowd out local firms from product markets, and easy access to foreign knowledge sources and advanced machinery may lead to certain degrees of dependence on foreign technology.

Benchmarking national patenting capacities and patenting efficiency

Figures 13.4 and 13.5 compare the estimated patenting capacities and patenting efficiency of six major industrialised countries obtained from the SFA, with patents proxying for innovative output. By this measure, Japan has been the top non-U.S. country with the highest patenting capacity (Figure 13.4). Japan has not only done well in patenting output, it is also one of the most efficient patenting countries in the world (Figure 13.5). In terms of innovation capacities in patent production, the distance of the rest of the G7 countries from the world leader United States is substantial, and there is little sign of convergence in the 1990s. Compared with the G7 countries, the UK's innovation capacity in patent production is higher than that for Italy, but lower than that for France and Germany, and far below that for the United States and Japan. In terms of patenting efficiency, the UK is consistently ranked the lowest among the G7 countries and shows little sign of catch-up in this respect. Considering the UK's strong performance in scientific publications and citations (King, 2004), this suggests that issues of successful translation of ideas into commercialisation practices remain important. France is in a similar situation to the UK, although its overall performance has been slightly better.

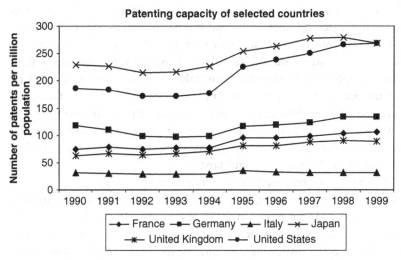

Figure 13.4 Patenting capacity of selected countries

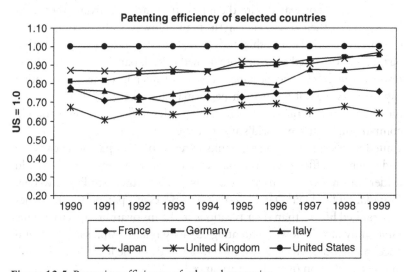

Figure 13.5 Patenting efficiency of selected countries

Italy has been the weakest among the G7 countries in terms of national patenting capacity. The number of U.S. patents it may produce based on its basic innovation inputs is far below that of the world leaders. However, Italy did fairly well in efficiently transforming its innovative inputs into outputs. Italy's estimated patenting efficiency has started to catch up since 1992, and this has placed it close to the world patenting frontier. This suggests that Italy has created an effective innovation system and mechanism to transform the innovative inputs into outputs. The main problem for Italy would appear to be the lack of innovation inputs. Different from the UK, France and Italy, Germany has been the best European country in terms of patenting capacities. It has also demonstrated a trend towards catch-up in patenting efficiency to the world frontier. Its patenting efficiency in 1999 was almost as high as that of the United States and Japan.

We have also compared the country patenting ranking from this study with those from several other studies that use similar data and variables but employ different methodology. These studies do not decompose the national innovation performance; instead, they incorporate innovation inputs and environment indexes into one model. Tables that summarise the rankings and the estimated efficiency scores using SFA can be found in Appendix 13.2. Both our capacity and efficiency rankings are, to a certain extent, correlated with the innovation rankings from other studies suggesting their consistency in the main. However, the decomposition exercise we carried out in this study reveals some interesting insights that distinguish our method from other methods. Japan has invested huge resources in R&D and became the world leader in terms of patenting capacity; its overall innovation performance ranked in other studies is mostly one or two ranks lower because it is less efficient in innovation in comparison with the world's most efficient innovative economies. The United States stands in the top ranks in terms of both patenting capacity and patenting efficiency. It is hence, with no surprise, ranked as the world leader in innovation performance by most other studies. Sweden, Canada, Finland and Denmark all have impressive patenting efficiencies that ranked higher than their positions in the innovation capacity league table. Italy has the lowest patenting capacity but an impressive performance in patenting efficiency. It therefore stands in the lower-middle rank in most studies on overall performance.

13.6 Benchmarking China against the world innovation frontier

Using data collected from OECD, Eurostat and the World Bank, following the same methodologies discussed earlier, we estimate the expected innovation capacity of China and other emerging economies for the period from 2005 to 2011 and compare it with the actual performance of these countries in terms of number of patents granted by the USPTO. The countries included in this analysis are China, Russia, Korea, Singapore and Argentina, in addition to the major industrialised countries such as the United States, the UK, Japan, Germany, France, Italy and Spain. The objective of this exercise is to, first, benchmark the innovation (patenting) performance of China and the other emerging economies against the world frontier and understand where China is in the global landscape after three decades of catch-up. Second, we decompose the gap between China and the world frontier into investment-based capacity and innovation efficiency and hence understand where the major gap lies.

As Figure 13.6 shows, the United States is the largest investor in R&D and remained the world's top innovator between 2005 and 2011 in terms of its expected innovation capacity estimated based on a country's investment and human capital for innovation. Japan ranks second in this respect. Amongst all the sampled countries, two have shown a clearly upward catching-up trend in expected innovation capacity and are ranked as the top fifth and sixth investors in 2011 in this sample. They are China and South Korea, which have invested heavily in R&D.

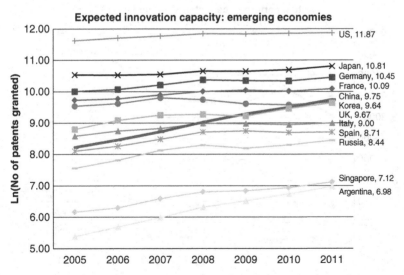

Figure 13.6 Expected innovation capacity: emerging economies

China also has the world's largest pool of trained scientists and engineers. However, looking at the actual performance in terms of the number of patents granted by the UPSTO, if we exclude the United States, which is the home country of the patent-granting authority, Japan is the largest owner of patents granted by USPTO. Korea is the second largest owner of granted patents by the USPTO in 2011, although its number of granted patents is about only a quarter of that of Japan. The number of granted patents of China in 2011 was 3473, which was about 8 per cent of that of Japan (Figure 13.7). However, as reported in Chapter 2, the R&D expenditure to GDP in China was 1.98 in 2011, which was 59 per cent of that of Japan. In terms of total R&D expenditure, China's was more than half (54 per cent) of that of Japan.

The differences between actual innovation performance and expected capacity based on R&D investment and personnel suggest the variations across countries in their efficiency in innovation. Using the stochastic frontier analysis method discussed earlier in this chapter, we can estimate the innovation efficiency of the sample countries. The estimated innovation efficiency scores are reported in Figure 13.8. As the diagram shows, Japan was the most efficient innovator in the world in most of the years over the sample period of 2005 to 2011. Korea was

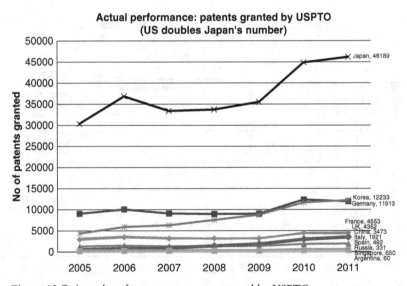

Figure 13.7 Actual performance: patents granted by USPTO

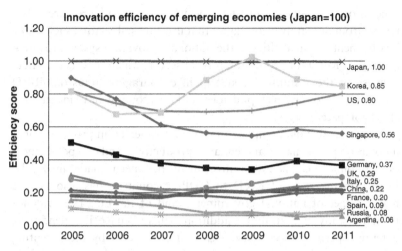

Figure 13.8 Innovation efficiency of emerging economies

the second most efficient in 2011, and the United States ranked third in the sample. In 2011, China's innovation efficiency score was only 22 per cent of that of Japan. In sum, there is a significant gap in innovation performance between China and the world leaders. Although a gap in R&D investment remains between China and the United States and Japan, the major gap lies in the low innovation efficiency in China.

13.7 Conclusions

This chapter has compared the determinants and performance of patenting among the OECD countries and benchmarked their patenting performance against the world patent production frontier. It finds that with respect to basic patenting capacity that is determined by physical innovation inputs, Japan and the United States have been the world leaders in the 1990s. The gap between the European countries and these leaders are substantial and there is no significant sign of convergence. With respect to national patenting efficiency, which is determined by institutional and structural factors in the national innovation system, Japan, Germany and Italy have been catching up during the sample period. The gap in patent production between the UK and the world leaders is substantial and lies in both basic patenting capacity and the patenting efficiency of the national innovation system. Both the generation of inputs and greater efficiency appear to be required. The results from our study also suggest that institutional factors, such as the involvement of universities in the national innovation system; the proportion of R&D funded by the private sector, which reflects the effectiveness of the institutional system in encouraging industrial R&D investment; and the development level of the economy have identifiable effects on patenting.

A number of policy implications are possible. To improve national innovation performance and enhance productivity and competitiveness of economies, considerable investment has been made in R&D. Increasing the ratio of R&D to GDP of countries has also been a major target of national governments and of the EU. The evidence from this study suggests that in addition to increased R&D expenditure, patenting performance is also significantly affected by the patenting efficiency of nations. In assessing the balance of effort in policy development between enhancing inputs and enhancing their conversion into outputs, countries should examine carefully the relative weakness in each aspect. We regard our findings as methodologically useful in distinguishing between inputs and efficient transformations.

In terms of developing current policy, a number of important issues arise. First, the development of better longitudinal data of an internationally comparable kind on innovation outputs is important. The development of a CIS-like sweep in the United States and Japan would, for example, help here. Second, we have presented relatively simple models that are parsimonious in relation to the variables included. The approach could be made richer if consistent data on the other system aspects were developed. Finally, our data end in 2002 so an update would inject interesting evidence as to whether this extensive policy commitment to EU innovation policy in the past five years (2009–14) has been translated into either patenting capacity or efficiency improvements.

Findings from the chapter indicate a significant gap in innovation performance between China and the world leaders. Although a gap in R&D investment remains between China and the United States and Japan, the major gap lies in the low innovation efficiency in China. This is the bottleneck that China has to tackle even if we take into account the limitations in using number of patents as a proxy of a country's innovation performance.

Appendix 13.1 Mean values of key variables for sampled countries

Country	Pat	Edu	RD	BERD	RDHE	GDPPC	OPEN	VC	IP	HITEC
Australia	445	5.37	1.57	46.05	26.50	20990	19	4.98	7.22	3.83
Austria	283	5.02	1.63	44.86	32.55	29887	40	4.61	7.82	5.4
Belgium	289	4.02	1.80	66.08	25.90	27840	72	5.42	6.91	4.85
Canada	2058	7.16	1.67	44.25	25.84	20186	37	6.12	7.19	5.03
Denmark	241	7.89	1.90	52.22	21.82	34835	37	6.34	7.28	4.63
Finland	423	7.22	2.56	61.21	19.82	26805	35	5.72	6.93	6.06
France	2811	5.47	2.29	49.50	16.69	27399	24	5.41	7.33	5.45
Germany	7037	4.34	2.37	62.38	17.48	30414	27	5.17	7.91	6.67
Greece	9	2.77	0.52	22.75	44.90	11685	19	3.38	5.55	2.08
Iceland	4	4.67	1.76	35.27	24.98	27361	35	3.91	6.34	2.15
Ireland	53	5.63	1.20	65.36	20.95	20070	76	5.73	6.57	9.12
Italy	1138	4.46	1.09	43.83	27.12	19322	24	3.70	5.51	4.88
Japan	23622	3.67	2.88	71.17	17.02	42767	10	4.30	6.67	6.65
Netherlands	689	4.11	1.98	47.31	28.59	27687	58	7.27	7.33	4.41
New Zealand	54	5.09	1.03	32.31	32.18	16439	31	4.52	7.14	3.33
Norway	141	6.91	1.67	47.87	26.99	34139	40	5.08	6.92	3.63
Portugal	3	6.31	0.64	21.42	39.35	11277	30	4.21	5.00	4.01
Spain	138	4.61	0.86	45.62	30.12	15368	23	4.10	5.40	4.44
Sweden	833	8.04	3.33	65.34	23.16	27809	38	6.04	6.91	6.15
United Kingdom	2163	5.36	1.97	49.40	18.75	19777	27	7.08	6.91	6.68
United States	62371	5.36	2.59	61.85	14.68	28407	11	7.92	7.54	6.75
Total	4991	5.40381	1.775381	49.3359	25.49429	24784	33.86414	5.319507	6.790071	5.057143

Appendix 13.2a *Estimated patenting capacity of sample countries (unit: patents per million population)*

	1990	1991	1992	1993	1994	1995	1996	1997	1998	1999
Australia	45	50	49	51	54	69	69	71	73	71
Austria	31	30	27	31	34	44	47	51	56	57
Belgium	34	36	35	39	40	51	54	61	66	67
Canada	52	51	51	54	55	75	78	78	80	79
Denmark	40	42	42	45	51	63	69	74	78	80
Finland	54	53	54	59	64	91	107	130	151	165
France	74	78	75	77	78	96	95	98	104	106
Germany	118	111	99	96	98	117	119	123	134	134
Greece	4	4	5	5	5	11	11	14	17	20
Iceland	14	14	15	16	20	22	37	43	47	52
Ireland	18	19	21	24	26	35	34	36	38	41
Italy	32	31	29	29	28	35	33	31	32	32
Japan	229	226	215	216	227	254	263	278	280	269
Netherlands	39	39	40	43	44	54	61	62	66	64
New Zealand	14	16	16	15	15	22	25	26	27	26
Norway	47	47	47	49	52	65	68	70	72	72
Portugal	7	8	8	10	11	15	17	20	21	23
Spain	19	19	18	20	20	26	28	33	33	40
Sweden	64	68	68	75	82	105	112	121	130	136
United Kingdom	63	67	64	67	71	81	81	88	91	89
United States	187	184	172	172	177	225	239	251	266	269
Average	56	57	55	57	60	74	78	84	89	90

Appendix 13.2b *Estimated patenting efficiency of sample countries*

	1990	1991	1992	1993	1994	1995	1996	1997	1998	1999
Australia	0.478	0.540	0.550	0.533	0.502	0.557	0.545	0.533	0.611	0.614
Austria	0.829	0.826	0.856	0.843	0.832	0.781	0.796	0.763	0.781	0.743
Belgium	0.698	0.664	0.730	0.744	0.791	0.769	0.742	0.769	0.773	0.732
Canada	0.858	0.865	0.870	0.866	0.871	0.859	0.865	0.874	0.879	0.875
Denmark	0.800	0.804	0.788	0.819	0.855	0.837	0.844	0.827	0.834	0.798
Finland	0.843	0.856	0.872	0.891	0.886	0.875	0.868	0.829	0.839	0.836
France	0.662	0.611	0.634	0.615	0.639	0.639	0.656	0.653	0.665	0.646
Germany	0.694	0.704	0.744	0.761	0.761	0.786	0.786	0.806	0.812	0.811
Greece	0.220	0.298	0.220	0.280	0.229	0.220	0.220	0.220	0.220	0.220
Iceland	0.883	0.844	0.756	0.707	0.554	0.726	0.815	0.737	0.816	0.774
Ireland	0.664	0.608	0.669	0.674	0.683	0.572	0.684	0.797	0.723	0.688
Italy	0.658	0.655	0.622	0.658	0.678	0.709	0.694	0.759	0.751	0.756
Japan	0.746	0.750	0.757	0.774	0.757	0.809	0.802	0.788	0.803	0.825
Netherlands	0.819	0.854	0.831	0.802	0.805	0.828	0.795	0.805	0.783	0.903
New Zealand	0.778	0.589	0.697	0.777	0.877	0.857	0.809	0.773	0.812	0.863
Norway	0.631	0.655	0.678	0.675	0.677	0.704	0.718	0.738	0.737	0.718
Portugal	0.220	0.220	0.220	0.220	0.220	0.220	0.220	0.220	0.220	0.220
Spain	0.233	0.220	0.227	0.220	0.231	0.264	0.220	0.220	0.220	0.220
Sweden	0.827	0.848	0.868	0.866	0.851	0.872	0.886	0.893	0.895	0.887
United Kingdom	0.575	0.524	0.566	0.561	0.572	0.601	0.607	0.565	0.582	0.547
United States	0.852	0.862	0.871	0.882	0.877	0.878	0.874	0.866	0.859	0.852
Average	0.665	0.657	0.668	0.675	0.674	0.684	0.688	0.687	0.696	0.692

Source: Authors' estimation using the SFA.

Appendix 13.2c Comparison of country rankings in innovation

Study	Our study: capacity	Our study: efficiency	Porter & Stern (1999)	Gans & Stern (2003)	OECD (2003)	INSEAD (2007)	EIU (2007)	EC (2008)
Year	1998	1998	1995	2000	1998	2007	2006	2007
Indicator	Predicted patents per mil pop	Efficiency score	Predicted patents per mil pop	Predicted patents per mil pop	Triad patents per mil pop	8 pillars of innovation	Innovation enabled	Average scores of 25 indicators
Japan	1	9	3	2	3	4	1	6
United States	2	3	1	1	6	1	3	9
Switzerland			2	3	1	6	2	2
Finland	3	4	6	5	4	13	5	3
Germany	4	8	5	7	5	2	6	7
Sweden	5	1	4	4	2	12	4	1
France	6	16	8	9	12	5	12	14
United Kingdom	7	18	14	13	14	3	18	8
Canada	8	2	9	10	16	8	13	16
Denmark	9	5	7	6	9	11	7	5
Australia	10	17	12	16	17	17	21	17
Norway	11	14	10	8	15	25	16	18

Ireland	12	10	11	11	7	9	9	13
Netherlands	13	12		12	11	15	14	15
New Zealand	14	11	13	15	13	22	11	12
Belgium	15	6		14	10	20		11
Austria	16	11		17	19	21	19	12
Iceland	17	19	17	20	22	27	25	23
Spain	18	13	16	18	18	24	20	21
Italy	19	5	15	19	20	28	22	22
Portugal	20	19		22	27	39	33	28
Greece	21	19		23	24	49	32	27

Sources: 1) Gans, Joshua and Scott Stern. (2003). Assessing Australia's Innovative Capacity in the 21st Century. 2) OECD. (2003c). OECD Science Technology and Industry Scoreboard. 3) INSEAD. (2007). The World Business/INSEAD Global Innovation Index 2007. 4) Economist Intelligence Unit (EIU) 2007. Innovation: Transforming the Way Business Creates. 5) European Commission. (2008). European Innovation Scoreboard 2007. [Relate to columns above]

14 | *Capabilities, incentives, institutions and national innovation performance*

14.1 Introduction

After more than 30 years of economic reforms and having transformed from a low- to a middle-income country, China now faces significant challenges in moving from imitation to innovation. The success of this transformation will be of crucial importance for China to avoid the middle-income trap and sustain its long-term economic growth (Wu, 2013).

The past fifteen years has seen an exponential increase in research and development (R&D) investment in China. Developing an innovation-driven economy in the coming decades is a major objective for China. Although many research papers and government reports discuss national innovation capabilities in China, most of them address this problem using the national innovation system (NIS) approach (e.g., Chen and Liu, 2008; OECD, 2008; MOST, 2010; Wu, 2010; Mu and Fan, 2011). The NIS framework is powerful in mapping out the major players in the innovation system and allows policy makers to identify the objects for policy intervention, but it does not explain how to increase the capabilities of players and strengthen the linkages between them. The question of how to enhance the innovation capabilities and performance of the country requires in-depth and systematic analysis.

This chapter examines policy choices for the development of innovation capabilities in China using the national innovation performance (NIP) framework developed by the OECD (1987) and Lall (1992) and modified and extended by Fu (2014). The importance of policy in enhancing national innovation performance vis-à-vis simply leaving it to the market is validated by several factors. First, given the nature of knowledge as a public good and the prevalence of externalities that may benefit other users of knowledge, government intervention is required to protect R&D investors and to encourage innovation activities. Second, innovation is risky and costly. Therefore, government financial support is needed to enable active innovation activities, especially in basic research where uncertainty is high because it is difficult to control the direction of the development of a technology and the cost of failure of an experiment is also high. Third, the presence of market failure caused by problems such as information asymmetries, externalities and public goods calls for policy intervention in information and knowledge provision. Finally, China is being forced towards a more skill-intensive and technology-intensive growth path, with the amount of surplus unskilled labour in China falling. This transformation can be realised through the operation of market forces, but long-sightedness by firms and government intervention are also required because of the long gestation periods involved.

The present chapter is organised as follows: Section 14.2 discusses the theoretical framework concerning the determinants of national innovation performance. Section 14.3 analyses the policy choices for boosting innovation performance in China based on analysis of China's innovation performance reported in earlier chapters, especially Chapters 2 and 13. Section 14.4 examines the space for innovation policy in the twenty-first century. Section 14.5 presents conclusions.

14.2 Determinants of national innovation performance: towards a theoretical framework

In a similar way to the overall growth performance of a country, national innovation performance (NIP) is a complex interaction of incentives, capabilities and institutional factors. It is the interplay of all these factors, in particular country settings, that determines how well countries use resources and develop their innovation capabilities. The OECD (1987:153) defines the role of incentives, capabilities and institutional factors as follows:

The *capabilities* define the best that can be achieved; while the *incentives* guide the use of the capabilities and, indeed stimulate their expansion, renewal or disappearance. In the advanced economies, the capabilities refer primarily to the supplies of human capital, of savings and of the existing capital stock, as well as to the technical and organizational skills required for their use; the incentives originate largely in product markets and are then more or less reflected in markets for factors supplies – thereby determining the efficiency with which capabilities are used. Both incentives and capabilities operate within an institutional framework: *institutions* set rules of the game, as well as directly

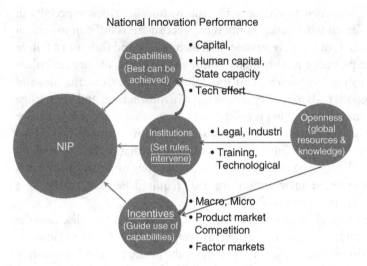

Figure 14.1 National innovation performance

intervening in the play; they act to alter capabilities and change incentives; and they can modify behavior by changing attitudes and expectations.

In this chapter, we first develop a model of the determinants of national innovation performance based on this three-pronged approach developed by the OECD (1987) and Lall (1992), taking into account the recent trend towards globalisation and the shift from a closed to an open innovation paradigm. This modified model, which is depicted in Figure 14.1, will create a framework to analyse the drivers of national innovation performance in China.

Determinant 1: Capabilities

Innovation capabilities include (1) the traditional elements of capabilities such as physical investment, human capital and technological efforts (Lall, 1992) and (2) the capabilities of the state.

Human capital. This term has a broad definition in this context. It not only refers to the skills in mastering and operating machines or the education level of the workforce but also includes creativity in the population – the creativity not only in the industrial but also in the research/ university and the public sectors and not only codified knowledge but also tacit knowledge (Fu, Pietrobelli and Soete, 2011). Skills can be developed through formal education but also informal or on-the-job training.

Physical investment. This refers to general investment in production facility, from investment in premier production equipment, production material and related infrastructure. Defining innovation in a broad sense to include the process from idea creation, R&D, production to commercialisation, physical investment is key for the commercialisation process.

Technological efforts. These are the efforts of productive enterprises to assimilate and improve on the relevant technology. This includes efforts through monetary investment in R&D but also involves non-monetary forms of effort, for example, risk taking and entrepreneurship.

Capabilities of the state. Because the state is regarded as a natural actor in the national innovation system through its role in supporting, facilitating and financing innovation, its ability to introduce correct intervention at the appropriate time is also important for the full functioning of the national innovation system.

In addition, because of information asymmetry, non-competitive markets and the public good nature of knowledge, market failures may occur, creating a justification for government intervention to remedy the failures. In light of the role of the state in the national innovation system, the costly and risky nature of innovation processes and the externalities that innovation will generate, the state may actively provide direct finance for innovation or support innovation through fiscal, financial, trade and industry policies. However, government policy does not necessarily lead to positive or expected outcomes. Therefore, the government's capacity to design and implement appropriate policies will also affect the outcome.

Determinant 2: Incentives

Because innovation is costly and risky, knowledge may generate externalities and the benefits are not easy to appropriate without stringent protection of intellectual property rights (IPR), innovation requires strong incentives to promote. Incentives will affect the (human and physical capital) resource allocation in the economy and determine how much and what kind of resources will flow to the innovative sector. The incentives of innovation include macroeconomic incentives: incentives (or disincentives) from product markets and competition; from factor markets; from economic system; and from proactive or responsive monetary, fiscal, trade and science and technology policy.

Macroeconomic incentives. Some elements of the macroeconomic policies will affect the incentives for innovation; economic growth;

and monetary, fiscal, trade and science and technology policy. A fast-growing economy indicates greater demand and markets for new products and hence greater incentive to invest in innovation. However, an adverse economic environment may also force firms to innovate and use process innovation to cut costs in particular to survive. A low interest rate will decrease the cost of borrowing and hence be a greater incentive to invest in innovation. So, too, will a low expansionary tax policy enable firms, small and medium enterprises (SMEs) in particular, to innovate. Of course, an economic environment in which it is easy to survive may make some firms/entrepreneurs lacking motivation begin to innovate. Empirical evidence is scarce in this respect. Finally, greater export orientation is found to be positively associated with innovation activity at the firm level (Coe and Helpman, 1995; Bustos, 2011; Kiriyama, 2012); therefore, an exchange rate that favours exports is likely to stimulate more innovation.

Competition and product market. Competition is a two-edged sword for innovation. On the one hand, rents from monopoly power will give firms greater incentives to innovate (Shumpeter, 1942). On the other hand, competition in the market will force firms to innovate so as to survive (Geroski, 1994). More recent research also argues that the relationship between competition and innovation follows an inverted U-shape (Aghion et al., 2005). Firms innovate to pursue profit or to take strategic leadership in a new or existing market. A product market that enables firms to appropriate the rents from innovation and minimises the rents from monopoly power is conducive to maintain firms' motivation to innovate and to direct financial resources to flow to the innovation sector.

The economic system of an economy may also affect the incentives for innovation. When some sectors are open for free competition while others have restrictions for entry, firms in the restricted sectors are able to enjoy abnormal returns from monopoly rents. As a result, capital and even talents may flow to the restricted sectors.

However, competition concerns domestic markets; it is also related to a country's trade policy. The debate on the role of industrial policy is inclusive. A wealth of literature suggests benefits from openness to innovation and growth through competition effects and knowledge transfer and spillover. The World Bank and a list of scholars have argued for openness to trade (and foreign direct investment) based on the success of the South East Asian economies and the recent rapid growth of China and India since the reforms (Kruger, 1974; Lin, 2011). Alternatively, the success of Korea and Japan inspired the 'infant industry' argument and arguments for selective 'winner-picking' industry policy, which protects local industry by restricting foreign entry based on the experience of Japan, Korea and Taiwan (Wade, 1990; Chang, 2003).

Factor markets. The efficiency of capital and labour markets will significantly affect the inter-firm and inter-industry resource allocation. Efficiency factor markets will direct and facilitate capital and labour flow to the sectors with higher return. Efficient labour markets should also transmit the higher returns to skills through wages and therefore attract talent to the innovative sectors.

Determinant 3: Institutions

Both incentives and capabilities operate within an institutional frame-work, which means they operate within various market and non-market institutions (OECD, 1987). With regard to national innovation capa-bilities, several sets of institutions are involved: the legal framework concerning science, technology and innovation; industrial institutions; education and training institutions; technological institutions; and IPR institutions:

- With regard to the legal framework, an intellectual property rights protection regime is the most important factor. This includes not only the availability of the relevant laws and regulations but also the strength in the implementation of the law.
- Industrial institutions refer to those that promote inter-firm linkages and intra-industry knowledge diffusion and co-ordinate the produc-tion of public innovative knowledge that benefits everyone in the sector. They also include those that provide support to SMEs.
- Training institutions include the formal higher education sector, vocational training institutions and institutions that provide training support for SMEs.
- Technology institutions include those market and non-market insti-tutions that promote the creation and diffusion of innovation within the country and between countries, for example, the technology exchange markets and technology transfer organisations that help

the diffusion of innovation. In recent years, government-supported innovation platform or innovation alliances have been widely used in the United States, Europe and China.

• A culture that encourages risk taking and tolerance to failure and does not over-emphasise short-term performance is also conducive to innovation activities of firms/organisations and individuals.

Therefore, a country's technological efforts, human capital and physical investment define the best that can be achieved in innovation, whereas incentives at macro and micro levels will guide the use of these capabilities and stimulate their expansion, renewal and disappearance. Incentives determine the efficiency with which capabilities are used. Both of these factors operate within an institutional framework: for example, legal institutions, such as IPR protection and economic and educational institutions. These institutions set the rules of the game and, through these, alter capabilities and change incentives.

Moderating Factor 1: Interplay

It is the interplay of the previously noted factors that shapes the national innovation capabilities of a country. Active and appropriate interactions between these factors require co-ordination and facilitators. In economies with well-developed markets, markets and prices will serve as moderating factors. If a market is unavailable (e.g., if there is no formal market for the trade of technology such as through a technology exchange or an intellectual property exchange), underdeveloped or subject to market failures, the state will play an important role. As the capabilities and initial level of development of countries and cultures differ, policies for innovation should be structured differently.

Moderating Factor 2: Openness

In the present context, openness refers to the international openness of innovation systems, primarily at the national level but also at the firm level (Chesbrough, 2003). With increasing globalisation and the internationalisation of innovation activities, the openness of innovation systems to foreign or transnational firms, organisations and researchers inevitably has a significant impact on all three determinants of innovation capabilities (Fu, 2008; Fu, Pietrobelli and Soete, 2011).

First, opening up the innovation system will affect capabilities through inflows and outflows of talent. Second, multinational enterprises (MNEs) change the landscape of competition and other incentive structures in the economy, leading to changes in institutions. Third, opening up the innovation system at both the national and firm levels also increases the importance of cross-border innovation collaboration, transforming the role of developing countries from innovation taker/acquirer to co-producer. These co-production activities will change the innovation capabilities of a nation, although the interactions will be dynamic and the causal relationships may operate in both directions (Fu and Zhang, 2011).

14.3 Boosting innovation performance in China: the policy choices

This section analyses the policy choices for boosting innovation performance in China based on analysis of China's innovation performance and efficiency reported in earlier chapters, Chapters 2 and 13 in particular.

Capabilities building

China has become one of the major global investors in R&D. This is a necessary step to promote the transformation process of new innovation. The Chinese government needs to continue to increase its investment in R&D, particularly in basic research. As noted earlier, China is now the third largest investor in R&D in the world. Moreover, comparing China with the OECD countries, the proportion of R&D investment by the private sector in gross domestic R&D expenditure in China has increased rapidly, from 60 per cent in 2003 to 74 per cent in 2011, and has taken over that of the major industrialised economies. For example, the proportion of R&D investment by the private sector in gross domestic R&D expenditure was 60 per cent in the United States in 2011, having fallen from a higher level of 70 per cent in 2003.[1] Therefore, in terms of encouraging private sector

---

[1] The data come from 'Gross domestic expenditure on R&D by sector of performance and source of funds' collected from the OECD website (http://stats.oecd.org). We cross-checked the China data in 'The 2nd National R&D census' available from the National Statistical Bureau website (http://www.stats.gov.cn), indicating 72 per cent for China in 2009.

investment in R&D in China, the business environment has improved over the past decade. In addition to having substantial investment in innovation, China has a large pool of trained scientists and engineers. The number of university graduates in science and engineering in China is the highest in the world, with 6.7 million graduates receiving undergraduate and postgraduate degrees in 2012.[2] This is also an advantage for China's innovation, particularly in terms of promoting the diffusion of innovation. Although the proportion of scientists and engineers in the total population in China is still comparatively low, at only 0.03 per cent in 2008,[3] their talents provide China the resources to make some breakthroughs in selected focused industries or disciplines, especially in the manufacturing sector.

The bottlenecks in China's capabilities lie in the creativeness of researchers and the labour force. Creativity is difficult to measure. In general, from a learning perspective, the Chinese education system emphasises respect for and attention to existing knowledge and doctrine, rather than fostering critical thinking and challenging existing limits. This emphasis may hinder the development of creativity for the younger generation (Li, 2006; Zi, 2013). Therefore, reforming the current education system is a crucial step in the development of national innovation capabilities over the long run. The development of creativity starts with nursery education, but the reform process should start by making changes to the university admissions process, followed by the exam system at middle and primary schools. This is a long-term process that needs to start now. China should also follow the best international practices in education, not only the experiences from the United States and Europe but also from Japan and Korea. Given the existing substantial literature and debate on education reform in China (e.g., Cheng, 2004; Shi, 2008; Wu, 2013), the present chapter will not expand the discussion in this regard.

Enhancing the skills of the labour force through on-the-job training should be prioritised. Innovation in the modern industrial sector necessitates increases in training and re-training. Because of the presence of externalities of knowledge and the lack of resources for training in the private sector, especially in the SMEs, workforce training decisions and

---

[2] This is calculated from data collected from the National Bureau of Statistics of China website, available from http://data.stats.gov.cn.

[3] This is calculated from data collected from the National Bureau of Statistics of China website, available from http://data.stats.gov.cn.

actions cannot be left purely in the hands of business. There is a role for policy intervention in the skill enhancement of the labour force. Since 1960, South Korea has insisted that companies spend at least 5–6 per cent of their total budget on education and training programs, hence involving the private sector in the education and innovation process in a meaningful way (McMahon, 1987).

In addition to the long-term or medium-term effects of education and training, the utilisation of international knowledge and talent will have both immediate short-term and long-term effects. China has started several programmes to attract highly skilled international researchers since 2008 and should continue to do so, while also paying attention to the necessary follow-up support. More research is needed on knowledge transmission mechanisms to transfer information, knowledge and skills from returnees to locally trained staff.

China needs to introduce effective foreign direct investment promotion policies to attract MNEs to invest more in R&D activities. Although there have been news headlines regarding MNEs, such as Microsoft having R&D labs in China and India, several pieces of research commissioned by the EU find that there has been no hollowing out effect on R&D activities within the EU (EC, 2013). In other words, most of the frontier R&D in the MNEs is still based in their headquarters and in OECD countries. The R&D intensity of the MNE subsidiaries in China is still not high.

Another constraint to address is the inequality in access to innovation resources and the need for greater support of SMEs (which form the most dynamic sector in the economy), as well as the private sector in general (the most efficient innovator in the economy). According to the EC (2013), SMEs have been the major driver of innovation growth in EU countries. In China, state-owned firms are currently the major beneficiary of government R&D programs. These firms also have much better access to bank loans than the private and SME sectors. Reform of the financial sector started recently in China, including liberalisation of interest rates. However, reforming the financial sector is a complex task that will take time to accomplish. Moreover, the constraint in access to financial resources by SMEs is a widely recognised problem even in developed economies. Therefore, even with a more liberalised financial sector in China, the government needs to set up targeted SME innovation funds and information support systems to promote the innovation activity of SMEs.

Strengthening incentives at multiple levels

As discussed in Section 14.2, the biggest gap between China and the most innovative countries is not physical infrastructure and investment, but the lack of effective incentives to stimulate efforts and creativity for novel innovation and to guide efficient allocation of resources, as well as the lack of soft skills in terms of innovation management and policy co-ordination.

Incentives are of crucial importance in guiding physical and human resources in the economy towards the innovative sectors and innovative firms. Incentives act to stimulate the expansion, renewal or disappearance of resources. Moreover, incentives at the micro level will greatly stimulate the efforts of researchers, managers and employers; reduce X-inefficiency[4]; and determine the efficiency of innovation. Despite high investment in R&D, China's incentive structure is not well developed or set appropriately, in the following aspects.

1. Greater role of the market in incentivising investment for innovation

The Chinese government needs to modify its role and learn to co-ordinate resource use more efficiently using a diverse set of tools. Problems in the funding allocation and administration system (to be discussed later) have led to inefficient use of R&D resources. Sometimes excessive intervention by various local governments leads to investment behaviour that seriously distorts market demand: for example, the lack of co-ordination among local governments and, hence, the overinvestment in the solar photovoltaic (PV) industry in China have led to a serious surplus in production capacity in this industry. This recommendation does not mean a full withdrawal by the state but, rather, less direct intervention than at present. Moreover, the government should extend the allocation of public funding more widely to include the private sector and SMEs and also use indirect tools in the labour market or in product markets to ensure that skills and innovative products are protected, for example, by influencing the price of and demand for skilled labour and innovative new products, such as subsidising customers using solar PV panels. Finally, the Chinese government

---

[4] X-inefficiency indicates the inefficiency that occurs in the absence of fear of entry and rivalry; it may occur in a monopoly since there is no competitive pressure to produce at the minimum possible costs.

should more actively employ policies to create an environment that fosters and encourages innovation in addition to increasing direct investment in R&D.

2. Enhance competition to motivate innovation

Reform of the economic system and competition policy is needed. Given the barriers to market entry and the abnormal profits that result from monopoly power and market failure, capital has tended to flow into sectors of the economy that are less innovative, such as the real estate sector and the stock market. Therefore, institutional reforms and marketisation that are intended to create a more efficient capital market will direct investment to the more innovative and productive sectors. Similarly, further increases in the openness of the economy and removal of protection against competition of certain groups of firms, such as state-owned enterprises (SOEs) in the transportation and telecommunication sectors, will have the same effect. Both Singapore and South Korea have used an approach whereby the government offers no protection but intervenes heavily in guiding investment (Krause, 1988).

3. Better use of human resource management practices

Better use of human resource management practices is crucial because of the entrenched unsuccessful practices currently used in many areas related to innovation in universities and research institutes. Better management practices might include, first, setting higher wages and rewards for personnel involved in innovation, not only R&D staff (scientists and engineers) but also production and marketing staff engaged with new product commercialisation. People are the crucial players in the creation of new knowledge. Internal brain drain of talent from the innovative sectors to the non-science and non-technology sectors has become a common problem faced by many countries, including China. This measure will not only attract more talent to participate in innovation and innovation-related activities in the business and public sectors but will also attract more young people to study science and engineering at universities.

Second, effective human resource management practices should be introduced to promote creative and innovative activities in firms, research institutions, universities and government departments. This includes, in particular, appropriate appraisal and reward/promotion systems. Of course, the emphasis should vary in different organisations.

Creativity comes from researchers and other innovation-related personnel, starting with top management and running through to R&D researchers and marketing staff. The motivation of each individual to foster innovation is one of the most important drivers of innovation. This is also an area in which China needs to improve. For example, the evaluation of top managers of firms (SOEs in particular) should be based on their performance not only in terms of the growth of sales or the total amount of profits but also in terms of the innovations (both technological and managerial) that the firm has introduced under their leadership.

With respect to researchers at universities and research institutes, human resource management policies can play several roles:

1. Give higher weight to the quality than to the quantity of research outcomes in appraisals. For example, in universities, the number of publications is the main criterion to evaluate a researcher's academic achievement, whereas the quality of the publications has not received enough attention. In fact, quality should be the main criterion instead of the quantity of papers, books and patents a researcher has published. In recent years, there have been changes in some research-oriented universities in this regard. However, such reform should be scaled up to the wider academic community in the country.

2. Use a researcher's/institution's ability to attract external funding as one of the appraisal criteria, but also use output as a more important appraisal criterion.

3. Set achievable targets that suit high-quality research in research performance appraisal. Major research performance evaluation should be carried out every three to four years instead every year. The emphasis should not be the quantity but the quality of research publications.

4. Set knowledge transfer as one of the appraisal criteria. In this respect, China can benefit from learning from international best practice. For example, in UK universities, the Research Excellence Framework (REF) exercise is carried out every five years, and only the four highest quality research outputs are required to be submitted for review by each academic staff member. Moreover, the REF exercise requires reporting on the impact that the research has on the economy and society.

5. Tolerate failure and have medium-term or longer-term vision in appraisals. Three to five years are necessary for high-quality research to be published. Although annual evaluations can still take place, major evaluations require a longer period of time. Of course, subject specificity should be taken into consideration.

Third, reform the R&D funding grant system and project appraisal methods:

1. Strengthen the appraisal of research projects.
2. The appraisal criteria should include not only the number of papers published but also the number of patents; also (a must) the value of knowledge transfer should be measured either in monetary terms or in terms of change in behaviour, practice and policy of firms, people and government.

Of course, for all these new policy and management practices to work, honesty is crucial. The government should ensure that there is a significant punishment if the code of conduct is broken. Moreover, a guide on research ethics should be introduced to researchers, teachers and students because there has been a weakness and lack of training in this regard in China (Cao et al., 2013).

4. Improve intellectual property rights protection to strengthen the internal motives for innovation

Given the high risk and costly nature of innovation, it is crucial to improve the protection of IPR in China to strengthen the motivation for innovation of investors and innovators. In the following subsection, we explain this in detail and examine institutional development.

The incentive bottleneck is currently a major problem that China faces. Breaking out of it will not only motivate innovative activities in China but also greatly increase efficiency in innovation.

Development of institutions

With respect to the development of institutions in building innovation capabilities, the most important task for China is to continue to strengthen the protection of IPR. China has made substantial progress, which may not be widely recognised (Bound et al., 2013). Nevertheless, relatively weak IPR protection in China has been widely cited by foreign investors and MNEs as a major barrier preventing them from using the most advanced technology in their production in China.

The strengthening of IPR protection will promote indigenous innovation because it will improve the motivation of investors and researchers to ensure that their investment and efforts will be properly rewarded and their rights protected. Moreover, it will not only help China attract R&D-intensive investment by multinationals but also promote international innovation collaboration between Chinese universities, firms and world-leading institutes. It will also incentivise existing MNEs in China to engage more with local firms and institutions for technology transfer. Moreover, correct signals will be passed to the factor markets and will further direct financial and human resources to the innovative sectors.

Investment in R&D, the commercialisation of new technology and the diffusion of innovation need to be greatly enhanced through using a scientific method for the pricing of IPR and intangible assets. The financing system for innovation is currently based on experience. For example, the value of a technology and the decision to invest or not in a technology commercialisation project is made mainly according to the experience of the venture capitalists. The lack of a widely accepted mechanism for the pricing of IPR has constrained the banks and other financial institutions from providing funding to innovation activities. This also hinders the trade and diffusion of the existing technology. With a new pricing system (e.g., with a more transparent and objective price evaluation mechanism), firms with international patents would more easily obtain funds for commercialisation. Investors, including the banks, would have a clearer idea about the value of the innovative technology to make a more informed decision. Investors in R&D and owners of intellectual property would have a tool to discover the value of an innovation outcome and a way to obtain the return at a market price. This will greatly enhance the incentives and resource use for innovation. This is a challenge facing firms not only in China but also in the developed countries. Venture capital and experienced investors have played a significant role to fill part of this gap. Nevertheless, developing a better system to finance innovation and commercialisation of inventions remains an important task for the governments in the world. Of course, progress in this area first requires a breakthrough in the research and the design of such an IPR pricing system, which is beyond the scope of what government policies can achieve. This should be a priority area for government support.

China needs to strengthen its technology market. The technology market is an intermediate market place for technology transfer and exchange. Although the technology market was introduced in China during the 1990s, it has not really prospered in the country. Indeed, the growth of the technology market should develop in parallel with the strength of IPR protection. Only when IPR and knowledge are properly valued will the technology market be able to serve as an effective marketplace to facilitate the transaction of technologies. In addition, when developing a domestic technology market to facilitate the intra-country diffusion of innovations, China should develop a reputable international technology exchange market to provide a respected, high-end platform for international technology transactions and exchange. This is an important institution to enhance the diffusion of innovation. Of course, the effectiveness of this institutional platform depends on the strength of IPR protection and the demand from the firms.

Strengthening co-ordination in policy making and implementation

The strength of the innovation capabilities of a country also depends on the interplay among the factors discussed earlier. The consistency of incentives and capabilities, as well as the co-ordination of the various policies, plays a key role in shaping the strength of the newly industrialised countries. Admittedly, the Chinese government has done a good job in treating the process of innovation as system engineering. A series of complementary policies were introduced in a sensible sequence to motivate and support innovation (Wu, 2010). A wide range of government departments have introduced policies relevant to innovation: for example, the 'Guidelines on Key Areas of Commercialisation of Prioritised High Technologies', jointly issued by the National Development and Reform Commission, the Ministry of Science and Technology, the Ministry of Commerce and the State Intellectual Property Office in 2007, and the 'Preferential Policies on Income Tax Related to Technology Innovation', jointly issued by the Ministry of Finance and the State Bureau of Taxation in 2006. Attempts at co-ordination in policy making and implementation have been made. For example, the innovation funds for SMEs are managed with co-ordination between the Ministry of Science and Technology and the Ministry of Finance under the direct support of the State Council. The government has also established a national Science, Technology and Education Leading Group to co-ordinate the policies between the Ministry of Science and Technology and the Ministry of Education.

Nevertheless, because of the disparate interests of different government departments and the existence of information asymmetry between different policy makers, overlaps and conflicts among policies still exist, and there is a lack of co-ordination between local governments (OECD, 2008; Wu, 2010, 2013). Therefore, the Chinese government should consider, first, setting up a central innovation leading group (CILG) led by the prime minister. Its members should include ministers of all the relevant departments, such as the National Development and Reform Commission, the Ministry of Science and Technology, the Ministry of Commerce, the People's Bank of China, the Ministry of Finance, the State Administration of Taxation, the General Administration of China Customs, the State Intellectual Property Office, the Ministry of Education, the Ministry of Human Resources and Social Security. Second, the government should set up an office for the CILG. The CILG would meet once every six months to make strategic decisions on the country's innovation policy and strategy and also to undertake co-ordinated initiatives requiring agreement at a high level. The office of CILG would be a regular agency responsible for policy research and implementing, evaluating and co-ordinating innovation policies within different departments. The office would report to the CILG and would also be responsible for the implementation of the decisions of the CILG.

Opening up the innovation system

The shift of innovation mode from closed to open innovation, the globalisation of the innovation system and the increasingly severe trade environment for China offer both opportunities and challenges. The Chinese government needs to actively use non-traditional modes to integrate China into the global innovation system, in particular by adopting the following measures.

First, the government must strengthen innovation collaboration and actively participate in international knowledge co-production. It should better provide some specified measures. Innovation has become a global and collaborative undertaking (OECD, 2008).

Second, the government should encourage international technology acquisition through cross-border mergers and acquisitions by offering support not only in a monetary sense but also in providing soft skills that are needed for successful knowledge acquisition. This could involve sponsoring research on strategy and the process management of mergers and acquisitions and also follow-up knowledge transfer to Chinese MNEs.

Third, the government should gradually open up the innovation system by actively attracting highly skilled world-leading researchers for innovation projects in China. China introduced the thousand-talent program in 2009, intended to attract overseas Chinese and foreign talent to support innovations in both academia and industry. The government should continue to invest in such programs and seek to improve them through careful evaluation of their impacts.

Finally, there should be active participation in international innovation activities through involvement in the global standard-setting activities of international organisations. Of course, active and successful participation requires high-calibre talented professionals who not only have expert knowledge in certain areas of science and technology but also international vision and excellent communication skills.

14.4 Space for innovation policy in the twenty-first century

There remains a large role for the government to play in promoting the technology and innovation capabilities of a country as the space for selective industry policy in the twenty-first century is becoming more limited. The world trading system is moving towards more free trade and away from protectionism. Countries are more capable of using non-tariff barriers, such as anti-dumping and anti-subsidy tools, to block the imports of goods that they regard as having benefitted from the exporting country's government protection and subsidies. Countries are now increasingly using anti-dumping and anti-subsidy sanctions and non-tariff barriers to protect domestic industries and to compete against major competitors. China has become one of the major targets of trade disputes. In fact, some industry policies have been rebranded and transformed into innovation policies, for example, policies supporting innovation networks or policies encouraging technology transfer instead of protectionist industrial policy based on the infant industry argument. Policy has been transformed from selective 'picking of winners' and protectionist policies into 'horizontal' policies that promote capabilities across sectors, such as those that improve infrastructure, institutions and universal capabilities building. Therefore, we have the following recommendations for policy design.

First, it is advisable to use pull rather than push policy measures to attract R&D-intensive MNEs and highly skilled talents to China. Examples of pull policies are improvements to IPR protection and the competitive market environment. The policy space for forcing MNEs to transfer technology and locate innovation activities in China has been limited according to the World Trade Organisation (WTO) rules since China's WTO entry in 2002. In this regard, continued strengthening of IPR protection in China is key to the removal of this bottleneck. Another relevant area involves helping MNEs and returning or foreign talented professionals to quickly integrate into the local research and social community and provide them with continued support after relocation.

Second, it is advisable to use more horizontal policies (e.g., policies supporting education, R&D, and improvement of infrastructure and institutions) rather than selective policies to promote the growth of certain industries. Selective policies, especially those through supply-side inputs (e.g., subsidies) are more likely to be a subject of trade disputes. Of course, this does not mean the abolition of selective policies. Rather, it means refraining from providing subsidies and preferential policy based on selective supply-side approaches. The Chinese government should allocate more resources and pay attention to policies that encourage demand, develop markets and improve the institutional environment. China should closely watch and take note of the relevant new developments in innovation policies that are introduced by other industrialised countries (e.g., the innovation platform, dedicated knowledge transfer funding programs and internship schemes) and should introduce them into China with the appropriate adaptation.

Third, government policy should focus on activities that suffer from market failure: for example, basic research that faces high risks and uncertainties and requires long-term investment to be sustained. The government should refrain from intervening in market-led activities such as the majority of the commercialisation process, especially the scaling up of production activities.

14.5 Conclusions

Building an innovation-driven economy has been highlighted by the Chinese government as one of its major tasks at the current stage of development of the country. In the present chapter, we examined the policy choices facing China when considering the goal of transforming from an imitator to an innovator. We have approached this question from the perspective of capabilities, incentives and institutions within the innovation capabilities framework. The analysis is subject to the limitation that the chapter only covers a few of the determinants of national innovation capacity in a wide range of macroeconomic, micro-economic, political, social and even cultural factors.

Analysis presented in this chapter suggests possible policy recommendations to enhance China's innovation performance, including the following.

First is to maintain the momentum of rapid growth in R&D investment and to ensure reforms will lead to more private sector investment growth; a wider allocation of the resources to the private sector and the SMEs sector; and a more efficient, market-driven funding allocation process.

Second is to encourage fair competition through reforms of the economic system, which should play a significant role in incentivising innovation at the firm level and in guiding the resources flowing to the innovation sectors to seek innovation rents instead of monopoly rents.

Third is to set appropriate incentives at multiple levels by introducing new, or modifying existing, human resource and funding management practices. This appears to be the key area for policy intervention at the current stage. The policy options include correcting misleading policies in appraisal and reward systems and in the management of research funding, as well as the introduction of new policies including heavy punishment for academic and professional dishonesty and wider criteria that will have an impact on the evaluation of researchers, projects and institutions.

Fourth is to encourage and facilitate international knowledge sourcing and co-production using unconventional methods. These unconventional methods include direct investment abroad, attracting highly skilled international talent and international innovation collaborations. China has made appropriate efforts in this regard and should continue to do so by refining the management process of these activities to ensure that Chinese firms will genuinely benefit from these methods. All these policies, if well designed and properly introduced, will have a significant impact on the propensity for, and efficiency of, innovation in Chinese firms and research institutions.

Fifth is the creation of institutions to co-ordinate the efforts and policies issued by different government departments; enhance the interplay between capabilities, incentives and institutions; and avoid possible contradiction and conflict among policies. In particular, the Chinese government should consider setting up a CILG led by the prime minister and involving ministers of all the relevant government departments. A regular agency such as the office of the CILG could also be set up to carry out the research, undertake assessment of innovation policies, co-ordinate the innovation policy of the different government departments and implement decisions made by the CILG.

Despite the important role that the state can play in fostering innovation capabilities, we have to realise that the space for innovation policies in the twenty-first century is smaller than what existed when Japan, Korea and other newly industrialised economies emerged. Therefore, the Chinese government should follow the global trend and use more horizontal policies rather than old selective policies that favour a few industries. More policies that address the pull factors should be used because the space for using push policies is becoming increasingly limited with respect to international knowledge sourcing and also in terms of promoting innovation in domestic firms.

Finally, we would like to highlight our expectations of government policy. As Stiglitz (1989, p. 202) argues, 'governments face information and incentive problems no less than does the private sector ... We need to recognise both limits and strengths of markets, as well as the strengths, and limits of government interventions aimed at correcting market failures'.

Conclusions

15 | *Conclusions: Open national innovation system and China's path to innovation*

China's industrial capabilities have increased significantly since the 1980s. Transforming the country into an innovation-driven economy has now become its top priority. This book attempts to provide a systematic, comprehensive and rigorous study of China's path to innovation from the 1980s to the present and for the future. This chapter summarises the major findings of the study and discusses the policy implications for China and other countries.

Open national innovation system and China's path to innovation

In the main, evidence reported in the book suggests that China has followed a path of an open national innovation system (ONIS) since the reforms and the take-off stage in the 1980s. An ONIS is a national innovation system (NIS) that is opened up to international knowledge, resources and markets. This model has the following characteristics: (1) It has dual knowledge sources and uses a dynamic combination of foreign and indigenous innovation that evolves over time. It has an NIS making efforts to foster indigenous innovation capabilities while opening up to external knowledge or resources for knowledge production at all stages of the innovation chain, from research to development to commercialisation. (2) It has multiple driving forces: the state, the private sector and the MNEs and uses a combination of the state and the market to guide the direction of innovation and allocate the resources. (3) It encompasses both the outside-in and inside-out branches of the open innovation model, though the inside-out branch becomes more relevant at the later stage of technology development. (4) It employs multiple knowledge diffusion channels and uses a combination of multi-channel, multi-layer knowledge sourcing strategy, which is again dynamic, evolving at different stages of technology development for international and domestic knowledge diffusion. These characteristics will be elaborated in the following sections of the chapter.

Before the reforms in the 1980s, the science and technology system in China was a closed innovation system developed following the former Soviet Union model (Xue, 1997). Since the opening up and system reforms in the 1980s, following the ONIS path, China's national innovation system has had a high degree of openness to external knowledge from the start. There has been investment in indigenous innovation over the years but with varying efforts at different stages of development: a small amount at the start that was mostly spent on absorption of foreign technology and development, followed by a lane change to emphasise indigenous innovation starting in the late 1990s, after about two decades of openness, while maintaining high openness to external knowledge. The system has even become more active in knowledge sourcing, using unconventional channels that are not often used in developing countries, for example, outward direct investment, international innovation collaboration and attraction of highly skilled migrants.

In principle, this is an appropriate path for a developing country along its development trajectory. China succeeded in embarking on a fast industrialisation trajectory as a result of this technological development strategy. However, the emphasis on indigenous R&D and innovation started later than it should have: policies encouraging indigenous innovation were introduced around 2000 when the dependency on foreign core technology acquisition had become a significant constraint in some industries. In comparison, although the model of innovation and technology development in Japan and South Korea is widely regarded as an inward looking, indigenous capability building–oriented model supported by strong employment of import-substitution strategy and industrial policy, in fact, Japan and South Korea have heavily relied on foreign technical assistance and aid provided by the Western countries, especially after World War II and the Cold War. In terms of knowledge sources for innovation and technical progress, they have not closed their doors, although they have closed their markets to foreign competition. Moreover, in the history of Japan's industrial catch-up, technology transfer from MNEs has also have played its role (Cantwell, 1992; Cantwell and Zhang, 2009). Although MNEs have not played a prominent role in the catch-up process in South Korea and Taiwan, international knowledge transfer through diasporas and highly skilled returned migrants has been crucial in building up local technological capabilities in these two economies (Dahlman, 1994; Wong, 1999).

Research presented in this book also suggests that ONIS is not a static but a dynamic model, evolving with the advancement of the innovation capability of a country. Leading Chinese firms have started to use unconventional methods of international knowledge sourcing, for example, international innovation collaboration with foreign partners including foreign universities and direct cross-border investment and acquisition. Although the full effect may need some time to appear, these unconventional knowledge sourcing activities are significantly associated with a greater likelihood of creating radical novel innovations in the Chinese firms. International operations have also allowed some Chinese MNEs to upgrade their overall capabilities and competitiveness, as the case studies of Huawei and ZTE reveal. In addition, China has also successfully sourced international knowledge through human flows and social networks. In the 1980s and 1990s, diasporas have been important foreign investors in China, through which superior technologies (though not the most advanced) were transferred to China (Fu, 2004). Since 2000, especially the introduction of the indigenous innovation strategy in 2006, highly skilled diaspora workers and many Chinese students educated abroad returned to China. They have played an important role in the development of some high-technology industries and the so-called strategic emerging industries such as renewable energy, electrical cars and biotechnology (Wang, 2012). This type of sequencing is also observed among the East Asian economies. As Lee, Jee and Eun (2011) find, at the macro and aggregate levels, China follows the "East Asian sequencing" rather than the Washington Consensus.

Therefore, for the way ahead, a rational strategy for China's path to innovation will be to continue to enhance innovation by harnessing internal and external resources as suggested by the ONIS model, and guiding it with a well-defined incentive structure and fully developed institutions.

Relationship between foreign and indigenous innovation in the ONIS model

The ONIS model suggests that opening up to foreign technology transfer and investment in indigenous innovation should go hand in hand. Despite the potential offered by globalisation and a liberal trade regime, the benefits of international technology diffusion can only be delivered with parallel indigenous innovation efforts and the presence of modern institutional and governance structures and a dynamic innovation system. In this sense, indigenous and foreign innovation efforts are complementary. Without proactive indigenous innovation efforts, foreign technology remains only static technology embedded in imported machines that will never turn into real indigenous technological capability. This conclusion is compounded by the expected inappropriateness of technologies created in the industrialised economies for countries in the developing South, which calls for greater efforts to develop indigenous innovation crucial for technological change and catch-up, especially in the middle-income countries.

As regards diffusion and adoption then, first, technology diffusion and adoption are not costless and unconditional. The speed of diffusion and adoption, and thereby of technological capabilities building, depends on the firms' absorptive capacity and complementary assets. Empirical evidence from Chapter 3 illustrates this and is supported by evidence from emerging economies (Fu, Pietrobelli and Soete, 2010). Second, only in the presence of local innovation capacity will MNEs adopt a more integrated innovation practice, which has greater linkages with the local economy and thereby enables greater opportunities of knowledge transfer (Franco et al., 2011). Hence, the encouragement of indigenous R&D and innovation activities remains an indispensable centrepiece of an innovation strategy targeting the assimilation and adaptation of foreign technology and the acceleration of technological learning and capabilities building.

Admittedly, developing countries face a dilemma of resource constraints to meet the high investment costs and high-risk challenges of innovation (Erdilek, 1984; Hoekman et al., 2005). Experience from China suggests that to maximise the benefits from innovation and accelerate catching-up, the explicit and well-focused encouragement of indigenous innovation and acquisitions of foreign knowledge must work in parallel. Neither autonomous innovations nor FDI-reliant strategies can be used independently. Relying solely on one of them would not be optimal for technological capability development and catching-up. The Chinese ONIS model proposes a strategy to maximise the benefits for the developing country. *How* to select and shape the best combinations at different stages of development and for different countries and industries is a question of utmost relevance for future research.

Evolution of the indigenous-foreign combination at different stages of development

The ONIS model is a dynamic model with continuous adjustment of this indigenous-foreign combination at different stages of development. It suggests a high openness to external knowledge from the early stage of technological development of a country and that indigenous innovation capacity building should also start from an early stage instead of purely depending on foreign technology transfer. However, given the resource constraints and the skills available in the domestic economy of the developing countries, the emphasis on indigenous innovation could increase with the level of economic and technological development of the developing country. The channels used for foreign technology transfer should also evolve with the advancement of technical progress at different stages of development. Along China's path to innovation and technology upgrading, imports of machinery and equipment and transfer of technology through licensing have been major channels of foreign technology acquisition in the 1980s. Direct adoption of these technologies and learning how to use the imported machines were the main efforts made by domestic firms and institutions.

In the 1990s, technology transfer through direct foreign investment has been a new focus. Huge amounts of FDI since then have flowed into China. China's overall industrial and technological capabilities increased significantly, supported mainly by those subsidiaries of MNEs especially in the high-technology industries. However, although there has been some learning by the indigenous partner in the joint ventures and spillovers to local companies in the same and linked industries, as evidenced in the book, the benefits to the technological and innovation capabilities from the FDI are limited. Therefore, since the late 1990s, acceleration of science and technology development has been given priority policy attention. Since 2006, indigenous innovation has been formally stated as one of the government's strategic priorities. At the same time, the channels used by China for foreign knowledge sourcing also started to change as analysed in Part III of the book. First, the Chinese government modified its inward FDI policy to attract knowledge-intensive FDI. Second, the go global strategy was introduced in 1998. Since then, China has started a more active international knowledge-sourcing strategy. Third, the intensity of international innovation collaboration increased rapidly, especially in recent years when more specific funding programmes were set up to encourage internationally collaborative research.

The experience of the solar-PV industry in China and India as analysed in Chapter 10 provides a classic example of catch-up and leapfrogging using a strategy of mixing and sequencing of different technology transfer and indigenous innovation mechanisms at different stages of technology development. Most leading solar-PV companies in both countries started from international technology transfer through licensing and joint ventures with MNEs. At the same time, all of them have put increasingly substantial effort into in-house R&D for the assimilation and adaptation of transferred technologies and the development of indigenous technological capabilities. However, once the basic production and technological capabilities were built up, they started more active knowledge acquisition and creation through indigenous innovation, international R&D collaboration and cross-border mergers and acquisitions. Such experience suggests that to accomplish such catch-up processes requires a combination of international technology transfer and indigenous innovation. Technology transfer will be a feasible and evidence-proven entry point for developing countries, although this should be accompanied with substantial indigenous efforts in assimilation and learning. In this respect, attractive bundles of trade, investment and technology policies are important mechanisms to leverage technology transfer.

The effectiveness of knowledge-sourcing channels at different stages

Given the availability of a variety of channels for international knowledge sourcing, choosing the most effective channels for countries of different industry structures and at different stages of development is important. China's experience in the past three decades offers some examples and lessons.

First, international knowledge and innovation exchange and collaboration, through inter-firm and intra-firm networks and global value chains (GVC), is now regarded as an important route for developing country firms to access knowledge and enhance learning and innovation. Integration into the GVC through engaging with processing and assembly activities is a widely used method by many developing countries, with the expectation of substantial learning and consequent development of technological capabilities in the local firms in related industries. The evidence from this book demonstrates that processing trade-FDI has generated significant positive information spillover effect (e.g., market intelligence, export management) on the export performance of indigenous firms. However, the technology spillover effect on the development of international competitiveness in indigenous firms is limited and in fact exerts a significant depressive effect on the propensity to export in these firms. Indigenous innovation, economies of scale and productivity are found to be the main drivers of export performance in indigenous firms in the high-technology industries.

China's experience in the acquisition of tacit knowledge within the Chinese optical fibre and cable industry also suggests that in industries where tacit knowledge is a more important component of technological learning than codified knowledge, internal R&D activities and domestic peers are important knowledge sources. Additionally, universities are shown to be an important asset in creating learning organisations and providing effective knowledge sources of both tacit and codified knowledge. However, imports of equipment and licensing are a less effective learning channel in the acquisition of tacit foreign technology.

Second, the experience of China's leading technology-intensive firms, Huawei and ZTE, and evidence from a survey of firms in Guangdong Province on the impact of going global indicate that firms can benefit from employing more active knowledge-sourcing channels for catch-up at a more advanced stage. For example, international operations allowed some of these leading Chinese MNEs to upgrade their overall capabilities, not only technological capabilities but also design and marketing capabilities for greater control at the two ends of value chains, where most of the value added is generated. Moreover, international innovation collaboration with foreign partners including foreign universities and direct cross-border investment and acquisition are significantly associated with a greater likelihood of creating radical novel innovations in the Chinese firms.

Leading players in the ONIS model: is the Chinese ONIS model state led?

Findings of the book also indicate that although the state-owned enterprises (SOEs) have been a major force in the Chinese economy, especially before and at the early stage of the reforms, in respect to innovation, the foreign invested and domestic privately owned firms are not only investing more in R&D than the SOEs, they are also more efficient in innovation and are producing more innovative outputs. Moreover, instead of having the SOEs taking a lead in pushing forward the technology frontier among Chinese firms, foreign invested (FIEs) and privately owned (POEs) enterprises are the leading players in the high-technology and low- and low-medium technology industries, respectively. That said, SOEs remain a leader in the high-medium technology industries. So the SOEs, POEs and FIEs all have played their roles in China's technology upgrading and innovation. Therefore, instead of a pure market-driven model of innovation or the often assumed state-led model of innovation, China's path to innovation follows a multi-driver model led by a mix of players – the state, the private sector and the MNEs, with each of them playing a leading role in different segments of the economy and the innovation system. Therefore, the ONIS model in China is led by a combination of the state and the market, although the actual practice so far is neither perfect nor mature.

Of course, the multiple-driver model of ONIS does not undermine the role of the state in ONIS and the role of policies in promoting innovation. Analysis of China's innovation policy in the past in Chapter 6 and policy choices for the future in Chapter 14 both suggest a role for the state in guiding and supporting the innovation process. The nature of innovation as public goods, the externalities that it may generate for long-term growth and its risky and costly nature all suggest a role for the state. Therefore, the state may play a more important role in areas of greater externality (e.g., supporting basic research) and in areas of greater capital intensity and uncertainty (e.g., the capital-intensity heavy industries). However, in areas where the market functions well (e.g., commercialisation and labour-intensive industries), the private sector will be more efficient in guiding the allocation of innovation resources and incentivising innovation.

Open innovation as a response to constraints and risks and the role of universities

Developing country firms often face resource, capabilities and institutional constraints for innovation. Evidence from the book shows how Chinese firms use open innovation as a response to the constraints and risks of innovation that they face. It is found that institutional, financial and knowledge- and skills-related risks and constraints are all significantly associated with firms' depth and breadth of openness in innovation. The responses, however, vary across firms of different ownership types. Foreign invested firms appear to be most responsive and take action to widen and deepen their openness in innovation. Privately owned firms have made significant responses to market- and institution-related and finance- and risk-related impediments but not to knowledge- and skills-related impediments. State-owned firms appear to be least responsive to the use of open innovation. Firm size and industry-specific effects also appear to have significant moderating effect on firms' responses to the various constraints. These findings are consistent with those from an in-depth study of the Chinese semiconductor industry by Teece and Chesbrough (2005).

Among the various possible partners that firms can collaborate with for innovation, universities are ones that have received substantial attention. Research reported in the book finds that domestic universities have played a significant role in the promotion of the diffusion of frontier technology and the creation of new products or processes that are new to the country or the firm, although their contribution to the creation of groundbreaking innovations is limited in China. International innovation collaboration with foreign universities, especially those in the newly industrialised economies and the emerging South, appears to be fruitful in enhancing the creation of groundbreaking innovations in Chinese firms. The experience of the Chinese optical fibre and cable industry also suggests that universities are an important asset in creating learning organisations and provide effective knowledge sources for both tacit and codified knowledge.

Incentives and institutions and the efficiency of innovation

Heavy investment in R&D is not equal to a strong innovation performance. There is a need for appropriate incentives to guide the use of the resources and stimulate their expansion, renewal or disappearance to transform potentially strong into actually strong performance. Institutions also affect this by setting the rules, modifying behaviour by changing attitudes and expectations, altering capabilities and changing incentives (OECD, 1987).

Research on the innovation potential and actual performance of the advanced economies indicates that institutional factors such as competition, openness and international property rights (IPR) protection are significantly associated with the patenting efficiency of an economy. Comparing China and the OECD and other emerging economies in recent years reveals that the gap in patenting performance between China and the world frontier is the result of relative underperformance mainly in the efficiency of innovation production. Therefore, developing institutions and reforming incentives are important areas to enhance innovation performance in China. In fact, evidence at sub-national level from Chinese regions suggests that the strength of technology spillovers to the domestic Chinese firms depends on the availability of absorptive capacity and the presence of innovation-complementary institutions in the host region. The type and quality of FDI inflows and the strength of local absorptive capacity and complementary assets in the host regions are crucial for FDI to serve as a driver of knowledge-based development. These innovation-complementary institutions include not only technology exchange markets but also training and financial institutions for innovation in start-ups and SMEs, for example, incubators, IPO market, venture capital, polytechnic institutions and information provision services for SMEs.

One of the areas that is of particular importance for the ONIS to work is the introduction, development and the implementation of regulation on IPR protection. Given the high risk and costly nature of innovation, effective protection of IPR will not only incentivise the investors and innovators to invest in innovation but also will ensure that the owners of advanced technology that their entitled rights are protected when they transfer and use advanced technologies in foreign countries or invest in R&D in foreign host countries. Relatively weak IPR protection in China has been widely cited by foreign investors and MNEs as a major barrier preventing them from using the most advanced technology in their production in China, although substantial progress has been made in the country (Bound et al., 2013). Of course, it is also argued that the requirement made by the industrialised countries and the MNEs for strong IPR protection in host developing countries is actually somewhat unfair given that Western countries also have practised imitation in their own catchup several centuries ago (Chang, 2003). Therefore, the design of the IPR protection regulation may need to take into account the nature of the technology and the stage of development of the recipient country. In-depth research in this area is needed.

The role of South-South technology transfer in the developing world

The analysis of the role of indigenous innovation and foreign technology presented in the book points to the inappropriateness of foreign technology in developing countries. Supplementing the earlier literature on appropriate technology and directed technical change that discusses the general appropriateness of foreign technology at the aggregate level, research in this book moves the analysis down to the industry level, taking into account the different characteristics in different industries. It argues that technologies created in labour-abundant countries may be unskilled-labour augmenting. In low-technology industries that use unskilled labour intensively, labour-augmenting indigenous technology will be more efficient than foreign technology. In contrast, foreign technology from industrial countries will be skilled-labour augmenting, and it will be more efficient than indigenous technology in the technology-intensive sector that uses skilled labour intensively. This is testified to by the empirical evidence presented in Chapter 5, where collective indigenous innovation efforts are found to be a major driver of indigenous technical change in China, and the indigenous firms are the leading forces on the technology frontier in the low- and medium-technology industries, whereas the MNEs dominate the frontier of the high-technology industries.

Therefore, middle-income countries such as China can reap the gains from South-South technology transfer, and the less developed countries can benefit from acquiring more appropriate technology. In fact, South-South technology transfer and the possible gains from it are highly consistent with the inside-out branch of open innovation. The innovative South can reap the gains of innovation from commercialisation of the innovative ideas/technologies not only in the domestic market but also in the market of other developing economies. Moreover, technologies created and first used in China and other middle-income countries may also later be diffused to the industrialised countries through reverse innovation (Immelt, Govindarajan and Trimble, 2009). Such South-North technology transfer is also beneficial to producers and customers in both the South and the North.

Findings of the book suggest that there are multiple and multi-tier choices of technology rather than the simple bi-dimensional North-South divide. Technologies developed in labour-rich emerging economies will be more appropriate to the factor endowments mix in other populous developing countries; technologies created in land- and resource-rich emerging economies will be more appropriate to other land- and resource-abundant countries. They will also be easier to diffuse and absorb by other local firms. Following this rule of thumb, South-South trade and FDI will represent effective vehicles for the diffusion of these technologies, and policies should consequently follow suit on a consistent basis.

Growth and developmental impact of innovation in China

Innovation is one of the most important drivers of long-term economic growth. It is not only relevant for the developed economies but also important for developing countries. Evidence based on regional data from China presented in Chapter 3 of the book attested to its role as an important determinant of economic growth in Chinese regions. Innovation also has important developmental effects. The unbalanced development in innovation and technological capabilities across Chinese regions has been a factor contributing to the increasing regional income inequalities in China. A review of the recent development of the regional distributions of R&D expenditure and patents documented in Chapter 2 suggests the increasing regional gap in innovation capability between the coastal and the inland regions in China. As innovation is increasingly playing an important role in China's economic growth, we can expect the pressure of continued and increasing regional income inequalities amongst Chinese regions. Therefore, how to accelerate the domestic diffusion of innovation from the leading to the following regions and how to encourage the type of innovation that leads to more inclusive and sustainable development are important topics for future research.

Policy choices for China at the crossroads

For China at the crossroads of structural change and great transformation into an innovation-driven economy, there are several policy priorities for the Chinese government to consider.

First, China should continue to increase its investment in R&D and in education. The government should maintain the momentum of rapid growth in R&D investment and to ensure that reforms will lead to more private sector investment growth; a wider allocation of the resources to the private sector and the SMEs sector; and a more efficient, market-driven funding allocation process.

Second, an attempt should be made to strengthen the incentive system at the macro, meso and micro levels. This strengthening may include reforms to release the power of competition and guide resources towards innovative sectors; adopt appropriate human resource management, such as appraisal and remuneration systems; create effective policies for research funding management; and evaluate the efficiency of research to encourage the creativity of researchers, managers and employees.

To be more specific, the Chinese government should encourage fair competition through reforms of the economic system, which should play a significant role in incentivising innovation at the firm level and in guiding the resources flowing to the innovation sectors to seek innovation rents (i.e., the Schumpeterian rents that occur during the period of time between the introduction of an innovation and its successful imitation and are earned by innovators) instead of monopoly rents. China also needs to set appropriate incentives at multiple levels by introducing new, or modifying existing, human resource and funding management practices. This appears to be the key area for policy intervention at the current stage. The policy options include correcting misleading policies in appraisal and reward systems and in the management of research funding, as well as the introduction of new policies including heavy punishment for academic and professional dishonesty and wider criteria that will have an impact on the evaluation of researchers, projects and institutions.

Third, China should encourage and facilitate international knowledge sourcing and co-production using unconventional methods, as it has already done through policy and financial support. These unconventional methods include direct investment abroad, attracting highly skilled international talents and international innovation collaborations. China has made appropriate efforts in this regard and should continue to do so by refining the management process of these activities to ensure that Chinese firms will genuinely benefit from these methods. All these policies, if well designed and properly introduced, will have a significant impact on the propensity for, and efficiency of, innovation in Chinese firms and research institutions.

Finally, China should consider creating institutions to co-ordinate the efforts and policies issued by different government departments; enhance the interplay between capabilities, incentives and institutions; and avoid possible contradictions and conflict among policies. Therefore, China and other developing countries should set up a high-level policy co-ordination group headed by the top leader of the country and composed of the heads of the relevant ministries. The strategic policy making and policy co-ordination of such a group will be more effective than a post such as a chief science and technology advisor in the government.

Overall, China is on the right track with its pursuit of becoming an innovative nation, although some areas need improvement, as previously discussed. What is also crucial is the determination and patience of all key players as innovation and capabilities development are never achieved in a short time.

Limitations and issues for future research

This book has conducted a comprehensive and systematic analysis of China's path to innovation in the past three decades. Nevertheless, there are still areas that have not been discussed systematically in this book given the fact that innovation is sophisticated system engineering. These areas include the role of human mobility in international knowledge transfer, the role of IPR protection and innovation financing. Several important issues await further research. First is the impact of the incentive structure on the propensity, intensity and quality of innovation at macro, meso and micro levels. At the macro level, what is the impact of competition and marketisation on innovation in a transition economy such as China? What is the role of the state in the innovation system and in what areas, using what model, to what extent and in what sequence should policies be introduced to correct market failures? At the meso level, what are the factors that affect the efficiency of innovation at project and industry levels? What incentive structure should be introduced in the non-private sector? Where are the constraints or disincentives at the micro level towards innovation in China? Would a direct introduction and implementation of the incentives, for example, stock options, used in the Western countries be effective in promoting the propensity and intensity of innovation in firms and non-business sectors? What is the impact of culture on fostering innovation?

Second, the next stage of the transformation from imitation to innovation in China requires the harnessing of internal and external resources for more and better innovation. Challenges also exist for greater capabilities of commercialisation of innovation. All this requires greater capabilities to integrate knowledge from different sources and from different disciplines. To fully understand this process, firms need to know what strategies and pathways they can adopt: whether to acquire or to co-produce, how to choose the best partner, how to develop the capabilities to manage such sophisticated integration, how to share the value added between partners and how to protect intellectual property rights created in these open collaborative innovation activities. These are all important areas for future research to ensure that China's pursuit to build an innovation-driven economy is successful and is undertaken along an efficient and sustainable path.

Third, the role of financing and new financial institutions for innovation, especially for entrepreneurial technology start-ups, is likely to be of growing importance now and in the future. These institutions include venture capital, IPO markets and institutions that support innovations in SMEs and private enterprises in addition to the science parks and incubators. Therefore, research on reforms of the current state-dominated banking system and state-driven venture capital funding system is also of urgent need. Finally, as discussed earlier, understanding the nature of inclusive innovation and developing policies that encourage the type of innovation that leads to more inclusive and sustainable development are important tasks for future research.

References

Acemoglu, D. (2002). 'Directed technical change', *Review of Economic Studies*, 69(4), 781–810.

and Zilibotti, F. (2001). 'Productivity differences', *Quarterly Journal of Economics*, 116(2), 563–606.

Luc, A. and Varga, A. (2002). 'Patents and innovation counts as measures of regional production of new knowledge', *Research Policy*, 31(7), 1069–86.

Acs, Z. J. and Audretsch, D. B. (1990). *Innovation and Small Firms*. Cambridge, MA: MIT Press.

Adler, N. and Golany, B. (2001). 'Evaluation of deregulated airline networks using data envelopment analysis combined with principal component analysis with an application to Western Europe', *European Journal of Operational Research*, 132(2), 260–73.

Aghion, P., Bloom, N., Blundell, R., Griffith, R. and Howitt, P. (2005). 'Competition and innovation: an inverted U relationship', *Quarterly Journal of Economics*, May, pp. 701–28.

and Howitt, P. (1992). 'A model of growth through creative destruction', *Econometrica*, 60(2), 323–351.

(1998). *Endogenous Growth Theory*. Cambridge, MA: MIT Press.

and Tirole, J. (1994). 'The management of innovation', *The Quarterly Journal of Economics*, 109(4), 1185–209.

Ahrens, N. (2013). *China's Competitiveness: Myth, Reality, and Lessons for the United States and Japan (Case study: Huawei)*, CSIS report, Washington, DC.

Aitken, B., Hanson, H. G. and Harrison, A. E. (1997). 'Spillovers, foreign investment, and export behavior', *Journal of International Economics*, 43(1), 103–32.

and Harrison, A. E. (1999). 'Do domestic firms benefit from direct foreign investment? Evidence from Venezuela', *American Economic Review*, 89(3), 605–18.

Almeida, P. and Kogut, B. (1997). 'The exploration of technological diversity and the geographic localization of innovation', *Small Business Economics*, 9(1), 21–31.

Amsden, A. (1989). *Asia's Next Giant. South Korea and Late Industrialization*. Oxford, UK: Oxford University Press.
(1992). *Asia's Next Giant: South Korea and Late Industrialization*. New York: Oxford University Press.
(2001). *The Rise of 'the Rest'. Challenge to the West from Late-industrializing Economies*. Oxford, UK: Oxford University Press, chapters 1 and 6–10.
Andersson, T., Formica, P. and Curley, M. (2010). *Knowledge-Driven Entrepreneurship*. New York: Springer.
Anselin, L., Varga, A. and Acs, Z. (1997). 'Local geographic spillovers between university research and high technology innovations', *Journal of Urban Economics*, 42, 422–48.
Arcelus, F. J. and Arocena, P. (2000) 'Convergence and productive efficiency in fourteen OECD countries: a non-parametric frontier approach', *International Journal of Production Economics*, 66(2), 105–17.
Archibugi, D. and Iammarino, S. (2002). 'The globalization of technological innovation: definition and evidence', *Review of International Political Economy*, 9(1), 98–122.
Arellano, M. and Bond, S. (1991). 'Some tests of specification for panel data: Monte Carlo evidence and application to employment equations', *Review of Economic Studies*, 58(2), 277–97.
Arrow, K. J. (1962). 'Economic welfare and the allocation of resources for invention', in Nelson, R. R. (Ed.), *The Rate and Direction of Inventive Activity: Economic and Social Factors*. Princeton, NJ: Princeton University Press for N.B.E.R., 609–25.
Athreye, S. and Cantwell, J. (2007). 'Globalisation and the emergence of new technology producers', *Research Policy*, 36(2), 209–26.
Atkinson, A. B. and Stiglitz, J. E. (1969). 'A new view of technological change', *Economic Journal*, 79(315), 573–8.
Audretsch, D. and Feldman, M. (1996). 'R&D spillovers and the geography of innovation and production', *American Economics Review*, 86(3), 630–40.
Bai, J. (2009). 'Technology acquisition, open independent innovation and overseas investment strategy of Chinese enterprises', *REFORMATION & STRATEGY (Chinese)*, 25(6), 40–45.
Balasubramanayam, V. N., Salisu, M. and Sapsford, D. (1996). 'Foreign direct investment and economic growth in EP and IS countries', *Economic Journal*, 106(434), 92–105.
Baldwin, J. R. (1997). *The Importance of Research and Development for Innovation in Small and Large Canadian Manufacturing Firms*, Research Paper Series No. 107. Ottawa: Statistics Canada.

Baldwin, J. R. and Lin, Z. 2002. 'Impediments to advanced technology adoption for Canadian manufacturers'. *Research Policy*, 31(1): 1–18.

Balzat, M. and Hanusch, H. (2004). 'Recent trends in the research on national innovation systems', *Journal of Evolutionary Economics*, 14(2), 197–210.

Banker, R. D., Datar, S. M. and Rajan, M. V. (1987). 'Measurement of productivity improvements: an empirical analysis', *Journal of Accounting, Auditing & Finance*, 2(4), 319–47.

Bao, Y., Chen, X. and Zhou, K. Z. (2012). 'External learning, market dynamics, and radical innovation: evidence from China's high-tech firms', *Journal of Business Research*, 65(8), 1226–33.

Barlow, T. (2013) *Between the Eagle and the Dragon: Who is Winning the Innovation Race?* California: Hansen House Publishing.

Barney, J. B. and Hansen, M. H. (1994). 'Trustworthiness as a source of competitive advantage', *Strategic Management Journal*, 15, 175–90.

Barrios, S., Görg, H. and Strobl, E. (2003). 'Explaining firms' export behaviour: R&D, spillovers and the destination market', *Oxford Bulletin of Economics and Statistics*, 65(4), 475–96.

Basu, S. and Weil, D. N. (1998). 'Appropriate technology and growth', *Quarterly Journal of Economics*, 113(4), 1025–54.

Battese, G. E. and Coelli, T. J. (1995). 'A model for technical inefficiency effects in a stochastic frontier production function for panel data', *Empirical Economics*, 20(2), 325–32.

Bayona, C., García-Marco, T. and Huerta, E. (2001). 'Firms' motivations for cooperative R&D: an empirical analysis of Spanish firms', *Research Policy*, 30(8), 1289–1307.

van Beers, C., Berghällb, E., and Poot, T. (2008). 'R&D internationalization, R&D collaboration and public knowledge institutions in small economies: evidence from Finland and the Netherlands', *Research Policy*, 37(2): 294–308.

Belderbos, R., Carree, M. and Lokshin, B. (2004). 'Co-operative R&D and firm performance', *Research Policy*, 33(10), 1477–92.

Bell, M. (1990). *Continuing Industrialisation, Climate Change and International Technology Transfer*. Brighton: Science Policy Research Unit, Sussex University.

and Pavitt, K. (1993). 'Technological accumulation and industrial growth: contrasts between developed and developing countries', *Industrial and Corporate Change*, 2(2), 157–209.

Bernard, A. and Jensen, B. J. (1999). 'Exceptional exporter performance: cause, effect, or both?', *Journal of International Economics*, 47(1),1–25.

Bernard, A. and Jensen, B. (2004). 'Why some firms export', *Review of Economics and Statistics*, 86(2), 628–39.

Bernard, A., Eaton, J., Jensen, B. and Kortum, S. (2003), 'Plants and productivity in international trade', *American Economic Review*, 93(4), 1268–90.

Bessant, J., Caffyn, S. and Gilbert, J. (1996). 'Learning to manage innovation', *Technology Analysis & Strategic Management*, 8(1), 59–70.

Bhagwati, J. (1982). 'Directly unproductive profit seeking (DUP) activities', *Journal of Political Economy*, 90(5).

Birkinshaw, J., Bessant, J. and Delbridge, R. (2007). 'Finding, forming, and performing: creating networks for discontinuous innovation'. *California Management Review*, 49(3), 67–85.

BIS. (2013) First findings from the UK innovation survey 2011. UK Department of Business, Innovation and Skills. Available at www.gov. uk/government/uploads/system/uploads/attachment_data/file/200078/12-P106A-UKIS_2011First_findings_Apr13.pdf.

Blomqvis, K., Hurmelinna-Laukkanen, P., Nummela, N. and Saarenketo, S. et al. (2008). 'The role of trust and contracts in the internationalisation of technology-intensive Born Globals', *Journal of Engineering and Technology Management*, 25(1–2), 123–35.

Blomström, M. and Kokko, A. (1998), 'Multinational Corporations and Spillovers', *Journal of Economic Surveys*, 12, 3, 247–77.

Blundell, R., Griffith, R. and Van Reenen, J. (1999). 'Market Share, Market Value and Innovation in a Panel of British Manufacturing Firms.' *The Review of Economic Studies*, 66(3), 529–554.

Bördin, V. and Längnér, M. (2012). 'A Study on Actual Internal Changes due to Major External Internationalization in SMEs'. *Bachelor Thesis*, Göteborgs Universitet, Handelshögskolan.

Bound, K., Saunders, T., Wildson, J. and Adams, J. (2013). *China's Absorptive State*. London: NESTA.

Boutellier, R., Gassmann, O. and von Zedtwitz, M. (2002). *Future Competitiveness: Research and Analysis of Cases on Global R&D Management (in Chinese)*. Guangzhou: Guangdong Economics Publisher.

Braczyk, H. J., Cooke, P. and Heidenreich, M. (1998). *Regional Innovation Systems: The Role of Governance in a Globalized World*. London; New York: Routledge.

Breschi, S. and Lissoni, F. (2001). 'Knowledge spillovers and local innovation systems: a critical survey', *Industrial and Corporate Change*, 10(4), 975–1004.

Buck, T., Liu, X., Wei, Y. and Liu, X. (2007). 'The trade development path and export spillovers in China: a missing link?', *Management International Review*, 47(5), 683–706.

Buckley, P. J., Clegg, J. and Wang, C. (2002). 'The impact of inward FDI on the performance of Chinese manufacturing firms', *Journal of International Business Studies*, 33(4), 637–55.

Bustos, P. (2011). 'Trade Liberalization, Exports, and Technology Upgrading: Evidence on the Impact of MERCOSUR on Argentinian Firms', *American Economic Review*, 101(1), 304–40.

Cantwell, J. (1992). 'Japan's industrial competitiveness and the technological capabilities of the leading Japanese firms', in Arrison, T. S., Bergsten, C. F., Graham, E. M. and Harris, M. C. (Eds.), *Japan's Growing Technological Capability: Implications for the US Economy*. Washington DC: National Academy Press, 165–88.

(1995). 'The globalisation of technology: what remains for the product cycle model', *Cambridge Journal of Economics*, 19, 155–74.

and Piscitello, L. (2002). 'The location of technological activities of MNCs in European regions', *Journal of International Management*, 8(1), 69–96.

and Santangelo, G. (1999). 'The frontier of international technology networks: sourcing abroad the most highly tacit capabilities', *Information Economics and Policy*, 11(1), 101–23.

and Zhang, Y. (2009). 'The co-evolution of international business connections and domestic technological capabilities: lessons from the Japanese catch-up experience', *Transnational Corporations*, 18(2), 37–68.

Cao, C., Li, N., Li, X. and Liu, L. (2013) 'Reforming China's S&T system', *Science*, 342(6145), 460–62.

Carlsson, B. (2006). 'Internationalisation of innovation systems: A survey of the literature', *Research Policy*, 35(1): 56–67.

Cassiman, B. and Veugelers, R. (2006). 'In search of complementarity in innovation strategy: internal R&D and external knowledge acquisition', *Management Science*, 52(1), 68–82.

Caves, R. E. (1974). 'Multinational firms, competition and productivity in host-country markets', *Economica*, 41(162), 176–93.

(1996). *Multinational Enterprise and Economic Analysis*. 2nd ed. Cambridge: Cambridge University Press.

Chang, H.-J. (2003). *Kicking Away the Ladder: Development Strategy in Historical Perspective*. London: Anthem Press.

Chang, J., Fang, X. and Yen, D. C. (2005). 'China's telecommunication market for international investors: opportunities, challenges, and strategies', *Technology in Society* 27, 105–21.

Chang, Y., Shih, C., Luh, Y. and Wu, S. (2006). 'MNE's global R&D strategy in developing countries: a study of foreign-affiliated R&D centres in Taiwan', paper presented at IAMOT 2006, Tsinghua University, Beijing, 22–26 May.

Charnes, A., Cooper, W. W. and Rhodes, E. (1978). 'Measuring the efficiency of decision making units', *European Journal of Operational Research*, 2(6), 429–44.

Chen, J. (1994), 'Learning model: from technology introduction to indigenous innovation', *Science Research Management* (Chinese), Vol. 2, pp. 16–20.

Chen, J. and Qu, W. G. (2003). 'A new technological learning in China', *Technovation*, 23, 861–867.

and Liu, X. (eds.) (2008). *Indigenous Innovation and Prosperity of Country*, Beijing: China Science Press (zhong guo ke xue chu pan she).

Chen, K. and Kenney, M. (2007). 'Universities/research institutes and regional innovation systems: the cases of Beijing and Shenzhen', *World Development*, 35(6), 1056–74.

Chen, Y. F. (2009). 'Improving the indigenous innovation capabilities in Chinese enterprises through open innovation'. *SCIENCE OF SCIENCE AND MANAGEMENT OF S&T (Chinese)*, 4, 81–86.

and Chen, J. (2008). 'The influence of openness to innovation performance', *STUDIES IN SCIENCE OF SCIENCE (Chinese)*, 26(2), 419–26.

Chen, Y. T., He, L. and Si, C. (2007). 'A study on relationship between open innovative culture, market driven and innovative performance of high-technology enterprises: empirical study on Jiang/Zhe/Hu/Min regions', *STUDIES IN SCIENCE OF SCIENCE (Chinese)* 25(3): 567–72.

Chen, Y. T., Ning, Z. and Si, C. L. (2006). 'Indigenous innovation modes of integrating external innovation sources: an empirical study on 241 firms in China'. *Economic Management (Chinese)*, 17, 11–15.

Cheng, V. M. Y. (2004). 'Progress from traditional to creativity education in Chinese societies', in Lau, S., Anna, N., Hui, N. and Ng, G. Y. C. (Eds.), *Creativity: When East Meets West*. Singapore: World Scientific Publishing Company, 137–68.

Chesbrough, H. (2003). *Open Innovation: The New Imperative for Creating and Profiting from Technology*. Cambridge, MA: Harvard Business School Press.

(2006). *Open Business Models: How to Thrive in the New Innovation Landscape*. Cambridge, MA: Harvard Business School Press.

and Crowther, A. K. (2006). 'Beyond high tech: early adopters of open innovation in other industries', *R&D Management*, 36(3), 229–36.

Vanhaverbeke, W. and West, J. (2006). *Open Innovation: Researching a New Paradigm*. London: Oxford University Press.

Cheung, K. and Lin, P. (2004). 'Spillover effects of FDI on innovation in China: evidence from the provincial data', *China Economic Review*, 15, 25–44.

Child, J. and Rodrigues, S. B. (2005). 'The internationalisation of Chinese firms: A case for theoretical extension'. *Management and Organization Review*, 1(3): 381–410.

Christensen, J. F., Olesen, M. H. and Kjar, S. (2005). 'The industrial dynamics of open innovation: evidence from the transformation of consumer electronics'. *Research Policy*, 34(10), 1533–49.

402   *References*

Climate Group. (2009). *China's clean revolution II: opportunities for a low carbon future*. The Climate Group. Available at http://www.theclimate group.org/_assets/files/Chinas-Clean-Revolution-II.pdf.

Coe, D. and Helpman, E. (1995). 'International R&D spillovers', *European Economic Review*, 39(5), 859–87.

Coelli, T. (1996). *A Guide to DEAP* Version 2.1, *CEPA working paper*, 96/08.

Cohen, W. and Levinthal, D. (1989). 'Innovation and learning: two faces of R&D', *Economic Journal*, 99, 569–96.

(1990). 'Absorptive capacity: A new perspective on learning and innovation', *Administrative Science Quarterly*, 35, 128–52.

Nelson, R.R. and Walsh, J.P. (2002). 'Links and impacts: The influence of public research on industrial R&D'. *Management Science*, 48, 1–23.

Conti, J.P. (2007). 'Profile Huawei: from China with love'. *Communications Engineer*, (8), 26–31.

Cookson, C. (2005). 'R&D spending falls further behind target', *Financial Times*, 24 May 2005.

Cooper, W.W., Seiford, L.M. and Tone, K. (2000). *Data Envelopment Analysis: A Comprehensive Text with Models, Applications, References and DEA-Solver Software*. Boston/Dordrecht/ London: Kluwer Academic Publishers.

Correa, C.M. (2005). 'Can the TRIPS agreement foster technology transfer to developing countries?', in Maskus, K.E. and Reichman, J.H. (Eds.), *International Public Goods and Transfer of Technology under a Globalised Intellectual Property Regime*. Cambridge: Cambridge University Press, 227–56.

Cosh, A., Fu, X., and Hughes, A. (2012) 'Organisation, Structure and Innovation Performance in Different Environments', *Small Business Economics*, 39(2), 301–317.

Cosh, A., Fu, X., and Hughes, A. (2004). 'How much does informality in management matter for SME innovation', 35th Entrepreneurship, Innovation and Small Business (EISB) Conference, Barcelona, Spain, September 2005, 'European Best Paper Award'.

and Hughes, A. (2001). *Innovation. The Contribution of European SMEs, in Enterprises in Europe: Sixth Report*. Luxembourg: Eurostat.

and Lester, R.K. (2006). *UK PLC: Just How Innovative Are We?* Cambridge MA; Cambridge UK: MIT Institute, Centre for Business Research and Industrial Performance Centre.

Cragg, John G. (1971). 'Some Statistical Models for Limited Dependent Variables with Application to the Demand for Durable Goods.' *Econometrica* 39(5): 829–844.

Criscuolo, C., Haskel, J. and Slaughter, M. (2005). *Why Are Some Firms More Innovative? Knowledge Inputs, Knowledge Stocks and the Role of Global Engagement*, NBER Working Paper No. 11479 (June).

Dahlman, C. J. (1994). 'Technology strategy in East Asian Developing Economies', *Journal of Asian Economics*, 5(Winter), 541–72.

Darby, M. R., Zucker, L. G. and Wang, A. (2003). *Universities, Joint Ventures, and Success in the Advanced Technology Program*'. NBER working paper no. 9463.

Darcy, J., Krämer-Eis, H., Guellec, D. and Debande, O. (2009). 'Financing technology transfer', *EIB Papers*, 142: 54–73.

Dasgupta, P. and David, P. A. (1994). 'Toward a new economics of science', *Research Policy*, 23, 487–521.

De Bondt, R. (1997). 'Spillovers and innovative activities', *International Journal of Industrial Organisation*, 15(1): 1–28.

Deng, P. (2007). 'Investing for strategic resources and its rationale: The case of outward FDI from Chinese companies', *Business Horizons*, 50(1): 71–81.

Department of Trade and Industry (DTI). (2002). *The 2002 R&D Scoreboard: Commentary and Analysis*. London: Department of Trade and Industry.

Department of Trade and Industry (DTI). (2003a). *Competing in the Global Economy – The Innovation Challenge*, DTI Economics Paper No. 7.

Department of Trade and Industry (DTI). (2003b). *Competing in the Global Economy – The Innovation Challenge*, DTI Innovation Report-Overview.

Department of Trade and Industry (DTI). (2003c). *The 2003 R&D Scoreboard: Analysis*.

Department of Trade and Industry (DTI). (2005). *The 2005 R&D Scoreboard: Analysis*.

Department of Trade and Industry (DTI). (2008). *Persistence and Change in UK Innovation, 2002–2006*. London, UK: Department for Business, Innovation & Skills.

Driffield, N. and Love, L. H. (2007). 'Linking FDI motivation and host economy productivity effects: conceptual and empirical analysis'. *Journal of International Business Studies*, 38(3), 460–73.

and Love, J. (2003). 'Foreign direct investment, technology sourcing and reverse spillovers', *The Manchester School*, 71(6), 659–72.

Drucker, P. F. (1985). *Innovation and Entrepreneurship*. New York: Harper & Row.

Du, P. and Cao, Y. (2010). 'Ethical reflection on new energy: the case of PV industry', in Chinese Academy of Science (Ed.), *High Technology Developement Report of China*. Beijing: Science Publisher.

Dunning, J. (1993). *Multinational Enterprises and the Global Economy*. Reading, MA: Addison Wesley.

(1994). 'Multinational enterprises and the globalization of innovatory capacity', *Research Policy*, 23, 67–88.

Kim, C. and Park, D. (2007). *Old Wine in New Bottles: A Comparison of Emerging Market TNCs Today and Developed Country TNCs Thirty Years Ago*. Oxford University TMCD (Technology and Management Centre for Development) Working Paper, No 011.

and Lundan, S. (2009). 'The internationalisation of corporate R&D: a review of the evidence and some policy implications for home countries'. *Review of Policy Research*, 26(1–2): 13–33.

and Narula, R. (1995). 'The R&D Activities of Foreign Firms in the United States'. *International Studies of Management & Organization*, 25: 39–73.

and Narula, R. (1996), 'The Investment Development Path Revisited: Some emerging issues,' in Dunning, J. H. and Narula, R., eds., *Foreign Direct Investment and Governments: Catalysts for Economic Restructuring*. London and New York: Routledge.

Lim, C. and Kim, J. (2001). 'Incorporating trade into the investment development path: a case study of Korea and Taiwan', *Oxford Development Studies*, Vol. 29, pp. 145–154.

Eaton, J. and Kortum, S. (1995). *Engines of Growth: Domestic and Foreign Sources of Innovation*, NBER Working Papers 5207, National Bureau of Economic Research, Inc.

(1996). 'Trade in ideas: patenting and productivity in the OECD', *Journal of International Economics*, 40(3–4), 251–78.

(1999). 'International technology diffusion: theory and measurement', *International Economic Review*, 40(3), 537–70.

Economist Intelligence Unit (EIU) (2007). *Innovation: Transforming the way Business Creates*. Available at http://graphics.eiu.com/upload/portal/Cisco InnoSmallFile.pdf.

EC (European Commission). (1995) *Green Paper on Innovation*, December, EC, DG XIII.

(2002). *European Innovation Scoreboard*. Available at http://trendchart. cordis.lu/Reports/index.cfm?fuseaction=ReportInnovationHome.

(2005). *European Innovation Scoreboard*. Available at http://trendchart. cordis.lu/Reports/index.cfm?fuseaction=ReportInnovationHome.

(2008). *European Innovation Scoreboard 2007*. Luxembourg: Office for Official Publications of the European Communities, 2008.

(2013). *Innovation Scoreboard, 2013*. Brussels: European Commission.

Elango, B. and Pattnaik, C. (2007). 'Building capabilities for international operations through networks: a study of India', *Journal of International Business Studies*, 38(4), 541–55.

Enkel, E., Gassmann, O. and Chesbrough, H. (2009). 'Open R&D and open innovation: exploring the phenomenon', *R&D Management*, 39(4), 311–16.

Eom, B.-Y. and Lee, K. (2010). 'Determinants of industry-academy linkages and their impact on firm performance: the case of Korea as a latecomer in knowledge industrialization', *Research Policy*, 39, 625–39.

Erdilek, A. (1984). International Technology Transfer in the Middle East and North Africa, *Management Decision*, 22(2), 45–49.

Ernst, D. (2006). 'Innovation off-shoring: Asia's emerging role in global innovation networks'. *East-West Center Special Reports* 10, 1–50.

et al. (2004). *Searching for a New Role in East Asian Regionalization: Japanese Production Networks in the Electronics Industry, Economics Study Area* Working Papers 68. Geneva: East-West Center.

Ettlie, J. E. (1983). 'Organizational policy and innovation among suppliers to the food processing sector'. *Academy of Management Journal*, 26, 27–44.

Etzkowitz, H. and Leydesdorff, L. (1997). *Universities and the Global Knowledge Economy: A Triple Helix of University-Industry-Government Relations*. London: Continuum.

2000, 'The dynamics of innovation: from national systems and "Mode 2" to a triple helix of university–industry–government relations', *Research Policy*, 29(2), 109–23.

Eun, J.-H., Lee, K. and Wu, G. S. (2006). 'Explaining the "University-run enterprises" in China: a theoretical framework for university–industry relationship in developing countries and its application to China', *Research Policy*, 35, 1329–46.

Eurostat. (2004). Available at www.europa.eu.int/comm/eurostat.

Evangelista, F. (2005). 'Qualitative insights into the international new venture creation process', *Journal of International Entrepreneurship*, 3(3), 179–98.

Faber, A., Kemp, R. and Van der Veen, G. (2008). 'Innovation policy for the environment in the Netherlands and the EU', in Nauwelaers, C. and Wintjes, R. (Eds.), *Innovation Policy in Europe: Measurement and Strategy*. Northampton, MA: Edward Elger, chapter 6.

Faber, J. and Hesen, A. B. (2004). 'Innovation capabilities of European nations: cross-national analyses of patents and sales of product innovations', *Research Policy*, 33(2), 193–207.

Fagerberg, J. (1994). 'Technology and international differences in growth rate', *Journal of Economic Literature*, 32(3), 1147–75.

Mowery, D. C. and Nelson, R. R. (2005). *The Oxford Handbook of Innovation*. New York: Oxford University Press.

Fan, P. L. (2006). 'Catching up through developing innovation capability: evidence from China's telecom-equipment industry'. *Technovation*, 26, 359–68.

Fang, X. (2007). 'Formation, evolution and reform of the Chinese S&T system', in Fang, X. (Ed.), *Chinese Technological Innovation and Sustainable Development (in Chinese)*. Beijing: Science Press.

Färe, R., Grosskopf, S., Norris, M. and Zhang, Z. (1994). 'Productivity growth, technical progress, and efficiency change in industrialized countries', *The American Economic Review*, 84(1), 66–83.

Farhoomand, A. F. and Ho, P. (2006). *Huawei: Cisco's Chinese Challenger*. University of Hong Kong Case HKU599 (Available through Harvard Business School, pp. 9–10).

Feldman, M. P. (1999). 'The new economics of innovation, spillovers and agglomeration: a review of empirical studies', *Economics of Innovation and New Technology*, 8, 5–25.

Feng, M. T. (2009) *Technology Transfer from University to Industry: Insight Into University Technology Transfer in the Chinese National Innovation System*. London: Adonis & Abbey Publishers Ltd.

Figueiredo, P. N.. (2003). 'Learning processes features: how do they influence inter-firm differences in technological capability-accumulation paths and operational performance improvement?' *Industrial and Corporate Change*, 12(3), 607–43.

Filatotchev, I. and Piesse, J. (2009). 'R&D, internationalisation and growth of newly listed firms: European evidence', *Journal of International Business Studies*, 40(8), 1260–76.

Findlay, R. (1978). 'Relative backwardness, direct foreign investment and the transfer of technology: a simple dynamic model', *Quarterly of Journal of Economics*, 92(1), 1–16.

Fosfuri, A. (2006). 'The licensing dilemma: understanding the determinants of the rate of technology licensing', *Strategic Management Journal*, 27(12), 1141–58.

 and Motta, M. (1999). 'Multinationals without advantages', *The Scandinavian Journal of Economics*, 101(4), 617–30.

 and Ronde, T. (2001). 'Foreign direct investment and spillovers through workers' mobility', *Journal of International Economics*, 53(1), 205–22.

Franco, E., Ray, S. and Ray, P. K. (2011). 'Patterns of innovation practices of multinational-affiliates in emerging economies: Evidences from Brazil and India', *World Development*, 39(7), 1249–60.

Freeman, C. (1987). *Technology and Policy and Economic Performance: Lessons from Japan*. London: Pinter.

 (1994). 'The economics of technical change', *Cambridge Journal of Economics*, 18(5), 463–514.

 (1995). 'The national system of innovation in historical perspective', *Cambridge Journal of Economics*, 19, 5–24.

and Soete, L. (1997). *The Economics of Industrial Innovation*. London: Pinter.

Fritsch, M. and Slavtchev, V. (2007). 'What Determines the Efficiency of Regional Innovation Systems?' Jena Economic Research Paper No. 2007–006. Available at SSRN: heep://ssrn.com/abstract=1018593.

Fu, X. (2004a). 'Limited linkages from growth engines and regional disparities in China', *Journal of Comparative Economics*, 32(1), 148–64.

(2004b). *Exports, Foreign Direct Investment and Economic Development in China*. London and New York: Palgrave McMillan.

(2005). 'Exports, technical progress and productivity growth in Chinese manufacturing industries', *Applied Economics*, 37(7), 725–39.

(2007). 'Trade-cum-FDI, human capital inequality and the dual economy in China: the Signer perspective', *Journal of Economic Change and Restructuring*, 40(1), 137–55.

(2008). 'Foreign direct investment, absorptive capacity and regional innovation capabilities: Evidence from China', *Oxford Development Studies*, 36(1), 89–110.

(2012a). 'How does openness affect the importance of incentives for innovation?' *Research Policy*, 41(3), 512–23.

(2012b). 'Managerial knowledge spillovers from FDI through the diffusion of management practices', *Journal of Management Studies*, 49(5), 970–99.

(2014). 'What potential does open innovation hold for Asia', *The Economist*, Oct 10, 12–16.

and Balasubramanayam, V. N. (2003). 'Township and village enterprises in China', *Journal of Development Studies*, 39(4), 27–46.

Cosh, A., Yang, Q. and Hughes, A. (2006). 'World innovation frontier and the EU-US innovation gap', paper presented at the 9th North America Workshop of Efficiency and Productivity Analysis, Stern Business School, New York University, New York.

Cosh, A., Hughes, A., De Hoyos, R. and Eisingerich, A. (2006). 'The experiences of UK mid-corporate companies in emerging Asian economies', *UK Trade & Investment*, London. 2006 (URN 06/1137).

and Gong, Y. (2008). *Indigenous and Foreign Innovations Efforts and Drivers of Technological Upgrading: Evidence from China*, SLPTMD Working Paper No 018, University of Oxford.

and Gong, Y. (2010). *Absorptive Capacity and the Benefits from Global Reservoirs or Knowledge: Evidence from a Linked China-OECD Dataset*, SLPTMD Working Paper 31, University of Oxford.

(2011). 'Indigenous and foreign innovation efforts and technological upgrading in emerging economies: firm-level evidence from China', *World Development*, 39(7), 1213–25.

Liu, S. and Li, T. (2013). *Determinants and Impact of Outward Direct Investment from China: Evidence from a Firm-level Survey in*

Guangdong Province. TMD *Working Paper No:* TMD-WP-49, University of Oxford.

Pietrobelli, C. and Soete, L. (2011). 'The role of foreign technology and indigenous innovation in the emerging economies: technological change and catching-up'. *World Development* 39(7), 1203–12.

and Soete, L. (2010). *The Rise of Technological Power in the South.* London and New York: Palgrave Macmillan.

and Xiong, H. (2011). 'Open innovation in China: policies and practices', *Journal of Science & Technology Policy in China*, 2(3), 196–218.

and Yang, Q. (2009). 'World innovation frontier: exploring the innovation gap between the EU and the US', *Research Policy*, 38(7), 1203–13.

and Zhang, J. (2011). 'Technology transfer, indigenous innovation and leapfrogging in green technology: the solar-PV industry in China and India,' *Journal of Chinese Economic and Business Studies*, 9(4), 329–47.

Funke, M. and Niebuhr, A. (2000). *Spatial R&D Spillovers and Economic Growth – Evidence from West Germany*, HWWA Discussion Paper No 98.

Furman, J. and Hayes, R. (2004). 'Catching up or standing still? National innovative productivity among "follower" countries, 1978–1999', *Research Policy*, 33, 1329–54.

Porter, M. and Stern, S. (2002). 'The determinants of national innovative capacity', *Research Policy*, 31, 899–933.

Galia, F., and Legros, D. (2004). 'Complementarities between obstacles to innovation: evidence from France', *Research Policy*, 33(8), 1185–99.

Gans, J. S., Stern, S., (2003). 'Assessing Australia's Innovative Capacity in the 21st Century'. *Intellectual Property Research Institute of Australia Working Paper.*

Gans, J. and Hayes, R. (2008). 'Measuring innovative performance'. *Melbourne Review*, Vol 2, No 1. 2006. 70–77.

Gao, X., Liu, J., Chai, K. H. and Li, J. (2007). 'Overcoming "latecomer disadvantages" in small and medium-sized firms: evidence from China', *International Journal of Technology and Globalization*, 3(4), 364–83.

Gassmann, O. (2006). 'Editorial: opening up the innovation process towards an agenda', *R&D Management*, 36(3), 223–28.

Gassmann, O., Enkel, E. and Chesbrough, H. 2010. *Editorial: The future of open innovation, R&D Management*, 40(3), 213–221.

and von Zedtwitz, M. (1998). 'Organization of industrial R&D on a global scale', *R&D Management*, 28(3), 147–61.

Geroski, P. A. (1990). 'Innovation, technological opportunity, and market structure', *Oxford Economic Papers*, 42(3), 586–602.

(1994). *Market Structure, Corporate Performance, and Innovative Activity.* Oxford: Oxford University Press.

and Mazzucato, M. (2002). 'Learning and the sources of corporate growth,' *Industrial and Corporate Change*, 11(4), 623–44.

Gilman, D. (2010). *The New Geography of Global Innovation*, Global Market Institute, Goldman Sachs, report.

Girma, S. (2005). 'Absorptive capacity and productivity spillovers from FDI: a threshold regression analysis', *Oxford Bulletin of Economics and Statistics*, 67, 281–306.

Gong, Y. and Görg, H. (2009). 'What determines innovation activity in Chinese state-owned enterprises? The role of foreign direct investment', *World Development*, 37(4), 866–73.

Greenaway, D. and Wakelin, K. (2001). 'Who benefits from foreign direct investment in the UK?' *Scottish Journal of Political Economy*, 48, 19–33.

Goes, J. B. and Park, S. H. (1997). 'Interorganizational links and innovation: the case of hospital services', *Academy of Management Journal*, 40(3), 673–96.

Gompers, P. (2006). 'Venture capital', in Eckbo, B. E. (Ed.), *Handbook of Corporate Finance: Empirical Corporate Finance*. Amsterdam; Boston: Elsevier/North-Holland, chapter 9.

Görg, H. and Greenaway, D. (2004). 'Much ado about nothing? Do domestic firms really benefit from foreign direct investment?' *World Bank Research Observer*, 19, 171–97.

and Strobl, E. (2001). 'Multinational companies and productivity spillovers: a meta-analysis', *Economic Journal*, 111(475), F723–39.

Granstrand, O. (1999). 'Internationalisation of corporate R&D: A study of Japanese and Swedish corporations. *Research Policy*, 28(Special issue), 275–302.

Bohlin, E., Oskarsson, C. and Sjoberg, N. (1992). 'External technology acquisition in large multi-technology corporations', *R&D Management* 22, 111–33.

Håkanson, L. and Sjölander, S. (1993). 'Internationalisation of R&D – a survey of some recent research', *Research Policy*, 22(5–6), 413–30.

Greenaway, D. and Kneller, R. (2004). 'Exporting and productivity in the UK', *Oxford Review of Economic Policy*, 20(3), 358–71.

Sousa, N. and Wakelin, K. (2004). 'Do domestic firms learn to export from multinationals?' *European Journal of Political Economy*, 20(4), 1027–43.

Upward, R. and Wright, P. (2002). *Sectoral and Geographic Mobility of Labour Markets and Structural Adjustment*, mimeo, University of Nottingham.

Greene, W. (1997). 'Frontier production functions', in Pesaran, M. H. and Schimidt, P. (Eds.), *Handbook of Applied Econometrics, vol. II: Microeconomics*. Oxford: Blackwell Publishers.

Greene, W. (2003). *Econometric analysis, 5th Edition*. London: Prentice-Hall.

Griffith, R., Harrison, R. and Reenen, J. V. (2006). 'How special is the special relationship? Using the impact of U.S. R&D spillovers on U.K. firms as a test of technology sourcing', *The American Economic Review*, 96(5), 1859–75.

Redding, S. and Van Reenen, J. (2003). 'R&D and absorptive capacity: theory and empirical evidence', *Scandinavian Journal of Economics*, 105(1), 99–118.

Griliches, Z. (1979). 'Issues in assessing the contribution of R&D to productivity growth', *Bell Journal of Economics*, 10(1), 92–116.

(1990). 'Patent statistics as economic indicators'. *Journal of Economic Literature*. 28 (4), 1661–1707.

Grossman, G, M. and Helpman, E. (1991). *Innovation and Growth in the Global Economy*. Cambridge, MA: MIT Press.

(1994). *Technology and trade*. NBER Working Papers 4926, National Bureau of Economic Research, Inc.

Guan, J. and Ma, N. (2003). 'Innovative capability and export performance of Chinese firms', *Technovation*, 23, 737–47.

(2007). 'China's emerging presence in nanoscience and nanotechnology: A comparative bibliometric study of several nanoscience "giants"', *Research Policy*, 36(6), 880–86.

Gulati, R. (1999). 'Network location and learning: the influence of network resources and firm capabilities on alliance formation', *Strategic Management Journal*, 20, 397–420.

Hagedoorn, J. (2002). 'Inter-firm R&D partnerships: an overview of major trends and patterns since 1960', *Research Policy*, 31(4), 477–92.

Hall, B. (2004). *Exploring the Patent Explosion*, Centre for Business Research, University of Cambridge, Working Paper no WP291.

Hansen, L. (1982). 'Large sample properties of generalized method of moments estimators', *Econometrica*, 50(4), 1029–54.

Harzing, A. and Noorderhaven, N. (2006). 'Knowledge flows in MNCs: an empirical test and extension of Gupta and Govindarajan's typology of subsidiary roles', *International Business Review*, 15(3), 195–214.

Hayhoe, R. (1996). *China's Universities, 1895–1995: A Century of Cultural Conflict*. New York: Garland Publishing.

He, X. and Mu, Q. (2012). 'How Chinese firms learn technology from transnational corporations: A comparison of the telecommunication and automobile industries', *Journal of Asian Economics*, 23, 270–87.

He, Y. (2008). 'Shenyang shukong: open innovation'. *People's Daily* (Chinese), 4 May.

Hershberg, E., Nabeshima, K. and Yusuf, S. (2007). 'Opening the ivory tower to business: university-industry linkages and the development of knowledge-intensive clusters in Asian cities', *World Development*, 35(6), 931–40.

Hiebert, D., 2002. The determinants of the cost efficiency of electric generating plants: a stochastic frontier approach. *Southern Economic Journal* 68 (4), 935–946.

Hippel, E. von and Krogh, G. von. (2003). 'Open source software and the private-collective model: issues for *organization science*', *Organization Science*, 14(2), 209–23.

HM Treasury. (2003). *Lambert review of business-university collaboration*, available at www.lambertreview.org.uk.

Hobday, M. G. (1995). *Innovation in East Asia: The Challenge to Japan*. Cheltenham, UK: Edward Elgar.

Rush, H. and Bessant, J. (2004). 'Approaching the innovation frontier in Korea: the transition phase to leadership', *Research Policy*, 33, 1433–57.

Hoekman, B. M., Maskus, K. E. and Saggi, K. (2005). 'Transfer of technology to developing countries: unilateral and multinational policy options', *World Development*, 33(10), 1587–1602.

Hoffman, K., Parejo, M., Bessant, J. and Perren, L. (1998). 'Small firms, R&D, technology and innovation in the UK: a literature review', *Technovation*, 18(1), 39–73.

Hoffmann, W. and Schlosser, R. (2001). 'Success factors of strategic alliances in small and medium-sized enterprises: an empirical survey', *Long Range Planning*, 34(3), 357–81.

Hofler, R. and Payne, J. E. (1993). 'Efficiency in social versus private agricultural production: The case of Yugoslavia', *The Review of Economics and Statistics*, 75(1), 153–57.

Hollanders, H. and Esser, F. C. (2007). *Measuring Innovation Efficiency*, INNO-Metrics Thematic paper, available at http://www.pedz.uni-man nheim.de/daten/edz-h/gdb/07/eis_2007_Innovation_efficiency.pdf

Hong, W. (2006). 'Technology transfer in Chinese universities: is "mode 2" sufficient for a developing country?' in Law, P., Fortunati, L. and Yang, S. (Eds.), *New Technologies in Global Societies*. Singapore: World Scientific Publishers, 21–50.

(2008). 'Decline of the center: The decentralizing process of knowledge transfer of Chinese universities from 1985 to 2004', *Research Policy*, 37(4), 580–95.

Hoskisson, R. E., Hitt, M. A., Johnson, R. A. and Grossman, W. (2002). 'Conflicting voices: the effects of institutional ownership heterogeneity and internal governance on corporate strategies'. *Academy Management Journal*, 45, 607–716.

Hou, C. (2009). 'Weichai: open innovation', *CHINESE MANUFACTURING INFORMATION (Chinese)*, 8, 52–53.

Hsiao, C. (2003). *Analysis of Panel Data*, Cambridge University Press, Cambridge.

Hu, A. and Jefferson, G. (2002). 'FDI impact and spillover: evidence from China's electronic and textile industries', *World Economy*, 38(4), 1063–76.

and Qian, J. (2005). 'R&D and technology transfer: firm-level evidence from Chinese industry,' *The Review of Economics and Statistics*, 87(4), 780–86.

Hu, A. (2011). *China in 2020: A New Type of Superpower*. Washington, DC: Brookings Institution Press.

Huang, Y. (2003). *Selling China*. New York: Cambridge University Press.

Huawei Press. (2011). *Huawei is the leading contributor to LTE standards*, Huawei press release, 29 November. Available at www.huawei.com/en/about-huawei/newsroom/press-release/hw-104732-huaweiltestandards.htm.

Hughes, A. (2003). *Knowledge Transfer, Entrepreneurship and Economic Growth: Some Reflections and Implications for Policy in the Netherlands*. University of Cambridge Centre for Business Research Working Paper no 273.

(2008). 'Innovation policy as cargo cult: myth and reality in knowledge-led productivity growth', in Bessant, J. and Venables, T. (Eds.), Creating Wealth from Knowledge. Meeting the Innovation Challenge. Cheltenham, UK: Edward Elgar.

(2010). 'The multifaceted role of universities', ESRC Society Now IN FOCUS, no. 8.

and Scott Morton, M. S. (2006). 'The transforming power of complementary assets', *MIT Sloan Management Review, Summer*, 47, 50–58.

Hwang, Y., Kim, S., Byun, B., Lee, G. and Lee, H. (2003). *Strategies of Promoting Industry-Academia-Research Institute R&D Partnerships to Cooperation with New Technologies: Focusing on Industry-Research Institute Inter-firm R&D Partnerships*. Science & Technology Policy Institute.

Immelt, J. R., Govindarajan, V. and Trimble, C. (2009). 'How GE is disrupting itself', *Harvard Business Review*, October.

India Semiconductor Association. (2010). *Solar PV industry 2010: contemporary scenario and emerging trends*. India Semiconductor Association. Available at http://www.isaonline.org/documents /ISA_SolarPV Report_May2010.pdf.

INSEAD. (2007). *The World Business/INSEAD Global Innovation Index 2007*.

International Labour Organization. (2003). *Report of the Committee on Employment and Social Policy*, GB.286/15, ILO, Geneva.

Iwasaki, I., Csizmadia, P., Illessy, M., Mako, C. and Szany, M. (2010), *Foreign Direct Investment, Information Spillover, and Export Decision: The Concentric-circle Model with Application to Hungarian Firm-level Data*, Institute for Economic Research, Hitotsubashi University, working paper, no 527.

Iyer, K. N. S. (2002). 'Learning in strategic alliances: an evolutionary perspective', *Academy of Marketing Science Review*, 10, 1–16.

Jaffe, A. (1989). 'Real effects of academic research', *American Economic Review*, 79, 957–70.

Trajtenberg, M. and Henderson, R. (1993). 'Geographic localization of knowledge spillovers as evidenced by patent citations', *The Quarterly Journal of Economics*, 108, 577–98.

Jakobson, L., (Ed), 2007. *Innovation with Chinese Characteristics, High-Tech Research in China*, Palgrave Macmillan/Finish Institute of International Affairs, Hampshire UK/New York, USA.

Jaumotte, F. and Pain, N. (2005). *From Ideas to Development: The Determinants of R&D and Patenting*, OECD Working Paper, ECO/WKP, 44.

Javorcik, B. S. (2004). 'Does foreign direct investment increase the productivity of domestic firms? In search of spillovers through backward linkages', *American Economic Review*, 94(3), 605–27.

(2008). 'Can survey evidence shed light on spillovers from foreign direct investment?' *World Bank Research Observer*, 23(2), 139–59.

Jensen, M. C. (1993). 'The Modern Industrial Revolution, Exit, and the Failure of Internal Control Systems'. *Journal of Finance*. 48: 831–80.

Jiang, J. H. (2009). 'Research on the cost determinants of knowledge transfer and influencing mechanisms for the latecomer firms', *Science Research Management*, 306, 1–8.

Jiang, X. J. (2004). 'Comprehension of technical globalization', *MANAGEMENT WORLD (Chinese)*, 6, 4–13.

Jin, J. and von Zedtwitz, M. (2008). 'Technological capability development in China's mobile phone industry', *Technovation*, 28(6), 327–34.

Johanson, J. and Mattsson, L. (1988). 'Internationalization in industry system: a network approach', in Hood, N. and Vahlne, J.-E. (Eds.), *Strategies in Global Competition*. London, UK: Routledge, 287–314.

and Vahlne, J.-E. (1977). 'The internationalization process of the firm – a model of knowledge development and increasing foreign market commitments'. *Journal of International Business Studies*, 8(1), 23–32.

Johnson, J. E. (2004). 'Factors influencing the early internationalisation of high technology start-ups: US and UK evidence', *Journal of International Entrepreneurship*, 2(1–2), 139–54.

Jones, C. I. (1995). 'R&D-based models of economic growth', *Journal of Political Economy*, 103(4), 759–81.

Kafouros, M., Buckley, P., Sharp, J. and Wang, C. (2008). 'The role of internationalisation in explaining innovation performance', *Technovation*, 28(1–2), 63–74.

Kamiyama, S., Sheehan, J. and Martinez, C. (2006). *Valuation and Exploitation of Intellectual Property*, OECS Science, Technology and Industry Working Paper No 2006/5.

Katila, R. and GautAm, A. (2002). 'Something old, something new: a longitudinal study of search behavior and new product introduction', *Academy of Management Journal*, 45(6), 1183–94.

Kaufmann, A. and Todtling, F. 2001. 'Science-industry interaction in the process of innovation: the importance of boundary-crossing between systems', *Research Policy*, 30, 791–804.

Keesing, D. B. and Lall, S. (1992). 'Marketing, manufactured exports from developing countries: learning sequences and public support', in Helleiner, G. K. (Ed.), *Trade Policy, Industrialization, and Development: New Perspectives*. Oxford: Clarendon Press.

Kessler, E. H., Bierly, P. E. and Gopalakrishnan, S. (2000). 'Internal vs. external learning in new product development: effects on speed, costs and competitive advantage', *R&D Management*, 30(3), 213–23

Keupp, M. M. and Gassmann, O. (2009). 'Determinants and archetype users of open innovation', *R&D Management*, 39(4), 331–41.

Kim, L. (1997a). *Imitation to Innovation: The Dynamics of Korea's Technological Learning*. Boston: Harvard Business School Press.

  (1997b). 'The dynamics of Samsung's technological learning in semiconductors', *California Management Review*, 39(3), 86–100.

  and Nelson, R. R. (Eds.). (2000). *Technology, Learning and Innovation: Experiences of Newly Industrializing Economies*. Cambridge: Cambridge University Press.

Kim, Y. and Lee, K. (2003). 'Technological collaboration in the Korean electronic parts industry: patterns and key success factors', *R&D Management*, 33(1), 59–77.

King, D. A. (2004). 'The scientific impact of nations', *Nature*, 430, 311–16.

Kiriyama, N. (2012). 'Trade and Innovation: Synthesis Report', OECD Trade Policy Papers 135, OECD Publishing.

Kitson, M., Howells, J., Braham, R. and Westlake, S. (2009). *The Connected University: Driving Recovery and Growth in the UK Economy*. London: NESTA.

Kleinknecht, A. (1996). 'New indicators and determinants of innovation: an introduction', in Kleinknecht, A. (Ed.), *Determinants of Innovation. The*

Message from New Indicators. Hampshire and London: Macmillan, 1-12.

Kneller, R. and Pisu, M. (2007). 'Industrial linkages and export spillovers from FDI', *World Economy*, 30, 105-34.

and Stevens, P. A. (2006). 'Frontier technology and absorptive capacity: evidence from OECD manufacturing industries', *Oxford Bulletin of Economics and Statistics*, 68, 1-21.

Koellinge, P. (2007). 'Why are some entrepreneurs more innovative than others', *Small Business, Economics*, 31, 21-37.

Kogut, B. and Zander, U. (1993). 'Knowledge of the firm and the evolutionary theory of the multinational corporation', *Journal of International Business Studies*, 24(4), 625-46.

Kokko, A., Tansini, R. and Zejan, M. C. (1996). 'Local technological capability and productivity spillovers from FDI in the Uruguayan manufacturing sector', *Journal of Development Studies*, 32(4), 602-11.

(2001). 'Trade regimes and spillover effects of FDI: evidence from Uruguay', *Weltwirtschaftliches Archiv*, 37(1), 124-49.

Koopman, R., Wang, Z. and Wei, S. J. (2008). *How Much of Chinese Exports Is Really Made in China? Assessing Domestic Value-Added When Processing Trade Is Pervasive*, NBER Working Paper 14109.

Koruna, S. (2004). 'External technology commercialization policy guidelines', *International Journal of Technology Management*, 27(2/3), 241-54.

Koschatzky, K. (2001). 'Networks in innovation research and innovation policy – an introduction', in Koschatzky, K., Kulicke, M. and Zenker, A. (Eds.), *Innovation Networks: Concepts and Challenges in the European Perspective*. Heidelberg: Physica Verlag, 3-23.

Krause, L. (1988). 'Hong Kong and Singapore: twins or kissing cousins?' *Economic Development and Cultural Change*, 36(3), 45-66.

Kroll, H. and Liefner, I. (2008). 'Spin-off enterprises as a means of technology commercialization in a transforming economy: Evidence from three universities in China', *Technovation*, 28, 298-313.

Krueger, A. (1974). 'The political economy of rent-seeking society', *American Economic Review*, 64(3), 291-303.

Krugman, P. (1991). 'Increasing returns and economic geography', *Journal of Political Economy*, 99(3), 483-99.

Kuemmerle, W. (1997) 'Building effective R&D capabilities abroad', *Harvard Business Review*, 3/4, 61-70.

Kuo, K. (2006). *China pursues Africa deals, red herring*, 11 December. Available at www.siemens.be/cmc/newsletters/index.aspx?id=13-621-17892.

Lall, S. (1982). *Developing Countries as Exporters of Technology*. London: Macmillan Press.
  (1987). *Learning to Industrialise: The Acquisition of Technological Capability by India*. London: Macmillan.
  (1992). 'Technological capabilities and industrialization', *World Development*, 20(2), 165–86.
  (1996). *Learning from the Asian Tigers – Studies in Technology and Industrial Policy*. London: Macmillan.
  (2001). *Competitiveness, Technology and Skills*. Cheltenham, UK: Edward Elgar.
  (2003). 'Foreign direct investment, technology development and competitiveness: issues and evidence', in Lall, S. and Urata, S. (Eds.), *Competitiveness, FDI and Technological Activity in East Asia*, published in association with the World Bank, Cheltenham, UK: Edward Elgar.
Lall, S., and Urata, S. (Eds.) (2003). *Competitiveness, FDI and technological activity in East Asia*. Cheltenham, UK: Edward Elgar.
Laursen, K. and Salter, A. (2006). 'Open for innovation: the role of openness in explaining innovation performance among UK manufacturing firms', *Strategic Management Journal*, 27(2), 131–50.
Lécuyer, C. (2006). *Making Silicon Valley: Innovation and the Growth of High Tech, 1930–70*, MIT Press, Cambridge, MA.
Lee, J., Bae, Z. and Choi, D. (1988). 'Technology development processes: a model for a developing country with a global perspective', *R&D Management*, 18(3), 235–50.
Jee, M. and Eun, J. H. (2011). 'Assessing China's economic catch up at the firm level and beyond: Washington consensus, East Asian consensus and the Beijing model', *Industry and Innovation*, 18(5), 487–507.
  and Lim, C. (2001). 'Technological regimes, catching-up and leapfrogging: findings from the Korean industries', *Research Policy*, 30(1), 459–83.
Lee, S., Park, G., Yoon, B. and Park, J. (2010). 'Open innovation in SMEs – an intermediated network model', *Research Policy*, 39(2), 290–300.
Lema, R. and Lema, A. (2012). 'Whither technology transfer? The rise of China and India in green techonology sectors', *Innovation and Development*, 1(2), 23–44.
Leonard, D. and Sensiper, S. (1998). 'The role of tacit knowledge in group innovation', *California Management Review Berkeley*, Spring (electronic). Available at http://connection.ebscohost.com/c/articles/738860/role-tacit-knowledge-group-innovation.
Leonard-Barton, D. (1995). *Wellsprings of Knowledge: Building and Sustaining the Sources of Innovation*. Cambridge, MA: Harvard Business School Press.

Lerner, J., Sorensen, M. and Stromberg, P. (2008). *Private Equity and Long-Run Investment: The Case of Innovation*, in Globalization of Alternative Investments Working Papers Volume 1: The Global Economic Impact of Private Equity Reports: World Economic Forum, 27–42.

Levinthal, D. A. and James, G. M. (1993). 'The myopia of learning', *Strategic Management Journal*, 14(S2), 95–112.

Lewis, J. I. (2007). 'Technology acquisition and innovation in the developing world: wind turbine development in China and India', *Studies in Comparative International Development*, 42(3–4), 208–32.

Li, H. and Atuahene-Gima, K. (2001). 'The impact of interaction between R&D and marketing on new product performance: an empirical analysis of Chinese high technology firms', *International Journal of Technology Management*, 21(1/2), 61–75.

Li, J. and E. Martinot. 2007. Powering China's development: the role of renewable energy. Worldwatch Institute. http://www.worldwatch.org/node/5491.

Li, J. and Kozhikode, R. K. (2009). 'Developing new innovation models: shifts in the innovation landscapes in emerging economies and implications for global R&D management', *Journal of International Management*, 15, 328–39.

Li J. L. (2007). 'Little Swan: building open innovation systems', *Economic Times* (Chinese), 17 November.

Li J. T. (2010). 'Global R&D alliances in China: collaborations with universities and research institutes', *IEEE Transactions on Engineering Management*, 57(1), 78–87.

Li, K. (2006). *Please train talents that are needed in the 21st century*, Zhongguo Jiaoyu Xinwen (China Education News), 9 November. Available at www.jyb.cn/high/gdjyxw/200611/t20061109_47908.html.

Li, X. B. (2009). China's regional innovation capacity in transition: an empirical approach. *Research Policy* 38, pp. 338–357.

(2011). Sources of external technology, absorptive capacity, and innovation capability in Chinese state-owned high-tech enterprises. *World Development* 39(7), 1240–48.

Lichtenthaler, U. (2008). 'Open innovation in practice: an analysis of strategic approaches to technology transactions', *IEEE Transaction on Engineering Management*, 55(1), 148–57.

(2009). 'Outbound open innovation and its effect on firm performance: examining environmental influences', *R&D Management*, 39(4), 317–30.

and Holger, E. (2007). 'External technology commercialization in large firms: results of a quantitative benchmarking study', *R&D Management*, 37(5), 383–97.

and O. de Barros. (2009). 'The growth of Brazil's direct investment abroad and the challenges it faces.' *Columbia FDI Perspectives* 13(17 August).

Lin, J. Y. (2011). 'New structural economics: a framework for rethinking development', *World Bank Research Observer, World Bank Group*, 26(2), 193–221.

Liu, C. Z. (2007). 'Lenovo: an example of globalization of Chinese enterprises', *Journal of International Business Studies*, 38, 573–77.

Liu, L. (2008). 'The Evolution of China's Science and Technology Policy (1975–2007)', *OECD Review of Innovation Policy: China*, 381–93.

Liu, X., Strangway, D. W. and Feng, Z. (2012) *Environmental Innovation in China*. Southampton: WIT Press.

Liu, X. H. and Buck, T. (2007). 'Innovation performance and channels for international technology spillovers: Evidence from Chinese high-tech industries', *Research Policy*, 36(3), 355–66.

Liu, X. L (2010). 'China's development model: an alternative strategy for technological catch-up', in Fu, X. and Soete, L. (Eds.), *The Rise of Technological Power in the South*. London: Palgrave MacMillan, 89–106.

   (2001). 'Comparing innovation systems: a framework and application to China's transitional context', *Research Policy*, 30, 1091–114.

Lokshin, B., Belderbos, R. and Carree, M. (2007). *The Productivity Effects of Internal and External R&D: Evidence from a Dynamic Panel Data Model'*, UNU-Merit Working Paper Series 2007–026, United Nations University: Maastricht Economic and Social Research and Training Centre in Innovation and Technology.

Lovell, C. A. K. (1996). 'Applying efficiency measurement techniques to the measurement of productivity change', *Journal of Productivity Analysis*, 7(2/3), 329–40.

Lowe, M., George, G. and Alexy, O. (2012). 'Organizational identity and capability development in internationalisation: transference, splicing and enhanced imitation in Tesco's US market entry', *Journal of Economic Geography*, 12, 1021–54.

Lu, J. W. and Beamish, P. W. (2001). 'The internationalization and performance of SMEs', *Strategic Management Journal*, 22, 565–84.

Lu, Qiwen. (2000). *China's Leap into the Information Age: Innovation and Organization in the Computer Industry*. Oxford: Oxford University Press.

Lundvall, B. (1992). *National Systems of Innovation: Towards a Theory of Innovation and Interactive Learning*. London: Pinter.

Ma, A. and Van Assche, A. (2010). 'The role of trade costs in global production networks: Evidence from China's processing trade regime', paper presented at 22nd CEA annual conference, Oxford.

Ma, W. (2004). *From Berkeley to Beida and Tsinghua: The Development and Governance of Public Research Universities in the US and China*. Beijing: Educational Science Press.

MacDonald, G., Yit-Seng, Y. and Xing, L. (2008) *Innovation in China: The Dawning of the Asian Century*. London: Adonis & Abbey Publishers Ltd.

Mairesse, J. and Mohnen, P. (2002). 'Accounting for innovation and measuring innovativeness: an illustrative framework and an application', *American Economic Review* Papers and Proceedings, 92(2), 226–30.

Malerba, F. (2002). 'Sectoral systems of innovation and production', *Research Policy*, 31(2), 247–64.

(2006). 'Innovation and the evolution of industries', *Journal of Evolutionary Economics*, 16(1), 3–23.

Mallett, A., Ockwell, D. G., Pal, P., Kumar, A., Abbi, Y. P., Haum, R., MacKerron, G., Watson, J. and Sethi, G. (2009). *UK-India collaborative study on the transfer of low carbon technology: phase II final report*. Sussex University and Institute of Development Studies. Available at https://www.sussex.ac.uk/webteam/gateway/file.php?name=decc-uk-india-carbon-technology-web.pdf&site=264.

Mansfield, E. and Lee, J. Y. (1996). 'The modern university: contributor to industrial innovation and recipient of industrial R&D support', *Research Policy*, 25, 1047–58.

Marin, A. and Giuliani, E. (2011). 'MNC subsidiaries' position in global knowledge networks and local spillovers: evidence from Argentina', *Innovation and Development*, 1(1), 91–114.

Markusen, J. R. (2002). *Multinational Firms and the Theory of International Trade*. Cambridge, MA: MIT Press.

Martinot, E. and Li, J. (2007). *Powering China's Development: the Role of Renewable Energy*. Washington, D.C.: Worldwatch Institute.

Maskus, K. E. (2000). *Intellectual Property Rights in the Global Economy*. Washington, DC: Institute for International Economics.

McDougall, P. and Oviatt, B. (2005). 'Defining international entrepreneurship and modeling the speed of internationalization', *Entrepreneurship Theory and Practice*, 29(5), 537 S.

McMahon, W. W. (1987). 'Education and industrialization', *Background Paper for the 1987 World Development Report*. Washington, DC: World Bank.

Melitz, M. J. (2003). 'The impact of trade on intra-industry reallocations and aggregate industry productivity', *Econometrica*, 71(6), 1695–725.

Metcalfe, S. (1997). 'Technology systems and technology policy in an evolutionary framework', in Archibugi, D. and Michie, J. (Eds.), *Technology,*

Globalisation and Economic Performance, Cambridge: Cambridge University Press.

Meyer, K. E. (2004). 'Perspectives on multinational enterprises in emerging economies', *Journal of International Business Studies*, 35(4), 259–76.

Milberg, W. (2007). *Export Processing Zones, Industrial Upgrading and Economic Development: A Survey*, Background paper for ILO Governing Board.

Miles, M. and Huberman, A. (1984). *Qualitative Data Analysis*. Beverly Hills, CA: Sage Publications.

Ministry of Education. (1999). The Regulation Regarding the Protection and Management of Intellectual Properties in Higher Education Institutions. Act 3, No. 8120.

MNRE (Ministry of New and Renewable Energy, government of India). (2006). *XIth plan proposals for new and renewable energy*. Available at www.mnre.gov.in/pdf/11th-plan-proposal.pdf.

MOF (Ministry of Finance of China). (2001). *Accounting System for Business Enterprises*. Available at www.mof.gov.cn.

MOFCOM (Ministry of Commerce of China). (2010). *Statistics of foreign investment*. Available at www.mofcom.gov.cn.

MOFTEC (2000). *Almanac of China's Foreign Economic Relations and Trade*, China Foreign Trade Press, Beijing.

Mohr, J. and Spekman, R. (1994). 'Characteristics of partnership success: partnership attribute, communication behavior and conflict resolution techniques', *Strategic Management Journal*, 15(2), 135–52.

MOST (Ministry of Science and Technology of China). (2010a). *Statistics of science and technology*. Available at www.most.org.cn.

MOST (Ministry of Science and Technology). (2010b). *Survey of Major Specific Areas of S&T work and Studies on the 12th Five-year Plan S&T Development Strategy*, Ministry of Science and Technology, Beijing, China (in Chinese).

MOST (Ministry of Science and Technology, China). (2010c). '2009 Innovation in environmental protection and energy conservation industries', in *Ministry of Science & Technology 2010 Annual Report*, 10.

Moulton, B. (1990). 'An illustration of a pitfall in estimating the effects of aggregate variables on micro units', *Review of Economics and Statistics*, 72(2), 334–38.

Mowery, D. C., Oxley, J. E. and Silverman, B. S. (1996). 'Strategic alliances and interfirm knowledge transfer', *Strategic Management Journal*, 17, 77–91.

and Sampat, B. N. (2005). 'Universities in national innovations systems', in Fagerberg, F., Mowery, D. C. and Nelson, R. R. (Eds.), *The Oxford Handbook of Innovation*. New York: Oxford University Press, 209–39.

Mu, Q. and Lee, K. (2005). 'Knowledge diffusion, market segmentation and technological catch-up: the case of the telecommunication industry in China', *Research Policy*, 34(6), 759–83.

Mu, R. and Fan, Y. (2011). 'Framework for building national innovation capacity in China,' *Journal of Chinese Economic and Business Studies*, 9(4), 317–27.

Nakai Y. and Tanaka, Y. (2010). 'Chinese company's IPR Strategy: How Huawei Technologies succeeded in dominating overseas market by sideward-crawl crab strategy', *Technology Management for Global Economic Growth (PICMET) 2010 Proceedings*, 18–22 July, Phuket, Thailand.

Narula, R. (2002). 'Innovation systems and "inertia" in R&D location: Norwegian firms and the role of systemic lock-in', *Research Policy*, 31, 795–816.

Narula, R. (2003) Globalisation and Technology: Interdependence, Innovation Systems and Industrial Policy. Cambridge: Polity Press.

Narula, R. and Zanfei, A. (2004). 'Globalisation of innovation: the role of multinational enterprises', in Fagerberg, J., Mowery, D.C. and Nelson, R.R. (Eds.), *Handbook of Innovation*. New York: Oxford University Press, 318–45.

National Bureau of Statistics (NBS) (2013). *China Statistical Yearbook*, Beijing: China Statistics Press.

Needham, J. (2004). *Science and Civilisation in China*. Cambridge: Cambridge University Press.

Nelson, R.R. (1959). 'The simple economics of basic scientific research', *Journal of Political Economy*, 67, 297–306.

(1986). 'Institutions supporting technical advance in industry', *American Economic Review*, 76, 186–89.

(Ed.). (1993). *National Innovations Systems: A Comparative Analysis*. Oxford: Oxford University Press.

and Winter, S. (1982). *An Evolutionary Theory of Economic Change*. Cambridge, MA: Harvard University Press.

Nickell, S.J. (1996). 'Competition and corporate performance', *The Journal of Political Economy*, 104(4), 724–46.

Niosi, J. (1999). 'The internationalization of industrial R&D: from technology transfer to the learning organization', *Research Policy*, 28, 107–17.

Nolan, P. (2001). China and the Global Business Revolution. Basingstoke, UK: Palgrave.

Norman, M. and Stoker, B. (1991). *Data Envelopment Analysis: The Assessment of Performance*. Chichester, UK: John Wiley.

OECD. (1987). *Structural Adjustment and Economic Performance*. Paris: OECD.

OECD. (1997). Proposed Guidelines for Collecting and Interpreting Technological Innovation Data: The 'Oslo Manual', Organization for Economic Development and Co-operation, Paris.

OECD. (2002). *Frascati Manual 2002: Proposed Standard Practice for Surveys on Research and Experimental Development*, The Measurement of Scientific and Technological Activities, OECD Publishing.

OECD. (2003a). *The Sources of Economic Growth in OECD Countries.* Paris: OECD.

OECD. (2003b). OECD Science Technology and Industry Scoreboard. OECD. Paris.

OECD. (2004). *OECD Information Technology Outlook 2004.* Available at http://www.oecd.org/internet/ieconomy/oecdinformationtechnologyout look2004.htm.

OECD. (2005). *OSLO Manual: Guidelines for Collecting and Interpreting Innovation Data*, Paris: OECD.

Pack, H. and Saggi, K. (2006). 'Is there a case for industrial policy? a critical survey', *The World Bank Research Observer*, 21(2), 267–97.

Pack, H. and Westphal. L. E. (1986). 'Industrial strategy and technological change: theory versus reality', *Journal of Development Economics*, 22(1), 87–128.

Pacter, P. and Yuen, J. (2001). 'New comprehensive accounting system adopted in China', *China Financial Reporting Update*, 2.

Padilla, R. and von Tunzelmann, N. (2008). 'Technological capabilities and global-local interactions. The electronics industry in two Mexican regions', *World Development*, 36(10), 1980–2003.

Parsaye, K. (1989). *Intelligent Databases.* New York: Wiley.

Pavitt, K. (1980). 'Industrial R&D and the British Economic Problem', *R&D Management*, 10, 149–158.

Pearce, R. D. (1999). 'Decentralised R&D and strategic competitiveness: globalised approaches to generation and use of technology in multinational enterprises', *Research Policy*, 28(2–3), 157–78.

(2005). 'The globalisation of R&D: key features and the role of TNCs', in *Globalisation of R&D and Developing Countries: Proceedings of an Expert Meeting.* New York and Geneva: UNCTAD, United Nations.

Polanyi, M. (1967). *The Tacit Dimension.* London: Routledge & Kegan Paul.

Pomfret, J. (2010). 'History of Telecom Company illustrates lack of strategic trust between U.S., China',*Washington Post*, 8 October. Available at w ww.washingtonpost.com/wp-dyn/content/article/2010/10/07/AR2010 100707210.html?wprss=rss_business.

Porter, M. E. (1985) *Competitive Advantage*, Free Press, New York, 1985.

(1990). *The Competitive Advantage of Nations.* New York: Free Press.

and Stern, S. (1999). *The New Challenge to America's Prosperity: Findings from the Innovation Index.* Washington, DC: Council on Competitiveness.

Powell, W. W. and Grodal, S. (2005). 'Networks of innovators', in Fagenberg, J., Mowery, D. C. and Nelson, R. R. (Eds.), *The Oxford Handbook of Innovation.* New York: Oxford University Press, 56–85.

Koput, K. W. and Smith-Doerr, L. (1996). 'Inter-organizational collaboration and the locus of innovation: networks of learning in biotechnology', *Administrative Science Quarterly,* 41(1), 116–45.

Prabhu, J. C., Chandy, R. K. and Ellis, M. (2005). 'The impact of acquisitions on innovation: poison pill, placebo, or tonic?' *Journal of Marketing,* 69(1), 114–30.

Prange, C. (2012). 'Ambidextrous internationalization strategies: the case of Chinese firms entering the world market', *Organizational Dynamics,* 41, 245–53.

Prasso, S. (2011). 'What Makes China Telecom Huawei So Scary?' *Fortune,* July 28.

Pylyshyn, Z. (1981). 'The imagery debate: Analogue media versus tacit knowledge'. *Psychological Review,* 88, 16–45.

Rigby, D. and Zook, C. (2002). 'Open-market innovation', *Harvard Business Review,* 80(10), 80–89.

Roberts, M. and Tybout, J. (1997). 'The decision to export in Colombia: an empirical model of entry with sunk costs', *American Economic Review,* 87, 545–564.

Rodrik, D. (2004). *Industrial policy for the twenty-first century.* Available at www.hks.harvard.edu/fs/drodrik/Research%20papers/UNIDOSep.pdf

Romer, P. (1994). 'The origins of endogenous growth', *Journal of Economic Perspectives, American Economic Association,* 8(1), 3–22.

Romer, P. M. (1990). Endogenous Technological Change, *Journal of Political Economy,* 98 (5), part II, S71–S102.

Royal Society. (2011). *Knowledge, Networks and Nations: Global Scientific Collaboration in the 21st Century.* London: Royal Society.

Ruane, F. and Sutherland, J. (2005). 'Foreign direct investment and export spillovers: how do export platforms fare?', IIIS Discussion Paper No 58.

Sainsbury, Lord of Turville. (2007). *Race to Top: Sainsbury Review of Science and Innovation.,* London: HM Treasury.

Sasidharan, S. and Kathuria, V. (2008). *Foreign Direct Investment and R&D: Substitutes or Complements – a Case of Indian Manufacturing after 1991 Reforms.* Oxford University SLPTMD Working Paper, no 021.

Schumpeter, J. (1942). *Capitalism, Socialism, and Democracy.* New York: Harper & Bros.

Schumpeter, J. A. (1994). *Capitalism, Socialism and Democracy.* London: Routledge.

Schwaag, S. (2006). 'China, from shop floor to knowledge factory', in Karlsson, M. (Ed.), *The Internationalization of Corporate R&D*. Stursund: Swedish Institute for Growth Policy Studies, 227–66.

Shi, Z. (2008). 'Does Chinese traditional culture handicap the cultivation of creative talents?' *Zhongguo Jiaoyu Xuekan (Journal of the Chinese Society of Education)*, 8, 1–6.

Simon, D. F. and Cao, C. (2009). *China's Emerging Technological Edge*. Cambridge: Cambridge University Press.

Siotis, G. (1999). 'Foreign direct investment strategies and firms' capabilities', *Journal of Economics & Management Strategy*, 8(2), 251–70.

Sjoholm, F. (1999), 'Technology gap, competition and spillovers from direct foreign investment: evidence from establishment data', *Journal of Development Studies*, 36(1), 53–73.

Skrondal, A. and Rabe-Hesketh, S. (2004). *Generalised Latent Variable Modeling: Multilevel, Longitudinal and Structural Equation Models*. Boca Raton, FL: Chapman & Hall/CRC.

Smith, K. (2004). 'Measuring innovation', in Fagerberg, J., Mowery, D. C. and Nelson, R. R. (Eds.), *The Oxford Handbook of Innovation*. New York: Oxford University Press, 148–77.

Soete, L. (1985). International diffusion of technology, industrial development and technological leapfrogging. *World Development*, 13(3), 409–422.

Someren, T. C. R, and Someren-Wang, S. (2013). *Innovative China: Innovation Race between East and West*. Berlin: Springer.

State Statistical Bureau of China (SSB). (2000–2006). China Statistical Yearbook. Beijing: China Statistics Press.

Steensma, H. K., Barden, J. Q., Dhanaraj, C. and Lyles, M. (2004). 'The influence of power, learning, and conflict on the internationalzation of international joint ventures', *Academy of Management Proceedings*, 1, L1–L6.

Stewart, F. (1983). 'Macro-policies for appropriate technology: an introductory classification', *International Labour Review*, 122(3), 279.

Stiglitz, J. (1989). *The Economic Role of the State*. London and New York: Wiley-Blackwell.

Stockdale, B. (2002), UK Innovation Survey, Department of Trade and Industry, London, available at: www.dti.gov.uk/iese/ecotrends.pdf October 2004.

Strangway, D., Liu, X. and Feng, Z. (2009). 'Policy report of China Council for International Cooperation on Environment and Development', in Chinese Academy of Science (Ed.), *Building an Environmentally-friendly Society through Innovation: Challenges and Choices*. Mimeo.

Sun, H. and Xu, Z. Q. (2009). 'On paths from open to indigenous innovation: a case study of coal liquefaction technological innovation', *S&T AND ECONOMY (Chinese)*, 127(22), 7–9.

Sun, Z., Xie, W., Tian, K. and Wang, Y. (2014). 'Capability accumulation and the growth path of Lenovo', in Yu, F.-L. T. and Yan, H.-D. (Eds.), *Handbook in East Asia Entrepreneurship*. London: Routledge. Available at www.tmd-oxford.org/content/publications.

Symeonidis, G. (2001). *Price Competition, Innovation and Profitability: Theory and UK Evidence*. CEPR Discussion Paper No. 2816. London: Centre for Economic Policy Research.

Takahashi, K. I., Tatemichi, H., Tanaka, T., Nishi, S. and Kunioka, T. (2004). 'Environmental impact of information and communication technologies including rebound effects', *International Symposium on Electronics and the Environment (ISEE'04)*, 13–16.

Tan, Y. (2011) *Chinnovation: How Chinese Innovators are Changing the World*. Singapore: John Wiley & Sons.

Teece, D. J. (1986), 'Profiting from technological innovations,' *Research Policy*, 15(6), 285–306.

and Chesbrough, H. W. (2005). *Globalisation of R&D in the Chinese Semiconductor Industry*. Report to the Alfred P. Sloan Foundation.

and Shuen, A. (1997). 'Dynamic capabilities and strategic management'. *Strategic Management Journal*, 18(7), 509–33.

Tether, B. (2002). 'Who co-operates for innovation, and why: an empirical analysis', *Research Policy*, 31(6), 947–67.

Tobin, J. (1958). 'Estimation of relationship for limited dependent variables', *Econometrica*, 26(1), 24–36.

Trajtenberg, M. (1990). *"Patents as Indicators of Innovation," Economic Analysis of Product Innovation*. Cambridge (MA): Harvard University Press.

Tsai, W. (2001). 'Knowledge transfer in intraorganizational networks: effects of network position and absorptive capacity on business unit innovation and performance', *Academy of Management Journal*, 44(5), 996–1004.

Tsang, E. W. (1999). 'A preliminary typology of learning in international strategic alliances', *Journal of World Business*, 34(3), 211–29.

Tushman, M. L. and Anderson, P. (1986). 'Technological discontinuities and organization environments', *Administrative Science Quarterly*, 31(3), 439–65.

UNCTAD. (1997). *World Investment Report: Transitional Corporations, Market Structure and Competition Policy*. New York and Geneva: United Nations.

UNCTAD. (2005a). *World Investment Report: Transnational corporations and the internationalization of R&D.* New York and Geneva: United Nations.

UNCTAD. (2005b). *Globalisation of R&D and Developing Countries: Proceedings of an Expert Meeting.* New York and Geneva: United Nations.

UNCTAD. (2014). Trade Statistics Database, available at www.unctad.org.

Varum, C. A. and Huang, C. (2007) *China: Building An Innovative Economy.* UK: Chandos.

Von Hippel, E. (1988). *Sources of Innovation.* New York: Oxford University Press.

Von Tunzelmann, N. and Acha, V. (2005). 'Innovation in low-tech industries', in Fagerberg, J., Mowery, D. C. and Nelson, R. R. (Eds.), *The Oxford Handbook of Innovation.* New York: Oxford University Press, 407–32.

Vrande,V. van de, de Jong, J. P. J., Vanhaverbeke, W. and de Rochemont, M. (2009). 'Open innovation in SMEs: trends, motives and management challenges', *Technovation*, 29(6/7), 423–37.

Wade, R. (1990). *Governing the Market: Economic Theory and the Role of Government in East Asian Industrialization.* Princeton, NJ: Princeton University Press.

Walz, R. (2008). 'Technological competencies in sustainability technologies in BRICS countries 12', paper presented at SLPTMD conference for Confronting the Challenge of Technology for Development: Experiences from the BRICS, 29–30 May. Oxford, UK.

Wang, E. C. and Huang, W. (2007). 'Relative efficiency of R&D activities: A cross-country study accounting for environmental factors in the DEA approach', *Research Policy*, 36, 260–73.

Wang, H. (2012). *Globalizing China: The Influence, Strategies and Successes of Chinese Returnees.* Bradford, UK: Emerald Publishing.

Wang, H. Y. and Liu, X. (2007). Changes, decision-making and trends of Chinese S&T policy', in Fang, X. (Ed.), *Chinese Technological Innovation and Sustainable Development* (Chinese). Beijing: Science Press.

Wang, L. 2006. 'CHUN-LAN: building open innovation platform', *Economic Times* (Chinese), 12 April.

Wang, X. (2008). 'Huawei, Global Marine Systems in telecom JV', *China Daily*, 18 December.

Willoughby, K. W. (1990). 'Technology choice: a critique of the appropriate technology movement' (Book), *Futurist*, 24(4), 45.

Wong, P. K. (1999). 'National innovation systems for rapid technological catch-up: an analytical framework and a comparative analysis of Korea, Taiwan and Singapore', paper presented at the DRUID Summer Conference on National Innovation Systems, Industrial Dynamics and Innovation Policy. Rebild, Denmark.

World Bank. (1996). *Industrial Restructuring: Experience, Future Challenges.* A World Bank Operations Evaluation Study. Washington, DC: World Bank.

——— (2005). *Economic Growth in the 1990s: Learning from a Decade of Reform.* Washington, DC: World Bank.

World Bank and Development Research Center of the State Council. (2013). *China 2030: Building a Modern, Harmonious and Creative Society.* Washington DC: World Bank.

Wu, G. (2010). 'Research on the content and development trend of science and technology policy, economic policy and innovation policy', Centre for Innovation Research, Tsinghua University, unpublished project report.

Wu, G. S., Wang, Y., Xiong, H. R. and Wang, Z. F. (2009). 'Study on the contents and trends of Chinese S&T policy, economy policy and innovation policy', Internal Research Report (Chinese), Beijing Municipal Science & Technology Commission.

Wu, J. (2013). *Choices of China's Growth Model.* Shanghai: Shanghai Far East Publisher (in Chinese).

Wu, W. P. (2007). 'Cultivating research universities and industrial linkages in China: the case of Shanghai', *World Development*, 35(6). 1075–93.

Xie, W. (2004). 'Technological learning in China's color TV (CTV) industry', *Technovation*, 24, 499–512.

Xie, W. and White, S. (2004). 'Sequential learning in a Chinese spin-off: the case of Lenovo Group Limited', *R&D Management*, 34(4), 407–22.

Xie, W. and Wu, G. (2003). 'Differences between learning processes in small tigers and large dragons learning processes of two color TV (CTV) firms within China', *Research Policy*, 32(8), 1463–79.

Xiong, H. R. and Li, J. Z. (2008). 'Innovative strategy of resource distribution for latecomers: perspective from opening', *China Economic Herald* (Chinese), 3 June.

Xu, B. (2000). 'Multinational enterprises, technology diffusion, and host country productivity growth', *Journal of Development Economics*, 62(2), 477–93.

Xu, Z., Chen, Y. T. and Ke, W. (2009), 'The mechanism of corporate venture capital for open innovation strategy', *Science of Science and Management of S&T* (Chinese), 4, 130–4.

Xue, L., (1997). 'A historical perspective of China's innovation system reform: a case study', *Journal of Engineering and Technology Management*, 14, 67–81.

Yli-Renko, H., Autio, E. and Tontti, V. (2002). 'Social capital, knowledge, and the international growth of technology-based new firms', *International Business Review*, 11(3), 279–304.

Yu, K.L. and Wang, Y.M. (2008). 'The influence of open innovation on indigenous innovation: a M&A perspective', *MANAGEMENT WORLD (Chinese)*, 4, 150–59.

Yu, M. (2010). *'Processing Trade, Firm's Productivity, and Tariff Reductions: Evidence from Chinese Products*, Peking University, China Center for Economic Research,Working Paper No. E2010007.

Yuan, J. (2002). *The Institutional Logic of University Start-Ups*. Xuzhou, China: The Chinese Mining University Press.

Zahra, S.A. (1996). 'Governance, ownership, and corporate entrepreneurship: the moderating impact of industry technological opportunities', *Academy of Management Journal*, 39(6), 1713–35.

Ireland, R. and Hitt, M.A. (2000). 'International expansion by new venture firms: international diversity, mode of market entry, technological learning and performance', *Academy of Management Journal*, 43(5), 925–50.

Zain, M. and Ng, S.I. (2006). 'The impacts of networks relationships on SMEs internationalization process', *Thunderbird International Business Review*, 48(2), 183–205.

Zeng, M. and Williamson, P. (2007). *Dragons at Your Door: How Chinese Cost Innovation Is Disrupting Global Competition*. Cambridge, MA: Harvard Business School Press.

Zhang, J. (2003). *The Development of High-tech Enterprises in China's Universities*. Wuhan: Huazhong Science and Technology University Press.

Zhang, K.H. (2009). 'Rise of Chinese Multinational Firms.' The Chinese Economy, 42(6): 81–96.

Zhang, Y. (2009). *Alliance-based Network View on Chinese Firm's Catching-up: Case Study for Huawei Technologies Co. Ltd.* UNU-MERIT Working Papers, ISSN 1871–9872.

Zheng C. (2014). 'The inner circle of technology innovation: a case study of two Chinese firms', *Technological Forecasting & Social Change*, 82, 140–48.

Zheng, G., He, Y.B., Chen, J. et al. (2008). 'How Chinese manufacturing enterprises improve the international competitiveness by indigenous innovation: A case study from CIMC', *SCIENCE RESEARCH MANAGEMENT (Chinese)*, 29(4), 7, 95–102.

Zhou, C. and Li, J. (2008). 'Product innovation in emerging market-based international joint ventures: an organizational ecology perspective', *Journal of International Business Studies*, 39, 1114–32.

Zhou, K.Z. and Li, C.B. (2012). 'How knowledge affects radical innovation: knowledge base, market knowledge acquisition, and internal knowledge sharing', *Strategic Management Journal*, 33, 1090–102.

Zhou, X., Zhao, W., Li, Q. and Cai, H. (2003). 'Embeddedness and contractual relationships in China's transitional economy', *American Sociological Review*, 68, 75–102.

Zhou, Y. (2006). 'Features and impacts of the internationalisation of R&D by transnational corporations: China's case', in *Globalisation of R&D and Developing Countries*. New York and Geneva: UNCTAD, United Nations.

Zhu, Y. (2010). 'An Analysis on Technology Spillover Effect of Foreign Direct Investment and Its Countermeasures,' *International Journal of Business and Management*, 5(4), 178–192

Zhu, Z. H. and Chen, J. (2008), 'Explorative learning and exploitative learning: antinomy or synergy?', *Studies in Science of Science* (Chinese), Vol. 26 No. 5, pp. 1052–60.

Zi, Z., (2013). '*The purpose of education*,' Zhongguo Jiaoyu Bao (China Education Paper), 9 December. Available at www.xxyedu.net/Article Detail.aspx?articleid=4743.

Index

Printed in the United States
By Bookmasters